P9-CEI-969

World Leaders of the Twentieth Century

MAGILL'S CHOICE

World Leaders of the Twentieth Century

Volume 1
Konrad Adenauer–Nikita Khrushchev
1–418

edited by

The Editors of Salem Press

SALEM PRESS, INC.
Pasadena, California   Hackensack, New Jersey

Original essays which appeared in *Great Lives from History: American Series*, 1987, *British and Commonwealth Series*, 1987, *Twentieth Century Series*, 1990, *American Women Series*, 1995, and *Dictionary of World Biography: The 20th Century*, 1999, have been updated and reformatted; new material has been added.

∞ The paper used in these volumes conforms to the American National Standard for Permanence of Paper for Printed Library Materials, Z39.48-1992 (R1997).

Library of Congress Cataloging-in-Publication Data

World leaders of the twentieth century / edited by the editors of Salem Press.
p. cm. — (Magill's choice)
Includes bibliographical references and index
ISBN 0-89356-337-4 (set : alk. paper). — ISBN 0-89356-338-2 (v. 1 : alk. paper). — ISBN 0-89356-339-0 (v. 2 : alk. paper).
1. Heads of state—Biography. 2. Statesmen—Biography. 3. Biography—20th century. I. Salem Press. II. Series.
D412.W67 2000
920′.009′04—dc21 99-17017
[B] CIP

First Printing

Printed in the United States of America

Contents

Publisher's Note

World Leaders of the Twentieth Century contains 111 essays. With the exception of fifteen freshly commissioned articles, all these articles are drawn from Salem Press's thirty-volume *Great Lives from History* series. Although these essays represent only a small percentage of the thousands of essays in the *Great Lives* series as a whole, they constitute nearly 40 percent of its essays on political leaders who were prominent between 1901 and 2000. Moreover, since they have been selected on the basis of the leaders' importance in world and regional affairs, they represent a large portion of the twentieth century's key global leaders.

As in the original *Great Lives* books, the chronological and geographical scope of *World Leaders of the Twentieth Century* is broad, with articles on leaders ranging from the early twentieth century British prime minister Arthur Balfour to current Russian president Boris Yeltsin. Selections span the Eastern and Western Hemispheres, covering every major geographical and cultural region. Most of the figures covered were, or are, national heads of state or government; however, the selection also includes outstanding military and social leaders who helped shape the political destinies of whole nations.

Articles in *World Leaders of the Twentieth Century* range in length from two thousand to three thousand words and follow a standard format. All articles begin with ready-reference listings, including birth and death details, concise identifications, and brief statements summarizing the leaders' contributions to their nations and their legacies. The articles then divide into three parts. "Early Life" sections provide facts about the leaders' early lives and the environments in which they were reared, setting the stage for the core sections, subtitled "Life's Work." These sections provide straightforward accounts of the periods in which the leaders made their most significant contributions. The final, "Summary," sections do not recapitulate earlier discussions but rather provide overviews of the leaders' places in history. Essays are supplemented by annotated bibliographies, which provide starting points for deeper research.

Like the original *Great Lives* books, the volumes of *World Leaders of the Twentieth Century* contain several features distinguishing them from other biographical reference works. Their articles combine breadth of coverage with a format that offers users quick access to the particular information needed. For convenience of reference, articles are arranged alphabetically by leaders' names, and an appendix at the end of the second volume lists leaders' names by their countries. (A few names are entered under more than one country.) Finally, a detailed index provides references to additional information on individual leaders, as well as events, organizations, laws, places, and names of other persons discussed throughout the set.

All the essays in this work have been written and signed by academicians specializing in the areas they discuss. The Editors of Salem Press wish to extend their appreciation to all those involved in development and production of this work; without their expert contribution, projects of this nature would not be possible. A full list of contributors and their affiliations appears at the beginning of this volume.

Contributors

Stanley Archer
Texas A&M University

Bryan Aubrey
Maharishi International University

Mario Azevedo
University of North Carolina

Iraj Bashiri
University of Minnesota, Minneapolis

Donald S. Birn
State University of New York at Albany

Steve D. Boilard
California Legislative Analyst's Office

John A. Britton
Francis Marion College

J. R. Broadus
University of North Carolina at Chapel Hill

William S. Brockington, Jr.
University of South Carolina at Aiken

Kendall W. Brown
Hillsdale College

Dallas L. Browne
York College of the City University of New York

William H. Burnside
John Brown University

Edmund J. Campion
University of Tennessee, Knoxville

Byron D. Cannon
University of Utah

Frederick B. Chary
Indiana University Northwest

Peng-Khuan Chong
Plymouth State College

Donald N. Clark
Trinity University

Robert G. Clouse
Indiana State University

Thomas H. Conner
Hillsdale College

Bernard A. Cook
Loyola University

James J. Cooke
University of Mississippi

Frances A. Coulter
Ouachita Baptist University

Loren W. Crabtree
Colorado State University

David A. Crain
South Dakota State University

Victoria Hennessey Cummins
Austin College

John C. K. Daly
Illinois State University

Nathaniel Davis
Harvey Mudd College

Andrew J. DeRoche
Community College of Aurora

David R. Dorondo
Western Carolina University

Kathleen E. Dunlop
East Carolina University

Stephen C. Feinstein
University of Wisconsin, River Falls

Richard B. Finnegan
Stonehill College

Richard G. Frederick
University of Pittsburgh at Bradford

Peter K. Frost
Williams College

Corinne Lathrop Gilb
Wayne State University

Margaret C. Gonzalez
Southeastern Louisiana University

Daniel G. Graetzer
University of Washington Medical Center

William I. Hair
Georgia College

Gavin R. G. Hambly
University of Texas at Dallas

Fred R. van Hartesveldt
Fort Valley State College

Carlanna L. Hendrick
Francis Marion College

Michael Craig Hillman
University of Texas

Ron Huch
Dickinson State University

Alphine W. Jefferson
College of Wooster

Charles T. Johnson
Valdosta State University

Wm. Laird Kleine-Ahlbrandt
Purdue University, West Lafayette

Shlomo Lambroza
St. Mary's College of Maryland

Eugene S. Larson
Los Angeles Pierce College

Jack M. Lauber
University of Wisconsin, Eau Claire

Terrance L. Lewis
Clarion University of Pennsylvania

John W. Long
Rider College

Raymond M. Lorantas
Drexel University

David C. Lukowitz
Hamline University

Reinhart Lutz
University of Pacific

Arthur F. McClure
Central Missouri State University

Paul D. Mageli
Independent Scholar

Michael E. Meagher
University of Missouri, Rolla

David W. Moore
Loyola University

Ronald O. Moore
University of Tennessee at Chattanooga

Gordon R. Mork
Purdue University, West Lafayette

Keith W. Olson
University of Maryland at College Park

Gary B. Ostrower
Alfred University

Joyce M. Parks
Independent Scholar

William E. Pemberton
University of Wisconsin, La Crosse

Richard V. Pierard
Indiana State University

Clifton W. Potter, Jr.
Lynchburg College

Edna Quinn
Salisbury State University

John D. Raymer
Indiana University at South Bend

Leo P. Ribuffo
George Washington University

Edward A. Riedinger
Ohio State University Libraries

Carl E. Rollyson
Baruch College of the City University of New York

Joseph Rosenblum
University of North Carolina at Greensboro

John Scheckter
Long Island University

Helmut J. Schmeller
Fort Hays State University

J. Christopher Schnell
Southeast Missouri State University

Robert W. Sellen
Georgia State University

Narasingha P. Sil
Western Oregon University

Andrew C. Skinner
Ricks College

Robert W. Small
Massasoit Community College

Jane Marie Smith
Butler County Community College

Mortimer Snell
Independent Scholar

James E. Southerland
Brenau Professional College

Taylor Stults
Muskingum College

Robert D. Talbott
University of Northern Iowa

Alice F. Taylor
Shorter College

Anthony Tinsley
Appalachian State University

Jiu-Hwa Lo Upshur
Eastern Michigan University

Paul R. Waibel
Liberty University

Abiodun Williams
Georgetown University

Michael W. Williams
University of North Carolina at Charlotte

Thomas P. Wolf
Indiana University Southeast

Malcolm M. Wynn
Stetson University

World Leaders of the Twentieth Century

KONRAD ADENAUER

Born: January 5, 1876; Cologne, Germany
Died: April 19, 1967; Rhöndorf, West Germany

Between 1917 and 1933, Adenauer served his country as mayor of Cologne, becoming, after 1945, founder of the Federal Republic of Germany and its first chancellor.

Early Life

Konrad Adenauer was born in Cologne, Germany, on January 5, 1876. Adenauer's family, of modest means and devoutly Roman Catholic, had produced bakers, bricklayers, reserve army officers, and local officials. In short, he was imbued with the ideals of hard work, self-sacrifice, and persistence. Above all, his home was steeped in the Rhenish tradition of Roman Catholicism and moderately liberal social values. These characteristics informed Adenauer's entire life, and, like his lifelong affection for the Rhineland's hills and rivers, they never left him.

After receiving a classical Catholic education, Adenauer took a bank clerk's job while preparing for university studies. These studies eventually took him to universities in Freiburg im Breisgau, Munich, and Bonn. Passing the bar in 1899, Adenauer entered civil service in the state prosecutor's office in Cologne.

As a Catholic Rhinelander, Adenauer lived figuratively and literally on the periphery of the German Empire created in 1871 and was inherently suspicious of an imperial system dominated by Prussia's Protestant elite. He treasured his region's specific cultural identity and socioeconomic evolution, neither readily compatible with Prussia's oftentimes autocratic and militarist virtues. While Adenauer's Rhenish homeland was an integral part of Prussia, the Catholic western provinces had long resented distant Berlin's domination.

Life's Work

As with most politicians of stature, Adenauer's career began locally. Establishing himself in Cologne, he joined the Center Party, a minority political party representing German Roman Catholics.

Konrad Adenauer *(Library of Congress)*

Subsequently, Adenauer became administrative assistant to Cologne's lord mayor in 1906. Hard-working and politically loyal, he became a mayoral candidate in his own right in 1917, even as Germany collapsed at the end of World War I.

Adenauer's steady pragmatism and determination to succeed allowed him not only to become lord mayor but also to execute numerous major civic improvements in the face of Germany's defeat. In the process, Cologne became a European center of social and political progressivism. Adenauer soon built a solid base of political support, using his genuine gifts of persuasion—"oversimplification" his detractors said—to help keep the Rhineland part of Germany at a time of rumored annexation by France or a separate Rhenish state. Expediently, Adenauer too flirted with separatism, but his political acumen cautioned that Rhenish independence was chimerical.

By 1919, Adenauer valued such caution. No longer merely lord mayor of Cologne, he had become a skilled and tenacious regional politician. Eliciting strong support from his followers and outwitting his less skilled opponents, he quickly established a reputation as an effective civilian leader in a country traditionally respecting only those in uniform. His reputation would carry him far in the post-1945 era.

During the interwar period, Adenauer devoted his energies to his beloved Cologne. One of Adenauer's most important early tasks was the refounding of the city's university. Utterly determined, Adenauer convinced the Prussian state government—despite budgetary difficulties and strident opposition from the neighboring University of Bonn—to reestablish the University of Cologne in 1919-1920. More immediately beneficial were Adenauer's efforts to improve Cologne's appearance and commercial accessibility. Between 1919 and 1929, he directed the razing of Cologne's outmoded fortifications. He replaced them with an extensive ring of parks around the growing metropolis.

Additionally, Adenauer greatly expanded Cologne's commercial importance by modernizing the riverain harbor facilities in the city's heart. Improving and rationalizing the living conditions of the metropolitan area's population, he also directed the annexation of neighboring townships and oversaw the construction of numerous apartment projects. Adenauer greatly eased Cologne's transition from large provincial city to conurbation. More important, the office of lord mayor sharply honed his administrative and political skills, which would serve him well after the war.

With the coming of the Nazi horror in 1933, Adenauer found himself, like so many others, unable to prevent the impending catastrophe. Depression-era economic chaos had vastly exacerbated the still-nagging shock of Germany's loss of World War I and the revolution of 1918. Consequent political radicalization benefited extremists such as the Nazis and the communists. Feeding voraciously upon the country's discontent and privation, these groups completely paralyzed Germany's democracy. The ultimate results were dictatorship and war.

On March 13, 1933, Adenauer was forced from his office as lord mayor. Failing to convince Berlin's Nazi overlords to spare him and his family from persecution, Adenauer went into secret, self-imposed internal exile in the Catholic monastery of Maria Laach in northwestern Germany. Between 1934 and 1937, fearful sojourns followed in Berlin and at Rhöndorf on the Rhine near Bonn. In Rhöndorf, Adenauer eventually built a new home for his family; the Nazis had banned him from his native Cologne.

From 1937 to 1944, Adenauer and his family lived as normal an existence as the travail of dictatorship and war would allow. A devoted father and husband, Adenauer held such normality to be critically important. In 1944, however, this normality was shattered by his imprisonment following the failed attempt by German army officers to kill Adolf Hitler. Escaping with the help of a friend, Adenauer was later recaptured and sent to a Gestapo prison. By the end of 1944, however, he had been reunited with his family, surviving both the Nazi terror and the total defeat of Hitler's Germany.

Liberating Cologne, United States forces immediately reinstated Adenauer as lord mayor. He was summarily dismissed, however, as British units assumed control of the city. Ironically, this dismissal freed Adenauer for a major role in the larger, tortured process of Germany's reconstruction. A new political party, Christian Democratic Union (CDU), served as Adenauer's vehicle. Absorbing the old Catholic Center Party, it united the middle class, a German tradition of social progressivism, and moderate political values. Skillfully outmaneuvering his Berlin rivals, Adenauer became the dominant personality of the new party by 1947. Artfully exploiting the simultaneous rift between the superpowers, he also helped to persuade the United States, Great Britain, and France by 1948 that an entirely new, democratic German state should be created: the Federal Republic of Germany.

Adenauer was absolutely convinced that a Western-oriented, federated republic was Germany's sole hope for the postwar world. As head of one of the two strongest West German political parties, Adenauer assumed that he should play a leading role in that republic's formation. Throughout the difficult formative process in 1948-1949, Adenauer pursued a dual objective: to make the state-in-being acceptable to the Western allies and simultaneously to foil proposals from his domestic opposition, principally in the Social Democratic Party.

Born in May, 1949, the new German republic possessed an unmistakable Western alignment, enjoyed genuine democratic government, and operated, in nascent form, the socially responsive free-market system, which helped make the Federal Republic of Germany the economic miracle of the 1950's. As the republic's first chancellor, Adenauer would hold the office until his retirement in 1963.

Almost alone among German statesmen to 1949, Adenauer held that any new Germany must renounce nationalism for Europe's sake. Underlying the foreign policy he directed in his dual role as chancellor and foreign minister, this idea earned for Adenauer the sharp domestic criticism that such policies doomed Germany's reunification. Adenauer countered that only a federal republic, firmly anchored in a united, militarily strong Western Europe, could compel the Soviet Union to surrender its European satellites. In any case, Adenauer's anti-Prussian sentiments made accepting a supposedly temporary German division all the easier. Though this division proved much longer-lived than Adenauer ever anticipated, his policies eliminated Germany's ancient enmity toward France and incorporated the federal republic's enormous economic potential into the growing European community. In the process, Adenauer oversaw the transformation of his country from ruined enemy of the Western world to self-assertive ally and valued friend.

Summary

Throughout his long and productive career, Konrad Adenauer maintained that the Western world is a cultural and historical community possessing fundamental and unique values not common to the East. No great theorist, he nevertheless consistently attempted, as lord mayor of Cologne and as chancellor and foreign minister of the Federal Republic of Germany, to realize these values daily for his countrymen. Though often haughty and imperious, he possessed the unique ability to transform himself from local politician to international statesman. In doing so, he steadfastly opposed all tyrannies, even at the cost of his personal safety. Intolerant of incompetence, he earned the respect of both supporters and opponents and led much of Germany through one of its most trying periods.

While absorbed in his beloved Cologne before 1933, Adenauer transferred his public devotion to a larger cause after 1945: that of helping Germany recover from the Nazi era's shame and criminality. Shepherding the young Federal Republic of Germany through the pain of occupation and reconstruction, Adenauer saw his country reacquire full sovereignty in 1955. Furthermore, he demonstrated that his countrymen could successfully overcome past mistakes to become respected and valued allies. Though never mastering Germany's division, Adenauer's reconciliation of the federal republic with the West must be recognized as a historic achievement.

Less tangible but equally important, Adenauer represented an often overlooked German tradition of social responsibility and middle-class, liberal democracy. He guided this tradition to an unparalleled degree of popular acceptance in Germany. In a society traditionally too ready to glorify things martial, Adenauer proved decisively that civilian rule could lead effectively and provide economic success and societal well-being. In the final analysis, that accomplishment stands as his enduring legacy.

Bibliography

Adenauer, Konrad. *Memoirs*. Translated by Beate Ruhm von Oppen. Chicago: H. Regnery, 1966.

Alexander, Edgar. *Adenauer and the New Germany: The Chancellor of the Vanquished.* Translated by Thomas E. Goldstein. New York: Farrar, Straus, and Cudahy, 1957. In an early and enthusiastic biography, Alexander attempts to show, on two levels, Germany's objective achievements under Adenauer and Adenauer's personal development. Alexander presents an extensive section on German reunification and an epilogue by Adenauer himself.

Augstein, Rudolf. *Konrad Adenauer.* Translated by Walter Wallich. London: Secker & Warburg, 1964. The publisher of the weekly *Der Spiegel*, Augstein presents a sometimes unflattering picture of Adenauer. Augstein faults particularly Adenauer's acceptance of Germany's postwar division.

Craig, Gordon. *From Bismarck to Adenauer: Aspects of German Statecraft.* Rev. ed. New York: Harper & Row, 1965. A great American historian of Germany depicts Adenauer's statecraft in the diplomatic context, reaching back to Otto von Bismarck. In a brief, excellent account, Craig stresses the role played by Adenauer's personal characteristics in policy formulation.

Hiscocks, Richard. *The Adenauer Era.* Philadelphia: J. B. Lippincott, 1966. Hiscocks presents a rather straightforward biography of Adenauer. The work is fairly evenly divided between treatments of Adenauer's accomplishments after 1945 and a general examination of postwar Western German society and politics. Hiscocks includes a short introduction on the historical setting surrounding Adenauer's post-1945 achievements.

Pommerin, Reiner, ed. *The American Impact on Postwar Germany.* Providence, R.I.: Berghahn Books, 1997.

Prittie, Terence. *Konrad Adenauer, 1876-1967.* Chicago: Cowles, 1971. Prittie's work provides a well-written, balanced, and thorough examination of Adenauer's life and work. Adenauer's early life and services to Cologne receive fair treatment as do Adenauer's experiences during the Nazi period. A solid investigation of Adenauer's postwar career follows. Includes numerous representative illustrations.

Wighton, Charles. *Adenauer, a Critical Biography.* New York: Coward-McCann, 1964.

David R. Dorondo

CORAZON AQUINO

Born: January 25, 1933; Tarlac Province, the Philippines

Aquino became the first woman president of the Philippines. She led the revolution that ended twenty years of dictatorial rule and restored democratic government.

Early Life

Maria Corazon Cojuangco Aquino was born on January 25, 1933, in Tarlac Province, about fifty miles north of Manila. The sixth of eight children, "Cory," as she became known, was born with a silver spoon in her mouth. She belonged to a wealthy and politically influential landowning family in the Philippines. Her father, Jose Cojuangco, was a sugar baron who also managed the family bank and later served in the national assembly. Both her grandfathers were senators.

Aquino was educated at exclusive girls' schools in Manila, run by Roman Catholic nuns. In 1946, when her father moved to the United States, she continued her education at Raven Hill Academy in Philadelphia and Notre Dame School in New York, both Catholic high schools. As a young girl, she showed deep religious conviction that would continue to be a major influence in her life. While a student in the United States, she had a brief foray into American politics as a member of the Junior Republicans and supported Governor Thomas Dewey in the 1948 presidential campaign.

In 1953, Aquino graduated from Mount St. Vincent College in the Riverdale section of the Bronx, with a degree in French and mathematics. She returned to Manila to study law at Far Eastern University, not because she was contemplating a career in law but out of an interest in the discipline of law. Soon after her return to the Philippines, she began a courtship with Benigno "Ninoy" Aquino, Jr., a dynamic and intelligent journalist from a well-known family in Tarlac Province. They were married in 1954, and Cory Aquino ended her legal studies.

Life's Work

For the next thirty years, Aquino played the traditional roles of a dutiful and loyal wife and mother. She reared four daughters and a son and supported her husband unobtrusively but effectively in his meteoric political career. Shortly after their marriage, Ninoy was elected the youngest mayor in the Philippines. When he became governor of Tarlac Province in 1959, he was also the youngest in the country. He performed a similar feat in 1967 by winning a seat in the senate and at thirty-five became the youngest senator. As Benigno Aquino's career advanced, he became a formidable opponent of Philippine president Ferdinand E. Marcos.

Cory Aquino's life received a major jolt in 1972 when President Marcos suspended the constitution, imposed martial law, and arrested her husband on charges of murder, subversion, and illegal possession of firearms. Marcos was seeking an unprecedented third term in the presidential elections scheduled for 1973, and it was widely believed in the Philippines that his redoubtable foe, Benigno Aquino, would defeat him. Ninoy's imprisonment was the first in a series of acts of repression by Marcos that included incarcerating hundreds of other opponents, abolishing the congress, ending the independence of the judiciary, and muzzling the press.

During her husband's seven and a half years in prison, Cory Aquino became the only link between him and the world beyond the prison gates. When Benigno Aquino went on a hunger strike in 1975, she not only solicited the help of her family to persuade him to end his fast but also tried to raise international public opinion against the conditions that had prompted his hunger strike. She regularly smuggled out messages from him to his supporters and reporters. In 1980, Benigno Aquino suffered a heart attack, and Marcos allowed him to go to the United States for a bypass operation. He subsequently became a fellow at Harvard University's Center for International Affairs. The Aquino family lived in Newton, Massachusetts, where Cory later said they spent the three happiest years of their lives.

While in the United States, Benigno Aquino further developed and refined his political philosophy. He also felt an obligation to return to the Philippines and resume the struggle against Marcos. Although aware of the risks involved, he was undeterred. On August 21, 1983, Benigno Aquino was assassinated while disembarking from a plane at Manila International Airport. Initially, the Marcos government asserted that Benigno Aquino had been murdered by

Corazon Aquino *(Library of Congress)*

Rolando Galman, who they alleged was a communist agent and who was shot at the scene by security guards. Although the evidence pointed to a military conspiracy, the Marcos-appointed court eventually acquitted General Fabian Ver, the armed forces chief of staff, and twenty-five others who had been charged with murder.

The Philippine economy, which had been in decline since the mid-1970's, worsened dramatically after the assassination of Benigno Aquino. The gross national product declined, inflation increased, and the government was unable to make interest payments on its foreign debts. The national economic and fiscal crisis, which in part had been caused by mismanagement and corruption, had severe social costs. Unemployment rose, the standard of living of the majority of Filipinos fell, and the gap between the rich and poor widened even further. These economic and social problems fueled the communist insurgency mounted by the New People's Army (NPA), as large numbers of people, particularly in the rural areas, became disaffected with the existing order.

The assassination of Benigno Aquino galvanized the Filipino people into action. It resulted in widespread anger and frustration, and sparked demonstrations against the Marcos regime. Benigno Aquino became a national martyr, and his widow rapidly acquired the stature of a national saint. The scale and intensity of the attacks by the communist guerrillas also increased. The Roman Catholic church, led by the archbishop of Manila, Jaime Cardinal Sin, became more vociferous in its criticisms of Marcos, a significant development in a country where 85 percent of the people are Catholic.

Cory Aquino, the symbol of the newly energized opposition, used her growing popularity and prestige to campaign against Marcos in the May, 1984, National Assembly elections. The opposition won a third of the seats, and although Marcos retained control of the assembly, the national consensus was that the opposition would have won a majority in a completely free and fair election. Faced with continuing calls domestically and internationally for a return to democratic government, Marcos announced on an American television program in November, 1985, that elections would be held the following February.

From that moment, Aquino was encouraged to run for the presidency, for many were convinced that only she commanded the support necessary to defeat Marcos and had the stature to unify a split opposition. A self-effacing and private woman who had never considered going into politics, Aquino was a reluctant presidential candidate. After receiving a petition with a million signatures and having spent a day of fasting and meditation at a convent near Manila, Aquino took up the challenge and agreed to run for president. Cardinal Sin was instrumental in persuading Salvador Laurel, who had presidential aspirations of his own, to become her running mate under the banner of Laurel's United Nationalist Democratic Organization (UNIDO).

A political neophyte, Aquino was thus pitchforked into the political arena. What she lacked in political experience she compensated for with her sincerity, forthrightness, and moral courage. Her image as a modern-day Joan of Arc bolstered her popularity. In speeches across the country, she challenged Marcos directly, holding him responsible for the political decay, social dislocation, and economic malaise that had plagued the Philippines during his long and autocratic rule. Yellow—her husband's favorite color—could be seen in the cities, towns, and rural hamlets and came to symbolize the desire for change and the aspirations of a restive populace. As her campaign progressed, Aquino became not only a symbol of opposition but also a dynamic leader, who inspired a populist movement that came to be known as "People Power."

The election, which was held on February 7, 1986, was marked by fraud and intimidation of voters by supporters of Marcos. After both candidates claimed victory, there was a stalemate that lasted for more than two weeks. On February 25, 1986, Marcos and Aquino held rival inaugurations. Faced with intense domestic and international pressures to concede defeat, and after key military officers defected to the Aquino camp, Marcos fled into exile in the United States.

Aquino inherited many daunting political, economic, and social problems from the Marcos era: promulgation of a new constitution, a foreign debt of more than twenty-seven billion dollars, land reform, endemic corruption, and a communist insurgency. Shortly after her inauguration, she ordered the release of more than five hundred political prisoners, thus fulfilling one of her campaign pledges. She ruled by decree until a new constitution was overwhelmingly endorsed in a referendum in early 1987. The economy would show modest improvements, although many structural economic problems would remain to be corrected, in order to ensure sustained growth.

The newly elected congress, dominated by landowners, passed a compromise Land Reform Bill in June, 1988, that was riddled with loopholes and fell far short of a radical redistribution of agricultural land. Caught between the powerful landed aristocracy (to which she belonged) and nationalist, communist, and military factions that rose to challenge the new government, Aquino's popular support waned. An interim agreement was reached in October, 1988, with the United States, which guaranteed the operation of U.S. military bases in the Philippines until 1991. Under the agreement, the Philippines would receive $481 million annually. She declined to run for reelection in 1992.

Summary

From her childhood, Corazon Aquino possessed a strong religious faith, high ethical principles, and moral integrity. Her strength of character sustained her during the trying years of her husband's imprisonment and the arduous period following his assassination. She demonstrated the same moral and religious conviction as she mobilized the Filipino people against the Marcos regime. This essentially peaceful democratic revolution enhanced the stature of the Philippines in the Southeast Asian region and in the wider international community. She set a new standard of ethical conduct for leaders throughout the world and demonstrated that politics can be shrewd but humane.

Although naturally shy and unassuming, Corazon Aquino grew in confidence and self-assurance as a leader. Following her speech to a joint session of the U.S. Congress in September, 1986, House Speaker Thomas P. O'Neill, Jr., said that hers was the "finest speech" he had heard in his long congressional career. After surviving several coup attempts and domestic upheaval, she restored greater political stability to the Philippines. The tourist industry was invigorated, and there was an increase in new local and foreign investment in the economy. Aquino showed tact, compassion, and fairness in dealing with the practical problems of politics. Under her leadership, the Filipino people gained a new faith and pride in themselves and in their nation.

Bibliography

Burton, Sandra. *Impossible Dream: The Marcoses, the Aquinos, and the Unfinished Revolution.* New York: Warner Books, 1989. A lucid account of the Philippine revolution. It contains interesting anecdotes that throw light on the relationship between Aquino and her husband.

Haskins, James. *Corazon Aquino: Leader of the Philippines.* Hillside, N.J.: Enslow, 1988. A sympathetic biography of Aquino. Her early life is treated more briefly than her role as a political leader and public figure, which is the real focus of the study. Intended for young readers.

Johnson, Bryan. *The Four Days of Courage: The Untold Story of the People Who Brought Marcos Down.* New York: Free Press, 1987. A journalistic but thorough account of the Aquino-Marcos election campaign. Good use is made of interviews with government, military, and civilian participants in the revolution.

Karnow, Stanley. *In Our Image: America's Empire in the Philippines.* New York: Random House, 1989. One of the best historical accounts of the special U.S. relationship with the Philippines. It provides penetrating insights into the circumstances that led to Aquino's rise to power. The book includes information gained from exclusive interviews with Aquino before and after she became president.

Komisar, Lucy. *Corazon Aquino: The Story of a Revolution.* New York: George Braziller, 1987. Although written without the cooperation of Aquino or members of her family, this "unauthorized biography" gives a well-rounded account of her personality. It also contains a useful background chapter on the history of the Philippines. A detailed account is given of Aquino's first year as president.

Mercado, Monina Allarey, ed. *People Power: An Eyewitness History of the Philippine Revolution of 1986.* Manila: James B. Reuter Foundation, 1986. A collection of personal accounts of events leading to the fall of Marcos, as seen from the perspectives of people from various segments of Philippine society.

Reid, Robert H., and Eileen Guerrero. *Corazon Aquino and the Brushfire Revolution.* Baton Rouge: Louisiana State University Press, 1995.

White, Mel. *Aquino.* Dallas, Tex.: Word Publishing, 1989.

Abiodun Williams

YASIR ARAFAT

Born: August 4 or 24, 1929; Cairo, Egypt, or Jerusalem

Arafat was the founder of al-Fatah, a Palestinian revolutionary and sometimes terrorist organization that became the founding block of the Palestine Liberation Organization (PLO). A controversial figure who is a freedom fighter to his own people and a terrorist to Israelis and others, he has moved the Palestinians from near obscurity in the 1960's to the forefront of the world's attention.

Early Life

Mohammed Abd al-Rauf Arafat al Qudwa al-Husseini was born in Cairo or Jerusalem on August 4 or 24, 1929 (records are conflicting). His mother, Hamida, was a cousin of Hajj Amin al Husseini, the Mufti of Jerusalem and Palestinian leader during the British Mandate over Palestine. Arafat was one of seven children from his father's first marriage. His father, Abd al-Rauf Arafat al Qudwa, was from the Qudwa family of Gaza and Khan Yunis, and a member of the Muslim Brotherhood. Arafat's family moved back to Gaza from Cairo in 1939, and he was reared by an uncle after the death of his parents.

After World War II, when Arafat was in his teens, he became active in Palestinian student causes. He belonged to the group Futuwah, a youth organization affiliated with the Husseini clan that feuded with the rival Nashashibis. In 1946, he was active in smuggling arms into Palestine from Egypt. He fought in the 1948 Arab-Israeli war in battles south of Jerusalem. From 1951 to 1956, Arafat attended Fuad I University (later the University of Cairo) as a civil engineering student. He underwent commando training with a Gaza brigade in the Egyptian army in 1951 and later became involved in groups that staged hit-and-run operations against the British around the Suez Canal. In 1952, Arafat was elected president of the Union of Palestinian Students.

In August, 1956, Arafat attended the International Student Congress in Prague and then became chairman of the Union of Palestinian Graduates. This position allowed him to establish contacts with Palestinians in other countries. He began work as a construction engineer. In the October, 1956, Suez war, Arafat fought in the Egyptian army as a bomb disposal expert.

Life's Work

In 1956, Arafat, along with Khalid al-Wazir, formed al-Fatah (victory) and became its spokesman. The principle of the new organization was that its members should not belong to any Arab political party or other movement. This, he believed, was a way to demonstrate that Palestinians did not want to interfere in Arab internal politics. During 1957, Arafat moved to Kuwait and worked for the Kuwaiti government's department of water supply as a civil engineer; he also established a construction company that hired Palestinians. Many important Fatah contacts were made in this period. He established the first of Fatah's underground cells. In July, 1962, President Ahmed Ben Bella of Algeria became the first Arab head of state to recognize Fatah. Arafat met Bella in December, 1962, and opened a Fatah office in Algiers under the name Bureau de la Palestine. Fatah subsequently developed along collective leadership lines. Arafat believed that Arab unity was key to liberating Palestine and that unity had to come from the people. His idea was to capture the imagination of the Palestinian people.

In 1964, the Palestine Liberation Organization (PLO) was formed by the Arab States in Cairo, led by Ahmad al-Shuqayri but in essence controlled by Egypt. Arafat, trying to assert Palestinian independence, had many difficulties with Arab regimes that wanted to control Palestinian resistance. In May, 1966, Arafat, Abu Jihad, and twenty other Fatah members were arrested by the Syrian government on trumped-up murder charges after a Syrian plot backfired, leading to the deaths of two Fatah members.

During the June, 1967, Six-Day War, Arafat and Abu Jihad fought on the Syrian front as irregulars. Arafat's reaction to Arab defeat was despair but was also to begin a popular war of liberation. Arafat was in favor of immediate resumption of guerrilla warfare as a way to avert the psychological burden of Arab defeat. On June 23, 1967, the Fatah central committee confirmed the idea of returning to military confrontation, and Arafat was appointed military commander. Some small operations began in August, but Israeli security forces had uncovered most of the cells by the end of the year. Arafat believed that irregular fighting allowed the Palestinians to

Yasir Arafat *(Archive Photos/Imapress)*

fix their identity. Arafat stayed in the West Bank until the end of the year and then escaped to Jordan. The years 1968 to 1970 saw Jordan used as a base for attacks against Israel.

On March 21, 1968, the Battle of Karameh occurred between Israelis and Palestinian-Jordanian forces, marking the first Palestinian military victory over Israel since 1948. Karameh was viewed as a "resurrection of the Palestinian people." Many volunteers came to PLO circles. In addition, a Palestinian bureaucracy was established and intellectuals became involved in the revival of Palestinian culture. The relationship between Arafat and President Gamal Abdel Nasser of Egypt blossomed after Karameh, and Arafat became the chief spokesman for the PLO. Arafat's solution to the Palestine problem in 1968 was to espouse the idea of a Democratic State of Palestine, which from an al-Fatah perspective meant dismantling Israel by politics and nonviolence but to Israel appeared to be based on violence. The nonviolent solution was also rejected by the PLO, which sought the extinction of Israel through violent means according to its 1964 covenant.

In early 1969, Arafat took over the PLO and made it into an umbrella organization, independent of the Arab regimes. Arafat himself became a symbol of resistance, more than a freedom fighter to some. The PLO covenant bound all to "armed struggle." Arafat was elected chairman of the PLO executive committee. On November 3, 1969, the Cairo Agreement, which allowed the PLO to base itself in Lebanon, bear arms, use Lebanese territory to attack Israel, and have direct rule over the Palestinian refugee camps, was concluded. Arafat became supreme commander of the Palestine Armed Struggle Command (PASC).

During September, 1970, however, Arafat lost control of the extremists, particularly the Popular Front for the Liberation of Palestine (PFLP). Although the PFLP was suspended from the central committee of the Palestine Resistance, a civil war broke out in Jordan, and the PLO, including Arafat's forces, was defeated by the Jordanian army. There is some opinion that the PLO disaster in Jordan could have been averted if Arafat had used force to control the radicals. Arafat, however, seemed unwilling to restrain the leftists out of respect for the principle of national unity. Arafat also believed that use of violence against the Left would have destroyed "democracy" within the PLO.

The result was the rise of terror as a tactic by Palestinian groups after 1970. Black September, led by the PFLP, was the most violent early group, being responsible for the 1971 assassination of the Jordanian prime minister Wasfi Tal, the May, 1972, Lod Airport massacre, and the August, 1972, massacre of Israeli Olympic athletes in Munich. Arafat subsequently made a tactical alliance with the PLO Left and committed himself to armed struggle.

The first change toward moderation came in February, 1974, with a PLO working paper that indicated a willingness to accept a political settlement in exchange for a ministate on the West Bank and in Gaza. Unofficial contacts were established with Israelis by the end of 1973, but it was not until 1977 that the Palestine National Council supported the idea of negotiations on the ministate idea. At the Rabat Conference in 1974, the PLO was recognized as the sole legitimate representative of the Palestinian people.

On November 13, 1974, Arafat was invited to address the United Nations (U.N.) General Assembly, and he called for establishment of national authority on any land in the West Bank and Gaza. Arafat was treated as head of state. He asserted that, "Today, I have come bearing an olive branch and a freedom-fighter's gun. Do not let the olive branch fall from my hand." To critics, the gesture seemed hypocritical, while his appearance in traditional Arab dress appeared as an example of political transformation in a changing world: yesterday a terrorist, today a diplomat. U.N. General Assembly Resolution 3236 of November 14, 1974, recognized the PLO as a representative of the Palestinian people and the right of the Palestinians to self-determination, national independence, and sovereignty. Diplomatic recognition was achieved by the PLO from more than eighty states by the 1980's, as well as was observer status at the United Nations.

Arafat's 1974 successes, however, were short-lived. In 1975, the PLO became involved in the Lebanon civil war, bringing the PLO into conflict with Syria, which did not want an independent Palestinian movement. Arafat moved in and out of Lebanon during the late 1970's, trying to position PLO forces and arrange cease-fires. The November, 1977, Sadat Peace Initiative with Israel and Anwar Sadat's historic visit to Jerusalem soured the relationship between Arafat and Sadat, as the Egyptian president appeared to usurp a role specifically delegated to the PLO.

In January, 1978, the PLO appeared to splinter further over the issue of legitimate leadership and the issue of armed struggle. Abu Nidal established a faction (Black June) and insisted that he was the real representative of al-Fatah, not Arafat. Several Palestinian supporters of Arafat were assassinated by Abu Nidal's group, and he, in turn, was sentenced in absentia to death by Fatah leadership. In April, 1978, a mutiny within Fatah was led by Abu Daoud. Arafat tried to heal the rift by integrating all militias under Fatah. Arafat, in his attempt to maintain Palestinian unity, often gave contradictory statements about what exactly was the ultimate desire of the Palestinians. In 1978, for example, in a discussion with U.S. congressman Paul Findley, he indicated that he would accept a Palestinian state in the West Bank and Gaza but "would reserve the right, of course, to use nonviolent means to bring about the eventual unification of all of Palestine."

In 1982, U.S. president Ronald Reagan proposed a peace plan that Arafat considered but that the Palestine National Council (PNC) ultimately rejected. This plan would have required Arafat to work jointly with King Hussein I of Jordan on Palestinian rights, which was something that President Hafiz al-Assad of Syria did not want. Hussein desired a Palestinian state in confederation with Jordan, a situation that would narrow the independence of a PLO state. Arafat later accepted the idea of a joint Palestinian-Jordanian delegation, but Hussein insisted on including West Bank representatives in the delegation as well. Assad, in response, planned a Fatah rebellion. By 1985, Hussein indicated that the PLO would have to accept U.N. Resolution 242 of 1967, and an agreement was made between Arafat and Hussein accepting the land for peace principle. Yet PLO terrorist actions continued, undercutting Arafat's desire for moderation.

PLO leadership was caught short by the *intifada*, the Palestinian uprising on the West Bank and Gaza that began on December 8, 1987. That uprising was begun largely because Arab states had become more interested in the Iraq-Iran war that was drawing to a close than the Palestine question. While the *intifada* was spontaneous in its origins, PLO leadership moved in to control much of the activity and strikes and to provide financial support for those under Israeli occupation.

On November 15, 1988, the PNC declared an independent Palestinian state without specific borders and conditionally accepted U.N. Resolutions 242 and 338 and the 1947 Partition Plan. There was no straight answer from Arafat as to whether this meant recognition of Israel. During December, 1988, there were many clarifications, which finally led to American recognition of the PLO. In early December in Stockholm, Arafat indicated that he had accepted the existence of Israel. On December 13, he addressed a special session of the U.N. General Assembly in Geneva after having been refused a visa by the U.S. Department of State. In his address he fell short of a full renunciation of terrorism but called for peace talks. A day later, on December 14, another statement by Arafat provided another clarification on the "right of all parties concerned in the Middle East conflict to exist in peace and security . . . including the state of Palestine, Israel, and other neighbors."

Arafat also renounced all forms of terrorism. These statements satisfied the U.S. government and ended the diplomatic isolation of the PLO from Washington, D.C. At the same time, Arafat was critical of what appeared to be unconditional support of Israel by the United States, which encouraged hard-line positions within Israel.

Despite the recognition of Israel and renunciation of terrorism, questions still existed regarding Arafat's attitudes toward Palestinian moderates and the wishes of Palestinians under occupation. During January, 1989, threats were made by Arafat against moderates who suggested ending the *intifada*. Arafat's general position by the end of the 1980's was to support the creation of a Palestinian state on the West Bank, in Gaza, and in East Jerusalem, with support from an international conference involving all parties of the Arab-Israeli conflict.

By 1993 a significant shift had taken place in Palestinian-Israeli relations. After intensive negotiations, and pressed by the United States to come to an agreement, Arafat and Israeli prime minister Yitzhak Rabin signed the Oslo Peace Accords, in which Israel agreed to give up some of the occupied territories to autonomous Palestinian control. Rabin, however, was soon assassinated by a zealot opposed to the peace process, and relations between Arafat and the new conservative prime minister, Benjamin Netanyahu, were difficult. Again, under international pressure, the two leaders signed the Wye River Agreement in 1998. Netanyahu's pledged concession of West Bank land cost him the support of his party. Arafat in turn struggled to maintain the support of the more militant Palestinian factions, while pledging to suppress terrorism against Israeli targets. As a condition of the peace process, the Palestinian Authority expunged from its constitution its commitment to destroy Israel, but Arafat sought to appease his opponents by declaring his intention to form the long-awaited Palestinian state. A new condition of peace was now placed on the table—the recognition or renunciation of Palestinian independence.

Summary

Although by the end of the 1990's Yasir Arafat had not succeeded in creating a Palestinian state, he was ultimately the symbol of the Palestinian revolution. As a world traveler and charismatic leader, he appeared to be wedded to the Palestinian revolution and was able to be all things to all men. Part of his leadership success was his ability to keep the PLO's ideology simple, especially in rejecting extraneous issues and refusing to make his organization a tool of any specific Arab regime. Ideologically, Arafat's bottom line was that Palestine was Arab land and hence Israel would never be formally recognized. Arafat was also able to obtain large financial subsidies for the Palestinian cause from oil-producing Arab regimes, which in turn increased the financial power of the PLO in Lebanon through the summer of 1982.

Arafat, however, was often said to have talked out of both sides of his mouth. His obscure statements about renunciation of terrorism and recognition of Israel did not allow him to get full support of the United States or Western European powers for the Palestinian cause. During his tenure as PLO leader, Arafat was also criticized for his individualism—his insistence that he be free to take personal initiatives, which often led to broad promises without the support of all PLO groups. He was also criticized by other Palestinian groups for enriching himself and the leadership at the expense of those in the camps. The strategy of delaying peace until the Arabs were strong enough to dictate terms was also criticized by peace advocates outside the Middle East. Arafat's life is a testimony to the complexity of the Palestinian Arab question and the fact that it is intimately connected with Arab politics. The unanswered question is whether Arafat will become the leader of an independent Palestinian state.

Bibliography

Aburish, Said K. *Arafat: From Defender to Dictator.* Bloomsbury Publishing Place, 1998. Examination of contradictions in Arafat's personal nature by an experienced Palestinian political writer who sees Arafat as a threat to true peace in the Middle East because of his dictatorial tendencies.

Becker, Jillian. *The PLO.* London: Weidenfeld & Nicolson, 1984. A history of the PLO that defines the organization as terrorist and takes a negative view toward Arafat as a leader.

Curtis, Michael, Joseph Neyer, Chaim I. Waxman, and Allen Pollack, eds. *The Palestinians: People, History, Politics.* New Brunswick, N.J.: Transaction Books, 1975. A useful anthology of articles that explain the various dimensions of the Palestinian people and their political, social, and economic problems.

Friedman, Thomas. *From Beirut to Jerusalem.* New York: Farrar, Straus and Giroux, 1989. This is an exceptionally interesting examination of Israeli, Palestinian, and Lebanese politics by a Pulitzer Prize-winning bureau chief of *The New York Times* in Beirut and Jerusalem.

Hart, Alan. *Arafat: Terrorist or Peacemaker?* London: Sidgwick and Jackson, 1984. An exceptionally sympathetic portrait of the PLO leader and the Palestinian cause. There are many undocumented quotations from sources that are questionable and not cross-checked for accuracy.

Mishal, Shaul. *The PLO Under Arafat: Between Gun and Olive Branch.* New Haven, Conn.: Yale University Press, 1986. A structural examination of the PLO that in a scholarly way distinguishes Arafat from other Palestinian leaders and examines the mechanics of the PLO.

Nassar, Jamal R. *The Palestine Liberation Organization: From Armed Struggle to the Declaration of Independence.* New York: Praeger, 1991.

Rubenstein, Richard. *Alchemists of Revolution.* New York: Basic Books, 1987. A critical examination of the structure of terrorism as it developed during the 1970's and 1980's. Special attention is paid to Arafat as representative of a figure who is a freedom fighter to his own people and a terrorist to outsiders.

Schiff, Ze'ev, and Ehud Ya'ari. *Israel's Lebanon War.* Translated by Ina Friedman. New York: Simon & Schuster, 1984. An examination of the 1982 Lebanon War by Israeli war correspondents. It is fairly critical of Israeli actions during the conflict.

Wallach, Janet, and John Wallach. *Arafat: In the Eyes of the Beholder.* New York: Carol, 1990.

Stephen C. Feinstein

KEMAL ATATÜRK

Born: May 19, 1881; Salonika, Ottoman Empire (later Thessaloniki, Greece)
Died: November 10, 1938; Istanbul, Turkey

Through his skills as a politician, general, and statesman, Atatürk founded the modern state of Turkey in 1923 out of the ashes of the old Ottoman Empire.

Early Life

Kemal Atatürk, the "father of Turkey," was born in Salonika, a major port in what was then the Ottoman province of Macedonia (part of modern-day Greece). His parents, Ali Riza and his wife Zubeyde, gave him the name Mustafa in honor of an older brother who had died in infancy. Mustafa's early years were marked by his family's declining fortunes. His father lost all his money in a salt venture. When his application for readmission to the civil service was rejected, he took to drinking heavily and died of tuberculosis, leaving behind nothing for Zubeyde and her family. She was forced to sell the house and move to her brother's farm outside of Salonika. During his years in the country, Mustafa developed into a strong and muscular young man. Later in life he would suffer from a variety of illnesses, some, in part, brought about by his own problems with alcohol.

By age twelve Mustafa had decided on his future career. Without telling his mother, he convinced a friend's father who was a major in the army to allow him to sit for the entrance exam to the Military Secondary School in Salonika. Even when Mustafa passed the exam, he still needed his mother's written consent, which he received after she had a dream in which she envisioned a brilliant military career for her son. Mustafa proved to be an excellent student. He was so good in mathematics that his instructor began to call him Kemal (perfection). During his student days, he realized the importance of understanding cultures other than his own. To that extent he read extensively in European political thought while simultaneously learning French. By the end of his time at the

Kemal Atatürk *(Library of Congress)*

academy, he had begun to learn German. Thus Kemal's intellectual foundation was laid during a time of growing change within the Ottoman Empire.

This intellectual growth also fostered a strong sense of nationalism and a belief that for his nation to survive, it needed to be modernized along European lines. In 1906 (he was now a captain in the army), while stationed in Damascus, Kemal joined a secret society known as the Fatherland Movement.

Two years later, this organization, of which Kemal was a recognized leader, merged with another nationalistic group called the Young Turks. In 1908 a rebellion broke out against the sultan's rule. The end result was the election of a parliamentary government and the establishment of a constitution. Shortly after the revolt, Kemal broke with the leadership of the Young Turks, citing that a serving army officer should resign if he wished to participate in politics.

In 1912 Kemal was sent to Libya during the war between the Ottoman Empire and Italy. The defeat of the Ottoman army, coupled with other military defeats in the Balkans during that same year, caused Kemal to become highly critical of the government's handling of the conflicts. Despite his comments, Kemal's growing popularity prevented any public rebuke. In 1913 he was transferred to Sofia, Bulgaria, where he began to see the increasing German influence within the Ottoman state—something that Kemal feared would draw the nation into a European conflict. In late 1914 this fear became a reality when the Ottoman Empire entered World War I on the side of Germany.

Kemal's service in the war made him a hero. During the Gallipoli campaign, units under his command helped to repel an Allied attack that threatened to cut the Turkish army in two. From 1916 until the end of the war, Kemal served in a variety of capacities, including commander of a Turkish army in Syria. With the end of the conflict in November, 1918, Kemal returned to Constantinople in time to see the Allied navy arriving—a sign that the fate of his country was now in enemy hands.

Life's Work

The defeat of the Ottoman Empire in 1918 set the stage for Kemal Atatürk's greatest achievement—the creation of the modern Turkish state. While the sultan and his ministers acquiesced to the Allied demands laid out in the armistice, Kemal remained defiant. As with his earlier attacks against the sultanate, Kemal's popularity with the people and influence within the army prevented the government from undertaking any retribution. In an attempt to reduce his growing influence, Kemal was sent to Anatolia in May, 1919, to supervise the disbanding of the army in that region. Despite attempts to remove him from the center of events in Constantinople, Kemal used his new assignment to position himself as the de facto leader of the Turkish National Movement emerging in that area. In July the organization met at Erzurum, where they drafted the National Pact. This document called for the right of self-determination for the Turkish people and a pledge to defend the nation's natural boundaries at all costs.

In September a larger meeting was convened at Sivas. The sultan responded to the demands of the Nationalists by allowing a parliamentary election, in which they emerged victorious. Before the newly elected parliament could accomplish anything, however, British forces occupying Constantinople dissolved the body. Under Kemal's leadership, the Nationalists responded by convening their own Turkish Grand National Assembly in Ankara—the embryonic capital of the new Turkish republic—beginning in April, 1920.

The work of the assembly and the cause of Turkish nationalism were given a further boost by two events in June of 1920. The Treaty of Sevres, which formally ended the conflict between the Ottoman Empire and the Allies, became public knowledge. The document called for a drastic reduction in the size of the Turkish state, placed its finances under foreign control, and proposed that the Bosporus and Dardanelles straits be placed under international control. It was also in June that the Greeks, encouraged by their British allies, launched an invasion of Anatolia. For the next two years, the Turkish armies, under the leadership of Kemal, fought to free Anatolia from Greek occupation. By August, 1922, the Greeks had been defeated. As Kemal's armies approached the Dardanelles, Great Britain called for an Allied effort to prevent their reoccupation by the Nationalists. When no other nation voiced its support, the British were forced to enter into negotiations with the victorious Nationalists.

In November the sultan fled, and the sultanate was abolished. In the same month, negotiations for a new peace treaty with the Allies began in Lausanne, Switzerland. In the final document, signed in July, 1923, the Nationalists—now the only political party in Turkey—achieved virtually all their demands as outlined in the National Pact. On October 29, 1923, the Turkish Republic was proclaimed and the capital officially moved to Ankara. Kemal, now president and head of the nation's only political party, was in the position to focus on his ultimate goal: modernizing Turkey along Western lines.

For Kemal, westernization could not occur without first secularizing many traditional Turkish institutions. In early 1924 the caliphate (the religious equivalent of the sultanate) was abolished. Theological schools and the religious courts were also closed. Two years later the Islamic legal system was replaced by a civil code. The traditional fez was outlawed and replaced by western-style hats. The Gregorian calendar was adopted. In 1928 the Latin alphabet replaced Arabic characters. Six years later Kemal announced one of his most significant reforms when he granted voting rights to women and allowed them to run for seats in parliament. It was also in 1934 that all Turks were compelled to adopt surnames. Kemal himself selected Atatürk (father of the Turks).

The modernization of Turkey extended beyond social and cultural institutions. Economic reforms were adopted. The government invested heavily in industrialization. In 1934 a five-year plan, modeled along Soviet lines, was implemented. Western farming methods and machinery were adopted to make crop production more efficient. The government even subsidized certain crops by guaranteeing their prices. In the international field, Kemal negotiated a series of economic and defensive treaties with neighboring nations—most notably, the Treaty of Angora with Great Britain and Iraq (signed in 1926) and the Balkan Defense Pact with Greece, Romania, and Yugoslavia (signed in 1934)—that assisted in promoting regional security and stability. In 1932 Turkey further committed itself to internationalism by joining the League of Nations.

Kemal's reforms did not go unopposed. Religious conservatives resisted—without success—attacks against the traditional influence of Islam in society. In 1925 a revolt began in Kurdistan. One year later, members of the Young Turk movement attempted to assassinate Kemal. The Turkish president used many methods—some quite ruthless—to combat this opposition. To curb any public protests over his policies, Kemal utilized the Republican People's Party (RPP; founded in 1923) to foster nationalism and a sense of unity. As the only legally recognized party, the RPP also helped suppress all political opposition. The Kurdish revolt was brutally suppressed in April, 1925. The conspirators in the assassination attempt were publicly tried and executed.

The last months of Kemal's life were dominated by health problems. In March, 1938, a public announcement regarding his illness (cirrhosis of the liver) was made. On the same day that Adolf Hitler and Benito Mussolini met with the prime ministers of France and Great Britain to decide the fate of Czechoslovakia, Kemal fell into a coma. He recovered for a short time, but on November 10, 1938, he died, ironically, in the sultan's palace in Istanbul. A nation deeply mourned the man known to them as Father Turk.

Summary

Kemal Atatürk's greatest achievement and lasting legacy is the modern Turkish state. His exploits, however, go beyond building a new nation. At a time when Turkey faced invasion and occupation, it was Kemal who provided the iron-willed leadership to rally the Turkish people at what can arguably be considered their darkest hour. His policies, while challenged by some, not only stabilized the country but also enabled it to begin to compete with Western nations on a more even level. As a man, Kemal was somewhat of a contradiction. His scandalous private behavior and his seeming disregard for the Islamic faith offended and alienated the conservative religious element. Yet the vast majority of his people overlooked this side, choosing instead to focus on his achievements in the areas of social, economic, and political reform to define a man that continued to serve as an inspiration for many in Turkey.

Bibliography

Kazancigil, Ali, and Ergun Ozbudun. *Ataturk: Founder of a Modern State*. 1981. Reprint. London: Hurst & Company, 1997. A series of articles by scholars in the field that focus on Atatürk's influence on Turkey's cultural, political, and economic structure. Includes biographical notes on the various authors.

Kinross, Patrick Balfour. *Ataturk: A Biography of Mustafa Kemal, Father of Modern Turkey*. New York: William Morrow, 1964. Provides a detailed discussion of Atatürk's work before the end of World War I, his influence during the Turkish war of independence, and his work as the father of modern Turkey. Includes maps, pictures, and bibliography.

Metz, Helen Chapin, ed. *Turkey: A Country Study*. Washington, D.C.: Federal Research Division, Library of Congress, 1996.

Palmer, Alan. *Kemal Ataturk*. London: Sphere Books, 1991. A concise and highly readable narrative designed to appeal to the general reader. Includes a chronology, maps, and a brief bibliography.

Pettifer, James. *The Turkish Labyrinth: Ataturk and the New Islam*. London: Viking-Penguin, 1997. A detailed study of the influence of Atatürk's reforms on the shaping of the modern Turkish state after his death. Also discusses how these reforms influenced Turkey's relations with its immediate neighbors in Europe and Central Asia. Includes chronology and bibliography.

Pope, Nicole. *Turkey Unveiled: Atatürk and After*. London: John Murray, 1997.

Volkan, Vamik D., and Norman Itzkowitz. *The Immortal Ataturk: A Psychobiography*. 1984. Reprint. Chicago: University of Chicago Press, 1986. Those skeptical of any work subtitled a "psychobiography" should not let that prevent them from reading this insightful and thought-provoking work. This book is unique in that Volkan and Itzkowitz utilize little-known material from the memoirs of many people who worked with and served under Kemal.

Charles T. Johnson

ARTHUR BALFOUR

Born: July 25, 1848; Whittinghame, East Lothian, Scotland
Died: March 19, 1930; Woking, Surrey, England

As prime minister, and in many other high government offices, Balfour provided leadership to his country and made noteworthy contributions to world peace.

Early Life

Arthur James Balfour was born July 25, 1848, in Whittinghame, East Lothian, in Scotland. His mother, Lady Blanche Balfour, was the daughter of the second Marquess of Salisbury. James Balfour, his father, was descended from an old Scottish family which had grown wealthy from trade with India. Named Arthur, after his godfather, the duke of Wellington, Balfour could take wealth and contacts with influential people for granted as he grew up. His father, who died in 1856 of tuberculosis, was a member of Parliament. His mother's brother, Robert Cecil, third Marquess of Salisbury and later prime minister, became an important figure in Balfour's early career.

Lady Blanche had given birth to nine children when she was widowed at the age of thirty-one. She never remarried, and she provided close and rigorous supervision to her children. Arthur, the oldest son, was to win the greatest renown, although several of the other children who survived to adulthood also had distinguished careers: Gerald was a member of Parliament for twenty years, Frank was an authority on genetics and held a chair at Cambridge University, Eleanor became the principal of Newnham College, and Eustace was a successful architect. The family was close-knit; one sister, Alice, who like Balfour never married, devoted her later life to supervising his household. The Balfours were also devout, with a commitment to both the Church of England and the Presbyterian Church of Scotland.

When he was ten, Balfour was sent away from home to attend a private boarding school at Hoddeston in Hertfordshire. In 1861, he went on to study at Eton, where he was an indifferent student and not robust enough to take an active part in sports. Five years later,

Balfour began his studies at Trinity College, Cambridge. There he developed an interest in the study of philosophy, a subject to which he considered devoting his career. He enjoyed Cambridge much more than Eton, although he was not a diligent scholar. He now began to take part in sports and games, an interest that continued to the end of his life.

In 1869, when he came of age, Balfour inherited the family estates. With wealth came responsibility, and he was often occupied with family and business affairs. His mother's death in 1872 increased this burden. He turned to his uncle, Lord Salisbury, for guidance in these years and under his patronage began a career in politics by standing for Parliament in January, 1874. He was returned unopposed as the Conservative member for Hertford.

Life's Work

At first, Balfour appeared no more promising in politics than he had as a student. He hesitated to speak or play an active role in the House of Commons and occupied himself with foreign travel and work on a book of philosophy. Published in 1879 as *A Defence of Philosophic Doubt*, the treatise was the first of several books which marked him as a shrewd, but rather conventional, intellectual talent.

When Salisbury became foreign secretary in 1878, he asked Balfour to become his parliamentary private secretary. This gave the young politician contacts and firsthand experience in diplomacy as he attended the Congress of Berlin. By 1880, when the Liberals under William Ewart Gladstone swept into office and forced Balfour into opposition, he was emerging as an articulate rising member of the Conservative Party. He soon became identified, along with Randolph Churchill, with an outspoken faction of Conservatives known as the "Fourth Party," raising objections to their own party leadership as well as Gladstone's government. When the Conservatives returned to office under Salisbury in 1885, Balfour became president of the Local Government Board. The following year he was made a member of the cabinet.

In 1887, Salisbury made his nephew chief secretary for Ireland, a challenging assignment in this period of unrest in Ireland. Balfour succeeded in removing some economic grievances in that troubled colony and had the good fortune to face an increasingly divided nationalist opposition. Nationalists distressed at his hard-line policies dubbed him "Bloody Balfour" at home, among his fellow Con-

Arthur Balfour *(National Archives)*

servatives, he was lauded for his vigor and skills as an administrator.

In 1891, Balfour was promoted to First Lord of the Treasury and became his party's leader in the House of Commons. He acted as a deputy to his uncle, the prime minister, in formulating policy and was the chief Conservative legislative strategist and spokesman. His achievements in this role were mixed; he had success with the Irish Local Government Act and some other pieces of legislation. Not a reformer, Balfour still showed foresight in such areas as transportation and urban housing, and he was ready to undertake constructive change.

Balfour was the logical choice to succeed his uncle as prime minister in 1902. The party over which he presided made his tenure in that office a rather difficult one. It was divided over such contentious issues as free trade and tariff reform, and Balfour had to work hard to keep it united. Moreover, he had no great popular following in the country at large. Nonconformists were especially upset by his Education Act of 1902, which retained government support for denominational schools operated by the Church of England. Faced with this opposition, Balfour resigned in 1905 and was defeated by the Liberals in the ensuing elections.

Balfour's greatest contributions as prime minister came in the field of foreign policy. Coming into office in the aftermath of the Boer War (1899-1902), which had shown Great Britain to be dangerously isolated, he strengthened ties with other nations. This important reversal of British policy was marked by the Entente Cordiale with France in 1904. Moreover, he established the Committee for Imperial Defense to provide expert advice on military preparedness and responded forcefully to the German challenge in building warships. These accomplishments may not have helped him with the electorate, but they did secure his reputation in the area of foreign and defense policy and led to many future opportunities to serve his country.

Balfour's dismay at being thrown out of office was compounded when he lost his own seat in Parliament in 1906. A safer seat was soon found for him in the City of London, and he took up the position of leader of his party in opposition. These were difficult years for Balfour, as Joseph Chamberlain and other tariff reformers often railed against his leadership. Weakened in health and spirit, he became increasingly distrustful of the burgeoning democratic currents of the age. He resigned his leadership position in 1911, although remaining as a member of Parliament.

Troubled by the dangerous drift in international affairs, Balfour helped found the Garton Foundation in 1912 to work for world peace. When World War I erupted in 1914, he became an unhesitating supporter of the government's position. He was asked to resume membership on the Committee of Imperial Defense and in November, 1914, joined an inner cabinet known as the War Council. The following year he was made First Lord of the Admiralty in the Asquith coalition government. When Prime Minister David Lloyd George ousted H. H. Asquith from the new coalition in 1916, he made Balfour, by now a trusted almost nonpartisan elder statesman, his foreign secretary.

With the war over, Balfour left the Foreign Office in 1919. He remained a member of the cabinet, however, until 1922 as Lord President of the Council. He headed the British delegation to the Washington Naval Conference of 1921-1922, and enhanced his reputation as an astute diplomat and peacemaker there. At this conference, which achieved a substantial measure of naval disarmament, Balfour was able to cement good relations between Great Britain and the United States. He also was able to contribute to the work of the League of Nations organization in its early years, regularly representing his country there and chairing the first meeting of the League Council.

In 1922, Balfour was elevated to a peerage as the first earl of Balfour. Yet his political career did not end when he left the House of Commons. He was Lord President of the Council from 1925 until 1929, the year before his death. He was also president of the British Academy and a leader in other voluntary groups, such as the League of Nations Union.

Summary

To the British public, the tall, graceful figure of Arthur Balfour came to symbolize the aristocrat in politics. His languid manner, taking for granted that his wealth and connections should bring him to the top, fitted this image. Yet much of Balfour is difficult to typecast. His intellectual interests, for example, were serious, as the four books he wrote on philosophy attest. If he was an athlete, he did not participate in the usual aristocratic sports, but, rather, was interested in bicycling and tennis. A respected but not outstanding prime minister, Balfour had a career which was in some ways more noteworthy after he left 10 Downing Street, the official residence of the prime minister. The Balfour Declaration of 1917, which promised a

Jewish homeland in Israel, and his encouragement of the League of Nations and the cause of internationalism are the monuments to this second phase of his career.

Bibliography

Dugdale, Blanche E. C. *Arthur James Balfour, First Earl of Balfour*. 2 vols. New York: G. P. Putnam's Sons, 1937. Written by his niece, this popular work glosses over many aspects of Balfour's career.

Egremont, Max. *Balfour: A Life of Arthur James Balfour*. London: Collins, 1980. Based on manuscript sources but colorfully written, this is a good introduction to Balfour's career for the general reader.

Judd, Denis. *Balfour and the British Empire*. London: Macmillan, 1968. This scholarly work examines Balfour's attitudes toward the empire and places it in the context of a broader examination of "imperial evolution" from 1874 to 1932.

Mackay, Ruddock F. *Balfour: Intellectual Statesman*. Oxford: Oxford University Press, 1985. A scholarly reexamination of Balfour's career which concentrates on certain subjects on which the author has found new evidence.

Rasor, Eugene L. *Arthur James Balfour, 1848-1930*. Westport, Conn.: Greenwood, 1998. An up-to-date survey of Balfour's entire career, which the author places fully within the context of his times.

Tomes, Jason. *Balfour and Foreign Policy: The International Thought of a Conservative Statesman*. New York: Cambridge University Press, 1997. First thorough examination of Balfour's thoughts on such international issues as imperialism, relationships among European powers, Africa, the Middle East, central Asia and the Far East, World War I, the Russian Revolution, Zionism, the League of Nations and Anglo-American relations.

Zebel, Sydney H. *Balfour: A Political Biography*. Cambridge: Cambridge University Press, 1973. An account of Balfour's political career, this work is addressed to scholars and is well documented.

Donald S. Birn

MENACHEM BEGIN

Born: August 16, 1913; Brest-Litovsk, Russia (later Belarus)
Died: March 9, 1992; Tel Aviv, Israel

Begin placed pressure on the British Mandate government to withdraw from Palestine, enabling Israel to declare its independence and sovereignty over part of Palestine. He also served as a key opposition leader and eventually as prime minister of Israel from 1977 to 1983.

Early Life

Menachem (from Hebrew for "one who brings comfort") Begin was born on the eve of World War I in Poland's largely Jewish city of Brest-Litovsk, then occupied by czarist Russia. In 1918, Germany took the area from the Soviet Union in the Treaty of Brest-Litovsk, and, at the Versailles Conference in 1919, it became part of the reestablished nation of Poland. Menachem's father and mother were orthodox Jews who worked for Zionism, the return of Jews to Palestine.

As a child Menachem saw a growing anti-Semitism in Brest-Litovsk: Rocks broke windows in Jewish homes; confiscatory, discriminatory taxation on Jews was levied by the Polish government; Jewish students were beaten by their peers. Once he had to watch several leading Jewish citizens receive twenty-five lashes in a public park for alleged "sympathy with Bolsheviks." Begin decided as a youth that Jews should not take such treatment passively and helped organize resistance against unwarranted attacks by fellow students.

Early in life, Begin demonstrated a forceful and effective public speaking personality. He attended a Polish *Gymnasium* and received a good liberal arts education. He studied law in Warsaw and received the degree of *magister juris* from the University of Warsaw. Begin was greatly influenced by Vladimir Jabotinsky, an eloquent Russian journalist who preached Zionist activism and violence if necessary. Begin was a key organizer of the Polish chapter of Betar, Jabotinsky's activist youth organization, and eventually became its commander of seventy thousand.

Meanwhile, in Palestine a splinter group of young Jews broke from the Haganah (the Jewish self-defense organization), which at the time followed a passive self-restraint in trying not to alienate the British as they defended their lands against Arab terrorist attacks. The splinter group eventually adopted the name Irgun Z'vai Leumi, the National Military Organization. The new organization received training in sabotage and underground warfare from Polish army officers plus quantities of weapons in exchange for promises to recruit as many Jews as possible from Poland and take them to Palestine.

In the spring of 1939, Begin married Aliza Arnold, after warning her of the exceptionally difficult life she would lead as his wife. Serene and cheerful, she was one of the great strengths of Begin's life. She and Begin escaped Warsaw just ahead of the German Blitzkrieg. They went to the neutral city of Vilna, Lithuania, but Begin was arrested by the Soviet secret police and sentenced to eight years in a labor camp in Siberia. Aliza managed to escape to Palestine. After working fourteen hours a day for nearly a year in exceptionally cold conditions, Begin and other Polish prisoners were released to join the Polish Liberation Army. Their first assignment was Palestine, in which Begin first set foot in May, 1942.

Begin was already well known to the Irgun as the leader of the Polish Betar, Irgun's best source of recruits. Jabotinsky had recently died; many Irgun members had joined the British army; and a splinter group of the Irgun, the "Stern Gang," Lohamei Herut Yisrael (Fighters for the Freedom of Israel, or Lehi), had taken with them eight hundred Irgun members. Irgun, then, by the end of 1943, numbered scarcely five hundred members. It needed a dedicated, dynamic organizer, and Begin was chosen to lead the decimated Irgun.

Life's Work

Begin's principal purpose in life was to establish the State of Israel and build it up to survive in strength. He was willing to pay any price to accomplish that objective. "The God of Israel, the Lord of hosts, will help us," Begin declared in 1943. "[T]here will be no retreat. Freedom—or death." Begin's strategy was to demonstrate to the international community Great Britain's inability to govern Palestine—and thus hasten its departure. He did not want to destroy its ability to wage war against Germany and Japan and so did not raid British army bases or installations necessary to the war

Menachem Begin *(Library of Congress)*

effort. Instead, Irgun sought to harass nonmilitary targets: disrupt communications; destroy records against illegal Jewish immigration; hamper the collection of taxes; and raid police stations and warehouses for weapons stockpiling. Irgun avoided killing either British or Arab—except when "necessary." Irgun raided a British army payroll train and "confiscated" banknotes amounting to thirty-eight thousand pounds.

Most members of Irgun were part-time saboteurs or propagandists (depending on the division to which they were assigned). Full-time staff of Irgun never numbered more than thirty or forty. Discipline and military training were strict. Irgun had an underground radio station begun in 1944 and the Irgun newspaper, *Herut*. (Haganah's radio station did not begin broadcasting until October, 1945). One of Begin's strong points as a leader was the meticulous and detailed way in which he analyzed problems and planned missions for Irgun. His conduct of meetings was the same way; he even had specific questions detailed for the agenda.

Begin tried to enlist Arabs in an effort to rid Palestine of the British. Irgun leaflets distributed in Arab villages claimed Jewish willingness to see the Arabs as peaceful citizens in the future Jewish state—which was not quite the political arrangement Arabs had in mind.

In response to Irgun raids and bombings, the British in 1944 imposed a curfew on the three major cities, Jerusalem, Haifa, and Tel Aviv, and brought out an old law imposing the death penalty for possessing arms or placing explosive devices. In June, 1946, a British military court condemned to death two Irgun members for stealing weapons from a British military installation. Irgun kidnapped five British officers with the tacit warning that if the Irgun men were hanged, so too would the British die. In July, the high commissioner commuted the death sentences of the two Irgun raiders. Irgun then released the British officers, each with a one-pound note for compensatory damages. On the Sabbath, June 29, 1946, the British arrested thousands of Jews, including members of the Jewish Agency, and even sought to arrest David Ben-Gurion.

Haganah, Irgun, and Lehi all participated in the planning of the King David Hotel bombing on July 22, 1946. Warnings were telephoned to the hotel and nearby buildings a half hour before the bomb exploded, and some escaped as a result. Nevertheless, one wing of the hotel ignored the warnings, and more than one hundred people were killed in the blast. Haganah immediately and publicly condemned Irgun and disassociated itself from the terrorist act.

Begin detested the humiliation of flogging by British authorities and warned that flogging of Jews must stop or there would be retaliation in kind. When an Irgun suspect was flogged by British police, Irgun captured a British major and three noncommissioned officers and flogged each with eighteen lashes. Then they were set free with an Irgun communiqué showing the emblem of the two banks of the Jordan River and a rifle with the slogan "Only Thus." The British flogged no more Jews or Arabs during the remainder of their stay in Palestine.

Irgun's (and Begin's) greatest triumph was the successful storming of the supposedly impregnable Crusader fortress of Acre, where Jewish prisoners were kept and, in capital cases, executed. In the midst of an Arab city, Begin planned an elaborate operation that blew an enormous hole in the walls and freed 251 prisoners—131 Arabs and 120 Jews. Fifteen Jews were killed and fifteen captured. When three of those captured were executed, Irgun retaliated with the hanging of two innocent British sergeants, one of the most despicable actions ever taken by Irgun in the eyes of its critics. Equally despicable were the murders of five innocent Jews by British soldiers and policemen in Tel Aviv in retaliation for the hanging of the sergeants. No more Jewish terrorists or British soldiers were executed in the remaining year of British occupation. After Begin became prime minister of Israel, he refused to permit the execution of Arab terrorists.

When the British withdrew from Palestine and the War of Independence began in May, 1948, with the invasion of Palestine by Arab troops from Transjordan, Egypt, Syria, Lebanon, and Iraq, Begin and his Irgun were a thorn in the flesh for the new government of Israel under prime minister David Ben-Gurion. The Haganah needed all the help it could get, but neither Irgun nor Lehi was willing to relinquish control of its organization to the new government. They were willing to fight the Arabs. The massacre of Deir Yassin remains the most notorious of uncontrolled Irgun/Lehi actions.

Begin's willingness to cooperate with the new government but not to submit to its authority led to armed conflict between Haganah and Irgun over the disposition of weapons brought in by Irgun on the *Altalena.* Of Irgun's men, fourteen were killed and sixty-nine wounded. The government suffered two killed and six wounded. Much of the desperately needed ammunition had been destroyed. To Prime Minister David Ben-Gurion, Israel could not afford to have private armies that were not under the discipline of the government. To Begin's credit, he swallowed his pride and fought the common Arab enemy and did not let the Israeli cause perish in fratricidal conflict. He refused to fight fellow Jews and accepted the authority of the government. On September 20, 1948, Ben-Gurion presented Begin with an ultimatum ordering the immediate disbandment of the Irgun. Begin accepted the order and disbanded his organization.

As the war drew to an end, Begin helped organize the opposition Herut party in Israel. Herut proposed a vigorous capitalist system instead of the labor socialism of the ruling Mapai coalition. Herut also insisted that the Land of Israel include all of biblical Palestine—on both sides of the Jordan River. In the first election to the 120-member Knesset, Israel's parliament, Herut obtained fourteen seats, including one for Begin, a post he held for thirty years.

Though usually a key opposition leader to the government, Begin closed ranks during each of Israel's wars. By 1977 Begin had formed a right-wing coalition called the Likud bloc and controlled sixty-two Knesset seats, a majority. Begin became prime minister of Israel. He was supported partially because of his uncompromising stance on the West Bank captured by Israel in the 1967 war. It was Prime Minister Begin who signed the 1978 Camp David accords in an effort to normalize relations with Egypt (leading to his being corecipient of the Nobel Peace Prize of 1978 with Anwar Sadat), and it was also Begin who ordered the invasion of Lebanon and the war to end the Palestine Liberation Organization's attacks in Israel.

Summary

No one can doubt Begin's dedication to the cause of Israeli independence and strength. He was a realist. He was brutal when he thought he needed to be. He suffered much. He caused much suffering. He was intensely loyal and a capable commander who tried to protect his subordinates. He brought enormous pressure on the British, who finally were almost too glad to depart Israel, thereby making it possible for Israel to win independence and prevent Arab conquest of part of Palestine. Did the British leave and the Israelis win because of or in spite of Irgun and Begin? Would the British have left anyway, or would they have left in a context more favorable to Arab Palestinians? If the Israelis had refrained from all terrorism and sabotage, would the British have cooperated more or sided with the Arabs more? These are the imponderables of history, to which no more than tentative answers can be given.

The Arabs despised the Israelis for depriving the Palestinian Arabs of the land of their fathers, but many Arabs hated the Jews long before they had such a cause. Begin played a crucial role before 1948, but the Irgun could not win the war for independence. Only the Jewish Agency and the Haganah had the resources to do what seemed impossible at the time. Begin's role as an opposition politician and later as an unpopular prime minister continues to be clouded in controversy and conflict, both of which plagued Begin all of his life.

Bibliography

Bauer, Yehuda. *From Diplomacy to Resistance: A History of Jewish Palestine, 1939-1945.* Translated by Alton M. Winters. Philadelphia: Jewish Publication Society of America, 1970. Begin arrived in Israel in 1942 and his most significant historical contributions to Israel were in the years 1942-1948. This book analyzes in detail the historical situation during the critical years for Palestine. Bauer describes the intricate interrelationships and cooperation among Haganah, Irgun, and Lehi. The ambivalent attitudes of the British government and occupying army in Palestine and their relationship to both Arab and Jew are examined.

Begin, Menachem. *The Revolt.* Translated by Shmuel Katz. New York: Schuman, 1951. In all the controversies surrounding Begin, it is only fair to hear his side of the story. Begin tells of insights and detailed facts that a sweeping narrative cannot. Begin's account, however, ends with 1948 and so is valuable only for the early period.

Bell, J. Bowyer. *Terror Out of Zion: Irgun Zvai Leumi, LEHI, and the Palestine Underground, 1929-1949.* New York: St. Martin's Press, 1977. A well-written, fascinating insight into the intrigues, mentality, and troublesome times of the Israeli underground groups and their relationships and disagreements. One hundred pages follow Begin's career, especially after his arrival in Palestine. This book was published after Begin became prime minister, giving more historical perspective to the events described.

Haber, Eitan. *Menachem Begin: The Legend and the Man.* New York: Delacorte Press, 1978.

Hirschler, Gertrude, and Lester S. Eckman. *Menachem Begin: From Freedom Fighter to Statesman.* New York: Shengold, 1979. A sympathetic biography of Begin with many details of his family and early life. None of the stages of his life is neglected, and, in the various controversies of his career, Begin is presented in as favorable a light as the authors can persuasively find.

Hirst, David. *The Gun and the Olive Branch: The Roots of Violence in the Middle East.* New York: Harcourt Brace Jovanovich, 1977. A sharply critical analysis of Israeli actions in Palestine, including Begin's role in "Gun Zionism."

O'Brien, Conor Cruise. *The Siege: The Saga of Israel and Zionism.* New York: Simon & Schuster, 1986. A full history of modern Israel written by an Irishman and often placing an unusual interpretation on historical events. O'Brien wrote much about Begin, including his years as prime minister. This is a balanced, scholarly account.

Sachar, Howard. *A History of Israel.* 2d ed. New York: Alfred A. Knopf, 1996.

Silver, Eric. *Begin: The Haunted Prophet.* New York: Random House, 1984. A fascinating biography written by an Oxford-educated English journalist who lived in Israel for eleven years as a foreign correspondent. He sees Begin as the most consistent of men, unswerving in his dedication to Israeli security. He is often critical of Begin but detached in his observations and analysis.

William H. Burnside

EDVARD BENEŠ

Born: May 28, 1884; Kožlany, Bohemia, Austro-Hungarian Empire
Died: September 3, 1948; Sezimovo Ústí, Czechoslovakia

Beneš helped undermine Austro-Hungarian rule in the Czech and Slovak region during World War I and became foreign minister of the new republic there in 1918. A brilliant statesman, he negotiated numerous agreements, but as president he was unable to prevent the dismemberment of his country at Munich. During World War II, he headed the Czechoslovakian government in exile and after 1945 endeavored unsuccessfully to maintain Czechoslovakia's political freedom in the face of mounting communist pressures.

Early Life

Edvard Beneš was born in Kožlany, Bohemia, on May 28, 1884. The youngest of ten children, he was the son of a moderately successful farmer who was able to send him to secondary school at Vinohrady. As family funds were too meager to cover the cost of higher education, however, Beneš resorted to tutoring and free-lance writing to make ends meet. In 1903, he entered Charles University in Prague to study philology (he did become an accomplished linguist) but switched to philosophy and came under the influence of Tomáš Masaryk, the leading advocate of Czech nationalism. At Masaryk's urging, Beneš went to France to study at the Sorbonne and at Dijon, and he obtained a doctor of laws degree in political science and sociology from the latter. In Paris he met a Czech student, Hana Vlčkova, whom he married in 1909. She became his lifelong companion and source of constant encouragement.

In 1909, Beneš returned home, completed a Ph.D. at Charles University, and secured a teaching post in political science at the Academy of Commerce in Prague. He also turned away from Marxism, joined Masaryk's Progressive Party, and wrote for its organ. In 1912, he joined the faculty at Charles University as a lecturer in sociology. (After the war, he regularly lectured there on sociology.) In 1913, he also became a lecturer at the Technical College in Prague. By that time, he had become a prolific writer on politics and international affairs and active in the national liberation movement. He had developed a deep hatred for militarism, of both the Austrian and the German variety, but he was not called up for army service at the outbreak of World War I, because of a leg injury incurred in his youth when he was a star soccer player. In early 1915, he and Masaryk (who was now in exile) formed an underground organization called Maffia, which sought to promote a national uprising and to aid the Allies by supplying secret information about activities in Austria-Hungary. In September, 1915, Beneš left the country with a forged passport to avoid imminent arrest by the Austrian police and joined Masaryk in Switzerland.

Beneš's earlier sojourn in France had imbued him with Western political, economic, and cultural ideas that put him at odds with those Bohemian patriots who looked to Russia for salvation. Beneš and Masaryk became the leading spokespersons for the "Westernist" school in the liberation movement. They represented a "Europeanist" or "realist" stance; that is, they believed the nation must learn how to observe, analyze, and contemplate options carefully, rather than follow the romantic notions of nineteenth century pan-Slavism. Through their intensive efforts in the three years that followed, Beneš and Masaryk almost single-handedly achieved their goal of an independent Czechoslovak state.

Life's Work

At their meeting in 1915, Beneš and Masaryk discussed plans for their country's future, arranged to gather funds to carry on the work, and determined that they would persuade the Allies to support their movement. Beneš functioned essentially as Masaryk's chief of staff. In February, 1916, Beneš became general secretary of the Czechoslovak National Council, which was seated in Paris, where he had extensive ties.

A tireless propagandist, Beneš pounded the Allies with details about how the Czech and Slovak people were working for victory through army desertions and mutinies and civilian riots, sabotage efforts, and demonstrations against the authorities in Austria-Hungary. Their movement contributed materially to the demise of the Habsburg Empire and influenced the Allies to recognize the idea of a Czechoslovak republic. Through his French contacts, Beneš negotiated the specific mention of the liberation of the Czechoslovaks from foreign domination in the Entente's note to Woodrow Wilson in January, 1917, which spelled out their war aims, and Wilson in-

Edvard Beneš *(Library of Congress)*

cluded in his Fourteen Points in January, 1918, the demand that the peoples of Austria-Hungary should have the opportunity for autonomous development.

Once Masaryk had secured the formation of the Czechoslovak Legion in Russia in 1917, the Czechoslovak National Council in Paris began to function as the government in exile of a state that had hitherto existed only in the minds of its leaders. In May and June, 1918, Beneš obtained French and British recognition of Czechoslovakia as an allied and belligerent nation, and he effectively countered Italian opposition to this recognition. He also was in regular contact with nationalist leaders in Prague, and, when the Habsburg regime collapsed, Beneš was able to secure the establishment of an independent state under the National Council on October 28. Three days later, the Slovaks proclaimed independence and joined with the Czech provinces.

On November 14, a hastily convened parliament approved the émigré committee as the constitutional government, with Masaryk as president and Beneš as foreign minister, and the latter was commissioned to represent the new country at the Paris Peace Conference. After signing in 1919 the Treaty of St. Germain with Austria, which finalized the authority of the Czechoslovak government, Beneš returned home in triumph to take up the duties of foreign minister. He served in this post until 1935 with only a brief interlude from September 26, 1921, to October 7, 1922, as premier.

During his tenure as foreign minister, Beneš gained renown as a European statesman who was devoted to the struggle for international peace and collective security. His major achievement was the formation of the Little Entente with Yugoslavia and Romania in 1920-1921 to check Hungarian ambitions; this Little Entente, linked with the Treaty of Alliance and Friendship with France in 1924, was the foundation of the continental balance of power and the French deterrence system against Germany. Through this tie, Beneš was able to secure French assistance for construction of the Czechoslovak border fortifications, which might have saved the country from German conquest in 1938 if the Sedition region had not been lost through the ill-fated Munich Agreement.

Beneš also concluded one of the first European treaties with Soviet Russia (1922) and treaties of friendship with Poland (1921), Austria (1921), Italy (1924), and Germany (1925). He was an active participant in the Genoa Economics Meeting (1922), the Locarno Conference (1925), disarmament conferences in 1927, 1929, and

1932, and the Lausanne reparations talks (1932). In 1933, he negotiated the London Convention with the Soviet Union, Yugoslavia, Romania, and Turkey, which defined aggression and thereby applied the 1928 Paris Pact to Eastern Europe, and in 1935 he concluded an alliance (Treaty of Mutual Assistance) with the Soviet Union. He played a leading role in the League of Nations, first as acting vice president in 1920 and then as a member of the council (1923-1927), president of the assembly (1935), and chairs of various committees. In 1924, Beneš and Greek foreign minister Nicholas Politis drafted the celebrated Geneva Protocol, which was designed to prevent aggressive war by requiring that international disputes be submitted to peaceful negotiation and arbitration.

When the aged Masaryk decided to retire, the parliament named his protégé as the new constitutional head of state on December 18, 1935. Beneš tried to check Nazi expansion by means of collective security, but his efforts were torpedoed by France, which allowed Germany to remilitarize the Rhineland, cowered behind the Maginot Line, and refused to honor its treaty commitments. After the Austrian Anschluss, Adolf Hitler put pressure on Czechoslovakia to cede the area populated by German-speaking people (the Sudetenland), and when he began to concentrate troops on the border, Beneš ordered a general mobilization on May 21, 1938.

By putting the country on a war footing, Beneš forced the führer to back down, but by late summer it appeared certain that Germany would drag Europe into a general conflict over the Sedition issue. The British and French leaders succeeded in negotiating an agreement at Munich on September 29 that allowed Germany to annex the region. Neither the republic nor its Soviet ally was consulted about the matter, and Czechoslovakia, stripped of its border fortifications, was thrown to the wolves. In response to Hitler's demands, Beneš resigned on October 5 and went into exile in London.

He traveled to the United States in February, 1939, to teach at the University of Chicago, but when Hitler seized the remainder of Czechoslovakia on March 15, he agreed to assume the leadership of his country's liberation movement. He returned to London in July, established a popular government known as the Czechoslovak National Committee, and a year later converted it into the Provisional Czechoslovak National Government. In July, 1941, the United States, Great Britain, and the Soviet Union accorded recognition to Beneš' government in exile.

Beneš's wartime strategy was to pay official visits to the two men who would play the decisive roles in shaping the new order: Franklin D. Roosevelt and Joseph Stalin. He went to the United States in May, 1943, and to Moscow in December, 1943. He made it clear that Czechoslovakia would have a new and more cordial relationship with the Soviet Union after the war, and he agreed to the Czechoslovak-Soviet Treaty of Friendship, Mutual Assistance, and Postwar Cooperation that paved the way for the disaster that would befall his country after the liberation. He hoped that voluntary concessions to Stalin would make for goodwill, but his surrender of Ruthenia (Subcarpathian Ukraine), Czechoslovakia's easternmost province, gained nothing.

As the war drew to a close, the Red Army installed native communists in Slovakia. Beneš naïvely thought that he and his government would be able to oust these communists once he appeared on the scene, and journeyed to Russia and then to Slovakia in March, 1945, where he established provisional headquarters at Košice. He agreed to a coalition government that would include communists, most notably the Czech party leader Klement Gottwald. On May 8, Beneš went to Prague (also liberated by the Soviets), where he was joyously welcomed.

Although Beneš set out to prevent the communists from monopolizing power in Czechoslovakia, his program of strengthening public morale, treating the communists evenhandedly and having them share power responsibility in proportion to their strength, yielding to their demands in social and economic but not political matters, and keeping avenues to the West open while reducing Soviet influence in the country was a failure. His position steadily eroded, and in 1948 the communists carried off a coup. On February 25, Beneš reluctantly signed the death warrant for Czechoslovak freedom by accepting the resignation of the democratic ministers and naming a new government headed by Gottwald. By that time, Beneš was a sick man. He had already suffered a serious stroke the year before, and he resigned the presidency on June 7 and retired to his country home at Sezimovo Ústí. His physical condition deteriorated rapidly, and he died on September 3, 1948.

Summary

Edvard Beneš was the quintessential European statesman of the interwar years. However, the times were not ripe for a person with such a commitment to international peace through collective security. Although he was a Czechoslovak patriot, he had a broader conception of the international order. He was an eternal optimist and an ineffable proponent of democracy on the international scene, and thus he was no match for dictators such as Hitler and Stalin. Although he was a brilliant negotiator and understood the art of compromise, his critics questioned whether he really had the fortitude to stand up to tyranny.

Like that of his country, Beneš' life was a tragic story. A confirmed democrat, he was forced to compromise with antidemocratic forces. His allies never came through when they were needed, and, in the crucial years of 1938 and 1948, he and Czechoslovakia were left alone and ignored as the flame of democracy was extinguished. Whether he was a victim of forces beyond his control or he had contributed to the situation by his own ineptness is a matter for historians to debate. Yet he left his mark as a statesman and fighter for a democratic nation and world.

Bibliography

Beneš, Edvard. *Memoirs: From Munich to New World and New Victory*. Translated by Godfrey Lias. London: Allen & Unwin, 1954. Reprint. New York: Arno Press, 1972. Originally published in Prague in 1947, the Czechoslovak edition was a best-seller until its suppression after the communist coup. It was designed to justify his statesmanship after Munich and the process of undoing the agreement.

__________. *My War Memoirs*. Translated by Paul Selver. Boston: Houghton Mifflin, 1928. A detailed personal account of Beneš' activities in the Czechoslovak national movement, from the beginning of the war to Masaryk's return to preside over the new state.

Bruegel, J. W. *Czechoslovakia Before Munich: The German Minority Problem and British Appeasement Policy*. Cambridge, England: Cambridge University Press, 1973. Insightful treatment of the Sedition German question and Beneš' efforts to deal with it. Demonstrates that he failed to grasp the significance of having such a large German minority within his state until it was too late.

Crabitès, Pierre. *Beneš, Statesman of Central Europe*. London: G. Routledge & Sons, 1935. Typical of the popular biographies that were published in the interwar years—laudatory and based on *My War Memoirs* and secondary sources.

Korbel, Josef. *The Communist Subversion of Czechoslovakia, 1938-*

1948. Princeton, N.J.: Princeton University Press, 1959. Traces communist activities in the land from Munich to the coup. Includes the efforts of Beneš to deal with the communist exile regime and his losing struggle with Gottwald to retain democracy.

__________. *Twentieth Century Czechoslovakia: The Meaning of Its History*. New York: Columbia University Press, 1977. A historical survey that focuses on the key role of Beneš and criticizes his apparent unwillingness to exercise forceful leadership during the Sedition crisis and the period before the communist coup.

Mamatey, Victor, and Radomír Luza, eds. *A History of the Czechoslovak Republic, 1918-1948*. Princeton, N.J.: Princeton University Press, 1973. A collection of seventeen detailed scholarly essays on various aspects of the republic's history. The central focus is on Beneš and his leadership.

Taborsky, Edward, *President Edvard Beneš: Between East and West, 1938-1948*. Stanford: Hoover Institution Press, 1981. An account by Beneš's personal secretary and legal adviser between 1939 and 1945 who fled to America after the coup. He relates the president's deeds during the war years and defends him against his critics.

Zeman, Z. A. B. *The Life of Edvard Beneš, 1884-1948: Czechoslovakia in Peace and War*. New York: Oxford University Press, 1997.

Richard V. Pierard

DAVID BEN-GURION

David Gruen

Born: October 16, 1886; Płónsk, Poland, Russian Empire
Died: December 1, 1973; Tel Aviv, Israel

Ben-Gurion dreamed of the state of Israel, then turned that vision into reality. As Israel's first prime minister and defense minister, he laid a solid foundation for the country's survival and prosperity; as its leading statesman, he established the principles that continue to guide it.

Early Life

The son of Avigdor and Sheindel (Friedman) Gruen, David Ben-Gurion was born in Płónsk, Poland, on October 16, 1886. His father was a local leader in Hovevai Zion (lovers of Zion), a forerunner of the Zionist movement, and a product of the Haskalah (Jewish enlightenment), which sought to fuse traditional and modern thought and to revive Hebrew as a living language. At the age of fourteen, he and two friends organized the Ezra Society to teach local children to speak and write Hebrew. Despite opposition from religious leaders who regarded Hebrew as too sacred for daily use, the group attracted 150 students.

Along with his love of Israel, the young Ben-Gurion was imbibing socialist principles. Harriet Beecher Stowe, Leo Tolstoy, and Abraham Mapu shaped his politics, and in 1905 he joined Poalei Zion (workers of Zion), which sought to build a workers' state in Israel. A natural organizer and orator, Ben-Gurion united the seamstresses of Płónsk to strike for a shorter workday, and he repeatedly outdebated non-Zionist opponents who argued for assimilation and socialist revolution in Europe.

Another lifelong belief also revealed itself in Płónsk, then ruled by czarist Russia. The country had witnessed numerous pogroms against the Jews, who rarely fought back against their attackers. Ben-Gurion, whose heroes were the Maccabees and Old Testament warriors, successfully urged his coreligionists to arm themselves for self-defense, as later he would organize the Haganah in Palestine to thwart Arab raids. Never a zealot, he did not want to turn Jews into wolves, but neither did he want his people to be sheep.

In 1906, Ben-Gurion's Zionist dream took him to Petach Tikva in Turkish Palestine, and for the next several years he worked in various settlements, living his idea of creating a Jewish state through labor. He was never physically strong, though, and Poalei Zion recognized that he could make a more significant contribution with his head than with his back. Appointed editor of the organization's newspaper, *Ahdut*, he took as his pseudonym the name of Yosef Ben-Gurion, a moderate leader of the Jewish revolt against the Romans in 66 C.E.

Life's Work

Believing that Turkey could be persuaded to grant a Jewish state, Ben-Gurion went to Constantinople in 1912 to pursue a law degree, after which he planned to enter the Turkish parliament and work for an independent Israel. The Balkan War interrupted his studies; the outbreak of World War I ended them. He returned to Palestine, where he urged support for Turkey against the Entente, fearing that if the Central Powers were defeated, anti-Semitic Russia would be awarded the ancient Jewish homeland. Indifferent to his pro-Ottoman stance, Turkish authorities arrested Ben-Gurion in February, 1915, for his Zionist activities and deported him.

Together with Itzhak Ben-Zvi, later to serve as Israel's president, Ben-Gurion went to the United States to encourage Jewish immigration; throughout his life, he believed that a Jewish state would arise and prosper only if Jews settled and worked the land. He made few converts, but one of them was a young girl from Milwaukee, Goldie Mabovitch; as Golda Meir, she would be Israel's prime minister. While in the United States, Ben-Gurion published *Yizkor* (1916) and *Eretz Yisrael* (1918) to promote Jewish settlement in Palestine. These volumes did little to further that cause, but they did enhance Ben-Gurion's reputation. While in the United States, he met and married Paula Munweis (December 5, 1917).

When the United States entered World War I, Ben-Gurion realized that Turkey and the other Central Powers were doomed. His shift of allegiance to the Entente was guaranteed by the Balfour Declaration (November 2, 1917), promising a Jewish homeland in Israel; he could not know that Great Britain was also pledging to give the same territory to the Arabs and to France. Urging the

David Ben-Gurion *(Library of Congress)*

creation of a Jewish Legion to support Great Britain, Ben-Gurion himself enlisted, leaving his pregnant wife. The legion saw little action, but it did return Ben-Gurion to the Middle East, where he immediately resumed his efforts to forge a united labor organization. Crucial to this goal was the Histadrut. Founded in December, 1920, with only 4,433 of the 65,000 Jews of Palestine, it grew throughout the decade, establishing its own bank, newspaper (*Davar*), construction company, and recreational facilities. Under Ben-Gurion's leadership, the various labor factions also joined politically, so that by 1930 his Mapai Party included 80 percent of the region's Jewish workers.

While Ben-Gurion's achievements and reputation grew in Palestine, he could not influence Zionist policy. The Fourteenth and Fifteenth World Zionist Congresses encouraged middle-class rather than worker immigration and favored urban instead of rural development. Ben-Gurion was philosophically opposed to this emphasis on bourgeois capitalism; he also recognized that businessmen, with no tie to the land, were likely to leave the country once prosperity ended, and so they did after 1927. Another disagreement, with Chaim Weizmann, president of the World Zionist Organization, arose over how far to press Great Britain to allow Jewish settlement in Palestine; Weizmann favored conciliation at almost any cost.

Unable to compete within the World Zionist Organization, Ben-Gurion in 1930 created a rival, the World Congress for Labor Palestine, dedicated to "a Jewish state, a laboring society, [and] Jewish-Arab cooperation." Through this new institution, Ben-Gurion hoped to enlist international Jewish support for his views, but Great Britain's efforts to placate the Arabs at Jewish expense were turning mainstream Zionists away from Weizmann. At the Seventeenth World Zionist Congress, the World Congress for Labor Palestine comprised the largest single bloc of votes, and its representatives received two seats on the executive committee. Two years later, when the organization convened again, the World Congress for Labor Palestine held 44.6 percent of the votes, thanks in large measure to Ben-Gurion's vigorous campaigning in Eastern Europe; Ben-Gurion himself was named to the Executive. By 1935, the World Congress for Labor Palestine had gained control, and Ben-Gurion became chairman of the Zionist Executive and head of the Jewish Agency.

Although he had refused the presidency of the World Zionist Organization in favor of Weizmann, the two men continued to disagree over unlimited immigration and relations with Great Britain. Realizing that Great Britain never would willingly fulfill the promise of the Balfour Declaration, Ben-Gurion in 1936 began training the Haganah, the underground Jewish army, for future conflicts with the Arabs and British. Throughout World War II, he opposed guerrilla warfare against Great Britain, but as soon as Germany surrendered he went to the United States to secure money for weapons. In October, 1945, he ordered the Haganah to use force if necessary to protect Jews entering Palestine illegally, Great Britain having refused to lift tight restrictions on Jewish immigration, and he supported a number of attacks against British installations. Great Britain responded by arresting Jewish leaders and confiscating weapons, but it also resolved to abandon its mandate, agreeing to a partition plan adopted by the United Nations on November 29, 1947.

After almost two thousand years, after a third of their number had been killed in the Nazi holocaust, the Jewish people were to have a country of their own—if they could defend it from the armies of five Arab nations poised to invade as soon as the British mandate ended. George Marshall, the American secretary of state, urged Ben-Gurion not to declare independence but to wait five or ten years more. Instead, on May 14, 1948, in the Tel Aviv Museum, Ben-Gurion declared the "establishment of the Jewish State in Palestine, to be called the State of Israel."

Ben-Gurion had been modern Jewry's Moses, leading it to the promised land. Now he would also be its Joshua, as the army he had trained and supplied turned back the invaders. At the same time, he overcame threats from Menachem Begin's Irgun Z'vai Leumi on the right and from the Palmach on the left, each seeking to maintain autonomous military organizations. He thus established the principle of civilian control over the military. Over the next four years (1949-1953), he led the fledgling nation as prime minister and defense minister, doubling the nation's Jewish population and securing international financial support.

At the end of 1953, he temporarily retired—for two years, he said—to Sde Boker, a kibbutz in the Negev desert, fifty miles south of Beersheba. He wanted a rest, a chance to read and write, but he also wanted to foster in others the pioneer spirit that had brought him to Israel almost fifty years earlier. Moreover, he regarded settlement of the Negev as crucial to the country's security against Egypt and hoped others would follow him into this area.

His absence from government actually lasted more than a year. A scandal in the defense ministry led to the resignation of Pinhas Lavon, and Ben-Gurion replaced him. After the 1955 elections, he also resumed the post of prime minister, leading the country to victory in the 1956 Suez campaign. Although much of the victory was annulled by pressure from the United States to return to prewar borders, Israel had secured freedom of navigation through Elath. Also, France, which had helped Israel during the fighting, agreed to build a nuclear reactor at Dimona.

At the same time that Ben-Gurion was making Israel the strongest military power in the region, he also wanted it to be one of the world's great moral forces. To the newly independent states of Africa and to Burma he sent technicians and scientists, and from these countries came students who would be doctors, nurses, and teachers in their homelands.

Well into his seventies, Ben-Gurion exemplified his definition of a leader: "You must know when to fight your political opponents and when to mark time. . . . And . . . you must constantly reassess chosen policies." In the 1960's, though, he became increasingly inflexible and out of touch with reality. He refused to recognize the evidence that exonerated Pinhas Lavon, who had been forced to leave the defense ministry in 1955 after perjured testimony and forged documents caused him to be blamed for terrorist acts in Egypt.

While Ben-Gurion recruited the next generation of Israel's leaders, among them Moshe Dayan, Shimon Peres, and Abba Eban, he antagonized many of his older colleagues, such as Moshe Sharett and Golda Meir, by seeming to ignore them in favor of younger protégés. His close ties to Germany brought Israel many benefits, but he failed to gauge the hostility that many of his countrymen harbored against that country. In 1963, amid growing opposition to his leadership, he resigned from the government; two years later he left the Mapai Party he had done so much to create, challenging it in the 1965 elections. His faction won ten seats, Mapai forty-five. When tension with Egypt increased in 1967, there were calls for Ben-Gurion's return to the prime ministry, but only from those unaware that he was urging peace. It was his disciple, Dayan, who as defense minister led the nation to its swift, overwhelming victory in the Six-Day War.

In 1970, Ben-Gurion left the Knesset, Israel's parliament, for what he thought was the last time, but, on his eighty-fifth birthday, he spoke to a special session called in his honor and received a standing ovation from friends and opponents alike. He then returned to the Negev, and there, after his death on December 1, 1973, he was buried, overlooking the Wilderness of Zin, where Israel's saga had begun three millennia before.

Summary

David Ben-Gurion observed that "history would have been quite different if there had been no Churchill." History would also have been different had there been no Ben-Gurion. As a young pioneer in Turkish Palestine, he had resolved, "I have but a single aim: to serve the Jewish worker in the Land of Israel." He never strayed from that purpose. When others hesitated to pressure Great Britain to declare Israeli independence and to open Israel's borders to unlimited immigration, he pressed boldly on. Though he might have shifted tactics, supporting the Central Powers and then the Entente in World War I, opposing guerrilla warfare against Great Britain and then favoring it, he never altered his goal of building a secure, moral Jewish nation.

Ben-Gurion sacrificed much for his dream. As a young man he was often ill, lonely, and hungry, as he sought work, frequently unsuccessfully, in a malaria-ridden land. Later he would have virtually no family life, traveling around Europe and the United States to cajole and coerce others into sharing his dream. His insistence on principles above politics alienated many former friends. Nor did he accomplish all that he sought, never reconciling Sephardic Jews from Africa and Asia with the European Ashkenazis, certainly not achieving peace with the Arabs. His hope of making Israel a leader among Third World nations remained unrealized.

For what Ben-Gurion did accomplish, though, he will remain, as Charles de Gaulle described him in 1960, the symbol of Zionism and "one of the greatest statesmen of [the twentieth] century." He had built his castles in the air, then had put solid foundations under them. The state of Israel is his legacy; he shaped its history and left a blueprint for its future—to do justly, to love mercy, and to walk humbly with its God.

Bibliography

Avi-hai, Avraham. *Ben-Gurion, State-Builder: Principles and Pragmatism, 1948-1963.* New York: John Wiley & Sons, 1974. This work argues that Ben-Gurion was successful in shaping modern Israel, because he could find practical ways to fulfill his ideals. It ends with Ben-Gurion's resignation as prime minister in 1963.

Bar-Zohar, Michael. *Ben-Gurion: A Biography.* New York: Delacorte Press, 1978. Bar-Zohar spent much time with Ben-Gurion and interviewed other Israeli leaders. Presents not only the public figure but also the private man behind the decisions.

Ben-Gurion, David. *David Ben-Gurion in His Own Words.* Edited by Amram Ducovny. New York: Fleet Press, 1968. Ducovny provides a brief biography of the Israeli leader and then arranges Ben-Gurion's statements under such headings as "The Philosopher" (chapter 2) and "The Scholar" (chapter 7). Includes a useful chronology through 1968.

Jabotinsky, Vladimir. *The Story of the Jewish Legion.* New York: Ackerman, 1945.

Kurzman, Dan. *Ben-Gurion: Prophet of Fire.* New York: Simon & Schuster, 1983. Based on extensive interviews and archival research as well as published material, this work provides a comprehensive survey of Ben-Gurion's life. Contains fascinating photographs and an extensive bibliography.

Teveth, Shabtai. *Ben-Gurion and the Holocaust.* New York: Harcourt Brace, 1996.

__________. *Ben-Gurion and the Palestinian Arabs: From Peace to War.* Oxford: Oxford University Press, 1985. Maintains that Ben-Gurion determined Israel's attitude toward the Arabs within its borders. Traces the evolution of Ben-Gurion's thoughts on Jewish-Arab relations. Ends with the establishment of the state of Israel.

__________. *Ben-Gurion: The Burning Ground, 1886-1948.* Boston: Houghton Mifflin, 1987. A scholarly companion to Avi-hai's work about Ben-Gurion after 1948. Ben-Gurion's papers are voluminous, and this work draws heavily on them. Ends at 1948 because official documents thereafter are inaccessible and because he sees Ben-Gurion as changing after Israel gained its independence.

Zweig, Ronald. *David Ben-Gurion: Politics and Leadership in Israel.* Portland, Oreg.: Frank Cass, 1991.

Joseph Rosenblum

HABIB BOURGUIBA

Born: August 3, 1903; Monastir, Tunisia

Bourguiba organized Tunisians to confront French rule and was the catalyst for independence, leading his people to nationhood in 1956. For thirty-one years, Bourguiba served as Tunisia's only president, until he was toppled from power in a bloodless coup d'état in Tunis.

Early Life

Habib Bourguiba was born in Monastir on August 3, 1903. Monastir, located on the north-central coast of Tunisia, was the site of a large, ancient Islamic fortress that was a constant reminder of Tunisia's ties to Islam. Bourguiba's family was one of modest means, being members of the lower-ranking civil service. When Bourguiba was five, his mother died, and his father then sent him to Tunis to reside with his elder brother Muhammad. There was no question about the young Bourguiba's intelligence, and, after training in the local Koranic schools, he went to the elementary school of Sadiki College. Later, he attended the college itself, an important center of Tunisian learning, as well as the Lycée Carnot. It was at Sadiki College and the Lycée Carnot that Bourguiba learned the best of both the French and the Tunisian worlds. Sadiki College would prove to have a profound impact on the young Habib Bourguiba and a dramatic impact on the course of Tunisian history.

Founded in the 1860's, Sadiki College trained generations of Tunisians who would become the leaders of the nationalist movement. These young Tunisians sought to blend a modern Tunisian nationalism with old Arab, Islamic values, and with the best that France had to offer. It was into this environment that Bourguiba entered as a student. Never in good health, Bourguiba had bouts of illness that slowed his studies, but eventually he went on to Paris to study law in 1924.

While in Paris, Bourguiba saw and adopted many French and Western European ideas, and before returning to Tunisia in 1927 he married a French woman. As a young intellectual, deeply impressed by life in the sophisticated French capital, Bourguiba was not simply content to practice law in Tunis. In 1922, he joined the Tunisian Destour (constitution) Party. While composed of forward-looking young Tunisians, the Destour Party did not have a coherent program or specific ideology. While it admired things French and modern, praising traditional French ideals (which were so often forgotten in the imperialist scheme of things), Destour looked backward to a supposed golden age of reform before the establishment of the 1881 protectorate.

Life's Work

Bourguiba and his circle of friends rejected the program of the Destour Party as the way to independence, and in 1933 they prepared the groundwork for the establishment of a new organization, the Neo-Destour Party. In 1933, Bourguiba and others founded the newspaper *L'Action tunisienne*, which was highly critical of the Destour leadership and which called for stronger action to end the French protectorate, an action designed to provoke the French. At Kasr Hillalin in March, 1934, the mavericks formed a vigorous new party, the Neo-Destour, with Bourguiba as its leading light. Many of the Neo-Destourians were from small towns, and a high number were from the ranks of Sadiki College graduates. From 1934 to 1936, Bourguiba and many of his Neo-Destour colleagues found themselves in jail for anti-Protectorate agitation. From 1938 to 1943, Bourguiba was again in jail. Following a series of riots in Tunis in April, 1938, the Neo-Destour was outlawed, and its leadership was arrested and incarcerated by the French.

The French Republic had good reason to fear unrest in Tunisia. Fascist Italy, with which France had had decent relations up to 1938, began a concentrated effort to extend its control over several French holdings, including Tunisia. Italian colonial claims to Tunisia in 1881 were substantial, and the young Italian government suffered a deep humiliation when Tunisia was added to the French Empire. The issue surfaced again in 1896 and, again, briefly, after the end of World War I. Benito Mussolini, with his dreams of a revitalized Roman Empire and feeling secure in his newfound friendship with Adolf Hitler, began to pressure the much-weakened Paris government over Tunisia. The result was a panic in Paris and repression in Tunisia.

That Bourguiba regarded Fascism as he did Marxism there can be little doubt, and the shrewd North African could see no future with either the Roman fasces or the Russian hammer and sickle.

Pressured by the Fascists during his incarceration in Rome in 1942 and 1943, Bourguiba continued to urge support for France but warned that support did not mean an end to Neo-Destourian agitation for an end to the protectorate. Once liberated from Fascist imprisonment, Bourguiba went back to work as an organizer.

By 1948, Bourguiba was perhaps the most popular nationalist leader in Tunisia, with a great following among those Tunisians who had served in the allied armies against the Axis and among young, well-educated Tunisians in general, but there seemed to be no relief from the short-lived de Gaulle government (1944-1946). The change finally came in 1954, when France, reeling under the Indo-Chinese War and facing continual problems (but not yet revolution) in Algeria, changed its imperialist policy.

In that year, French premier Pierre Mendès-France visited Tunisia and on July 31, 1954, proclaimed the self-government of Tunisia within a French union. Even Bourguiba, back in prison, hailed the French move and praised the French as keeping faith with their own revolutionary heritage. For two years, negotiations took place between Tunisia and the French, looking forward to the 1956 target. In 1955, Bourguiba returned to Tunis and was given a hero's welcome by the people. By the time of independence in 1956, there was no more popular figure in Tunisia than Bourguiba.

Bourguiba's tenure as Tunisia's first president represented moderation. He rejected virulent Arab nationalism, cautioned against Tunisia's being too deeply embroiled in the Arab-Israeli conflict (even though that conflict had not yet drawn distinct lines), urged nonalignment, promoted a Tunisian brand of Arab socialism (the Neo-Destour Party changed its name in 1964 to the Parti Socialist Desturien), encouraged French help (assistance among equals), and tried to come to grips with the thorny and ever-present problem of state-Islam relations. Bourguiba did give sanctuary to the Algerian rebels, who were locked in a bloody life-and-death struggle with France, but he feared the rampant nationalism of the Algerians; he worried lest the Algerians infect Tunisian youth who saw the Algerian Front de Libération Nationale and their army as a set of true North African heroes.

Bourguiba's relationship with Islam was a rocky one. While the 1956 constitution proclaimed Islam as the religion of the state, there was a quiet contest between Bourguiba and Islam. In 1960, this contest came to a head when Bourguiba prescribed the dates for Ramadan, the month of fasting, one of the five great pillars of the

Muslim faith. The month of Ramadan tries the patience of the believers, and it can seriously hinder commerce and industry. Also, the end of Ramadan is marked by *al-Futur*, a feast of celebration which can also tax the faithful. Bourguiba, citing national goals, tried hard to curtail Ramadan, without success. Bourguiba had shown, however, a tendency to interpret Islam in the context of the modern nation-state. In 1960, this was an issue, but by the 1980's, with Islam flexing a strong and militant muscle, the picture would be different indeed.

As early as 1957, Bourguiba officially began to address the needs of Tunisian women in the modern world. He personally attacked the veil as a relic of the past that was not rooted in Islam. In 1957, over strong objections by traditionalists, he encouraged the formation of the Union des Femmes de la Tunisie (UNFT), and he continued his support of Tunisian women by assuring them the vote in municipal elections in 1957 and in all subsequent national and local elections. More than forty thousand women were enrolled in the UNFT by 1960, and the future seemed quite bright for Tunisian women. By the 1980's, however, the bright banner of the UNFT had become tarnished, as had many once so promising national institutions, because of the lack of direction from the rapidly aging Bourguiba.

In creating Tunisia, Bourguiba built a one-party state with power resting mainly in his hands and, to a much lesser extent, in the hands of the Neo-Destour cadres. If Bourguiba had had to rely only on his own position as president or on his role as head of the party, it is doubtful that he could have lasted thirty-one years. His charisma, his role in Tunisian independence, and his basic moderation, keeping Tunisia relatively free of embroilment in the ongoing Arab-Israeli conflict and stemming the tide of Islamic revivalism and fundamentalism, made Bourguiba the figure of stability and continuity for Tunisia.

Bourguiba never did come to grips with the question of an orderly succession, nor did he, throughout the 1970's and early 1980's, encourage the emergence of new leadership within the party. While the future looked good for Tunisia, there were troubling signs, such as rising unemployment and an economic slowdown. Four major problems would come to plague Bourguiba's last few years in power: Bourguiba's health and the succession issue, the atrophy of the one-party state, Islamic revivalism and fundamentalism, and relations with Tunisia's North African neighbors, Algeria and Libya.

In the early 1980's, rumors emanated from Tunis that Bourguiba was suffering from a number of ailments and that old age had begun to take its toll on the leader. Bourguiba's son had been named as a likely successor, but this was destined not to be. No one seemed to be sure what Bourguiba had in mind, and there were reports that his behavior was becoming more erratic. This had its impact on the political faithful who saw their position challenged by more youthful political aspirants.

In 1983, the Bourguiba government froze wages, but inflation continued until, in 1984, there were severe food riots which shook the foundation of the government. There were signs of an Islamic revival. The Movement de la Tendance Islamiste became something of a force in the towns and on campuses. Labor problems beset the government. Muhammad Mzali, the prime minister and the man selected by Bourguiba to succeed him at some unspecified time, found it difficult to deal with the rising tide of religious, political, and economic discontent.

Libya continued to be a clear threat to Tunisia, and neither Bourguiba nor Mzali seemed able to curb the open enthusiasm for Libya's anti-Western posturing. Libya's position fitted well with the Muslim revivalists and with those who called for radical change in Tunisia.

In November, 1987, in a bloodless coup, Tunisian security chief (appointed by Bourguiba) Zin al Abidin bin Ali removed the ailing, eighty-four-year-old president. The new leader simply stated that Bourguiba was "mentally unfit" to remain in power, and he was placed in house arrest near Tunis. For all practical purposes, Bourguiba, a sick, aged man, passed from the political scene.

Summary

Despite Habib Bourguiba's removal from power there remained his legacy: an independent Tunisia. His accomplishments were many, and will, in the long run, overshadow the last years of his rule. Bourguiba's first and greatest accomplishment was the nurturing of the ideal of independence, which grew into the reality of a bloodless transition from colonial status to new nationhood. He helped bring Tunisia to independence without the bitter ideological baggage that weighted down so many new states of the Third World. Bourguiba's second feat was to steer a moderate course when other African and Arab states were mired in wars and successive, destructive *coups d'état*. It was always clear that Bourguiba led an Arab, Islamic state, but his reasonable approach brought him respect from all sides, and he was able then to suggest answers and compromises to feuding factions.

In the late 1970's and early 1980's, however, Bourguiba, frustrated with the course of Arab-Israeli relations, did involve Tunisia more and more with the Palestine Liberation Organization, allowing them to maintain offices and camps, especially for orphaned and traumatized children, in the Tunis area. Ironically, it was this evidence of Tunisia's Arab status that brought violence in the form of an Israeli air raid and assassinations. As Bourguiba reasoned, it was perhaps inevitable that the conflict would touch even the most moderate Arab state.

Bourguiba also left behind one of the most prosperous North African states, with concrete achievements in education, wage earning levels, and women's rights. By the last half of the 1970's Bourguiba's prestige was at its highest, but as he aged this prestige began to slip away. Perhaps Bourguiba believed that only he, the man who gave life to independent Tunisia, had the insights to keep it on its course. As Bourguiba's force waned so did the basic direction of the state, and this led to his removal in 1987. Despite the inglorious end to his career, his achievements cannot be tarnished.

Bibliography

Brown, Leon Carl. *The Tunisia of Ahmad Bey, 1837-1855.* Princeton, N.J.: Princeton University Press, 1974. This is a study critical to understanding the reform period which deeply affected the Tunisian nationalists of the twentieth century.

Hopwood, Derek. *Habib Bourguiba of Tunisia: The Tragedy of Longevity.* New York: St. Martin's Press, 1992.

Micaud, Charles A. *Tunisia: The Politics of Modernization.* New York: Praeger, 1964. Despite its date, this work contains valuable information on the course of Tunisian politics and society after independence.

Moore, Clement Henry. *Politics in North Africa: Algeria, Morocco, Tunisia.* Boston: Little, Brown, 1970. This useful volume compares the politics of the three former French North African states since independence. It is detailed and makes serious comparisons.

__________. *Tunisia Since Independence.* Berkeley: University of California Press, 1965. This book remains one of the better studies on the emergence of Tunisian elites after independence.

Murphy, Emma C. *Economic and Political Change in Tunisia: From Bourguiba to Ben Ali.* New York: St. Martin's Press, 1999.

Sylvester, Anthony. *Tunisia*. London: Bodley Head, 1969. Sylvester's work is a serious study of the entire fabric of Tunisian history. What this work does is to relate the developments of the twentieth century to Tunisia's past. Well written, this book helps the reader to see the whole history of Tunisia in a usable, compact form.

Zartman, I. William, ed. *Political Elites in Arab North Africa*. New York: Longman, 1982. This important work includes the former French colonies and also Libya and Egypt. The scholarly, well-researched articles by leading authorities tie together all of Arab and Islamic North Africa, regardless of former colonial status. While focusing on the elites, this book sheds great light on the complexities of inter-North African diplomacy and relations.

James J. Cooke

BOUTROS BOUTROS-GHALI

Born: November 14, 1922; Cairo, Egypt

Boutros-Ghali is best known for his extensive involvement in international affairs as a diplomat, jurist, and scholar. An Egyptian statesman who became the first United Nations secretary-general from an Arab nation, Boutros-Ghali strongly supported mediation in post-Cold War conflicts, led the international celebration of the United Nation's fiftieth anniversary, and proposed organizational reforms that were opposed by the United States.

Early Life

Boutros Boutros-Ghali was born a descendent of one of Egypt's most distinguished and wealthy Coptic Christian families and a grandson of former Egyptian prime minister Boutros Pasha Ghali. Boutros-Ghali received a bachelor of laws degree from Cairo University in 1946 and diplomas in political science, economics, and public law before earning his doctorate in international law from Paris University in 1949 with a thesis on the study of regional organizations. While holding a professorship in international law and international relations at Cairo University from 1949 to 1977, Boutros-Ghali traveled extensively, lecturing at universities in Africa, Asia, Europe, Latin America, and North America. Among other early honors, he was a Fulbright Research Scholar at Columbia University from 1954 to 1955, director of the Centre of Research of the Hague Academy of International Law from 1963 to 1964, and visiting professor on the faculty of law at Paris University from 1967 to 1968.

As a public figure in an Islamic society, Boutros-Ghali faced the challenges of being married to a Jewish wife, Leia Maria Boutros-Ghali. He also developed a reputation for not liking to delegate authority or meet with the press and for being a poor communicator in his third language of English. A brilliant analyst known for dissecting problems from all possible angles, Boutros-Ghali's training was instrumental in his development of an intellectual arrogance that compelled him to stand up to authorities even when it was politically detrimental to do so.

Life's Work

Boutros-Ghali first gained international notoriety when he was appointed Egypt's minister of state for foreign affairs in October, 1977, after his predecessor resigned in protest against Egyptian-Israeli rapprochement. Boutros-Ghali accompanied Egyptian president Anwar Sadat on his historic first trip to Jerusalem to address the Israeli Knesset and helped orchestrate the landmark negotiations between Egypt and Israel at the Camp David Summit Conference held in the United States in 1978 under the administration of President Jimmy Carter. Boutros-Ghali headed Egypt's delegation to the United Nations General Assembly in 1979 and also to the 1982 and 1990 sessions following Sadat's October, 1981, assassination.

In addition to representing Egypt in meetings of the Organization of African Unity, the Movement of Non-Aligned Countries, and the Summit Conference of the French and African Heads of State, Boutros-Ghali's impressive résumé included serving as vice president of the Socialist International, as part of the secretariat of the National Democratic Party, and as a member of the International Law Commission, the International Commission of Jurists, and the central committee and political bureau of the Arab Socialist Union.

His considerable involvement in law, international affairs, and political science was also evident by his active membership in numerous professional and academic associations such as the Institute of International Law, the International Institute of Human Rights, the African Society of Political Studies, the Curatorium Administrative Council of the Hague Academy of International Law, the Scientific Committee of the Académie mondiale pour la paix (in Menton, France), the Institute affari internazionali (in Rome, Italy), and the Committee on the Application of Conventions and Recommendations of the International Labour Organisation. Boutros-Ghali served as president of the Egyptian Society of International Law and president of the Centre of Political and Strategic Studies and founded the publication *Alahram Iqtisadi*, which he edited from 1960 to 1975, and *Al-Seyassa Al-Dawlia*, which he edited until 1991.

Boutros-Ghali served as Egypt's deputy prime minister for foreign affairs from May, 1991, until December 3, 1991, when he was appointed by the General Assembly of the United Nations as its sixth secretary-general. He began his five-year term on January 1, 1992, as the first secretary-general following the Cold War and also the first from the Arab world. Within his first fourteen months in office, the United Nations conducted seventeen different peacekeeping operations, which severely depleted its financial resources.

Policy disagreements over the lengthy, difficult, and eventually disastrous United Nations peacekeeping efforts in Bosnia and Herzegovina, Somalia, and Rwanda led to much internationally discussed evaluation of his administration by the major powers. Boutros-Ghali responded by rebuking several United Nations member states for not supporting the post-Cold War peacekeeping efforts he strongly supported in Africa and accused the North Atlantic Treaty Organization (NATO) of Eurocentrism. Failure of the parties involved to agree on an effective strategy to end the Yugoslav war placed United Nations peacekeepers in Bosnia in an "untenable" position, motivating Boutros-Ghali to propose reforms that included formation of a standing rapid-response military force under United Nations command.

During his term as secretary-general, Boutros-Ghali received numerous honors from over twenty-four countries. Notable credits from North America include honorary degrees from the School of Foreign Service at Georgetown University in Washington, D.C., and Canada's University of Laval in Quebec, University of Moncton in New Brunswick, and Carleton University. He was the recipient of the Onassis Award for International Understanding and Social Achievement, the Man of Peace award sponsored by the Italian-based Together for Peace Foundation, the Arthur A. Houghton, Jr., Star Crystal Award for Excellence from the African-American Institute, the Christian A. Herter Memorial Award from the World Affairs Council, and a doctorate *honoris causa* from the Catholic University of Louvain, Belgium.

After initially indicating his desire to serve only one term, Boutros-Ghali informed United States secretary of state Warren Christopher in June, 1996, that he would seek reelection at age seventy-four, later stating, "only stupid people never change their minds." Although six months earlier U.S. president Bill Clinton had publicly thanked him for his "leadership, energy, resolve, and vision of the world for the next 50 years," his administration abruptly declared that they would veto his reelection following his numerous disputes with United Nations ambassador Madeleine Albright.

Article 15 of the United Nations Charter states that the "Secretary-general shall be appointed by the General Assembly upon the recommendation of the Security Council," but the real power of appointment resides with the fifteen-nation Security Council's five permanent members (the United States, the United Kingdom, France, China, and Russia), each of which possess veto power. His reelection was supported by most African nations and fourteen of fifteen Security Council members, with his supporters hoping that the other "Big Five" countries would retaliate by vetoing all candidates supported by the United States, thus forcing the Security Council to extend Boutros-Ghali's term as it had done in 1950 when it extended Trygve Lie's term for three more years.

Clinton claimed that Boutros-Ghali had not done enough to reduce United Nations bureaucracy even though he had cut departments and offices from twenty to twelve and high-level posts in the secretariat from forty-eight to thirty-seven (40 percent less than ten years earlier), phased out over one thousand positions representing a staff reduction of 20 percent from 1986, and implemented a zero-growth budget that included reductions of $117 million, later to include another $154 million. Many felt the United States vetoed Boutros-Ghali because U.S. policymakers considered his leadership "too independent" and chose to make him a "scapegoat for American domestic politics" whereby Clinton's Democratic Party wished to deny its Republican opponents the opportunity to attack their foreign policy as he sought reelection at the end of the year. The American image of the United Nations had become clouded at the beginning of this U.S. presidential election year as Boutros-Ghali continually stood in the way of bombing the Serbs. Republican Party presidential candidate Bob Dole became upset even at the sound of Boutros-Ghali's name and stated that a United Nations commander would never order U.S. troops into battle if he were elected.

With United States opposition deciding for 184 other countries, Boutros-Ghali became the first secretary-general since the 1945 creation of the United Nations to serve only one term. He was succeeded by Khofi Annan from Ghana, the United Nations' first black African secretary-general, on January 1, 1997. Boutros-Ghali left Annan with the challenge of developing reforms to increase United Nations economic efficiency and responsiveness, convincing the United States to pay over $1.5 billion in back dues, and dealing with Iraq's defiance of weapons inspections against which the United States had threatened military intervention.

Summary

Boutros Boutros-Ghali, an Egyptian diplomat and scholar who served as the United Nations secretary-general from 1992 to 1996, was the first U.N. secretary-general from the Arab world and also the first from Africa to hold the post. Boutros-Ghali personally considered his biggest success to be getting the international community to focus on how to cope with the awesome problems of globalization as the planet's population exceeded six billion. This was accomplished by four major conferences that offered guidelines for the twenty-first century: in Rio de Janeiro on the environment, in Vienna on human rights, in Cairo on population, and in Beijing on women and development. He considered his biggest failure to be his inability to convince the United States of the importance of the United Nations. Boutros-Ghali's participation in the affairs of international law, human rights, economic and social development, decolonization, the Middle East question, international humanitarian law, the rights of ethnic and other minorities, nonalignment, development in the Mediterranean region, and Afro-Arab cooperation extended over four decades.

Bibliography

Barnett, Michael N. "Bringing in the New World Order: Liberalism, Legitimacy, and the United Nations." *World Politics* 49 (July, 1997): 526-551. Containing information on the "Agenda for Peace" by Boutros-Ghali, this report evaluates the development of a liberal international order that is assisted by the United Nations by concluding that force alone cannot sustain order.

Boudreau, Tom. *Sheathing the Sword: The U.N. Secretary-General and the Prevention of International Conflict*. New York: Greenwood Press, 1991. This text documents the secretary-general's role in past settlements of international disputes.

Boutros-Ghali, Boutros. *Egypt's Road to Jerusalem: A Diplomat's Story of the Struggle for Peace in the Middle East*. New York: Random House, 1997. Boutros-Ghali describes the rocky road toward Middle East peace with his personal diary describing the tense international drama beginning with Sadat's sudden trip to Jerusalem through the Camp David agreements.

__________. *The Road to Jerusalem*. New York: Random House, 1997.

Buckley, William F., Jr. "The Price of Boutros Boutros-Ghali." *National Review* 48 (December 31, 1996): 58-59. This manuscript evaluates why Clinton opposed another term for Boutros-Ghali and discusses France's support of Boutros-Ghali, involvement of U.S. troops in Bosnia under United Nations authority, and unpaid

U.S. dues to the United Nations.

Ignatieff, Michael. "Alone with the Secretary-General," *The New Yorker*, Aug. 14, 1995, 33-35. Interview with Boutros-Ghali during his last full year as secretary-general.

Kirdar, Uner, and Leonard Silk. *People: A Global Agenda*. New York: New York University Press, 1995. With a forward by Boutros-Ghali, this 420-page text intended for a collegiate audience focuses on issues such as economic development, peace, poverty, and social policy.

Kitfield, James. "Not So United." *National Journal* 29 (January 11, 1997): 69-72. This well-written article describes the strained political relationships that developed between the United States and United Nations when some congressional policymakers, after deciding that Boutros-Ghali had resisted much-needed organizational reforms, generated pressure by refusing to pay the over $1.5 billion the United States owes the United Nations and vetoing Boutros-Ghali's reelection.

McGeary, Johanna. "The Unforgiven." *Time* 148 (December 2, 1996): 46-47. This article describes Boutros-Ghali's relationship with the United States with a contrast of the reasons Clinton wanted his resignation and the 14 of 15 Security Council members who voted for his reinstatement.

Rajan, M. S., ed. *United Nations at Fifty and Beyond*. New Delhi, India: Lancers Books, 1996. This 368-page book was published under the auspices of the Indian Society of International Law in New Delhi and contains contributed papers from a 1995 seminar held in New Delhi to commemorate the United Nations' fiftieth anniversary from its beginnings with World War II relief efforts.

United Nations. *The United Nations and Human Rights, 1945-1995*. New York: United Nations Department of Public Information, 1995. With an introduction by Boutros-Ghali, this book celebrates the United Nations' fiftieth anniversary by highlighting its most significant contributions.

Williams, Ian. "Must the UN Find a New Pope?" *New Statesman* 125 (September 6, 1996): 20-21. This article evaluates the reasons for the lack of U.S. support for Boutros-Ghali's reelection for political reasons versus concern for protecting the financial soundness of the United Nations.

Daniel G. Graetzer

WILLY BRANDT

Born: December 18, 1913; Lübeck, Germany
Died: October 8, 1992; Unkel, near Bonne, Germany

Brandt was awarded the Nobel Peace Prize (1971) for his efforts in improving relations between West Germany and Eastern Europe. He was instrumental in creating a competitive political party system in West Germany. In 1985, Brandt received the Albert Einstein Peace Prize and the Third World Prize.

Early Life

Willy Brandt, who never knew his father, was the son of an unwed salesclerk who gave him the name Herbert Ernst Karl Frahm. His maternal grandfather, Ludwig Frahm, upon returning from service in World War I, became the principal influence in Brandt's childhood. When he was five, Brandt went to live with his grandparents and subsequently saw his mother regularly but infrequently. As had his father, Ludwig had been a farm laborer. Dissatisfied with those working conditions, he took a factory job and, after the war, was a truck driver. Even before leaving farm work, he was a socialist, one who read widely the works of leading socialist thinkers. Young Brandt picked up this political orientation, which not only was unpopular then but also was considered to be subversive by many.

Unlike many socialists who denounce religion, the Frahms were Protestants, who baptized their children but did not let them attend religious classes in public school. Brandt continued to follow the Christian ethos as an adult but rarely in a conventional fashion, as set out in a strict denominational way. A bright pupil, he won a scholarship to a prestigious *Realgymnasium* (college preparatory high school). There, he had a difficult time as one of the few students from a working-class family. This disparity was compounded by his outspoken political views and his occasional attire, the uniform of the socialist youth organization.

At this time, Brandt's active career as a socialist began. First, he wrote pieces for the Lubeck Social Democratic newspaper. Its editor, Julius Leber, a Social Democratic Party (SPD) member of the Reichstag, offered encouragement and advice to the young man, who adopted the pen name Willy Brandt. Although the required age was eighteen, with Leber's endorsement, Brandt became a member of the SPD in 1930 at the age of sixteen. The next year, the close tie between Leber and his protégé was severed. Considering the SPD insufficiently radical and indecisive toward the Nazi threat, Brandt joined the Socialist Workers Party (SAP), an offshoot of the SPD but which pursued direct action, taking on the Nazis in street fights.

When the Nazis came to power in 1933, leftist parties, such as the SPD and the SAP, prepared to go underground. SAP plans included establishing centers abroad in key cities. Brandt was sent to Oslo for this purpose when the man initially selected to head that activity was arrested by the Nazis. Thus, when only nineteen, Brandt was in a leadership post that permitted him to travel across Europe, in Belgium, in Berlin, and in Spain, covering the civil war in 1937 as a correspondent for Scandinavian newspapers. He also briefly attended a Norwegian university. In 1941, he married a Norwegian socialist, Carlota Thorkildsen, whom he divorced in 1947, after a 1943 separation. He later married Rut Hansen, a member of the wartime resistance in Norway. They were divorced in 1980. The first marriage produced a daughter, the second, three sons.

Brandt had not yet been granted Norwegian citizenship when the Nazis invaded Norway in 1941. Wearing a friend's army uniform, Brandt was captured with the friend's unit. His fluent Norwegian enabled him to deceive the Nazis, who released him with other members of the unit. Then he went across the border to Sweden, a neutral nation where he spent the rest of the war, receiving his Norwegian citizenship and writing or coauthoring six books. His principal activity at that time was journalism.

As soon as hostilities ceased, he returned to Norway, before departing in October, 1945, to cover the Nuremberg War Crimes Trials. In 1946, Brandt became press attaché with the Norwegian military mission in West Berlin.

Life's Work

Now Brandt's life came to a crossroads. At both Nuremberg and Berlin, he had met several figures who hoped to, and in many cases would, shape postwar Germany. After some hesitation, he decided to renounce his Norwegian citizenship and resumed that of Germany in 1947. At that time, he legally became Willy Brandt, the name that he had used for years.

On the recommendation of Kurt Schumacher, leader of the SPD, Brandt became a party official in Berlin, where he came under the tutelage of Mayor Ernst Reuter, whose aide he was during the dramatic Airlift of 1948-1949. In addition to offices within the SPD,

Willy Brandt *(The Nobel Foundation)*

Brandt continued his journalistic career and was elected to local and national legislatures. He emerged as a national, perhaps international, figure in 1956, when he quelled an unruly Berlin rally protesting the use of Soviet troops to crush the Hungarian Revolution.

The next year, Brandt was elected mayor of Berlin, a post he held during two key events in postwar Germany: the 1959 Bad Godesberg SPD conference, at which he played a minor role in the party's renunciation of three historic goals—pacifism, anticlericalism, and nationalization of the economy—and the erection of the Berlin Wall in 1961. He was disappointed by what he considered an inadequate U.S. response to the Berlin Wall, but international attention focused on Berlin thrust him into the spotlight: He emerged as the leading figure in the SPD, a role magnified by his fluent English.

Brandt was the SPD chancellor candidate in the September, 1961, 1965, and 1969 Bundestag elections. Although the SPD increased its share of the vote in each successive try, it did not become the largest Bundestag party until 1969 and even then needed the support of the small Free Democratic Party (FDP) to form a government. The stage was set for this success in 1966, when the Grand Coalition was created. This arrangement between West Germany's two largest parties was precipitated by the nation's faltering economy and what was regarded as the weak leadership of Ludwig Erhard, who had led the Christian Democratic Union (CDU) to its fifth successive headship of a coalition government in 1965. Following negotiations between the CDU and the SPD, Erhard resigned, and a CDU/SPD government, with Brandt as vice chancellor and foreign minister, took office.

With his foreign policy portfolio, Brandt first strengthened West Germany's links with the Western Alliance, especially France. Then he turned to Eastern Europe, cautiously reinstating diplomatic ties with Romania and Yugoslavia. His efforts to create closer ties with Eastern Europe accelerated when he became chancellor and were supported by his foreign minister, Walter Scheel, head of the FDP. In a series of negotiations, Brandt pursued his *Ostpolitik*, or Eastern policy. In a relatively short period, treaties were signed with Eastern European communist nations, most important the Soviet Union, Poland, and East Germany. These treaties produced more normal relations with these nations; especially key were easier trade, relaxed travel restrictions on West Germans to East Germany, and West Germany's pledge not to use force to seek return of the Oder-Neisse territories, which were parts of pre-1939 Germany that had been placed under Russian and Polish "administration" in 1945.

Ostpolitik was the high point of Brandt's career. His efforts to achieve modest domestic goals were frustrated: SPD radicals, seeking more purely socialist programs, diluted his support within the party; members of the FDP, opposing his economic policies or questioning his conciliatory overtures toward the Communist bloc, defected from the governing coalition; and voters wanted more government services but no higher taxes to fund them. To compound the situation, the West German economy stagnated.

With the coalition's majority down to one vote, Brandt used the unique "constructive vote of nonconfidence" of the Basic Law (constitution) to force a Bundestag election, the first in which the parliament had not lasted its maximum four-year term. In the November, 1972, election, the SPD with a plurality of seats formed another coalition with the FDP. Despite the coalition's comfortable majority, Brandt faced more obstacles: public workers' strikes, SPD losses in state elections, continued SPD factionalism, and communist governments that delayed implementing *Ostpolitik*.

In April, 1974, the final act of Brandt's chancellorship began with the arrest of his close aide, Günter Guillaume, who was charged with being an East German spy over a period of eighteen years. Amid rumors about his personal life and doubts about his leadership, Brandt resigned on May 7, 1974. Brandt was involved with women before and after his first marriage, a practice not uncommon in Europe. The women with whom he was closely associated tended to be active in public life. Susanne Sievers, whom he met in Bonn in 1951 while he served in the Bundestag and she was a Bundestag employee, was said to be one reason for his 1974 resignation. Rumors purported that she was about to release details of their affair or had been paid a large sum of money not to reveal their former relationship.

This event did not end Brandt's public career. He served in various capacities, often in the international arena, including an unsuccessful effort to mediate the 1984 election in Nicaragua. He was chairman of the Independent Commission on International Development Issues (the Brandt Commission), a body of fifteen distinguished statesmen from across the globe. Appointed by Robert McNamara, president of the World Bank, the commission issued a lengthy document, the North-South, or Brandt Report, in 1980 that called for extensive economic aid from the industrial nations to the Third World. Despite a generally favorable reception and its inclusion on the agenda of the 1981 Cancún (Mexico) economic summit conference, the report was not acted upon. In 1983, he married his third wife, Brigitte Seebacher.

When he resigned as chancellor, Brandt retained his post as chairman of the SPD, a position that he held while his successor, Helmut Schmidt, was chancellor. This position gave Brandt a platform from which he could speak out within and beyond the party. Often he seemed to be undercutting Schmidt. Brandt continued as party leader under the CDU chancellor, Helmut Kohl, until 1987, when he abruptly gave up the party leadership. Brandt's resignation as SPD chairman was also the result of his association with a woman. He stepped down amid the clamor over his intention to appoint Margarita Mathiapoulos, a friend of his wife, to be press spokesperson for the SPD. Critics of his decision noted that his choice was neither a German citizen nor an SPD member and was not familiar with the party organization. Moreover, her fiancé was a prominent CDU official. Yet, after the tumultuous events in the two Germanys in late 1989, Brandt once again rose to prominence and was even elected in February, 1990, honorary president of the East German Social Democratic Party.

Summary

Willy Brandt's personal and public lives cannot be separated. In the aftermath of defeats, and sometimes victories, within the SPD and in his public official roles, he frequently manifested an indifference or malaise, if not depression, that might occupy him for days or weeks. He was also criticized for being indecisive. Brandt, however, illustrated the complexities that may be found in the makeup of a prominent national and world leader: impressive qualities of command but also traits of weakness. Yet there was a persistent pattern in his life of seeking a better life for the oppressed and impoverished, whether victims of Adolf Hitler's Third Reich, East Germany's communist regime, or economic adversity in the Third World.

Bibliography

Barnet, Richard J. *The Alliance: America-Europe-Japan, Makers of the Postwar World.* New York: Simon & Schuster, 1983. Chapter 7, "The Double Detente: Mr. Nixon and Herr Brandt Look East," focuses on Brandt's Ostpolitik in the context of general East-West relations.

Binder, David. *The Other German: Willy Brandt's Life and Times.* Washington, D.C.: New Republic Book, 1975. Completed shortly after Brandt's resignation as chancellor; one of the few works that comments on the Brandt-Sievers affair.

Brandt, Willy. *Arms and Hunger.* Translated by Anthea Bell. New York: Pantheon, 1986. Examines the issues and politics that the Brandt Commission faced.

__________. *People and Politics: The Years 1960-1975.* Translated by J. Maxwell Brownjohn. Boston: Little, Brown, 1978. The second installment of Brandt's memoirs, covering the zenith of his career. Includes an index.

__________. *My Life in Politics.* London: Viking, 1992. Posthumously published memoirs.

Drath, Viola Herms. *Willy Brandt: Prisoner of His Past.* Radnor, Pa.: Chilton, 1975. Bibliography of both English- and German-language sources. More on the Guillaume affair than most sources have.

Harpprecht, Klaus. *Willy Brandt: Portrait and Self-Portrait.* Translated by Hank Keller. Los Angeles: Nash, 1971. Largely composed of excerpts from Brandt's writings. Not analytical but illustrates Brandt's views and impressions on some issues and events.

Homze, Alma, and Edward Homze. *Willy Brandt: A Biography.* Nashville: Thomas Nelson, 1974. Brief, complimentary biography, mentions Brandt's resignation as chancellor in only one paragraph.

Kellerman, Barbara. "Mentoring in Political Life: The Case of Willy Brandt." *American Political Science Review* 72 (June, 1978): 422-433. Assesses the impact of three key mentors—his grandfather, Julius Leber, and Ernst Reuter—on Brandt's life.

Prittie, Terence. *Willy Brandt.* New York: Schocken Books, 1974. The Standard biography on Brandt. Finished before Brandt's 1974 resignation, but a postscript comments on that. Contains a extensive bibliography in English and German.

Wechsberg, Joseph. "The Outsider." *The New Yorker* 49 (January 14, 1974): 35-40, 42, 44, 46-50, 52-57. This gives an impression of Brandt's managerial style with civil servants, other politicians, and the public. Also offers observations on *Ostpolitik.*

Zudeick, Peter. "Willy Brandt." In *The German Chancellors*, edited by Hans Klein. Chicago: Edition Q, 1996.

Thomas P. Wolf

LEONID ILICH BREZHNEV

Born: December 19, 1906; Kamenskoye, Ukraine, Russian Empire
Died: November 10, 1982; Moscow, Soviet Union

Brezhnev directed the Soviet Union for nearly two decades (1964-1982). His administrative record as party chief and head of government was characterized by emphasis on continuity and the status quo in domestic policy, an increase in military strength, and a mixture in foreign policy of cautious adventurism, arms control agreements with the United States, and military intervention in two neighboring states.

Early Life

Leonid Ilich Brezhnev was born in Kamenskoye (later Dneprodzerzhinsk), Ukraine, on December 19, 1906. Of ethnic Russian background, Brezhnev was the son and grandson of factory workers in the local steel mill. He began work in the same plant at age fifteen. As a young boy at the time of the 1917 revolutionary period and the following civil war, he recalled the strikes and turmoil in his native town. Brezhnev joined the Komsomol in 1923 at age seventeen. He graduated (1927) from an institute in Kursk as an agricultural specialist and moved to the Urals region to work as an economic administrator and a local government official. He joined the Communist Party in 1931 at age twenty-five and entered a metallurgical institute in Dneprodzerzhinsk the same year. Graduating in 1935, he entered a Red Army training school for tank drivers. In 1937, Brezhnev became the vice chairman of the Dneprodzerzhinsk soviet but soon after moved into administrative work in the Communist Party.

He became (February, 1939) secretary of the regional party committee in Dnepropetrovsk, a major industrial center in the Ukraine. After the start of the war in Europe, Brezhnev was selected for the newly created post of Secretary for the Defense Industry in the region, responsible for overseeing the transition of local plants for possible war production. In 1941, following the Nazi invasion of the Soviet Union, he volunteered for military service and served in the

Leonid Ilich Brezhnev *(Library of Congress)*

role of a political officer. By war's end, he was a major general and chief of the political department of the Fourth Ukrainian Front. He saw some limited military combat service in the Black Sea, Caucasus, and Ukraine regions. Following the war, he became party head of the Zaporozhye region in the Ukraine (1946-1947) and then held the same post in the Dnepropetrovsk region of the Ukraine. His primary task was to oversee economic reconstruction of the areas damaged by the war.

Life's Work

Brezhnev made his record as a loyal party administrator who provided steady leadership and fulfilled the responsibilities assigned to him. He slowly but steadily rose in the Communist Party apparatus to higher positions, eventually culminating with his selection as first secretary of the Communist Party in October, 1964, replacing Nikita Khrushchev. (The office was retitled "general secretary" in 1966.)

At age forty-three, Brezhnev was selected to be first secretary of the Moldavian Republic Communist Party and worked there from 1950 to 1952. He then rose to national party positions in late 1952, with his election to the Communist Party central committee, the party secretariat, and (as a candidate member) the Communist Party Presidium. Scholars interpret this advancement as part of Joseph Stalin's preparations to purge the older party leadership in favor of new and younger subordinates. Brezhnev, in his mid-forties, apparently was being groomed for new leadership responsibilities, but, with Stalin's death in March, 1953, Brezhnev lost his secretariat and presidium positions.

During 1953-1954, Brezhnev worked in the Ministry of Defense as the first deputy chief of the main political administration with the rank of lieutenant general. His responsibility was to ensure ideological and political loyalty to the party and government. He returned to direct party service in early 1954 as second secretary of the Kazakh Communist Party and was later promoted to first secretary in August, 1955. During the mid-1950's, Brezhnev implemented Khrushchev's "Virgin Lands" scheme and won more fame for the initial success of this ambitious agricultural undertaking. He was reelected to the central committee of the party in 1956, as well as returning to both the secretariat and the ruling Party Presidium as a candidate member. He was raised to full membership in the Presidium in June, 1957. These promotions marked Brezhnev as a Khrushchev associate who benefited from loyalty to his chief.

By 1960, Brezhnev's relations with Khrushchev seem to have weakened, as Khrushchev was entering the final period of his rule. Brezhnev again gave up his secretariat position in 1960 and was elected Chairman of the Supreme Soviet Presidium (the titular head of state or "president"), with primarily ceremonial functions.

He resumed duties in the secretariat in mid-1963 and relinquished the head of state position in June, 1964. Khrushchev's ouster as party head in October, 1964, immediately resulted in Brezhnev's selection as first secretary, and he held that responsibility until his death in November, 1982. It was in this office that he made his mark and left a mixed legacy to his successors.

The years of collective leadership—Brezhnev as party head and Aleksei Kosygin as government head—worked reasonably well until the latter's resignation in October, 1980, and death soon after. In fact, Brezhnev steadily expanded his influence and visibility over the period. During the Brezhnev years, the Soviet Union saw a number of achievements: continued manned space efforts, growing emphasis on military strength, the celebration of the fiftieth anniversary of the Bolshevik Revolution, expanded relations with other world communist parties, and the holding of important party congresses. Brezhnev expanded his functions and titles, becoming Marshal of the Soviet Union in May, 1976 (the only party leader besides Stalin to hold that rank) as well as chairman of the Defense Council. In 1977, he became chairman of the Supreme Soviet Presidium and held that position until his death.

On the domestic scene, the Brezhnev era soon developed a reputation as a conservative and status quo administration. The party apparatus was more tightly controlled, and few significant changes in the Communist Party Presidium (renamed the "Politburo") and other agencies occurred until the early 1970's. Literary dissidents felt continued harassment, beginning with the arrest of Andrei Donatovich Sinyavsky and Yuli Markovich Daniel in 1965 and their trial in early 1966. The problems with Aleksandr Solzhenitsyn, which led to the author's forcible deportation in February, 1974, are widely known. Andrei Sakharov's human rights activity from 1968 onward eventually led to his banishment to the city of Gorky in 1980. Despite promises of domestic reform and human rights, as specified in the 1975 Helsinki Accord, repression continued throughout the Brezhnev years as a dominant motif.

Economic policies returned to the more centralized system, as the later Khrushchev experiments were terminated. Virtually no innovations appeared during the Brezhnev years after 1965, and the economy suffered as a result of the old ideological priorities and institutional administrative structure. Improved relations with the United States in the early 1970's permitted substantial imports of grain to cover shortages in Soviet agriculture. Industrial growth rates fell, and both quality and quantity suffered. This was especially true in the late 1970's and early 1980's during the remaining years of the Brezhnev leadership.

In foreign policy, the Soviet Union showed a diversity of options and tactics. Military buildup in conventional and nuclear systems dominated the budgetary priorities for the period. The party's tough and uncompromising attitude can be seen in the military intervention in Czechoslovakia in August, 1968, to oust the reform movement of Alexander Dubček, in what came to be known as the Brezhnev Doctrine. In the Western Hemisphere, the Soviet Union continued its role as the major patron of Fidel Castro's Cuba and also began the penetration of Central America by its support of the Sandinista movement in Nicaragua. The Soviet decision to shape events in Afghanistan eventually led to the introduction of Soviet troops in December, 1979, and the emergence of a full-scale war, which lasted a decade in that neighboring state.

Soviet relations with the United States varied widely, affected by the Glassboro Summit (1967), the Czech intervention (1968), the era of détente in the early 1970's with the Strategic Arms Limitation Treaty (SALT) I (signed 1972), a cooling in the mid- and later 1970's, and the signing of SALT II (1979). Throughout the Brezhnev era, Soviet foreign policy remained in the hands of the experienced and competent Andrei Gromyko as foreign minister. Relations with the People's Republic of China remained poor, including Sino-Soviet skirmishes on the Ussuri River frontier in 1969. Soviet influence in the Middle East fluctuated, especially in Egypt in the early 1970's. Brezhnev traveled widely in the 1960's and 1970's to both communist and noncommunist nations.

By the time of the Twenty-fifth Party Congress in 1975, Brezhnev's health and abilities began a marked deterioration. This decline continued for the remaining years of his life, until his death in Moscow on November 10, 1982, at the age of seventy-five.

Summary

The latter years of Leonid Ilich Brezhnev's life gave ample evidence of his faltering leadership and the problems he was not able to face and resolve. Since his death, the deleterious effects of his rule have become all too painfully evident. During the era of Mikhail Gorbachev, the inadequacies and damage of the Brezhnev period were widely publicized as what is called the "era of stagnation." Economic problems were the usual focus along with the Brezhnev "command" system of decision making, the existence of cronyism, and corruption within the Communist Party. The attacks on Brezhnev, who was given an official state funeral in 1982, affected members of his immediate family even to the imposition of jail sentences. Brezhnev's name was also removed from towns, schools, and streets that had been named in his honor.

On the positive side, Brezhnev's leadership reveals strengths and positive attributes. He ended Khrushchev's increasingly desperate efforts to find a "quick fix" for domestic and foreign problems. Brezhnev provided stability and a sense of continuity in both domestic and foreign policy. The Soviet economy grew during his years in office, although not at rates sought. The standard of living for many Soviet citizens improved, and construction of new housing was an ongoing priority. Food prices were kept low by heavy state subsidies. Medical care was expanded, and educational programs absorbed large numbers of Soviet youth. Space technology efforts had extensive funding and successes. No one doubts that the Soviet Union became militarily stronger and more formidable under Brezhnev's efforts to provide greater national security, but an unfulfilled agenda remained at his death to challenge his successors.

Bibliography

Academy of Sciences of the U.S.S.R. *Leonid I. Brezhnev: Pages from His Life.* New York: Simon & Schuster, 1978. This revealing Soviet biography of Brezhnev is notable for its omissions of important information, excessive praise, and overstated ideological fervor. It does cover the main outlines of his life and presents Brezhnev as an excellent leader and world statesman.

Anderson, Richard D., Jr. *Public Politics in an Authoritarian State: Making Foreign Policy During the Brezhnev Years.* Ithaca, N.Y.: Cornell University Press, 1993.

Breslauer, George W. *Khrushchev and Brezhnev as Leaders: Building Authority in Soviet Politics.* London: Allen & Unwin, 1982. A carefully researched study of Brezhnev's leadership since 1964, with penetrating assessment of the results as affected in three time periods, by economic concerns, and by party issues. Portrays Brezhnev as a "consensus" leader. Provides alternative interpretations of Brezhnev's policies but indicates the author's own preference.

Dornberg, John. *Brezhnev: The Masks of Power.* New York: Basic Books, 1974. Readable account of Brezhnev's background, rising career in the Communist Party, and first decade as general secretary. Portrays him as an ideological and political conservative who brought stability to his nation. Anecdotes reveal Brezhnev's personality in the period before the onset of the "era of stagnation" and other problems in the later Brezhnev era.

Gelman, Harry. *The Brezhnev Politburo and the Decline of Detente.* Ithaca, N.Y.: Cornell University Press, 1984. Gelman effectively studies the objectives and techniques underlying Soviet foreign policy in the Brezhnev era. He includes the external and domestic factors. Factions and disputes within the Politburo and the party apparatus are reviewed. The author sees the Soviet Union seeking foreign policy opportunities but not according to a "master plan."

Murphy, Paul J. *Brezhnev: Soviet Politician.* Jefferson, N.C.: McFarland, 1981. This straightforward political biography gives a detailed account of Brezhnev's early party career and rise to power in 1964. Provides good coverage of his political maneuvering and leadership from 1964 to 1980. Portrays Brezhnev as capable, shrewd and scheming, and essentially a Stalinist in outlook.

Smith, Hedrick. *The Russians.* New York: Ballantine Books, 1984. A well-known account by a Pulitzer Prize recipient describing the Soviet Union in the 1970's. Excellent balance of anecdotal description and careful analysis of the nation's people, leaders, ideology, and daily life. Brezhnev's leadership and influence are assessed, especially for his last years.

Taylor Stults

GEORGE BUSH

Born: June 12, 1924; Milton, Massachusetts

As forty-first president of the United States (1989-1993), Bush culminated a career that included service as U.S. ambassador to the United Nations, chairman of the Republican National Committee, director of the Central Intelligence Agency, and vice president to Ronald Reagan.

Early Life

On June 12, 1924, George Herbert Walker Bush was born in Milton, Massachusetts, to Dorothy Walker Bush and Prescott Sheldon Bush. His father, who made a fortune as a Wall Street banker and eventually became the managing partner of the banking firm of Brown Brothers, Harriman and Company, also represented Connecticut as a Republican U.S. senator from 1952 to 1963. Bush's family lived in Greenwich, Connecticut, and he attended a private day school in the affluent New York City suburb before entering Phillips Academy, an exclusive preparatory school in Andover, Massachusetts. He excelled as a student and athlete at Phillips and was elected president of his senior class. After his graduation in 1942, Bush deferred his admission to Yale University and enlisted in the U.S. Navy, becoming its youngest pilot.

From 1943 to 1944, Bush was assigned as a bomber pilot to the USS *San Jacinto*. While he was flying a mission in September, 1944, his plane was hit by antiaircraft fire. Forced to parachute into the Pacific, he was rescued several hours later by a U.S. submarine. His courageous service earned him the Distinguished Flying Cross and three Air Medals. In December, 1944, he was reassigned to a base in Virginia as a flight instructor and remained there until his discharge in September, 1945.

On January 6, 1945, shortly after his return to the United States, Bush married Barbara Pierce of Rye, New York, the daughter of a prominent magazine publisher. After the war ended, the young couple moved to New Haven, Connecticut, where Bush enrolled at Yale University. In 1948, after only three years of study, the economics major and varsity baseball captain graduated Phi Beta Kappa. The new graduate then moved his fledgling family to Texas, where he worked in the oil industry as a salesman for Dresser Industries.

As a businessman, Bush was a success. In 1951, he and a colleague, John Overby, formed the Bush-Overby Oil Development Company. The business expanded into Zapata Petroleum Corporation, and by 1954, Bush was president of a Zapata subsidiary, Zapata Offshore, which developed offshore drilling equipment.

George Bush *(Library of Congress)*

Bush's family also grew. By 1959, he and Barbara had become the parents of four sons and two daughters. Their first daughter, Robin, died of leukemia in 1953.

Life's Work

During his years in Texas, Bush became active in Republican politics. By 1964, he was party chairman in Harris County, and he took a leave of absence from the oil business to make a bid for a U.S. Senate seat. His opponent, Democrat Ralph Yarborough, was an ally of President Lyndon B. Johnson. Bush's bid, though unsuccessful, was impressive. In a year of overwhelming victory for the Democrats, he garnered a noteworthy 43.5 percent of the vote against a favored incumbent. He did not remain politically unsuccessful for long. In 1966, he was elected to the U.S. House of Representatives from the 7th District of Texas, the first Republican representative from the city of Houston. Bush quickly made his presence known in Washington. He was named to the influential House Ways and Means Committee, becoming the only freshman legislator to earn that honor in sixty years. Two years later, he ran unopposed for his seat in the House.

A staunch supporter of President Richard Nixon, Bush followed the president's advice and resigned his seat in Congress to run for the Senate in 1970. His opponent this time was Lloyd Bentsen, a conservative Democrat. Despite campaign support from both Nixon and Vice President Spiro Agnew and substantial financial contributions from the oil industry, Bush could not defeat Bentsen in Texas, historically a Democratic state.

Despite this setback, Bush continued his career in politics. Shortly after the election, Nixon appointed him to serve as U.S. ambassador to the United Nations, where Bush learned the ground rules of foreign policy. Despite his lack of diplomatic experience, he performed well. In 1973, however, Nixon asked him to become chairman of the Republican National Committee, and he resigned his U.N. post.

As news of the Watergate scandal began to surface, Bush found his new appointment to be increasingly difficult. Initially, he was a resolute defender of the president; as evidence against the president mounted, however, he was forced to recognize Nixon's complicity in the affair. Thereafter, Bush tried to focus his attention as chairman on maintaining party strength in the face of Nixon's troubles. Finally, on August 7, 1974, concerned that Nixon's troubles would have negative repercussions on the Republican Party, Bush sent the president a letter asking for his resignation; Nixon announced his resignation the following day.

When Gerald Ford succeeded to the presidency, he rewarded Bush's loyalty to the Republican Party by allowing him his choice of several posts. Bush decided to move to Beijing as chief of the U.S. Liaison Office to the People's Republic of China. Given Nixon's renewal of U.S. relations with the communist country in 1972, his service there came at a crucial and delicate time. Again, he performed well.

Bush continued in the China liaison position until December, 1975, when President Ford surprised him with a request to return to Washington to replace William Colby as head of the Central Intelligence Agency (CIA). The CIA's reputation had suffered severely in the face of revelations of its involvement in such illegal activities as assassination plots against foreign officials. Bush helped to restore the agency's credibility and morale, earning him bipartisan praise.

After Ford's loss to Jimmy Carter in the 1976 presidential election, Bush resigned his CIA post and returned to Houston, where he played an active role in several political campaigns. Frustrated with the Carter administration, he announced his own presidential candidacy in May, 1979. Despite victories in the Iowa caucus and several primaries, including Massachusetts, Connecticut, and Pennsylvania, he lost the Republican nomination to Ronald Reagan.

At the Republican National Convention in July, 1980, Reagan initially approached former president Ford as a potential running mate. Ford, however, declined, and in a bid for party unity, Reagan asked Bush to join his ticket. Bush's extensive foreign-policy experience, more moderate stand on social issues, and relative youth all contributed to Reagan's electoral success. As in his previous positions, Bush proved to be a hard, loyal worker, and he earned the respect of many of his colleagues and constituents.

That work ethic dominated Bush's eight years as vice president, during which time his responsibilities focused primarily on foreign-policy issues. Building upon his diplomatic experience, he frequently traveled overseas to represent the White House. He also managed Reagan administration involvement in worldwide efforts to halt both international terrorism and the drug trade. Toward the end of Reagan's second term, Bush again announced his intentions to seek the presidency.

Robert Dole, Senate majority leader from Kansas, offered Bush his stiffest competition in the 1988 primaries. Before the Republican convention, however, Bush had won enough delegates to secure his party's nomination. He and his running mate, Dan Quayle of Indiana, defeated Massachusetts governor Michael S. Dukakis and Texan Lloyd Bentsen, the Democratic presidential and vice presidential candidates, in an electoral landslide. Reagan campaigned vigorously for Bush, who promised to continue his predecessor's economic policies and not raise taxes.

As president, Bush tackled several critical issues. Domestically, he faced the possible demise of the savings and loan system, continued the war against illegal drugs, signed a controversial deficit-reduction bill, and—despite his campaign pledge—agreed to increase taxes. In the international arena, his administration dealt with significant changes in Eastern Europe and the Soviet Union beginning with the 1989 fall of the Berlin Wall, long a symbol of communist dominance. In meetings with Soviet president Mikhail Gorbachev, he negotiated START I and START II, historic arms-reduction treaties. Committed to a policy of international free trade, he spearheaded efforts that culminated in the eventual signing of the North American Free Trade Agreement (NAFTA).

Bush's greatest challenge came during the Persian Gulf War, which commanded his attention during the fall and winter of 1990-1991, following Iraq's invasion of Kuwait in August, 1990. When the Iraqi government refused to withdraw its troops in compliance with a United Nations-imposed deadline of January 15, 1991, a U.S.-led international coalition of troops launched a major offensive, Operation Desert Storm. The allied forces quickly succeeded in driving the Iraqis from Kuwait, and Bush's popularity soared.

During the next year, however, U.S. voters turned their attention to issues closer to home, primarily a sagging economy. By January, 1992, Bush's approval rating had plummeted, and his reelection, deemed a sure thing after the Gulf War, seemed in doubt. In the 1992 election, he was defeated by Governor Bill Clinton of Arkansas, whose campaign focused on such domestic issues as the economy and health care.

After leaving office, Bush and his wife returned to their adopted state of Texas. He continued his public service in many ways, including acting as a political adviser and serving on the board of the Episcopal Church Foundation.

Summary

Bush made his most significant contributions in the area of foreign affairs. From his early days as ambassador to the United Nations to his final days as president, he displayed an ability to grasp how the United States could most effectively relate to its fellow nations. In China, he helped to smooth the way for improved relations between the two countries. As vice president, Bush acted as an intermediary between other nations and Reagan, who was more skilled at home than abroad. As president, Bush's relationship with Soviet president Mikhail Gorbachev helped bring a peaceful end to the Cold War. His leadership in the Persian Gulf War helped to establish the importance of the United States in a post-Cold War world and to demonstrate the effectiveness of international cooperation in collective security measures.

Bush's domestic achievements are harder to assess. Many of his contemporaries point to the anemic state of the American economy at the end of his presidency and to his inability to gain a second term as evidence of his domestic failures. Nevertheless, several laws adopted during his tenure—especially the North American Free Trade Agreement, the Americans with Disabilities Act, and the Clean Air Act—had significant and widely lauded effects on domestic policy.

Bibliography

Beschloss, Michael R., and Strobe Talbott. *At the Highest Levels: The Inside Story of the End of the Cold War*. Boston: Little, Brown, 1993. Focuses on the roles Bush and Gorbachev played in ending the Cold War. An inside look at the intricacies of foreign-policy maneuvers.

Bush, George, with Victor Gold. *Looking Forward: An Autobiography*. New York: Doubleday, 1987. Released to coincide with the beginning of Bush's 1988 campaign, this autobiography provides insight into Bush's perceptions of himself and his quest for the presidency.

Campbell, Colin, and Bert A. Rockman, eds. *The Bush Presidency: First Appraisals*. Chatham, N.J.: Chatham House, 1991. Though written only halfway through Bush's term in office, this compilation of essays provides a solid assessment of various aspects of his work, from his leadership style to his choice of cabinet members.

Duffy, Michael, and Dan Goodgame. *Marching in Place: The Status Quo Presidency of George Bush*. New York: Simon & Schuster,

1992. A compelling, well-documented assessment of Bush's leadership style. Written by two *Time* magazine White House correspondents.

Hyams, Joe. *Flight of the Avenger: George Bush at War*. San Diego: Harcourt Brace Jovanovich, 1991.

King, Nicholas. *George Bush: A Biography*. New York: Dodd, 1980. A straightforward account of Bush's life up to the time of his selection as Reagan's running mate.

Mervin, David. *George Bush and the Guardianship Presidency*. New York: St. Martin's, 1996. Mervin defines and judges Bush as a guardian president, a conservator of the status quo rather than an advocate of change. Extensive bibliography.

Parmet, Herbert. *George Bush: The Life of a Lone Star Yankee*. New York: Scribner's, 1997.

Whicker, Marcia Lynn, James Pfiffner, and Raymond Moore. *The Presidency and the Persian Gulf War*. Westport, Conn.: Praeger, 1993. A collection of well-written, thought-provoking essays that assess Bush's role in the Gulf War.

Woodward, Bob. *The Commanders*. New York: Simon & Schuster, 1991. Woodward examines Bush as commander-in-chief in this study of U.S. military policy just prior to the Gulf War. While the book has been popular, some analysts have questioned Woodward's scholarship.

Jane Marie Smith

LÁZARO CÁRDENAS

Born: May 21, 1895; Jiquilpan, Mexico
Died: October 19, 1970; Mexico City, Mexico

The energetic and controversial president of Mexico from 1934 to 1940, Cárdenas carried out bold policies intended to benefit peasants and workers. In 1938, he posed a major challenge to the United States and Great Britain by his nationalization of their Mexican oil properties. His assertion of the authority of the Mexican government left an indelible imprint on his times and provided precedents for other developing nations after World War II.

Early Life

A humble son of provincial Mexico, Lázaro Cárdenas had few of the characteristics associated with success in Mexican politics. The eldest male among eight children, he grew up in the household of a struggling merchant in the town of Jiquilpan in the state of Michoacán. He was a solemn youth who took his six years of schooling seriously and developed strict views on moral issues, particularly gambling and the use of alcohol. After the completion of grammar school, Cárdenas worked as an assistant to the local tax collector.

As the thirty-four-year-old dictatorship of Porfirio Díaz collapsed in 1911, sixteen-year-old Cárdenas was drawn to the excitement and idealism of the revolutionary movement led by Francisco Madero. Although the overthrow of Madero's presidency in 1913 greatly disappointed him, he joined the forces of Venustiano Carranza, who carried on in the deposed president's name. A courageous and at times impetuous field commander, Cárdenas rose to the rank of brigadier general by 1920. During these years of combat, he developed an awareness of social and economic issues. The Indian part of his ancestry (he was a mestizo, or a person of mixed Indian and European descent) gave him a special sensitivity to the needs of the rural poor.

Although increasingly involved in politics, Cárdenas decided to remain in the army as zone commander of the units stationed in Tamaulipas from 1925 to 1927. The young general quickly learned that United States and British oil companies expected him to accept expensive gifts in exchange for special favors, a common practice among zone commanders in the oil region. Cárdenas also saw that Mexican laborers received a fraction of the pay of their foreign counterparts for doing the same work. Oil company managers and engineers lived in the comfort of segregated compounds while Mexican workers endured in makeshift housing in the hot, humid coastal environment. Cárdenas rejected the bribe offers but retained a vivid memory of the difficulties faced by his fellow Mexicans.

Life's Work

In 1928, Cárdenas left active military service to become governor of Michoacán. After fifteen years on the battlefields of the revolution and in the command centers of the army, he ventured into the arena of politics with a combination of idealism and determination that was unusual in Mexico of the late 1920's. He pursued a vigorous policy of distributing farmland to the peasants while improving public education throughout the state. He led in the mobilization of peasants and workers in a statewide political party with a broad platform that included prohibition and women's rights. Although these efforts did not always bring the results he wanted, Cárdenas built an impressive image as governor and began to gain national attention.

One of the effects of the worldwide economic depression in Mexico was to make an already uncertain political situation even more unstable. Cárdenas emerged in this environment as a competent state governor who had a brief tenure as head of the recently formed Partido Nacional Revolucionario (PNR, or National Revolutionary Party). In 1933, Plutarco Elías Calles, Mexico's dominant politician, approved of Cárdenas as the PNR's presidential candidate for the election of 1934. This nomination virtually ensured victory, but Cárdenas chose to conduct a strenuous campaign anyway. In the process, many residents of isolated villages saw a presidential candidate for the first time. The man they saw was, at a glance, hardly an imposing personality. He was not a fiery public speaker, and the receding chin beneath his fleshy cheeks, along with a quiet manner, created an impression of reserve. Cárdenas, nevertheless, managed to generate excitement. He relished his personal meetings with the common people, and his simple life-style with his new bride, Amalia Solórzano of Michoacán, won for him the admiration of peasants and workers. After easily winning the election, Cárdenas converted his popularity with the voters and his respect among generals and politicians into a major coup—the peaceful expulsion of the nation's political boss, Calles, not only from Mexican politics but also, in 1936, from Mexico itself.

Lázaro Cárdenas *(Library of Congress)*

In spite of his limited formal education, Cárdenas had an awareness of the importance of ideas in shaping a presidential administration. The PNR had adopted a six-year plan as a campaign platform. A conglomeration of Western liberalism and Soviet economic planning grafted onto Mexico's Constitution of 1917, the six-year plan was both a help and a hindrance to the new president. It established a central goal of massive social and economic change, a goal that Cárdenas readily accepted. It also contained vague Marxist slogans and made socialist theory the main doctrine in education. Such radicalism caused widespread protests from irate Catholics. Although he was anticlerical, Cárdenas backed away from strict enforcement of socialist education and eventually moderated the government's commitment to Marxist ideas.

By contrast, Cárdenas ventured far to the Left in land reform. The heavy concentration of land in a few large estates, or haciendas, was the product of centuries-old traditions in Mexico. Since the early years of the revolution, leaders such as Emiliano Zapata had made clear the importance of the breakup of the haciendas for the benefit of the peasants. After twenty years of rhetorical promises, however, land reform had made little progress. An impatient Cárdenas quickly implemented controversial policies: government expropriation of haciendas, which were then converted into collective farms, or *ejidos*, for the peasants. Yet the young president realized that this transfer of property was only the first step. If the *ejidos* were to be successful, they needed credit to support their large-scale operations and technical skills to cultivate and market their products. Consequently, the Cárdenas government provided loans and technical training for the *ejidos*. In spite of this comprehensive approach, the farmers brought more enthusiasm than expertise to their work. Widely hailed as a political success by the peasant farmers and a daring innovation by leftist observers, the *ejidos* did not achieve sufficient levels of productivity.

The rise of Cárdenas to the presidency coincided with the appearance of a new labor organization known as the Confederación de Trabajadores de México (CTM, or Mexican Confederation of Workers). Numerous spontaneous and disruptive strikes testified to the dynamism of the movement, but the Cárdenas administration established more orderly procedures through its close relationship with the CTM. Under the constant urging of the president, the CTM expanded to include many small unions and eventually reached a total membership of 600,000. In return for the allegiance of the

CTM, Cárdenas transformed some benefits for the working class from theory into practice, particularly in technical education and government support in strike settlements.

The greatest challenge faced by Cárdenas came when the oil workers of the CTM struck for better wages and working conditions against United States and British petroleum corporations. The dispute went to the Mexican supreme court, which ruled in favor of the union. The corporations refused to comply and thereby openly defied not only the court but the entire Cárdenas government as well. Cárdenas responded with his own defiance: the nationalization of the oil corporations' properties on March 18, 1938. Faced by aggressive Fascism in Europe, the British wanted military seizure of the oil fields, but the United States was committed to its Good Neighbor Policy. Presidents Franklin D. Roosevelt and Cárdenas initiated negotiations that resulted in a settlement for all parties in 1942. Cárdenas confronted the two foreign powers with the largest investments in Mexico and won a signal victory.

With these accomplishments in oil nationalization, labor organization, and land reform, Cárdenas obligated his government to expensive programs that weighed heavily on Mexico's limited financial resources. The complex process of land reform reduced agricultural production, which combined with higher wages for workers to create inflation. United States and British oil companies refused to purchase Mexican oil, which cut into the government's tax revenues. Plagued by this economic crisis, Cárdenas took a more moderate course after 1938.

Cárdenas left the presidency in 1941, but he continued to exercise influence in Mexican affairs until his death in 1970. He was especially active in regional economic development in Michoacán and in commentary on international affairs, in which he was a consistent opponent of imperialism. He and his son Cuauhtémoc Cárdenas—who was elected mayor of Mexico City in the 1990's—came to symbolize the independent Left in twentieth century Mexico.

Summary

The legacy of Lázaro Cárdenas contains the contradictions and disappointments of a political leader who attempted to change a nation's entrenched hierarchical economic structure by peaceful methods. In order to deal with this structure, Cárdenas relied on a powerful government bureaucracy which, after he left the presidency, stressed stability and security over experimentation and change. The government and political party that Cárdenas helped to build for the benefit of the masses came to dominate them and eventually came to stifle local initiative.

Yet Cárdenas did make significant contributions to Mexican history in terms of the principles he espoused. He aroused Mexican peasants and workers in the name of peaceful social and economic change and, within limits, oversaw the early stages of land reform and labor organization for their benefit. He accumulated extraordinary personal power but willingly relinquished the presidency to his successor. He chose not to meddle in politics thereafter, thereby breaking with the authoritarian tradition of the imposition of continued influence by extraconstitutional means.

Caught between the world of his roots, the isolated mountain village, and the world of power politics, the intermeshed international economic system, Cárdenas used decisive if controversial methods to meet the challenges of modernization that have confronted most developing nations in the twentieth century. He committed Mexico to the adoption of modern technology and values in agriculture, industry, and education. He sought to redistribute wealth in his country through the nationalization of the property of foreign-owned corporations, a path that other nations would follow. In the process, he maintained a course independent of both communism and liberal capitalism. Operating in the context of the 1930's, Cárdenas underwent experiences that anticipated struggles elsewhere in Latin American, Africa, and Asia later in the century.

Bibliography

Ankerson, Dudley. *Agrarian Warlord: Saturnino Cedillo and the Mexican Revolution in San Luis Potosí*. DeKalb: Northern Illinois University Press, 1984. This book is a valuable account of the rise and fall of one of the Cárdenas administration's main antagonists. Provides a careful explication of Cedillo's point of view.

Ashby, Joe C. *Organized Labor and the Mexican Revolution Under Lázaro Cárdenas.* Chapel Hill: University of North Carolina Press, 1963. The author focuses on the expansion of organized labor and its participation in politics and the oil expropriation.

Bantjes, Adrian. *As If Jesus Walked on Earth: Cardenismo, Sonora, and the Mexican Revolution.* Wilmington, Del.: Scholarly Resources, 1998.

Becker, Marjorie. *Setting the Virgin on Fire: Lázaro Cárdenas and the Redemption of the Mexican Revolution*. Berkeley: University of California Press, 1995.

Carr, Barry. "Crisis in Mexican Communism: The Extraordinary Congress of the Mexican Communist Party." *Science and Society* 50 (Winter, 1986): 391-414; and 51 (Spring, 1987): 43-67. Penetrating analysis of the internal and external problems of the Mexican Communist Party during the last years of the Cárdenas presidency.

Daniels, Josephus. *Shirt Sleeve Diplomat.* Chapel Hill: University of North Carolina Press, 1947. Daniels was United States ambassador to Mexico from 1933 to 1942. His sympathies for Cárdenas were evident in the resolution of the oil expropriation controversy and also in this account of his years in the United States embassy in Mexico City.

Hamilton, Nora. *The Limits of State Autonomy: Post-Revolutionary Mexico.* Princeton, N.J.: Princeton University Press, 1982. Hamilton explains the origins and weaknesses of Cárdenas's political alliance and the limits of its power within the context of national and international economic structures.

Michaels, Albert L. "The Crisis of Cardenismo." *Journal of Latin American Studies* 2 (May, 1970): 51-79. While this article concentrates on the crisis after the oil expropriation, it also provides an evaluation of the entire six-year presidency.

Prewett, Virginia. *Reportage on Mexico.* New York: E. P. Dutton, 1941. Prewett, a conservative journalist, was generally skeptical and at times critical of the Cárdenas administration in contrast to Daniels's *Shirt Sleeve Diplomat.*

Tannenbaum, Frank. "Mexico's Man of the People." *Reader's Digest* 31 (October, 1937): 43-44. A brief but insightful portrait by a Columbia University historian who knew him well.

Townsend, William Cameron. *Lázaro Cárdenas, Mexican Democrat.* 2d ed. Waxhaw, N.C.: International Friendship, 1979. This highly laudatory study of Cárdenas and his presidency is the only biography available in English. Useful because of the author's long-term personal relationship with Cárdenas.

John A. Britton

JIMMY CARTER

Born: October 1, 1924; Plains, Georgia

As president, Jimmy Carter was a conservative in some policies and a liberal in others. On one hand, he attacked government bureaucracy, moved away from détente with the Soviet Union, and increased military spending; on the other, he supported racial equality, took seriously the problems of underdeveloped countries, and pressured repressive regimes to respect human rights.

Early Life

James Earl Carter, Jr., thirty-ninth president of the United States, was born on October 1, 1924, in Plains, Georgia, a town of 550 in Sumter County. Jimmy, as he liked to be called, was the first child of James Earl Carter, Sr., an up-and-coming farmer and rural businessman, and Lillian Gordy Carter, a registered nurse. Along with his sisters Gloria and Ruth and his brother William (Billy), he grew up on the family farm three miles from Plains. After being graduated from Plains High School in 1941, he briefly attended Georgia Southwestern College and Georgia Institute of Technology. Appointed to the U.S. Naval Academy in 1943, Carter graduated three years later, standing fifty-ninth in a class of 820. On July 7, 1946, he married Rosalynn Smith, a friend of his sister Gloria. He and Rosalynn had four children: John William (Jack), James Earl III (Chip), Jeffrey (Jeff), and Amy.

After two years' work on battleships, Carter transferred to the Navy submarine service in 1948 and then to the nuclear submarine program in 1951. Subsequently he served on the precommission crew of the nuclear submarine *Seawolf* and rose to the rank of lieutenant commander. Following his father's death in 1953, Carter returned to Plains, took charge of the family businesses, and quickly became a local leader. Between 1955 and 1962, he chaired the Sumter County Board of Education. In 1962, he was elected to the Georgia Senate. During two terms, he advocated governmental efficiency, regional planning, and better schools. In 1966, Carter lost the Democratic nomination for governor but ran a strong third in a field of six.

Carter's defeat produced a mild depression that led in turn to an important though undramatic religious experience. He had been reared a Baptist, conducted Bible classes in the Navy, and taught Sunday school at the Plains Baptist Church. Following his primary loss, however, Carter began to feel insufficiently devout. Guided by his sister, evangelist Ruth Carter Stapleton, he was "born again" and vowed to live a more godly life.

This religious conversion caused no basic change in his personality. On the contrary, Carter's determination to be a better Christian fitted into his long-standing habit of placing high demands on himself. He worked systematically, sometimes taking special courses to improve his memory, reading speed, and knowledge of art, music, and Spanish. He disciplined his body as well as his mind. A cross-country runner at Annapolis, he jogged in middle age to keep fit. In his late forties, Carter stood five feet, ten inches tall and weighed a trim 160 pounds. His stern commander in the nuclear submarine program, Admiral Hyman Rickover, reinforced his perfectionism. Carter set high standards for his family and subordinates. Anyone who fell short risked "the look," as Carter's staff called a piercing stare from his hazel eyes.

Nor did spiritual rebirth dampen Carter's political ambition. Between 1967 and 1970, he both visited northern cities as a missionary and prepared for his next gubernatorial campaign. In 1970, he defeated former governor Carl Sanders in the Democratic primary and easily won the governorship.

Life's Work

Governor Carter's inaugural address in January, 1971, attracted national attention when he declared that the "time for racial discrimination is over." Although Carter sometimes courted segregationist voters, he had remained personally moderate on civil rights issues. Now moving in a more liberal direction, he appointed African Americans to state office and displayed a portrait of Martin Luther King, Jr., in the executive mansion. As governor, Carter worked hardest to streamline state agencies, but discrediting prejudice as a political issue was his greatest accomplishment. In 1972, he was mentioned as a dark-horse contender for the Democratic vice-presidential nomination. Yet, ineligible for reelection and more conservative than leading Democrats, he was not a major figure in party or national affairs.

Four years later, Carter used his image as an outsider to win the presidency of a nation unsettled by the Vietnam War, the Watergate scandal, the cultural upheaval of the late 1960's, and the energy crisis of the early 1970's. Carter's book, *Why Not the Best?* (1975), announced the central theme of his campaign: Government with effective leadership could be open, compassionate, and competent. Furthermore, claiming a governor's managerial skill, a nuclear engineer's technological expertise, and a born-again farmer's sound morality, Carter presented himself as uniquely qualified to lead. In addition, he blamed President Gerald R. Ford for high unemployment and Machiavellian foreign policy. Despite the wide appeal of these themes, Carter probably would have lost the Democratic nomination if liberal rivals had coalesced against him, and might have lost the general election if the economy had not been afflicted with rising unemployment and inflation. Carter beat Ford by 1.7 million votes.

Jimmy Carter *(Library of Congress)*

Although Carter won a narrow victory, the country greeted the start of his term with enthusiasm. By the end of 1977, however, his legislative program had bogged down in Congress and, according to polls, fewer than half of all Americans approved of his leadership. With some justification, Carter attributed these problems to prejudice against a rural southerner in the White House, but other factors were more significant. While continuing to think of himself as an outsider, the president presented a legislative agenda that would have taxed the skill of an old Washington hand. Moreover, impatient with loose ends, Carter offered what he liked to call "comprehensive" programs. In 1977, he backed bills to reorganize the civil service, restructure the welfare system, lift regulations on major industries, create two new cabinet departments, and end price controls on natural gas.

Furthermore, Carter and his aides initially underestimated the need to cultivate powerful senators and House representatives. More important than these considerations of style, temperament, and tactics, was Carter's ideological position to the right of most congressional Democrats. Unmoved by his rhetoric of efficiency, they resented his disinclination to promote national health insurance, full employment, and comparable liberal measures.

Conflicting aspirations, great expectations, and tactical errors also marked Carter's first efforts in international affairs. The president's chief foreign policy advisers symbolized his (as well as the country's) ambivalence about the Soviet Union: Secretary of State Cyrus Vance wanted to continue détente while National Security Council chairman Zbigniew Brzezinski took a tough anticommunist line. Giving mixed signals himself in 1977, Carter both decided against building a new intercontinental bomber and reneged on campaign promises to reduce military spending, while both repudiating the "inordinate fear of communism" and condemning Soviet suppression of freedom. This criticism of the Soviets may have hindered progress on a strategic arms limitation treaty to succeed the limited accord (SALT I) signed by President Richard M. Nixon. A more decisive factor was Carter's presentation of a typically comprehensive disarmament plan. Suspicious Soviet officials rejected it, accusing the United States of reopening issues seemingly settled with President Ford.

From the outset, President Carter showed unprecedented concern about human rights abroad. Regimes sanctioning harassment, imprisonment, or murder of dissenters risked White House censure and loss of American aid. Realpolitik, congressional pressure, and bureaucratic maneuvering rendered Carter's human rights policy less "absolute" than he had promised in his inaugural address. Nevertheless, there were notable successes. Carter's intervention saved lives in Argentina, Brazil, Chile, and other nations ruled by military juntas. His ambassador to the United Nations, Andrew Young, an African American, cultivated Third World delegates, and, in April, 1978, Carter became the first president to visit Africa. Also in April, 1978, he secured Senate ratification of treaties that would end American control of the Panama Canal in 1999. Carter's human rights campaign and empathy for the Third World, however, were less popular at home than abroad. By late 1977, Republican and Democratic cold warriors charged that his soft and self-righteous policies damaged American interests.

Despite growing criticism from both the Left and the Right, Carter secured impressive victories between mid-1978 and mid-1979. Congress revised the civil service system, eased regulations on airlines, and enacted decontrol of natural gas prices. After grueling negotiations at Camp David, Maryland, Carter persuaded Egyptian president Anwar Sadat and Israeli prime minister Menachem Begin to accept a "Framework for Peace in the Middle East." In December, 1978, he established full diplomatic relations with the People's Republic of China. At the Vienna summit conference in June, 1979, Carter and Soviet president Leonid Brezhnev finally signed a strategic arms limitation treaty (SALT II). Yet none of Carter's successes was unmixed. Liberals complained that decontrol of natural gas prices enriched big business. Conservatives condemned the recognition of China and viewed SALT II as a needless concession to the Soviets. Perhaps most disappointing to Carter, though he brokered an Egyptian-Israeli peace treaty in March, 1979, the Camp David accords inspired no other Middle East settlements.

During the summer of 1979, Carter faced a faltering economy, oil shortages, and an angry nation. "Stagflation," the combination of rising unemployment and inflation, reappeared after two years in remission. Furthermore, when a revolution that deposed the shah of Iran in January, 1978, also disrupted Iranian oil exports, the Organization of Petroleum Exporting Countries (OPEC) limited production and doubled prices. As American motorists clamored for scarce gasoline, Carter's bills promoting energy conservation and synthetic fuels stalled in Congress. On July 15, 1979, Carter attempted to rally the country against what he called a "crisis of the American spirit." This speech temporarily improved his standing in the polls and on Capitol Hill. Carter's subsequent decision, however, to remove several cabinet secretaries and fight inflation instead of unemployment cut short this resurgence. By the early fall, Senator Edward M. Kennedy had decided to contest the president's renomination.

In October, 1979, Carter made the most important decision of his presidency, allowing the exiled shah of Iran to enter the United States for medical treatment. On November 4, Iranian revolutionaries seized the United States embassy in Tehran; fifty-two of the original sixty-six Americans stationed there (fourteen were released after a few weeks) remained captive for 444 days. The Middle East situation deteriorated further when Soviet forces invaded Afghanistan in December. Carter responded by withdrawing SALT II from Senate consideration, halting grain sales to the Soviet Union, urging a boycott of the Olympic Games in Moscow, and asking for a large increase in military spending. According to the Carter Doctrine announced in January, 1980, attempts by outside forces to control the Persian Gulf would be "repelled by any means necessary, including military force." The president's rhetoric masked relative American weakness in the region. Indeed, a military mission to rescue the hostages failed in April when American helicopters collided far from Tehran.

Although Carter turned back Kennedy's challenge to win renomination, his inability to free the hostages combined with the faltering economy cost him the presidency. On November 4, 1980, Republican nominee Ronald Reagan defeated Carter by 8.4 million votes. During his last months in office, Carter, now a convinced cold warrior, stopped aid to the leftist Sandinista government in Nicaragua. Negotiations to free the hostages remained his chief concern. They were released minutes after Reagan took office on January 20, 1981, and former president Carter flew to greet them at an American base in Germany.

Carter resettled in Plains but secular and religious interests often pulled him away from home. He represented the United States at Anwar Sadat's funeral in Cairo, received accolades in Latin America for his human rights efforts, and joined a church group repairing slum housing in New York City. During the 1990's Carter's reputation was further enhanced when he helped negotiate a settlement in Haiti's government and helped build houses for Habitat for Humanity. Although his memoir *Keeping Faith* (1982) dealt primarily with foreign affairs, Carter also criticized Washington insiders who had opposed his domestic program. *The Blood of Abraham* (1985), his well-informed study of the Arab-Israeli conflict, rebuked President Reagan for failing to pursue the peace process begun at Camp David. By and large, however, Carter avoided public attacks on his successor.

Summary

Jimmy Carter was probably a more significant—and much better—president than his overwhelming defeat in 1980 suggests.

Ironically, part of his significance lay in legitimating themes, such as the need to shrink the federal government, that Reagan used against him during the campaign. Similarly, by lifting regulations on major industries, moving away from détente, and increasing military spending, Carter initiated policies later continued by Reagan. Notwithstanding these unintended contributions to American conservativism, Carter's most important accomplishments derived from his liberal side. In the White House, as in the Georgia state house, Carter, a white southern supporter of racial equality, discredited race prejudice as a political issue. His presidential appointments included many women and Hispanics as well as African Americans. In foreign policy, Carter encouraged Egyptian-Israeli peace by accepting an evenhanded approach to the Middle East, paid respectful attention to underdeveloped countries, and placed human rights on the international agenda.

Bibliography

Anderson, Patrick. *Electing Jimmy Carter: The Campaign of 1976*. Baton Rouge: Louisiana State University Press, 1994.

Califano, Joseph A., Jr. *Governing America: An Insider's Report from the White House and the Cabinet*. New York: Simon and Schuster, 1981. A critical retrospective by the liberal secretary of health, education, and welfare whom Carter fired in 1979. Califano presents the president as an incompetent conservative but credits him with a good record on minority recruitment.

Campagna, Anthony S. *Economic Policy in the Carter Administration*. Westport, Conn.: Greenwood Press, 1995.

Carroll, Peter. *It Seemed Like Nothing Happened: The Tragedy and Promise of America in the 1970's*. New York: Holt, Rinehart and Winston, 1982. A lively history of the decade, especially perceptive on cultural trends and the social development of minorities. Places Carter in context and views him as a conservative Democrat.

Carter, Jimmy. *The Blood of Abraham*. Boston: Houghton Mifflin, 1985. Carter brings together a detailed knowledge of the Bible, recent Middle Eastern politics, and his own experiences in the region. Cautiously hopeful about the possibilities of peace, he offers sensible policy recommendations.

__________. *Keeping Faith: Memoirs of a President*. New York: Bantam Books, 1982. This defensive memoir shows Carter and liberal Democrats talking past each other. Contains comprehensive accounts of the Camp David negotiations and the Iran hostage crisis.

Dumbrell, John. *The Carter Presidency: A Re-evaluation*. 2d ed. New York: Manchester University Press, 1995.

Glad, Betty. *Jimmy Carter: In Search of the Great White House*. New York: W. W. Norton, 1980. One of the best biographies of a sitting president. Glad presents the most detailed scholarly interpretation of Carter's youth, early career, religious beliefs, and 1976 campaign strategy. Relatively little on the presidency.

Lynn, Laurence E., Jr., and David deF. Whitman. *The President as Policymaker: Jimmy Carter and Welfare Reform*. Philadelphia: Temple University Press, 1981. This thorough account of Carter's unsuccessful attempt to restructure the welfare system effectively uses interviews with cabinet members, senators, representatives, and civil servants. Reveals Carter's strengths and weaknesses as a policymaker along with the institutional constraints he encountered.

Mazlish, Bruce, and Edwin Diamond. *Jimmy Carter: A Character Portrait*. New York: Simon and Schuster, 1979. A subtle psychobiography by an intellectual historian and media critic. Especially good on Carter's religious beliefs, family relationships, and rhetorical exaggerations.

Morris, Kenneth. *Jimmy Carter: American Moralist*. Athens: University of Georgia Press, 1996.

Smith, Gaddis. *Morality, Reason, and Power: American Diplomacy During the Carter Years*. New York: Hill and Wang, 1985. The best analysis of Carter's foreign policy. Smith places the administration in broad historical context, applauds his human rights record, and regrets his abandonment of détente.

Troester, Rod. *Jimmy Carter as Peacemaker: A Post-Presidential Biography*. Westport, Conn.: Praeger, 1996.

Leo P. Ribuffo

FIDEL CASTRO

Born: August 13, 1926 or 1927; near Birán, Cuba

Castro led a successful revolutionary struggle against the Cuban dictatorship of Fulgencio Batista y Zaldívar in the late 1950's. The revolutionary leader subsequently implemented Latin America's third social revolution of the twentieth century and transformed Cuba into the first communist state of the hemisphere in defiance of the United States.

Early Life

Fidel Castro Ruz was born on a large cattle estate near the village of Birán in Cuba's Oriente Province. Fidel was the third of seven children sired by a prosperous Spanish immigrant landowner and his second wife. Between 1941 and 1945, Castro completed his secondary education at the Colegio Belén, a prestigious Jesuit institution in Havana. Taller in stature than most Latin males, Castro was a natural athlete, excelling in many sports, especially basketball and baseball, which he played with near professional ability. Castro enrolled in the University of Havana's Law Faculty in 1945. There he became a student political activist in a frequently violent campus political setting. Castro joined one of the rival student political groups, became known for his speaking talent, and occasionally expressed nationalist and anti-imperialist sentiments, while condemning the exploitation of the poor by the rich.

While a university student, Castro became involved in two international incidents—first, an aborted attempt in 1947 to overthrow the Dominican Republic's dictator Rafael Leónidas Trujillo Molina, and then, in 1948, political disorders following the assassination of a prominent Colombian politician in Bogotá, where Castro was attending an anti-imperialist student congress. In spite of these extracurricular interruptions, Castro graduated in 1950 with a doctor of laws degree. The politically ambitious graduate began his career as an attorney who litigated on behalf of underprivileged clients. Castro also became active in the Havana organization of the Ortodoxo Party, which championed reform and crusaded against corruption. Most recent presidential regimes had succumbed to graft and gangsterism, frustrating popular sentiment in favor of economic nationalist policies and profound social reform. The young attorney was selected to run as an Ortodoxo candidate for congress in the general elections scheduled for June, 1952.

Life's Work

Events soon propelled Castro into a revolutionary career. On March 10, 1952, former president and political strongman Fulgencio Batista y Zaldívar seized power in a coup and canceled the elections. When it became clear that peaceful tactics could not dislodge Batista, Castro and his younger brother Raúl organized an armed conspiracy. On July 26, 1953, the rebels attacked the Moncada military barracks in Santiago, hoping to set off a general uprising. The effort ended in disaster as about one-third of the one-hundred-seventy-man force survived the clash and reprisals that ensued. At Castro's trial, the young rebel delivered a five-hour address in defense of his actions, which became known by its closing statement, "History will absolve me."

The court sentenced Castro to fifteen years' imprisonment. Yet Castro was released in May, 1955, through a general political amnesty. In July, Castro departed for Mexico to organize a new armed effort to topple Batista. Castro broke all ties with traditional political parties and called his new independent organization the 26th of July Movement. Joining the rebel leader abroad were his brother Raúl, other Cuban political refugees including survivors of the Moncada attack, and an Argentine-born physician, Che Guevara. After a period of secret military training, Castro's force, numbering eighty-two men, sailed at the end of November, 1956, from the Yucatán coast for Cuba in an overloaded old yacht called the *Granma.* A few days after they landed in Oriente Province, an army unit nearly wiped out the small invading force. A remnant of only twelve survivors reached safety in the nearby Sierra Maestra.

Eventually Castro's tiny force received the support of peasants and was also bolstered by recruits from the movement's urban organization. Publicity from journalistic interviews and news of rebel successes made Castro the focus of the popular resistance in Cuba. Moderate middle-class opposition groups signed an accord with the rebel leader on his terms in April, 1958. Shortly thereafter, the Cuban communists, who had previously criticized Castro's tactics, secretly agreed to support him. Meanwhile, Batista's severe

Fidel Castro and followers in the 1950's *(Library of Congress)*

repression had alienated his government. The dictator's large but ineffective army failed in its campaigns to eliminate the guerrillas. Castro's rebel armed forces, numbering fewer than one thousand, assumed the offensive in the summer of 1958, and the dictatorship collapsed as Batista fled Cuba on New Year's Day of 1959.

Now the most popular figure in Cuba and in control of the armed forces, Castro gradually pushed aside his moderate middle-class allies in the new government, who objected to his sweeping agrarian reform proposal and the growing influence of the communists in the revolutionary process. After mid-1959, the government consisted solely of Castro's youthful 26th of July Movement, revolutionary student organizations, and veteran communist politicians. As Cuba's prime minister, Castro sought a radical restructuring of Cuban society on behalf of the rural and urban lower classes and a diversified economy free from foreign dominance and dependency on sugar exports.

The question of whether Castro held but concealed Marxist and communist views during the struggle against Batista is still a matter of controversy and conjecture. In any event, the radical nationalist and socioeconomic goals of Castro's revolutionary government facilitated a working alliance with the Cuban communists.

United States-Cuban relations deteriorated steadily over the next two years. Castro reacted to Washington's hostility to his regime's orientation by nationalizing foreign-owned firms and seeking ever closer ties with Communist bloc countries. The United States severed relations with Havana in January, 1960, while the Central Intelligence Agency plotted to assassinate the Cuban leader and organized an unsuccessful invasion by anti-Castro exiles in April, 1961. Strengthened by this victory, Castro openly labeled his revolution "socialist." Then, in an effort to secure Soviet economic and military commitment to his revolution, the Cuban prime minister declared himself a Marxist-Leninist in December, 1961. United States influence, once a dominant force in Cuba's economic, cultural, and political life, disappeared as Castro aligned his country with the Soviet bloc states.

Castro established a one-party state amalgamating his movement and its political allies into a Marxist-Leninist party. The regime wiped out illiteracy, raised the living standards of rural laborers, and brought better health, educational benefits, and opportunities for social advancement to Cuba's masses. Castro's Cuba also made strides toward ending racial and sexual discrimination. Cuba became more prominent on the international scene. Castro sponsored international conferences, spoke out frequently on Third World issues, dispatched Cuban medical personnel, teachers, and technicians to a number of countries, and provided direct military aid to Marxist regimes in Ethiopia and Angola.

On the negative side, Castro did not succeed in achieving his original economic goals for Cuba. At an early date, industrialization efforts and attempts to diversify agricultural production failed and were set aside on Soviet advice in favor of renewed dependency on sugar exports. Production goals frequently fell short, and Cuba's economy became dependent on Soviet subsidies and technical aid. As the Soviet Union teetered toward collapse in the late 1980's, shortages of consumer items, as well as suppression of public and organized dissent and curbs on artistic freedoms, caused a significant number of Cubans to leave their homeland as exiles.

Castro is noted for his flamboyant, personal style of leadership. Called "Fidel" by most Cubans, he has a powerful charismatic appeal and macho qualities which are valuable assets in Latin American political culture. Castro is charming and entertaining in his personal contacts with individual Cubans, mass audiences, or foreign visitors to Cuba. He has frequently toured the island, dealing directly with his countrymen and their problems. The Cuban leader annually makes many public speeches on revolutionary anniversaries to audiences that number in the hundreds of thousands.

In early 1998 Castro's international stature received a new boost when he hosted an official visit by Pope John Paul II. Although Castro's speeches sometimes last several hours and may even cover mundane topics, Castro establishes a close rapport with listeners and mesmerizes crowds throughout the performance. Castro makes effective use of television to convey his powerful personal touch in messages and appeals to the Cuban public. These political talents and qualities have enabled the Cuban leader to retain the support of many of Cuba's ten million inhabitants despite his regime's authoritarian nature and lagging economic performance.

Summary

Fidel Castro has made himself the central player in modern Cuban history and has vigorously asserted his presence on the international scene. Twentieth century Latin America has witnessed three significant social revolutions: in Mexico (1910-1940), Bolivia (1952-1964), and Cuba. Furthermore, Castro personally directed his revolutionary movement to victory over the Batista dictatorship against great odds. In spite of Cuba's vulnerable geographic location within the U.S. sphere of interest, the Cuban leader founded the first communist state in the Western Hemisphere and survived the early U.S. attempts to isolate or topple him.

An interdependent relationship existed between the Soviet Union and its small Latin American ally. Castro's freedom of action was somewhat limited by Cuba's dependence on vital Soviet aid. Moscow was similarly restrained from asserting its leverage to the point of suffering a major political reverse by allowing Castro's revolutionary experiment to collapse. Therefore, Castro occasionally took positions contrary to Soviet views on international and domestic issues. After the collapse of the Soviet Union in 1989, Cuba's Soviet subsidies ended, and Castro's government was left to its own resources.

Among modern world leaders, Castro is one of the better known. Few heads of state have held power longer than the Cuban leader. Though Cuba is a small Caribbean nation whose influence in world affairs is relatively minor, Castro is an important although controversial world figure and statesman.

Bibliography

Balfour, Sebastian. *Castro*. New York: Longman, 1995.

Bourne, Peter. *Fidel: A Biography of Fidel Castro.* New York: Dodd, Mead, 1986. Bourne, a psychiatrist who met Castro while serving with the Carter presidential administration, attempts to explain some of Castro's actions and personality traits through psychoanalysis. The author is generally sympathetic to his subject.

Castro, Fidel. *Revolutionary Struggle, 1947-1958.* Edited by Rolando E. Bonachea and Nelson P. Valdés. Cambridge, Mass.: MIT Press, 1972. A collection of Castro's speeches, writings, and interviews during the period before he came to power. The long introduction provides a valuable portrait of the Cuban leader against the background of this era.

Guevara, Ernesto. *Reminiscences of the Cuban Revolutionary War.* Translated by Victoria Ortiz. New York: Monthly Review Press, 1968. This is a good historical account of Castro's guerrilla struggle against the Batista regime; it is based on the careful firsthand observations of one of Castro's leading military and political collaborators.

Lockwood, Lee. *Castro's Cuba, Cuba's Fidel.* New York: Macmillan, 1967. Lockwood's book is one of the most useful works on Castro's personality and leadership style. A series of interviews and events show the Cuban leader in a variety of situations. Illustrated with many photographs.

Quirk, Robert E. *Fidel Castro*. New York: W.W. Norton, 1993.

Ruiz, Ramón Eduardo. *Cuba 1933-Prologue to Revolution.* Ithaca, New York: Cornell University Press, 1972. An analysis of political and economic factors in the two decades preceding the start of

Castro's revolutionary career which contributed to his nationalistic and Marxist social revolution.

Szulc, Tad. *Fidel: A Critical Portrait.* New York: William Morrow, 1986. The most comprehensive and detailed biographical study of Castro. Szulc utilizes extensive and detailed personal interviews with Castro and knowledgeable Cubans of varying political persuasions. This is a balanced and objective treatment of the subject, unlike most previous biographical studies.

Thomas, Hugh. *Cuba: The Pursuit of Freedom.* New York: Harper & Row, 1971. A lengthy history of Cuba that is useful for placing Castro in the context of Cuban historical development. The relevant period from the 1940's through the 1960's makes up about half of the book. An objective study.

David A. Crain

NEVILLE CHAMBERLAIN

Born: March 18, 1869; Birmingham, Warwickshire, England
Died: November 9, 1940; Highfield Park, Heckfield, England

Chamberlain was a major voice in the Conservative Party for two decades, seeking modest and solid social reforms to improve the housing and health of the common people of Great Britain. As prime minister from 1937 to 1940, he sought in vain to avert World War II by appeasing Adolf Hitler.

Early Life

Arthur Neville Chamberlain was born March 18, 1869, into a well-to-do and politically prominent family in the rising industrial city of Birmingham. His father, Joseph Chamberlain, made a fortune manufacturing screws and went into politics, first locally and then in Parliament; eventually he became colonial secretary under Arthur Balfour. Neville's elder half brother, Austen Chamberlain, was educated for a political career and went into Parliament at the age of twenty-eight. Young Neville was expected to go into business and broaden the family fortune. He attended Rugby, but rather than going to Cambridge like his brother, studied engineering at Mason College in Birmingham and finished his formal education with an apprenticeship in an accounting firm.

At the age of twenty-one, Neville was sent off to manage a family estate in the Bahamas, which promised large profits growing sisal for rope on hitherto undeveloped land. For six years Neville toiled in an attempt to create a prosperous plantation, but the venture was risky at best and doomed to failure at worst. Heavy capital investment was necessary to clear and to develop the land, the plants grew poorly on the thin soil, the labor supply was unreliable, and the world price of sisal fell just at the time the harvests began. The investment was a sorry one, but Neville worked doggedly to try to make it pay, earning the respect of the local people in the Bahamas and of his family at home.

The Chamberlains belonged to the Victorian upper-middle class of Unitarian persuasion, which believed that hard work and dedication to duty would ultimately triumph in spite of adversity. The Bahamas experience did not shatter this ideal in Neville. Indeed, it tended to reinforce his penchant toward tenacity and even stubbornness under pressure. He developed a fine eye for detail, as his letters and diaries from the period testify, and a vigorous constitution. When he returned to England after the failure of the plantation, he possessed a toughness of mind, character, and body which was to remain with him throughout his life.

Back in Birmingham, Neville took over a small firm which made ships' berths. It prospered under his leadership, and he soon was recognized as a valuable entrepreneur throughout the business community. He diversified his commercial interests, and his financial future, and that of the family, was reasonably secure. Though never possessing great wealth, the family thereafter was comfortable in the lifestyle of the Victorian upper-middle class, and Neville could devote his administrative talents to charitable and political concerns. The extended family was closely knit. Neville discussed political matters regularly not only with his father, Joseph, and his brother, Austen, but also with two of his sisters, Ida and Hilda. Physically he was relatively tall—five feet, ten inches—and slim. He enjoyed the rigors of nature well into his later years, taking particular pleasure in unusual plants and in salmon fishing. In 1911, at the age of forty-one, he married Annie Vere, the daughter of a military officer, and eventually they had a son and a daughter. She remained a loyal helpmate throughout his career.

Life's Work

In 1911 Chamberlain entered the Birmingham city council, and in 1915 he was elected lord mayor. He wished to use his office to improve city planning, clear slums, build new housing for the working classes, and provide for broadly based health services. World War I, however, required a different set of priorities, and social and economic reforms had to wait. Chamberlain was too old to serve in the military himself, but several members of his extended family did so, and he was particularly depressed by the death of his cousin, Norman Chamberlain, who had been almost like a brother to him. He served a brief and frustrating tenure as director general of the national civilian labor service under David Lloyd George, an experience which permanently estranged him from the Liberal leader and convinced him that if he were to become active in national affairs he would first have to develop a solid political base.

In December, 1918, Neville won a seat in Parliament from Birmingham and served in the House until his death. As middle-class members of a dissenting religious group, the Chamberlain family

Neville Chamberlain *(Library of Congress)*

had traditionally been liberal rather than conservative, but political shifts early in the twentieth century split the Liberal Party, and the Chamberlains became leading members of the "Liberal Unionists," who cooperated with the Conservative Party. By the time Neville entered Parliament, cooperation had become amalgamation, and he always served as a Conservative, yet he retained some of the social ideals of the Nonconformist middle class and saw himself as a social reformer bent on bringing about steady improvements in the life and health of the British people through positive governmental programs. Peaceful social change, rather than revolutionary upheaval, was his goal.

After serving briefly in other cabinet posts, Chamberlain was minister of health in 1923 and then again, from 1924 to 1929, under Prime Minister Stanley Baldwin. He worked hard to improve conditions in hospitals and clinics, and to bring about better housing for the lower classes through cooperation between local government and the private sector under a national policy. His efforts were strongly criticized by the Liberals and the rising Labour Party as inadequate, but his ability to put any positive program through under the Conservative regime was praised by many.

After the Labour Party won the 1929 election, Neville Chamberlain became a staunch spokesman for the opposition, but he rejoined the cabinet in 1931, when Ramsay MacDonald formed a "national government" under the pressure of the Great Depression, and became chancellor of the Exchequer. In this important office, Chamberlain had an increasingly dominant voice in policy, as MacDonald's and then Baldwin's powers declined. In a private letter to his sister Hilda in 1935, Chamberlain referred to himself as "a sort of Acting P.M." Thus he began to think seriously about international affairs. Since childhood he had been well aware of the wider world, particularly from the standpoint of the British Empire. Now he had to consider Continental problems which might bring Great Britain again into a bloody war. When he spoke of Czechoslovakia as a "faraway country" and its population as "people of whom we know nothing," he was demonstrating the insularity of his view of the world.

Chamberlain had no sympathy for the Nazi dictatorship and referred to Adolf Hitler privately as the "bully of Europe," but he shared the isolationism which was widespread in both the United States and the United Kingdom at the time, denying the responsibility of his country for taking military action against Germany. His attitudes toward Italy were more ambivalent. He called Benito Mussolini's Ethiopian venture of 1935 "barbarous" but nevertheless looked to Rome as a potential counterweight to Berlin if British influence in Italy could remain strong. With the rest of the British cabinet, he agreed that Great Britain could not go to war over Hitler's violations of the Treaty of Versailles by rearmament in 1935 and remilitarization of the Rhineland in 1936.

By the middle of 1936 it was clear that Chamberlain would become prime minister when Baldwin finally retired, and he in fact assumed the office in May of 1937. At the age of sixty-eight, Chamberlain had finally achieved the rank which had eluded his father and elder brother. Tall and gaunt, almost birdlike, habitually clad in the wing collar of a bygone era, and given to Shakespearean allusions in his oratory, he sometimes appears in retrospect as a weak and bumbling incompetent, naïvely trying to appease ruthless dictators who were clearly bent on aggressive conquest.

Naïve Chamberlain may have been, but he had great personal courage and fortitude, and he was a highly competent administrator, fully in command of the detail of the many issues which crossed his desk. His immense capacity for paperwork, plus his active correspondence with his sisters, is worthy of admiration. He remained a moderate reformer at heart, seeking to avoid violent revolutionary upheavals by advocating peaceful change. This principle he applied to foreign affairs as well as to domestic questions. It is notable that he had as his chief diplomatic adviser Sir Horace Wilson, a man who had made his reputation as a negotiator in labor disputes rather than anyone from the Foreign Office.

Chamberlain was well aware of Hitler's potential for violence, but also aware that the dictator put his demands in the familiar and even acceptable language of "self-determination" for the German people; moreover, Hitler had written in *Mein Kampf* (1925-1927) that he sought a peaceful settlement with Great Britain. There were vocal opponents of appeasement in Great Britain, chiefly Winston S. Churchill. Given the relative weakness of British land and air forces, however, and given the lack of stability in the French Third Republic, in which government followed government almost on a monthly basis, it seemed that Great Britain could do little to stop Hitler's expansion to the east.

The word "appeasement" at the time was not a term of opprobrium, but rather was understood as a policy of conciliation which seemed realistic if not inevitable. Defenders of Chamberlain point out that he accompanied his appeasement policy with one of British rearmament, especially in air defenses. Nevertheless, it seems clear from both the public and the private record that Chamberlain's policy had as its goal not merely the postponement of war but its avoidance altogether.

Hitler's Anschluss (annexation) of Austria in February, 1938, was his first act of aggression against another state. Chamberlain had hoped to maintain good relations with Mussolini so that Italy would oppose Hitler's designs on Austria, as it had successfully done in 1934. Using private communications via his brother's widow, as well as regular diplomacy, Chamberlain hoped to split the Rome-Berlin Axis. The only result, however, was British rejection of a private appeal from President Franklin D. Roosevelt for closer cooperation and the resignation of Anthony Eden. When Austria fell without a shot, neither Great Britain nor France took action; Chamberlain consoled himself with the idea of "self-determination" for the German-speaking Austrians. Privately, he wrote to his sister that "force is the only argument Germany understands," but he also told her that should a military crisis arise, Great Britain did not have the means to help Czechoslovakia and would not do so.

The Munich crisis of September, 1938, was the high-water mark of appeasement and the moment in history at which Neville Chamberlain played his most important role. He saw his personal approach to Hitler, first by quickly called summit conferences with the führer at Berchtesgaden in the Bavarian Alps and Bad Godesberg in the Rhineland, and then at Munich itself, as bold maneuvers to save the peace. Chamberlain forced Czechoslovakia to give up her frontier territories, with more than three million German-speaking people, to Hitler's Reich, and he forced France to approve the arrangement. In return, he got Hitler's public promise that he had no further territorial demands in Europe, and his signature on a piece of paper pledging that Germany and Great Britain would never go to war with each other again. Returning to London after the Munich conference, Chamberlain stated publicly on September 30, 1938, that he had brought back "peace with honour" and "peace for our time."

Disillusionment was not long in coming. Hitler's troops marched into the rest of Czechoslovakia in March, 1939. Chamberlain, along with the French government, gave guarantees to Poland a few days later, and the stage was set for World War II. He made some attempt to reach an understanding with Joseph Stalin, but the mutual suspicion between the Birmingham conservative capitalist and the Moscow dictatorial communist was too great, and Stalin struck a deal with Hitler instead.

On September 3, 1939, Hitler's attack on Poland became World War II when Chamberlain announced that Great Britain had no choice but to declare war. Until the last, Hitler believed that Chamberlain would revert to the appeasement policy rather than fight. The führer was wrong. Chamberlain had appeased the dictators not out of fear but because he believed that he could preserve the peace by diplomatic agreements; now the aging prime minister showed that he could be as tenacious in pursuing war as in pursuing peace. He formed a War Cabinet, bringing in Churchill and several other opposition figures, and finally relinquished the office of prime minister to Churchill after the fall of Norway in May, 1940. Chamberlain's policy of peace had failed, and now his health was failing as well. He had a major operation for abdominal cancer in August, but died November 9, 1940, at Highfield Park, Heckfield, near Reading.

Summary

"War," said Neville Chamberlain, is "a senseless and cruel thing," and he did all he could to avoid it. As a businessman and a politician, he sought to do business with, and reach political agreements with, Adolf Hitler. When he wished, Hitler could be persuasive indeed. After returning to England from his first meeting with Hitler, Chamberlain wrote to his sisters, "I got the impression that here was a man who could be relied on when he had given his word." His attitude was not based upon any pro-German, let alone pro-Nazi, sentiments. Throughout his life he had had no special love for Germany, and he found Nazi ideology, especially its anti-Semitism, absurd and offensive.

Chamberlain did not, however, believe that Great Britain had either the obligation or the power to force another major European country to make itself over in a British image. He believed that national self-determination, for the Germans as well as for other major nationalities, was more or less inevitable. Rather than defend the status quo of the Treaty of Versailles, he wanted to see whatever changes were unavoidable come about with a minimum of bloodshed. Thus, Great Britain could retain its leading position in the world without the burden of another massive war, and the resources of that enlightened country could be turned to such good works as housing, hospitals, and education rather than to the machines of destruction.

Chamberlain's appeasement policy was a failure, and as a result he will never be regarded as a great prime minister. The most that can be said of him is that his motives were laudable and that he was strongly devoted to carrying out a policy which he believed to be both correct and righteous.

Bibliography

Baumount, Maurice. *The Origins of the Second World War*. Translated by Simone D. Ferguson. New Haven, Conn.: Yale University Press, 1978. This distinguished French historian sees Chamberlain as an old Englishman trying to hunt a tiger with an umbrella, but is also critical of the French governments.

Charmley, John. *Chamberlain and the Lost Peace*. Chicago: Ivan R. Dee, 1990.

Churchill, Winston S. *The Second World War*. Vol. 1, *The Gathering Storm*. Boston: Houghton Mifflin, 1948. The first volume of the war memoirs of Chamberlain's most gifted critic firmly states the case against the appeasement policy while giving insights into the major features of British politics from a particular point of view.

Dilks, David. *Neville Chamberlain*. Vol. 1, *Pioneering and Reform, 1869-1929*. Cambridge: Cambridge University Press, 1984. The first of two massive and well-researched volumes on Chamberlain by a British professor. Should be the standard biography of Chamberlain for many decades to come.

Feiling, Keith. *The Life of Neville Chamberlain*. London: Macmillan, 1947. An early biography which has been surpassed by those written by Macleod and Dilks.

Kleine-Ahlbrandt, W. Laird. *Appeasement of the Dictators*. New York: Holt, Rinehart and Winston, 1970. An anthology of views on the diplomacy leading to World War II, which points out that appeasement was not always regarded as foolish.

Macleod, Iain. *Neville Chamberlain*. London: Frederick Muller, 1961. A sympathetic biography of Chamberlain the man, emphasizing his role as a reformer and arguing that, given the military weakness of Great Britain, appeasement served the purpose of buying valuable time for rearmament and demonstrated the peaceful nature of the British.

Parker, R. A. C. *Chamberlain and Appeasement: British Policy and the Coming of the Second World War*. New York: St. Martin's Press, 1993.

Rock, William R. *Chamberlain and Roosevelt: British Foreign Policy and the United States, 1937-1940*. Columbus: Ohio State University Press, 1988.

Taylor, A. J. P. *The Origins of the Second World War*. New York: Atheneum Publishers, 1962. A gadfly among historians, this British scholar seeks to assemble a revisionist case on the coming of the war, more or less exonerating Hitler from major responsibility. He argues that Chamberlain and the appeasers actively encouraged Hitler's expansion and then trapped him into war by guaranteeing Poland. Few would agree.

Taylor, Telford. *Munich: The Price of Peace*. Garden City, N.Y.: Doubleday, 1979. A solid, prizewinning history by an American law professor who was one of the prosecutors at the Nuremberg trials. He sees Chamberlain as a man of courage, consistency, and logic, devoted to peace but unable to understand the nature of his enemies.

Wheeler-Bennett, John W. *Munich: Prologue to Tragedy*. New York: Viking Press, 1948. An older but well written history of the appeasement policy, critical of Chamberlain but balanced in tone.

Gordon R. Mork

CHIANG KAI-SHEK

Born: October 31, 1887; Chikow, China
Died: April 5, 1975; Taipei, Taiwan

Chiang was the most important man in the Kuomintang government during the Nanking decade. He led the government and Chinese armed forces through eight years of war against Japan (1937-1945) until Allied victory, was elected president, but lost the civil war to the Chinese Communist Party. He and his Kuomintang followers fled in 1949 to Taiwan, where he ruled until his death.

Early Life

Chiang Kai-shek was born on October 31, 1887, in the village of Chikow, in Fenghua county, Chekiang Province. Chiang's grandfather had begun a successful business as a salt merchant, which Chiang's father, Chiang Ch'ao-ts'ung, had continued. His mother, née Wang, was his father's third wife. Chiang had an elder half brother, half sister, a younger brother (who died as a child), and two young sisters by his mother. His schooling began at age five; his own and others' memory of his early years was that he was a mischievous boy. His grandfather's death in 1895, followed by that of his father in 1896, resulted in division of the family's property that left his mother in financially straitened circumstances for many years as she struggled to rear and educate her children.

At fourteen, Chiang married a girl chosen by his mother, née Mao. She bore him a son, Ching-kuo, in 1909, who became president of the Republic of China on Taiwan in 1978 and died in office in 1988. Chiang had a traditional Chinese education in the classics up to 1906, when he obtained his mother's permission to go to Japan to pursue a modern military education. Since he could not enter a military academy in Japan without Chinese government sponsorship, he first gained admission to a Chinese military academy, studied there for a year, then won a scholarship to study in Japan. There he met Ch'en Ch'i-mei, an associate of Sun Yat-sen, and joined the T'ung-meng hui (United League), which Sun had organized in 1906 with the goal of overthrowing the Ch'ing Dynasty in China.

Chiang graduated from the Shimbu Gakko (military preparatory school) in 1910 and served for a year in the 13th Field Artillery Regiment of the Japanese Army, until the outbreak of the revolution against the Ch'ing Dynasty in 1911. He then resigned from the Japanese army, sailed for Shanghai, and participated in military actions that overthrew the dynasty. With Sun's resignation as provisional president of the Chinese Republic early in 1912 and the eclipse of the Kuomintang by strongman Yuan Shih-k'ai and warlords, Chiang spent much of his time until 1918 in Japan or in Shanghai.

Life's Work

In 1918, Chiang received a summons to join Sun in his new government in Canton. He assisted Sun in military affairs and became the rising star of the Kuomintang. In 1923, he headed a group that visited the Soviet Union to study its party and military and political organizations and to inspect its military schools and facilities. While there, Chiang met Leon Trotsky, Georgi Chicherin, and other Soviet leaders. He submitted a report to Sun upon his return in 1924. It showed his keen appreciation of some Soviet policies that contributed to the strength of the Red Army, but he was suspicious of Soviet communism and its intentions in China. In 1924, Chiang was appointed commandant of the Whampoa Military Academy, which Sun had ordered him to establish to train officers dedicated to the Kuomintang cause. Chiang took personal command in the training of the first three classes of about two thousand cadets.

After Sun's death in 1925, Chiang took a centrist position in the party's ideological disputes and supported continued cooperation with the Soviet Union and the Chinese communists. After securing Kwangtung and neighboring areas for the Kuomintang, Chiang was appointed commander in chief of the National Revolutionary Army in 1926 and launched the Northern Expedition to unify China under the Kuomintang. Victorious against numerically superior warlord armies, Chiang's troops quickly drove through south China and captured Nanking and Shanghai in early 1927. Chiang thereupon broke with the left-wing Kuomintang government in Wu-han that was headed by Wang Ching-wei but that was manipulated by Soviet advisers, established a rival government in Nanking with the support of right-wing Kuomintang leaders, expelled Soviet advisers, and purged Chinese communists in areas under his control. The dissolution of the left-wing Kuomintang government in Wu-han in

Chiang Kai-shek *(Library of Congress)*

July, 1927, left the Nanking Kuomintang government without challengers as Chiang resumed leadership of the campaign to unify China in 1928. The Northern Expedition ended in triumph with the capture of Beijing and the peaceful accession of the northeast (Manchuria) at the close of 1928. Thereupon the Kuomintang (Nationalist) government received international recognition.

Chiang dominated the Nationalist government politically and militarily during the Nanking decade (1928-1937) and survived all challenges mounted by dissident politicians and generals who vied for power. His government was, however, pinched between the communists, who sought to launch their power in China through armed rebellion, and Japanese imperialism, which aimed to subjugate China before it could modernize and defend its sovereignty. Chiang believed that China must be unified and modernized before it could face Japan. Therefore, he launched campaigns to eliminate the communists and dissident warlords, on the one hand, while on the other he sought German military advice to modernize his army; he created an air force and supported measures to build industries, roads, and railways.

Professing adherence to Sun's political program for China, the government proclaimed in 1929 the beginning of a period of political tutelage, in preparation for constitutional rule. During the next years, new law codes and other reforms to modernize the Chinese economy and infrastructure were put into effect, but no land reform took place.

Chiang's marriage to Mei-ling Soong in 1927 obtained for his government assistance from the modern financial community in which the Soong family was prominent. All the while he negotiated and made concessions to Japan, trading space (Manchuria and parts of northern China) for time. He was, however, compelled to halt his anticommunist campaign, which had much reduced but not eliminated that group as a result of the Sian Incident in December, 1936. Chiang was kidnapped and held for two weeks by a powerful subordinate general but was freed on his verbal promise to stop the anticommunist campaign and head a united front of all Chinese parties against Japan. During the Sian negotiations, the Soviet Union pressured the Chinese communists to work for Chiang's release and support his leadership so that China could act as bulwark against Japanese designs on the Soviet Union. Japan's attack on China in July, 1937, which led to an eight-year war, sealed the United Front between the Kuomintang and the Chinese communists and catapulted Chiang to the height of power as supreme military commander and party leader.

Chiang led China through eight years of war, at first heroically as it resisted a militarily superior and brutal enemy. Japan conquered the coastal regions but could not defeat a determined Chinese government that had retreated to Chungking in the inaccessible interior. The stalemated war of attrition and accompanying inflation and other sufferings led to the deterioration of Chinese morale. The government became increasingly authoritarian and corrupt. After the Japanese attack on Pearl Harbor and U.S. and other Western colonies in Southeast Asia, the Chinese-Japanese War became part of World War II.

The initial drubbing the Japanese gave to the Westerners earned for the Chinese, who had fought and held out alone, international respect. Limited United States aid after it entered World War II led to friction between the two governments. Meanwhile, the United Front with the communists had long since broken down, as the communists took advantage of opportunities provided by the war to increase vastly their territory and power. On his part, Chiang reserved some of his best units to blockade the communists. Both the Kuomintang and the Chinese communists prepared for the civil war to come.

Chiang's prestige peaked as the China he led won international equality in 1943, after a century of humiliations by Western powers, with the abrogation of remaining unequal treaties with Great Britain and the United States. He met British prime minister Winston S. Churchill and U.S. president Franklin D. Roosevelt at the Cairo Conference in 1943 to discuss Allied war goals; China was promised return of all Japanese conquests since 1895. When titular chairman of the National Government Lin Sen died in 1943, Chiang was elevated to that position also. China was recognized as a Big Four Allied power, a founding member of the United Nations in 1945, and a holder of one of five permanent seats on its Security Council.

After victory against Japan on August 14, 1945, the government returned to Nanking. The National Assembly convened by the Kuomintang in 1946, but boycotted by the communists, adopted a constitution that ended the period of political tutelage. Chiang was elected president by a new National Assembly under the terms of the constitution in 1948, but his vice presidential candidate was defeated by a rival Kuomintang general Li Tsung-jen. The real contest for control of China had resumed between the Kuomintang and the Communist Party in renewed civil war in 1946. United States special ambassador George Marshall had attempted but failed to mediate a truce that he had hoped would be followed by the formation of a coalition government.

The Nationalists received economic and military aid from the United States up to 1948, and the Chinese communists received from the Soviet Union Japanese weapons that it had captured in Manchuria. From seeming strength in the beginning, the Nationalist position deteriorated rapidly in 1948. Chiang resigned the presidency in January, 1949, to let vice president Li Tsung-jen salvage what he could of the Nationalist debacle. When Li also failed to stem the communist advances, Chiang and his loyal supporters retreated to Taiwan. Mao Zedong proclaimed the establishment of the People's Republic of China on October 1, 1949.

Chiang resumed his presidency on Taiwan in March, 1950, but the precarious position of the Nationalist government did not improve until communist North Korea attacked South Korea in June, 1950. This action, and communist China's intervention on behalf of North Korea with more than a million "volunteers" led the United States to order its Seventh Fleet to patrol the Taiwan Strait and to sign a Mutual Defense Treaty with the Nationalist government in 1954. Taiwan received American military aid and economic aid until the mid-1960's to build up its war-ravaged economy. Meanwhile, Chiang supervised the reform of the Kuomintang and carried out a nonviolent land reform. These factors and a sound education system combined to bring about marked and sustained economic growth on Taiwan that has continued at an accelerated rate after Chiang's death. He was reelected to a second six-year term as president in 1954 by those members of the National Assembly who had been elected on the mainland seven years earlier and who had retreated to Taiwan with his government; suspending the constitutional provision that limited the presidency to two terms, he was elected to a third term in 1960, a fourth term in 1966, and a fifth one in 1972, dying in office in 1975.

Summary

Chiang Kai-shek was truly one of China's and the world's key history makers of the twentieth century. From the time he set out to unify China as commander in chief of the Northern Expeditionary Army in 1926 until the defeat of the Kuomintang by the communists in 1949, he was the dominant person in Chinese politics and played a pivotal role in the government. His authority, however, was always challenged, by rival generals and politicians in the Kuomintang and by the Chinese communists. Thus, while he was China to the world for two decades, he never was able to assert absolute dictatorial power as his critics claimed. Chiang was a complex person, a dedicated Chinese nationalist, follower of Sun Yat-sen, and, after his marriage to Mei-ling Soong and conversion, a sincere Christian. Above all, he was a soldier-politician. While his government was mired in corruption during its last years on the mainland, and while many of his relatives benefited from the corruption, he himself remained incorruptible and lived a sternly simple life. A man of monumental ego, he equated himself with China and could not brook a vision of China other than his own. Thus he was trapped by his own failings and by international circumstances beyond his control. He was caught in the vise of Japanese imperialism and communist armed insurrection. Even though the Allied cause finally triumphed over Japanese imperialism, the China that he had led was destroyed in the process. Thus he ended his career in eclipse on Taiwan, while his archenemy, Mao Zedong, ruled mainland China.

Bibliography

Chang, Hsin-hai. *Chiang Kai-shek: Asia's Man of Destiny.* Garden City, N.Y.: Doubleday, Doran, 1944. Sympathetic biography of Chiang's life up to the date of publication, with background information about China since its first defeat by Great Britain in 1842.

Chi, Hsi-sheng. *Nationalist China at War: Military Defeats and Political Collapse, 1937-1945.* Ann Arbor: University of Michigan Press, 1982. An analysis of the weaknesses in the Chinese military and political systems and how they could not withstand the strains of an eight-year war.

Crozier, Brian, with Eric Chou. *The Man Who Lost China: The First Full Biography of Chiang Kai-shek.* New York: Charles Scribner's Sons, 1976. A generally unsympathetic analysis of Chiang's career and by no means a "full" biography.

Furuya, Keiji. *Chiang Kai-shek: His Life and Times.* New York: St. John's University Press, 1981. At almost a thousand pages, even this abridged edition gives a great deal of information. Many subheadings makes this a good reference book.

Lattimore, Owen. *China Memoirs: Chiang Kai-shek and the War Against Japan.* Tokyo: University of Tokyo Press, 1991.

Linebarger, Paul M. *The China of Chiang Kai-shek: A Political Study.* Boston: World Peace Foundation, 1941. A sympathetic and laudatory study of Chiang up to the time of publication.

Morwood, William. *Duel for the Middle Kingdom: The Struggle Between Chiang Kai-shek and Mao Tse-tung for Control of China.* New York: Everest House, 1979. An account of the Kuomintang-communist struggle up to 1949, with emphasis on the two main protagonists.

Tong, Hollington K. *Chiang Kai-shek, Soldier and Statesman: Authorized Biography.* 2 vols. Shanghai: China Publishing, 1937. A detailed, fulsome, and laudatory account of Chiang up to the point of writing.

Jiu-Hwa Lo Upshur

CHOU EN-LAI

Born: March 5, 1898; Huaian, Jiangsu Province, China
Died: January 8, 1976; Beijing, China

Chou En-lai was the premier of the new People's Republic of China from its birth in 1949 until his death in 1976. He thereby guided the new China in solidifying the new order, led in domestic reform toward modernization, and was instrumental in having the new government accepted by the international community during trying times.

Early Life

Chou En-lai was born in Huaian, in China's Jiangsu Province on March 5, 1898. Although the Chou family was part of the aristocracy, it was in a state of decline. The increasingly impecunious position of the family made Chou's childhood most unstable and meandering. Before age one, he was taken by an uncle and aunt as a foster son to be nurtured and reared. His genteel and cultured foster mother was determined to prepare him for the civil service examination, passage of which was the ladder to success in imperial China. By age four, he was able to read; by age ten, he was devouring classical Chinese literature. Yet these days of security would end when his foster mother died. In 1910 and at age twelve, Chou was dispatched to live with another uncle in the far northeast of China. There he entered elementary school, which continued his learning of Chinese tradition but which also added some of the new learning of mathematics and science.

In 1913, Chou was enrolled at Nan-kai Middle School in Tientsin. This school, founded only in 1906, emphasized a modern curriculum with the goal of training Chinese to lead the country into modernization. Upon his graduation from Nan-kai, Chou left to study in Japan, being fascinated by, as were many other Chinese, Japan's great success in developing a modern society. He did not, however, pass the entrance examination for study in a Japanese university.

In 1917, the revolution in Russia "shook the world" and stirred Chou. He began to study Marxism. While Russia was in revolution, civil war, and tumult, China was to have her lesser, albeit societal, rattling upheaval as well, in May, 1919. Chou rushed back to his homeland and to Tientsin to participate. Students at Peking University demonstrated in the streets of their nation's capital when they learned that China had gained nothing from her participation in World War I. Disillusioned and disappointed, they expressed condemnation of their government's ineptitude and the continued presence of foreign imperialists on China's soil. Chou became a leader, organizer, and even editor of a newspaper.

In 1920, Chou went on a work-study program to France, where he hoped to learn more about Marxism and about how it might be used to restore and reinvigorate China domestically and internationally. Chou studied Marxism assiduously, and he helped form Marxist groups among the other Chinese who were working and studying in Western Europe at the same time.

Back in China, a small group met and formed the Chinese Communist Party (CCP) in Shanghai in July, 1921. Chinese Marxists inside and outside the country were enlisted as full-fledged members of the party. Chou was officially in the organization. Activities going on in China synchronized with his, and so he returned home in 1924.

Life's Work

Chou returned to China to find his country greatly divided. Yet he saw great hope for China's future; the nationalistic spirit loosed by the May Fourth upheaval was still widespread. Sun Yat-sen and his Kuomintang (KMT) had plans for the reunification of the Chinese homeland, and the fledgling CCP, small though it was, stood ready to contribute to the cause as best it could. Sun, although not a Marxist, could only receive the aid he needed for his plans of unifying China from the Soviet-dominated Comintern, and so he took it. The CCP would lend its support, and here Chou was to contribute crucially. This twenty-six-year-old suave and articulate Chinese communist brought his reputation of successful leadership in France home with him when he returned. Immediately, he was selected for the prominent post of working to develop an army for the KMT. He was appointed the political adviser to Chiang K'ai-shek, the commandant of the newly founded Whampoa Academy for the training of officers. Chou gained great respect from many of the student officers during his tenure at Whampoa; many of these would defect to the communists once the battle between the KMT and the CCP reached decision-making proportions in the civil war, 1946-1949.

By 1926, KMT leaders decided they were ready to tackle the warlords who were dividing China. Sun had died in 1925; Chiang had come to be the new leader, and he proclaimed a "northern

Chou En-lai *(Library of Congress)*

expedition" from his southern base in moving militarily to restore China to a unified nation. Chou moved from the military academy in Canton to Shanghai to aid the plan, and he was assigned the role of organizing the labor force in this largest of China's cities and making it ready to accept the KMT as the new leader of a unified China. Chou did his work as assigned, but the outcome was not what he expected. Chiang had come to distrust the CCP totally, saw it as detrimental to China's unity, and attempted to destroy it.

The KMT, instead of accepting Chou's delivery of Shanghai to its allegiance, tried to kill off all the communists; most were massacred. Chou escaped that fate and fled to a haven of safety at a communist camp in the hills of a rural base. At this base, Chou aided communist military leader Chu Teh in founding a Red Army for the party in order to survive. Chiang was determined to destroy the communists and kept up the attack. The war went on for years, with the communists mostly on the defensive, and culminated in the famous "Long March."

During the Long March, Mao Zedong had been selected to be the main spokesman and leader of the Chinese Communist Party. He would hold the title of leadership from that time until his death in September, 1976. Chou accepted Mao's leadership and would work hand-in-glove with the entitled chairman for the rest of his existence. Both were strong Chinese nationalists; both were Marxists. Both were determined to push forward to the success of Chinese nationalism with a Marxist society. Chou decided to work within the framework of the new society as an administrator and as a diplomat. He began his work almost immediately.

In 1936, Chiang reactivated his quest to rid China of what he viewed as the divisive communists. He decided to attack them at their new base of Yen-an in Shensi Province. His generals, however, were more concerned about the presence of the Japanese in China. The Japanese had launched an attack on China's northeastern section in Manchuria, were successful, and had established a puppet government. After intense negotiations between the KMT and the communists, the communists decided it would be in everyone's best interest for them to join forces with the KMT to drive out the Japanese.

The united front came into full play when Japan launched an attack on China proper in July, 1937. Japan's successful military surges in China forced Chiang to abandon much of his domain to foreign occupation and to flee to Chungking. Chou moved to

Chungking as the liaison of the CCP. Chou worked during most of the war in Chungking for the advantage of the communists. Chou's many contacts with foreign diplomats and foreign journalists during the war allowed him to display his cosmopolitanism, his cordiality, and his diplomatic flair for the benefit of his communist comrades. He did his work well, for those who had any association with him came away most impressed with his personal talents and came away believing that those in Yen-an were serving the war effort and Chinese society more adeptly and more energetically than were the KMT group in Chungking.

After World War II, the CCP-KMT cooperation came to an end, and old conflicts arose, creating civil war. Despite the material advantages of the KMT, it lost the support of the Chinese people, who saw the CCP as the organ to lead China to a better life and a more secure status internationally. On October 1, 1949, the communists, through the mouth of Mao, announced the creation of the People's Republic of China (PRC). Chou became the premier as well as the foreign secretary. The former office he would hold until his death in 1976; the latter he would assign to another in 1958, but he would still be present at any major contact with a foreign dignitary.

Chou, as the premier and head administrator of the new nationwide government, held the responsibility for putting into order policies and instruments of rule. Policies, programs, and agencies that had been used effectively in the "liberated areas" (as the territory under rule of the communist base in Yen-an was called) were now extended into all of China. The peasants were urged to form cooperatives and to attack the large landowners; Chinese entrepreneurs were asked to turn over their enterprises to public ownership; imperialist holdings were confiscated; Chinese intellectuals were cajoled and encouraged to support the "new." It was Chou who stood forth in making the pronouncements and the encouragements. He expounded the new laws for the equality of women.

Chou used all the talents that he could muster through counseling, persuasion, encouragement, and force to rally Chinese of all classes and categories to support the new system of Chinese communism and Chinese national unity. By 1951, when he was at the age of fifty-three, the premier then pronounced a new constitution and moved on to announce the start of Five Year Plans. Chou was instituting Marxism in China with finesse, flair, and success. The people's support expanded, agricultural and industrial production grew, diets improved, and diseases decreased.

Mao, ever the philosophical and revolutionary visionary, used his prominence to direct China toward major changes in 1957 and again in 1966. Chou, the ever-loyal administrator, made Mao's ideas public. In 1957, it was the Great Leap Forward; in 1966, it was the Great Proletarian Cultural Revolution. Both brought upheaval to Chinese society; both were formally announced and supported by Chou. Both saw major reorganizations of the Chinese power centers.

After the failure of the Great Leap Forward, Mao, although keeping his title and public eminence, had lost power. Others were able to wrest the control over policymaking, and Chou stood in support. Mao, however, would not stand by for long. In 1966, through the announcement by Chou, Mao launched the Great Proletarian Cultural Revolution. Leaders in communes, in factories, in art, in education, in government, and even in the party were ousted, criticized publicly, and sent to live in the countryside. Mao led the upheaval; Chou joined the new crusade, but he tried to keep some semblance of order and stability as the disruption of the Cultural Revolution proceeded for ten years, 1966-1976. It seems that Chou's levelheadedness made a mark, for the system still survived when he died in January, 1976.

Chou's diplomatic talents were as demanding as his domestic administrative ones. Chou was not only the prime minister of the new republic but also the leading actor in the foreign ministry. He carried the title of foreign minister from 1949 until 1958; he continued to be China's leading spokesman in that area until his death, trying to gain for his country acceptance by the world community. Chou was able to make headway in this respect at the Geneva Conference in 1954 and the Bandung Conference in 1955.

From its foundation in 1949 and during the Cold War, the PRC had to rely on an alliance with the Soviet Union, an alliance that was not overly cordial from the start and one that devolved into a break and increased bitterness after 1961. Chou's diplomacy at Geneva and at Bandung did bring solid relationships for China from other countries, even though they were of lesser stature, and he tried to build on these bases by traveling to numerous countries. He continued in his attempts to gain China's entry into the United Nations and in having formal diplomatic recognition from the United States.

In 1971, the PRC was voted membership in the United Nations (U.N.). In February, 1972, U.S. president Richard Nixon visited

China, although full relationships were not established between the two countries until January, 1979. Chou did not live to see the outcome of these relations; he died on January 8, 1976.

Summary

Chou En-lai was a transitional figure in twentieth century Chinese society. He was born into a family of status and had been inculcated with the values of old China; however, early during his adolescence, he came to be educated in schools that taught modern subjects. Both of these exposures guided him for the rest of his life. He believed that China should reassert and reestablish itself as the "middle" country that it had been throughout most of its early and long history, and he decided that it could only be done via the communist route.

Although China had difficulties in finding the type of communism it would follow, Chou, as the head administrator and directing diplomat, tried to keep his society functioning during these oscillations and continued to press for China's acceptance in the world community. Chou's persistent and stabilizing influences left their mark during his lifetime and after. Mao was hailed as the "helmsman" in his later years; Chou was the ballast, although not so entitled. Where Mao was the domineering patriarch, Chou was the warm, loving, and stable matriarch, if viewed from the perspective of the traditional Chinese society.

Bibliography

Archer, Jules. *Chou En-lai.* New York: Hawthorne Books, 1973. This is a work written for the general public; it is interestingly written but with little new information.

Chae-Jin Lee. *Zhou Enlai: The Early Years.* Stanford, Calif.: Stanford University Press, 1994.

Fang, Percy Jucheng, and Lucy Guinong J. Fang. *Zhou Enlai: A Profile.* Beijing: Foreign Languages Press, 1986. The only complete biography in English coming from the PRC. It is mostly favorable, but it includes information on his private life not found elsewhere.

Fitzpatrick, Merrilyn. *Zhou Enlai.* St. Lucia, Australia: University of Queensland Press, 1984. This work is forty-eight pages long and covers all major events of Chou's life.

Han Suyin. *Eldest Son: Zhou Enlai and the Making of Modern China, 1898-1976.* Edited by Paul De Angelis. Reprint ed. New

York: Kodansha International, 1995. Sympathetic, detailed, and smoothly written account of an inherently secretive leader, whose career is placed fully within the broader context of Chinese history.

Hsu, Kai-yu. *Chou En-lai: China's Gray Eminence.* Garden City, N.Y.: Doubleday, 1968. Hsu was the first of Chou's biographers. The book is well written and has an abundance of information from a favorable viewpoint.

Keith, Ronald C. *The Diplomacy of Zhou Enlai.* New York: St. Martin's Press, 1989. The only solid study of Chou's work in diplomacy, showing how he was a communist and a nationalist.

Kuo-Kang Shao. *Zhou Enlai and the Foundations of Chinese Foreign Policy.* New York: St. Martin's Press, 1996.

Li, Tien-min. *Chou En-lai.* Taipei, Taiwan: Institute of International Relations, 1970. This is a highly critical work, but it contains valuable factual information.

Wilson, Dick. *Zhou Enlai: A Biography.* New York: Viking Penguin Press, 1984. This is a book written in the style of a journalist, with much emphasis on personal acts and foibles.

Zhou, Enlai. *Selected Works of Zhou Enlai.* Vol. 1. Beijing: Foreign Languages Press, 1981. This is a collection of some of Chou's writings, 1926-1933. The only collection available in English.

Raymond M. Lorantas

JEAN CHRÉTIEN

Born: January 11, 1934; Shawinigan, Quebec

In both the 1993 and 1997 Canadian elections, Chrétien led his Liberal Party to absolute majorities in the Canadian House of Commons. His victory in 1993 put an end to nine years of Conservative Party rule in Canada.

Early Life

Joseph-Jacques Jean Chrétien was born on January 11, 1934, in the small Quebec town of Shawinigan, which is located near Trois-Rivières. He parents were French-speaking Catholics. His father, Wellie, worked in a paper mill and was active in the Liberal Party. His grandfather had served for thirty years as the mayor of St.-Etienne-des-Grés and was one of the organizers of the Liberal Party in Quebec. Jean was the eighth of nineteen children born to Wellie and Marie Chrétien. Nine of their children survived infancy. Jean was born deaf in his right ear and partially paralyzed on the left side of his face. Despite his physical problems, he was mainstreamed in local grammar schools and high schools. His parents worked hard to ensure that their children received excellent educations. For high school, he attended St. Joseph's Seminary in Trois-Rivières. Jean's brother Michel became a well-known endocrinologist in Montreal, while Jean studied at Laval University in Quebec City, where he received both his undergraduate and law degrees. While he was a law student, he married Aline Chaîne. They had a daughter named France and a son named Hubert. Jean was admitted to the bar in 1958, and he began working for a law firm in his native city of Shawinigan.

Life's Work

In 1963, Chrétien was successful in his first run for political office. The voters in St. Maurice, Quebec, elected him to represent them as a Liberal member of Parliament. Soon after his arrival in Ottawa, he began to study English because he realized that it was essential for his political career that he be able to express himself in both

French and English, the two official languages of Canada. Chrétien became fully bilingual. He soon impressed Lester Pearson, the Liberal Party leader who served as prime minister from 1963 to 1968. Within two years of his entrance into Parliament, Chrétien was appointed the parliamentary secretary to the prime minister. Just two years later, Pearson selected him to serve as minister of state for finance. At the age of thirty-three, he was the youngest federal minister in the history of Canada.

Jean Chrétien *(AP/Wide World Photos)*

From 1968 until 1984, the liberal Pierre Trudeau served as the prime minister of Canada, with the exception of a few months in 1979 when the conservative Joe Clark was prime minister. During the Trudeau years in Ottawa, Chrétien became an increasingly influential leader of the Liberal Party. Like Trudeau, he was fully committed to bilingualism in Canada, but he also shared Trudeau's opposition to the separation of Quebec and to granting special rights or a special legal status to the French-speaking majority in Quebec. Chrétien was a federalist who strove to maintain the unity of Canada while at the same time protecting the linguistic and political rights of all Canadians.

Between 1968 and 1984, Chrétien held diverse federal positions that enabled him to understand the rich complexity of Canada. As the minister of national revenue and minister of finance, he learned how the federal government's tax policies could encourage economic development throughout Canada in order to fight such serious problems as unemployment, inflation, and budgetary deficits. Chrétien grew up in a purely French-speaking town in Quebec and had little previous contact with Native Canadians. From 1968 until 1974, however, he served as the minister of Indian affairs and northern development. Chrétien came to understand that federal and provincial governments had mistreated Native Canadians by attempting to suppress their culture and by doing little to encourage economic development in areas of Canada with majority Native Canadian populations. He became involved in defending the rights of Native Canadians and in improving the quality of their lives. In 1972, Chrétien and his wife adopted an orphan from the Gwichin tribe whom they named Michel.

Chrétien later served as minister of justice and attorney general of Canada. In 1980, he played a central role in persuading Quebecers to vote against separation from Canada. He argued eloquently that French and English-speaking Canadians shared the same rights, which would be protected effectively only in a unified Canada. The 1980 referendum failed by a 20 percent margin in Quebec. English-speaking Canadians admired Chrétien's forceful defense of Canadian unity, but separatists in Quebec were angered by his successful efforts to prevent Quebec's secession from Canada.

Two years later, he successfully negotiated a significant change in the British North America Act of 1867, which had created Canada as an independent dominion within the British Empire. This old law required laws passed by the Canadian Parliament to be submitted for the approval of the English king or queen. Many Canadians viewed this requirement as an affront to their sovereignty. This law was changed in 1982 so that Canada gained the right to amend its own constitution. One effect of this 1982 law was that Quebec lost its ability to veto constitutional changes. Chrétien viewed this as a positive and democratic step because he believed that it was not conducive to Canadian unity to allow Quebec or any other province to frustrate the will of the majority.

As a member of the French-speaking minority in Canada, he was sensitive to their aspirations and to their fervent desire to protect their language and their culture from the English-speaking majority, but he felt that it served little purpose to modify the constitution by declaring that Quebec was a "distinct society" within Canada. If Quebec received special treatment under the law, then every group would demand and expect preferential treatment under the law. In 1984, Trudeau stepped down as prime minister, and the Liberals in the House of Commons selected John Turner as their new leader and prime minister. The Liberals under the leadership of Turner were soundly defeated by the Conservatives under Brian Mulroney in both the 1984 and 1988 federal elections.

In 1985, Chrétien published his autobiography *Straight from the Heart,* which was a best-seller in Canada. The next year, he resigned his seat in the House of Commons and temporarily withdrew from politics. He accepted a position with an influential Ottawa law firm and earned a good deal of money between 1986 and 1990. In hindsight, commentators realized that Chrétien was simply waiting for Canadian public opinion to turn against the policies of Mulroney. By 1990, unemployment and inflation had increased significantly in Canada, and Mulroney's solution to reducing the deficit was to impose a national goods and services tax on Canadians. When the budget deficit increased even after the imposition of this tax, the popularity of Mulroney plummeted. In 1990, Chrétien was reelected to the House of Commons, and then became the Liberal Party leader. In 1993, Mulroney resigned, and he was succeeded by Kim Campbell.

In the midst of turmoil, many conservatives joined the new Reform Party. In the October 25, 1993, federal election, the Liberal Party, under Chrétien, won 177 out of the 295 seats in the House of Commons. The Conservative Party won only two seats while the Reform Party, the New Democrats, and the separatist Bloc Québécois held the other 116 seats. During his first four years as prime minister, Chrétien ruled as a fiscal conservative and social liberal. His main goals were to create jobs by increasing exports to the United States and other countries, reduce the national deficit, maintain Canadian unity, and keep taxes low while ensuring quality education and medical care for all Canadians. He fully implemented the North American Free Trade Agreement (NAFTA) with the United States and Mexico and played a key role in persuading Quebec voters in October, 1995, to vote once more against separation from Canada.

One of the most traumatic events during Chrétien's first term as prime minister occurred on the morning of November 5, 1995, when a knife-wielding man named André Dallaire entered the Chrétien residence and wandered the halls for twenty minutes. Aline heard his steps and awakened her husband, who called the Royal Canadian Mounted Police agents stationed in their residence. It took the security officers seven minutes to reach the Chrétien's bedroom and arrest Dallaire. It later became public that this assassination attempt might well have succeeded had the quick-thinking Aline not locked the door to their bedroom from the inside.

In the spring of 1997, Chrétien called federal elections in which his party once again won an absolute majority. He was the first Liberal Party prime minister since Louis St. Laurent in the 1950's to win two successive absolute majorities in the House of Commons. In a June 2, 1997, election, the Liberals won 155 seats out of 295 in the House of Commons. The Liberals won a respectable number of seats in Quebec and elsewhere in Canada, but their main area of strength was in Ontario, where they won 101 out of 103 seats. Canadians expressed their support for Chrétien's efforts to improve their economy while at the same time maintaining national unity.

Summary

Jean Chrétien's political evolution was quite extraordinary. Until his election to the House of Commons in 1963, his interests did not extend beyond Quebec, and he spoke only French. Within a few years of his arrival in Ottawa, he became concerned with all aspects of Canadian society and politics, and he became a fervent federalist committed to defending individual rights of all Canadians within a unified Canada. Had it not been for a tradition within the Liberal Party for the party leadership to alternate between native speakers of English and native speakers of French, Chrétien would have most probably become prime minister in 1984 after the resignation of Trudeau. However, he would have been soundly defeated by Mulroney because Canadian opinion polls indicated that the Liberals could not have hoped to defeat the Conservatives in 1984.

The selection of Turner by the Liberals in 1984 was a blessing in disguise for Jean Chrétien because it was Turner and not Chrétien who lost the 1984 and 1988 federal elections. With the collapse in the popularity of the Conservative Party in the early 1990's, the Liberals became the sole political party with solid representation in the House of Commons from all Canadian provinces. The other four parties became largely regional in their appeal to voters. Chrétien developed a vision of a unified Canada that impressed both voters in English-speaking provinces and Quebecers opposed to separation from Canada.

Bibliography

Bothwell, Robert, Ian Drummond, and John English. *Canada Since 1945: Power, Politics, and Provincialism*. Revised. Toronto: University of Toronto Press, 1989. The pages on Chrétien describe the many different positions of influence that he held in the governments of Lester Pearson and Pierre Trudeau.

Chrétien, Jean. *Straight from the Heart*. Revised. Toronto: Key Porter, 1994. When it was originally published in 1985, this autobiography was a best-seller in Canada. It created a favorable impression on Canadian voters and helped prepare his return to national politics a few years later.

Martin, Lawrence. *Chrétien*. Toronto: Lester, 1995.

Mowers, Cleo, ed. *Towards a New Liberalism: Re-creating Canada and the Liberal Party*. Victoria, British Columbia, Canada: Orca, 1991.

Wilson-Smith, Anthony. "A House Divided: After a Narrow Win, Federalists Fear That the Real War Is Only Starting." *Maclean's* 108 (November 6, 1995): 14-17. This articles deals well the important role played by Jean Chrétien in creating a bipartisan coalition to defeat the Quebec separatist referendum and preserve the unity of Canada.

__________. "Today's Man: Jean Chrétien's Liberals Sweep to Power as Voters Radically Reshape the Political Map." *Maclean's* 106 (November 1, 1993): 8-11. This article in a Canadian weekly news magazine describes the reasons for Chrétien's landslide victory in the federal election of October 25, 1993.

Wilson-Smith, Anthony, and Mary Janigan. "Distinct Societies: The Election Leaves the Nation Splintered as Never Before." *Maclean's* 110 (June 9, 1997): 16-20. This article describes the victory of Chrétien and his Liberal Party in the general election of June 2, 1997.

Edmund J. Campion

SIR WINSTON S. CHURCHILL

Born: November 30, 1874; Bleinheim Palace, Oxfordshire, England
Died: January 24, 1965; London, England

One of Great Britain's greatest prime ministers and war leaders and one of the twentieth century's greatest public figures, Churchill was exceptionally influential in both war and peace.

Early Life

Winston Spencer Churchill was born on November 30, 1874, at Bleinheim Palace in Oxfordshire, England; he was two months premature. He was the son of Lord Randolph Churchill (1849-1895), a prominent Conservative politician and a descendant of the duke of Marlborough (1650-1722), a statesman and one of the greatest military commanders in history. Bleinheim Palace was the gift of a grateful nation to the duke of Marlborough for the first of his famous victories at Bleinheim (1704) in the War of the Spanish Succession (1701-1714). Churchill grew up within this background of military glory and patriotism and always had it in mind to preserve and to enhance the grandeur of the British Empire.

Churchill's mother, Jennie Jerome, was the daughter of Leonard Jerome, described as an "American freebooter" and the "King of Wall Street." Winston adored his mother, although she shared little of her fashionable life with him. In his efforts to shape American opinion during World War II and afterward, he made the most of his American ancestry. He worshipped and stoutly defended his reckless, flamboyant, and self-destructive father—even writing a biography of Randolph (1906) in justification of his father's life. All these qualities—filial piety, loyalty, pugnacity, grandiloquence, and enormous courage—were to make of Churchill a unique figure in the twentieth century, for he was almost a throwback to an earlier age, more like an eighteenth century soldier statesman and man of letters than a modern politician.

Churchill was educated at Harrow and Sandhurst, the latter a school for the training of military officers. From the beginning of his career, he combined his craving for military exploits with a talent for journalism. Thus, in 1895, he took a leave from the military to report on the war in Cuba for London's *The Daily Telegraph*. After serving in both India and South Africa, Churchill was assigned in 1899 to cover the South African War for *The Morning Post*. The story of his capture, imprisonment, and escape catapulted him to the forefront of British journalists. In these early adventures, Churchill was already the man he would become as prime minister: rambunctious, intrepid, a bit of a bully, but nearly always an engaging and inspiring leader and writer. He thrived on words, with his favorite mode of composition being dictation, in which he could galvanize himself and his readers with a vibrant language that seemed inseparable from the man himself.

In his early career, Churchill went from success to success: He was elected to Parliament as a Conservative in 1900 and appointed undersecretary for the colonies in the cabinet of Sir Henry Campbell-Bannerman; he also served as president of the Board of Trade (1908-1910) and as home secretary (1910-1911). In the latter post, he initiated important labor and pension legislation. In 1911, Churchill became first lord of the Admiralty and aggressively expanded and modernized the fleet. With the devastating failure of the Dardanelles campaign (1915) in World War I, however, he suffered not only his first major defeat but also a far more serious blow: He became branded as a reckless adventurer, a

Sir Winston S. Churchill *(The Nobel Foundation)*

loner in public life whose career might end as disastrously as his father's, whose life had ended sadly in a series of illnesses and rages brought on by syphilis.

Churchill's early setback was by no means a mere misfortune. He had often acted arbitrarily and outside the boundaries of normal party and governmental conduct. Elected as a Conservative, he switched to the Liberal Party, then switched back again to the Conservatives. As first lord of the Admiralty, he often ran roughshod over seasoned naval officers—sometimes with cause, sometimes only for the misguided gratification of his own ego. To many of his political colleagues, therefore, Churchill was not a man to be trusted; he was out to serve only himself. Although the defeat in the Dardanelles was not exclusively Churchill's fault (indeed, credible arguments can be advanced that his military plans were sound), his conspicuous touting of himself inevitably provoked the vehement reaction against him.

Life's Work

It became Churchill's life's work not only to rehabilitate his reputation but also to fulfill his early promise and destiny: to become prime minister and supreme military leader. Churchill's talents were not ignored, but in various cabinet positions he was not allowed to get near the center of power. He was, successively, minister of munitions (1917), secretary of state for war and for air (1918-1921), colonial secretary (1921-1922), and chancellor of the Exchequer (1924-1929). None of these offices required Churchill's broad-based talent for mobilizing a whole nation during periods of crisis, and he lacked real interest in domestic matters. From 1929 to 1939, he had no government position. As a member of Parliament he was a steadfast anticommunist and an early—if not always consistent—opponent of the Fascists.

By the time of Neville Chamberlain's "peace in our time" capitulation to Adolf Hitler at Munich in the summer of 1938, Churchill had become fixed in his country's imagination as the prophet who had foreseen Great Britain's involvement in World War II and who had demanded military preparedness. Whereas his vitriolic "empire first" speeches had once seemed dangerous and ridiculous affectations belonging to an earlier age, now his evocations of moral and military grandeur spoke eloquently to a nation that needed to be aroused to fight for its own freedom.

At various points in the 1930's, Churchill, physically and politically, had looked like an old man. War, however, energized him. He was sixty-six when he became prime minister in May of 1940. His appearance no longer seemed merely overweight. He now had the heft of a powerful man. There was a spring in his voice and in his step. His famous "V for victory" signs and his boyish grins bespoke a man who was reborn, and yet a man of years, of broad experience, equipped better than anyone else to stay the course and to excite a nation to arms. Just as he had sounded the alarm of war, so he now broadcast the call to victory. There is ample documented evidence that his public display of confidence was no sham. To be sure, he had his moments of despair, but observers of his private life testify to a man who was irrepressible, a demon for work, a demanding—sometimes unreasonable—chief executive. He drove his staff as mercilessly as he drove himself. If he commanded the power of the word, the word was transformed into actions. Churchill required results and was always quick to take action even at the risk of defeat. His task was to spur the government and the people onward.

As prime minister in time of war, Churchill's independence was a signal strength. Although a Conservative, he had never been much of a party man, and his claim to be serving the whole nation was never better supported than during the war. Although he opposed communism and socialism, some of his wartime measures heralded the welfare state Great Britain would become after the war. Loath to grant independence to any part of the British Empire, his vigorous prosecution of the war inevitably strengthened the successful movement of a free India.

It came as something of a shock for Churchill to be turned out of office at the end of World War II. In retrospect, however, it seems clear that the voters knew his finest hour had been during a time of military need. Now the Labour Party would set about putting into effect a postwar economy that would make good on promises of increased social security, health benefits, and other domestic improvements desperately desired by a people weary of war.

Summary

Winston S. Churchill was a world figure. With Franklin D. Roosevelt and Joseph Stalin, he helped shape the postwar world. Present at Yalta (1945) and other important wartime meetings, he shared Roosevelt's terrible responsibility in coming to some kind of terms with the victorious Red Army. Although Churchill is remembered for having been a staunch anticommunist, his treatment of Stalin was inconsistent. He seems to have thought on occasion that he could charm the Soviet leader into taking a moderate, peaceful view of postwar politics. Sometimes Churchill seems to have been cynical in suggesting to Stalin that there was an equitable way of dividing up Europe to the satisfaction of all the wartime allies. In truth, for all of his brilliance, Churchill had a weak hand to play as the representative of a declining empire and perhaps thought that he could make do with guile and with ingratiation.

Churchill's disappointment over the course of postwar events is readily apparent in his famous Fulton, Missouri, speech (1946), in which he coined the term "Iron Curtain" to describe the brutal way Stalin had cut Eastern and Central Europe off from the "free world." Churchill's rhetoric crystallized what many Americans and Western Europeans had not yet articulated, and his view of the menace of postwar communism came to dominate American foreign policy—especially in the formulation of the "containment" strategy by which American governments attempted to prevent the spread of communism throughout the globe. Elected prime minister twice after the war (in 1951 and 1955), Churchill was not a particularly effective leader, although his august position as world statesman was unassailable.

Whatever Churchill did not win through politics or through war, he won through the word. His many books consolidated his position in history. In 1953, he won the Nobel Prize for his writing and oratory. His six-volume history *The Second War* (1948-1954) and his *A History of the English-Speaking Peoples* (1956-1958) made him appear as a figure for the ages. These books are as much myth as they are history, for Churchill had no compunction about revising the past to portray his own part in it as illustriously as possible. Yet the books are also reflective of a great man who was able to stamp history in his own image and to make his word stand for the deed.

Bibliography

Bonham Carter, Violet. *Winston Churchill: An Intimate Biography*. New York: Harcourt, Brace and World, 1965. A sympathetic biography by a friend who first met Churchill in 1906 and was in a position to observe his public and private behavior, his leadership in times of war and peace, and his reactions to both victory and defeat.

Brendon, Piers. *Winston Churchill*. New York: Harper and Row, Publishers, 1984. A succinct, lively, and colorful one-volume biography.

Churchill, Randolph, and Martin Gilbert. *Winston S. Churchill*. London: Heinemann, 1966- . This is the definitive multivolume life begun by Winston's son, Randolph, and carried on by Gilbert, whose work is still in progress. This is a minutely detailed (sometimes day-by-day) account of every aspect of Churchill's life and career which is partial to his own view of himself.

Churchill, Winston. *The Complete Speeches of Winston Churchill*. Edited by R. R. James. New York: Chelsea House, 1974.

_________. *My Early Life*. London: T. Butterworth, 1940. One of Churchill's best books, written in his fluent, engaging style.

Gilbert, Martin. *Churchill: A Life*. New York: Henry Holt, 1991.

_________. *In Search of Churchill: A Historian's Journey*. London: HarperCollins, 1995.

Rose, Norman. *Churchill: An Unruly Life*. New York: Simon & Schuster, 1994.

Taylor, A. J. P., et al. *Churchill Revised: A Critical Assessment*. New York: Dial Press, 1969. Studies of Churchill the statesman by Taylor, the politician by J. H. Plumb, the military strategist by Basil Liddell Hart, and the man by A. Storr.

Thompson, R. W. *Generalissimo Churchill*. New York: Charles Scribner's Sons, 1973. A study of Churchill's skill as a military commander based on both secondary and primary sources, including interviews with his close friends and associates. Covers Churchill's "long apprenticeship" as a war leader and his overall performance in World War II.

Carl E. Rollyson

GEORGES CLEMENCEAU

Born: September 28, 1841; Mouilleron-en-Pareds, France
Died: November 24, 1929; Paris, France

Clemenceau was significant in French politics from 1871 to 1919. Although he influenced the nation's political course several times, Clemenceau is best known for his role as premier during the last eighteen months of World War I, when his determination to win inspired France despite enormous adversity.

Early Life

Born in the Vendée in 1841, Georges Clemenceau was the eldest son of Benjamin and Emma Gautreau Clemenceau. The family eventually consisted of three sons and three daughters. Oddly, as the region was strongly Catholic, the patriarch was an atheist and his wife Protestant. Georges followed his father in religion and in his leftist political views.

Clemenceau's early education was at home, but in 1853 he enrolled at the *lycée* in Nantes. Upon graduation in 1858, he entered medical school there. In 1861, he transferred to Paris. Although he graduated in 1865, he had spent so much time getting acquainted with leftist political circles—participation in an 1862 demonstration cost him two months in jail—that he got a poor residency. The articles he wrote in the early 1860's suggest that he had more talent as a political journalist than as a physician.

In 1865, frustrated by unrequited love, Clemenceau went to the United States for four years. At first he lived on a paternal allowance and the proceeds of his articles about the United States sold to the Paris press. When his father cut him off in an effort to get him home, he took a position teaching French at a Connecticut academy. He fell in love with a student named Mary Plummer, and, after some disagreement with her guardian over Clemenceau's distaste for religion, the two married on June 23, 1869. The match was unfortunate, for after the births of a son and two daughters the two were estranged. Mary had little part in Clemenceau's life after 1875, and they divorced in 1892. Tales of Clemenceau's callousness have circulated ever since, but although his wife spent much of the rest of her life in some isolation, there is no real evidence that he mistreated her.

Life's Work

Clemenceau's political career began in the turmoil of the Franco-Prussian War (1870-1871). Personally he had no use for the Second Empire or Napoleon III, but, a determined patriot, he could hardly hope for a French defeat. The disastrous defeat at Sedan, where the emperor himself was taken prisoner, led to the creation of the Third Republic. On September 5, 1870, Clemenceau was appointed mayor of Montmartre. Known for his leftist views, he organized the National Guard in his district and forbade religious instruction in the schools. A gulf began to open between the Left and the government, and, when municipal elections agreed to in the face of riots were canceled, Clemenceau resigned his post. A national plebiscite supported the government, but Clemenceau was reelected on November 5. The Left believed that the National Guard was the equal of the professional forces of Prussia, and, when France was forced to accept an armistice on January 28, 1871, Leftists cried treachery.

In February, Clemenceau was elected to the new National Assembly and voted against a peace that was to give Alsace-Lorraine to the Prussians. In March, he attempted to defuse the violence that erupted when the army tried to confiscate some cannons that had been left in Montmartre. He was too late, and two officers were murdered. The Radical Republicans and Socialists formed the Paris Commune, intending it to be the nucleus of a national government. On March 19, 1871, the mayors of Paris, including Clemenceau, met with the central committee of the commune; they were ready to represent the city's grievances before the national government, led by Adolphe Thiers, but not to rebel. Compromise failed, and Clemenceau was crushingly defeated in the ensuing communal elections. Pretending to be an American, he got out of the city for a conference of delegates from republican cities and was thus away during the bloody week of May 21-28, when the government crushed the Commune. For much of the rest of his career, however, he was damned by the Right as a supporter of the Commune and by the Left as a traitor for abandoning it.

For the first four years of the Third Republic, Clemenceau was in the political background. He served on the Paris Municipal Council, becoming president in 1875, and practiced medicine. In February, 1876, he was elected to the Chamber of Deputies, wherein his calls for amnesty for Communards and increased popular sovereignty quickly established him as one of the leaders of the Left. As Republicans gained more electoral strength, Clemenceau sought to offer the electorate a choice between radical and conservative Republican factions.

Georges Clemenceau *(Library of Congress)*

In the late 1870's, Clemenceau began a campaign for leadership of the Radical Republicans. He established a newspaper, *La Justice*, to express his views, created a party organization, and began making speeches in and out of Parliament. Like most political journals, Clemenceau's had a patron, Cornelius Herz, but, unlike many legislators, Clemenceau did not do favors in return for the money. The target of his campaign was a Radical Republican victory in 1885. The issues were constitutional reform, the condition of the working class, and colonial policy. Clemenceau wanted an elected judiciary and the abolition of the senate whose members served for life. Although the Senate was made an elective body, by 1885 Clemenceau found such reform was not of popular concern.

Although not a collectivist, Clemenceau supported trade unions and improved conditions for workers. He became more conservative over time, but during the 1880's he inspired some of the younger French socialists, such as Jean Jaurès and Léon Blum. In the mid-1880's, however, the major issue was colonial expansion in Tunis and Indochina. Clemenceau argued that the profits of colonies did not offset their expenses; that colonial conflict would divert military resources from European preparedness; and that aggressive colonialism would produce friction with Great Britain, leaving France alone against Germany.

In March, 1884, just as the premier Jules Ferry was making secret arrangements with China over Tonkin, Clemenceau, justifying his reputation as a brutal debater, crushed the government with information about military setbacks that later proved false. A caretaker government was appointed and a spirited electoral campaign followed, leading to elections in October of 1885. The Republicans, however, could not agree about issues or candidates, and the result of the first ballot was the biggest victory for the Right since the early 1870's. The feuding Republicans managed to combine their lists of candidates for the second ballot, resulting in a chamber divided in thirds: Right, Opportunists (moderate Republicans), and Radicals.

Clemenceau was perhaps lucky that his attacks on Ferry had angered enough Republicans that he got no office. The parliament of 1885-1889 was marked much more by scandal than reform. Efforts by Ferdinand de Lesseps to duplicate his Suez Canal building success in Panama led to failure and many bribes and special favors for legislators to ensure the profits of those at the top before the company fell. Also, in 1888, General Georges Boulanger, who had risen in politics as a protégé of Clemenceau, began to attack the failure of the republic to make reforms. A popular military hero, Boulanger, secretly in league with the royalists, seemed about to stage a coup. The Republican legislature, belatedly aware of the danger, trumped up charges against his lieutenants, causing Boulanger to panic and flee. Clemenceau then successfully initiated legislation that would force Boulanger's faction to form a structured party, which it lacked the unity to do. The Radicals had been forced to help the government without getting any reforms and lost much of their separate identity. The popular reaction was a drift to the Right, and so there would be no constitutional reforms before the defeat in World War II resulted in a new constitution.

The elections of 1889 reduced the influence of the Republicans and Clemenceau. Then three years later, the aftermath of the Panama Canal scandal virtually ruined him. No one ever directly charged Clemenceau with misconduct, but his longtime friend and backer Cornélius Herz was involved and had even attempted to blackmail government figures. Right-wing politicians, perhaps seeking revenge for the defeat of Boulanger, damned Clemenceau by association, using the charges to defeat him at the polls in August, 1893.

Clemenceau, forced out of politics, embarked on a career as a man of letters. He wrote almost daily for *La Justice*, until it failed in 1887, and often for other papers, and, before returning to politics, produced a novel and a play. His most important publications were the volumes of essays *La Mêleé sociale* (1895) and *Le Grand Pan* (1896).

The Dreyfus affair, which arose because of the indictment and hasty conviction for espionage of Alfred Dreyfus, the only Jew who had ever served on the French general staff, provided a cause that helped Clemenceau to focus his writing. His style improved markedly, and in the last years of the century he was writing almost daily about *l'affaire*. When Emile Zola, whose article "J'accuse" (1898) had made Dreyfus a national concern, was tried for libel, Clemenceau was allowed to join the defense team even though he was not a lawyer. Dreyfus was convicted largely because of anti-Semitism and sent to Devil's Island. Even after his innocence had been established, there was resistance to changing the verdict.

Clemenceau had once again become an influential figure, and in 1901 *Le Bloc*, a weekly newsletter written entirely by him, began to appear. Aimed at an elite audience, it was influential, but only a year later he gave it up to campaign for a senate seat, which he held for the rest of his political life. On March 14, 1906, he became minister of the interior. Clemenceau was quite influential from the beginning and became premier on October 9. The government has on occasion been criticized for failing to advance the program of the Left, but it accomplished much in adverse circumstances. Without battles over church-state relations and the Dreyfus affair, the Left had no unifying cause. There was no majority for a coalition of the far Left, and so the cabinet was made up of mostly moderate Republicans. Over its three years, this cabinet managed to nationalize the western railroad, get an income tax bill through the chamber (it failed in the Senate), and start work on an old-age pension bill that was finally passed in 1910. It was a respectable set of reform efforts for a government based on moderates.

The Clemenceau government had problems at home and abroad. During the Algeciras Conference (1906), which dealt with a German challenge over the growing French role in Morocco, Clemenceau's determination kept up French resolve. Ultimately, the *Entente cordiale*—the semiofficial connection between London and Paris—held firm, and the Germans backed down. When large-scale strikes led to violence, Clemenceau adroitly combined repression, using troops to keep order, and conciliation, blocking efforts to suppress the Confédération Générale du Travail and supporting reasonable wage and hour demands. Throughout his tenure Clemenceau was faced with labor problems, but, although the Socialists were not pleased, his policy was quite successful.

Clemenceau's fall from power came ostensibly over a question of naval preparedness but was actually a result of personality. He was challenged by Théophile Delcassé, whose efforts to create a British alliance and resist Germany had made him popular. Instead of defending his own program, Clemenceau attacked his foe, with whom he had previously had personal difficulties. The vote that brought down Clemenceau was really a vote of sympathy for Delcassé. It was difficult for Clemenceau to put personal feelings aside and react purely in political ways. The next few years were quiet. In 1911, Clemenceau spoke against concessions to Germany in the second Moroccan crisis and campaigned for extending the basic term of military service from two to three years, which was done in 1913. He also began to publish a new newspaper, *L'Homme libre.*

The outbreak of war in August, 1914, led to Clemenceau's finest hour. At first, however, he was a critic. In the senate and his newspaper, which he renamed *L'Homme enchaîné* in response to censorship, he demanded a more vigorous prosecution of the war while condemning the tactic of mass assaults. The Left was inclined to seek compromise, and the Right was loyal to the Sacred Union (the nonpartisan war government). By the time the horrendous butcher's bill from the Western front began to produce disillusionment, he was the only politician who had both criticized the handling of the war effort and demanded an all-out effort to win. His moment came in the summer of 1917 when the bloody failure of the Nivelle Offensive led to large-scale army mutinies.

While General Philippe Pétain restored discipline, Clemenceau attacked the government for tolerating defeatist attitudes, which the army blamed rather than admitting that the horrors of the front, added to the disgusting conditions in rest camps, had been the real cause of the revolt. Governments failed in October and November, and Clemenceau was asked to form a cabinet. The members were mostly Republicans, but none of prominence. No one from the Right was included, but that side was strongly supportive in any case. The Socialists abandoned the Sacred Union and went into opposition. The result was that Clemenceau was completely dominant and, unlike his predecessors, had no reason to adjust his policy to accommodate the Socialists.

At seventy-six in 1917, Clemenceau, who was short and rotund, was still in good physical condition. Fitness had long been important to him, and he was an expert horseman and fencer. He was dapper, with a high forehead and walrus mustache, but his dominant feature was his piercing eyes. His appearance did not belie his nickname, the "Tiger," earned by the ferocity of his debating.

Russia's withdrawal from the war because of the Bolshevik Revolution freed large numbers of German troops for the Hindenburg offensives of early 1918, but Clemenceau's oratory helped maintain the French will to fight. By making it clear to unions that he would support wage and condition improvement but crush any hint of pacificism or defeatism, he got such cooperation that the number of days lost to strikes fell dramatically. He pressed the British to increase the proportion of their young men drafted and promoted plans to make the aggressive Ferdinand Foch supreme Allied commander. When things went awry, he backed his generals, refusing to look for scapegoats. He frequently visited the front at considerable personal risk to show the *poilus* that he cared.

With the arrival of the Americans, the Germans were stopped and the tide ineluctably turned. Clemenceau worked for Allied unity and to ensure that peace arrangements would guarantee French security. He had to balance the idealism of Woodrow Wilson, the practical desires of British prime minister David Lloyd George for a revived Germany in European trade, and the demands of Foch and President Raymond Poincaré for the crushing of Germany. Clemenceau was influential at the Paris Conference as chairman of the Council of Ten (later reduced to the heads of the major powers) and, despite being shot by an anarchist, was able to get much of what he wanted in the Versailles Treaty.

A key question for Clemenceau was security. Foch and Poincaré demanded major territorial cessions by Germany, but, when it was clear that the Allies would not agree, Clemenceau accepted a fifteen-year occupation of the Rhineland and the separation of the Saar from Germany for a similar period with a plebiscite in the latter region to determine its final fate. In return, France was to get an Anglo-American guarantee of its borders. The guarantee was voided by the refusal of the United States to ratify the Versailles Treaty, and Clemenceau had to defend the arrangement as adequate. It bought time to rearm. The other great concern was reparations, and Clemenceau was as guilty as the other negotiators for the impossible burden imposed on Germany. Although more vindictive than the other negotiators, Clemenceau was little more responsible for the treaty's failure. He had to satisfy the political demands of the electorate and compromise with France's allies. Even had he wished to, he could not have changed the treaty much.

During the negotiations, Clemenceau was faced with labor unrest, financial problems, and an increasing Socialist challenge. There were some dramatic strikes, but on the whole the postwar boom prevented political danger. Although the government seemed in good shape, a change in electoral law made coalitions important, and, since the Socialists refused any coalition, the result was a massive victory for the right-center Bloc National in 1919. Clemenceau, despite the prestige of having led the nation to victory, had to resign.

After 1919, Clemenceau took little part in politics, though he did make some effort to help his protégé, André Tardieu. For a decade he devoted most of his time to travel and writing. He composed biographies of Demosthenes and Claude Monet and, most important, *Grandeurs et misères d'une victoire* (1930; *The Grandeur and Misery of Victory*, 1930). The latter was in part memoirs but was more intended as a response to Foch, who had continued to criticize the peace settlement and Clemenceau for agreeing to it. He died early in the morning of November 24, 1929, in Paris.

Summary

Georges Clemenceau was above all a politician. He was devoted to the liberal principles of separation of church and state, support for labor, and popular sovereignty. Although he became more conservative toward the end of his career, his support for those principles never wavered. Part of that conservatism came from his unyielding sense of patriotism, and his conviction that France had to be preparing to defend herself against Germany.

Present at the creation of the Third Republic in 1871, Clemenceau's combativeness slowed his political rise, for he made enemies more easily than friends. Guilt by association in the Panama Canal scandal also sidetracked his career. He carried on, using journalism to make his opinions known and to regain respect in the political arena. Getting a chance to serve in a government, he effectively furthered the program of the moderate Left. When he fell, he was an elderly man and could have retired with honor.

The summit of his career came in the darkest hours of World War I. Taking almost sole control of the government and war policy, Clemenceau's enormous willpower stiffened the resolve of the nation to make the final sacrifices and win. His importance to his nation was greater than that of any other war leader in any of the belligerents. His career ended with his influential role at the Paris Peace Conference, at which he did as much as was possible to protect the future interests of France.

Bibliography

Bruun, Geoffrey. *Clemenceau.* Cambridge, Mass.: Harvard University Press, 1943. Although in places outdated, Bruun's biography is a good, straightforward narrative that is still worth reading.

Churchill, Winston S. "Clemenceau." In *Great Contemporaries.* New York: G. P. Putnam's Sons, 1937. Churchill's eloquence and shrewd insights into human nature are evident in this biographical sketch. Churchill packs much information into a few pages.

Clemenceau, Georges. *Georges Clemenceau: The Events of His Life as Told to His Former Secretary Jean Martet.* Translated by Milton Waldman. New York: Longmans, Green, 1930. Although not always trustworthy, this book is one of the few sources available for the study of Clemenceau's early life. It is a must for any biographical research.

Dallas, Gregor. *At the Heart of a Tiger: Clemenceau and His World, 1841-1929*. New York: Carroll & Graf, 1993.

Douglas, L. "Clemenceau." In *The History Makers*, edited by Lord Longford and Sir John Wheeler-Bennett. New York: St. Martin's Press, 1973. Focused on Clemenceau's importance in the development of French history, this is a good introductory article for those interested in seeing the key elements of the subject's career.

Jackson, John Hampden. *Clemenceau and the Third Republic.* New York: Macmillan, 1948. A useful biography with a political slant. Jackson's judgments are judicious, and he is at times insightful.

King, Jere C. *Foch Versus Clemenceau: France and German Dismemberment, 1918-1919.* Historical Monographs series 44. Cambridge: Harvard University Press, 1960. Clemenceau was so intimately involved in the entire resolution of World War I that, although this book is really about Franco-German diplomacy, anyone seeking an in-depth knowledge of him should read it.

Lansing, Robert. "Georges Clemenceau." In *The Big Four and Others of the Peace Conference.* Boston: Houghton Mifflin, 1921. An eyewitness, Lansing offers an impressionistic but valuable view of Clemenceau's dominating role at the 1919 Paris Peace Conference. Although short on biographical data, this article is a good introduction to the administration of the peace talks.

Newhall, David. *Clemenceau: A Life at War*. Lewiston, N.Y.: Mellen, 1991.

Roberts, J. "Clemenceau the Politician." *History Today* 6 (September, 1956): 581-591. A popular article focused on Clemenceau's role in politics. Because so much emphasis is placed on his role in World War I, the article's emphasis is helpful in establishing a balanced view.

Watson, David Robin. *Georges Clemenceau: A Political Biography.* New York: David McKay, 1974. An excellent scholarly biography, Watson's volume is perhaps a little short on personal information and at times shows a tendency to be overly favorable to the subject.

__________. "Pillar of the Third Republic." *History Today* 18 (May, 1968): 314-320. By one of Clemenceau's biographers, this article is an effort to establish the subject's central role and importance in the development of the Third Republic of France. The popular approach makes it a valuable introduction to Clemenceau.

Fred R. van Hartesveldt

BILL CLINTON

Born: August 19, 1946; Hope, Arkansas

A five-term governor of Arkansas who was especially successful in improving education in his state, Clinton was elected the forty-second president of the United States in 1992; in 1996, he became the first Democratic president since Franklin D. Roosevelt to win election to two full terms.

Early Life

William Jefferson Blythe IV was born in the rural town of Hope, Arkansas, on August 19, 1946, three months after the death of his father in an automobile accident. Later, as a teenager, he changed his surname to that of his stepfather, Roger Clinton. He began to be popularly known as Bill Clinton at the start of his political career.

As an infant, Clinton was reared primarily by his grandparents and a nanny. His mother, although devoted to him, frequently had to be away. When he was seven, his family moved to Hot Springs, Arkansas, where he received his elementary and high-school education. He distinguished himself in both his class work and extracurricular activities, and his outgoing and congenial nature made him popular. He was elected president of his junior class and became a National Merit Scholarship semifinalist; he also played saxophone in his own band. As a senior, he was selected to participate in the Boys' Nation program in Washington, D.C. At the White House, he met his idol, President John F. Kennedy; for the young Clinton, the encounter was a momentous event that would help to determine his political dreams and ambitions.

Despite his academic and social successes, however, his home life was often fraught with instability and tension. Clinton's stepfather was an alcoholic who physically abused his wife; on some occasions, the young man had to intervene to protect his mother. He also helped to care for his younger half brother, Roger Clinton, Jr.

In 1964, Bill Clinton enrolled at Georgetown University, a Jesuit institution in Washington, D.C. He majored in international studies, and he was elected class president during his first two years there.

(Although he was brought up as a Southern Baptist, Clinton had significant experience of Catholic education; his primary education began in a parochial school.) While at Georgetown, he worked in the office of Arkansas senator J. William Fulbright, who became his political mentor.

Upon his graduation in 1968, Clinton went to England to study at Oxford University, having received the distinction of a Rhodes Scholarship. At the time, the United States was embroiled in the Vietnam War, and Clinton was eligible for the military draft. Although the number he received in the draft's lottery system was high enough to ensure that he would not be called into military service, some of his political opponents would later point to his time abroad as an instance of "draft dodging."

After returning to the United States, Clinton in 1970 began studies at Yale University Law School. There he met Hillary Diane Rodham, a fellow student whom he married in 1975. After receiving his law degree in 1973, he returned to his home state, where he accepted a position teaching law at the University of Arkansas in Fayettesville.

Life's Work

In the 1970's, Clinton began his professional political career. His first efforts, though, were less than auspicious. In 1972, he managed the Texas campaign of Democratic presidential nominee George McGovern, who was badly defeated; in 1974, Clinton himself campaigned unsuccessfully for an Arkansas congressional seat. In 1976, however, his political career gathered momentum: He managed the Arkansas campaign of victorious Democratic presidential candidate Jimmy Carter, and he was himself elected the state's attorney general.

Clinton proved popular as attorney general, and he was credited with helping to hold down utility and phone-service rates. In 1978, at the age of only thirty-two, he was elected to a two-year term as governor of Arkansas; however, he alienated key supporters by raising taxes to fund a highway-improvement project and by challenging major business interests. Moreover, he was identified with the Carter administration, which became particularly unpopular in Arkansas for relocating Cuban refugees in the state. When he ran for reelection in 1980, he was defeated.

Shocked by his defeat, Clinton and his staff perceived that he needed to modify his image as a youthful radical. He decided to

ss what issues he should address and how to pursue them. g this difficult period, he was consoled by the birth of his only child, a daughter, Chelsea. He regained the governorship in 1982, and he was reelected in 1984, 1986 (at which point a four-year term was established), and 1990. He made improving the quality of education a major theme of his administration, and he cultivated a less radical image.

The education issue brought him wide support, particularly from business interests that needed an educated workforce to improve their competitiveness as the South experienced an economic resurgence. Clinton lobbied for increased teacher qualifications and pay, more rigorous administrative standards, and more demanding attendance and testing requirements for students. Financing for these efforts came from increases in the state sales tax.

Clinton was soon dubbed the "education governor," and his national stature began to rise. He became chair of the National Governors Association at the end of 1986. At the 1988 Democratic National Convention in Atlanta, he gave the nominating speech for the party's presidential candidate, Michael Dukakis. In 1990, he chaired the Democratic Leadership Council, an organization of moderate and conservative Democrats. As a "New Democrat" reassessing the role of big government and emphasizing the role of the private sector, Clinton positioned himself to run for the presidency in 1992.

He began his bid to unseat Republican incumbent George Bush at the end of 1991. During the primaries, while he was competing for the Democratic nomination against numerous rivals, his campaign almost collapsed under allegations that he had been having an extramarital affair. Similar allegations had troubled him earlier during his tenure as governor.

With the support of his wife, Clinton overcame these difficulties and triumphed at the Democratic National Convention in New York City in July, 1992. In his campaign, he emphasized the human consequences of the recession and unemployment that were plaguing the nation and against which Bush seemed ineffective. He also emphasized the need for national health insurance and called for the federal government to balance the federal budget by increasing taxes in the higher income brackets and by reducing defense spending.

Clinton was elected the forty-second president of the United States on November 3, 1992. He received only 43 percent of the

Bill Clinton *(Library of Congress)*

popular vote; Bush received 38 percent, and an independent candidate, the mercurial billionaire H. Ross Perot, received 19 percent. Clinton garnered 370 votes in the electoral college to Bush's 168, Perot obtaining none. Clinton's running mate was Tennessee senator Al Gore, Jr., a fellow southerner and valuable adviser with whom Clinton established an exceptional rapport.

Sworn in on January 20, 1993, Bill Clinton was the first Democrat to be elected president in twelve years and the youngest since John F. Kennedy. He was also the first president born after World War II and the first since Herbert Hoover without military service. In addition, he was the first president to be inaugurated during the post-Cold War period, in a world without the Soviet Union.

Clinton made addressing domestic issues his top priority. The Clinton administration's most difficult task was to find ways to support essential government programs, trim or eliminate others, and balance the federal budget, which had accumulated an enormous deficit during the Reagan-Bush years (1981-1993). To staff his administration, Clinton assembled a team that emphasized representation of minorities and women. He appointed the first woman as attorney general, Janet Reno. In 1997, he appointed Madeleine Albright as the first woman to be secretary of state, the senior position in the cabinet.

During his first two years in office, he had the advantage of ıg with a Democratic Congress, and he was successful in .l areas of legislation, somewhat satisfying both liberal and conservative agendas. He obtained passage of a budget that included both higher taxes on the wealthy and cuts in federal programs. Landmark anticrime legislation was passed that included a ban on certain assault weapons and increased the number of police. He also lobbied successfully for passage of family-leave legislation. On the world economic stage, he was successful in obtaining tariff reductions through the North American Free Trade Agreement (NAFTA) and the Uruguay Round of the General Agreement on Tariffs and Trade (GATT). He also appointed two Supreme Court justices whom he hoped would restore a more moderate balance to the Court, which had become increasingly conservative after a series of Republican appointments.

In foreign relations, his administration's goals were principally economic in nature, rather than political or military. This emphasis represented a major shift in American foreign policy and vividly reflected the consequences of the post-Cold War period. Nevertheless, the Clinton administration dealt forcefully and immediately with renewed threats of Iraqi aggression against its neighbors. In Haiti, the U.S. forces restored civilian government; Clinton also sent peacekeeping forces into the tinderbox of the Balkans. A peacekeeping expedition to war-torn Somalia, however, was widely viewed as a fiasco. The administration also supported the emergence of market economies and democracy in the newly independent states of Eastern Europe and gave important backing to Russian president Boris Yeltsin. In the Middle East, the administration worked steadily for peace between Palestinians and Israelis.

On the domestic front, however, Clinton failed to obtain congressional approval of his prime legislative objective, national healthcare reform, a project headed by his wife. He was also forced to compromise with the military establishment over efforts to end discrimination against gays in the armed forces.

Moreover, the Clinton administration became the focal point for a number of highly charged moral, ethical, and legal issues that received continuous attention from the media and from political opponents. These issues included allegations of the improper dismissal of personnel from the White House travel office; charges against the president of sexual harassment; and questions about possible criminal involvement by the Clintons in Whitewater, a failed Arkansas land-development deal from more than a decade earlier. The Whitewater affair touched off an ongoing, wide-ranging independent counsel investigation that, though inconclusive, caused the Clintons substantial personal and political embarrassment.

Clinton's first-term troubles helped contribute to one of the most dramatic political reversals in U.S. history in the 1994 congressional elections. The Republicans obtained majorities in the House and Senate for the first time since the Dwight D. Eisenhower administration, reversing decades of Democratic congressional dominance. This was a blow as stunning to Clinton as that which he had suffered when he was defeated in his first bid for reelection as governor of Arkansas.

The 1994 reversal produced a similar reaction, as Clinton resolved to accommodate the conservative center on issues of reducing government size and cost. At the beginning of 1995, it seemed as if his presidency might become paralyzed by the powerful Republican Congress led by the new House speaker, Newt Gingrich.

The Republicans, however, lost popular support as wrangling over the federal budget resulted in the shutting down of federal government operations at the end of 1995 and the beginning of 1996. Clinton's popularity rose as he stood firm against proposed drastic reductions in Medicare and Medicaid funding. His support was further solidified in midyear when, to the dismay of liberals, he vowed "to end welfare as we've known it" and signed legislation terminating many federal subsidies for the poor but emphasizing that those leaving welfare had to be helped with job training. He also succeeded in persuading Republicans to raise the minimum wage in two stages in 1996 and 1997. Throughout his first term, he presided over a period of peace and relative prosperity, the recession abating and unemployment steadily diminishing.

Clinton was well positioned for the 1996 presidential race. No Democrat challenged him in the primaries, and he was overwhelmingly nominated at the party's August convention in Chicago. Clinton and Gore campaigned on a well-articulated platform of support for education, the environment, and Medicare, emphasizing that these would be the means of "building a bridge to the twenty-first century." His Republican opponent, Senator Bob Dole, did not articulate as extensive a program. In what was once again a three-way race, with Perot entering the campaign as the candidate of the new Reform Party, Clinton was reelected. He obtained 49 percent of the popular vote; Dole received 41 percent and Perot 8 percent. In the electoral college, Clinton obtained 379 votes to 159 for Dole; Perot eceived none. The Republican majority was also returned to ...ess.

Bill Clinton was inaugurated for a second term on January 20, 1997. He thus became the first Democratic president since Franklin Roosevelt to be inaugurated for two full terms. As the term began, budget conflicts with Congress abated because of increased federal revenue. The year 1997 saw the first federal budget surplus in over a generation. By the end of 1998, the United States had enjoyed the longest period of peacetime economic expansion in its history. This prosperity occurred in significant part because of Clinton's successful efforts to continuously reduce federal budget deficits. These efforts kept inflation and interest rates low, thereby supporting investments, which then resulted in high levels of employment, productivity, and tax revenue. As of 1997, nonetheless, growing economic recession in Asia posed a menacing hazard. Moreover, the United States continued to have the highest level of disparity between rich and poor of all industrialized nations.

The Republican Congress raised questions in early 1997 about Democrat fundraising in the previous year's campaign. It focused on misuse of the White House for raising funds and on contributions by the Chinese government to buy influence in the Clinton administration. Despite Senate and House committee investigations into these charges, the allegations remained unproven, although they left an air of suspicion about both parties. The head of the House committee, Republican congressman Dan Burton, was himself the subject of investigation for campaign irregularities and for the methods by which he conducted his committee proceedings. The Democratic Party returned significant amounts of contributions to the original donors. Campaign reform legislation supported by the president was thwarted by the new Republican majority leader in the Senate, Trent Lott.

At the beginning of 1998 the Whitewater investigation assumed a new responsibility. It began examining an allegation that President Clinton had an affair the previous year with a young White House intern, Monica Lewinsky, and that he might have persuaded her to lie under oath about the matter, thereby suborning perjury, an action possibly subject to impeachment. The investigation, headed by Republican conservative Kenneth Starr, had lasted for over four years at a cost of more than 40 million dollars. With offices in both Washington, D.C., and Little Rock, Arkansas, the investigation closed the latter at the beginning of 1998, making no charges against Clinton or his wife. At the same time, a sexual harassment case brought against Clinton by a former Arkansas government employee, Paula Jones, was thrown out of court as being without basis. The report on the Monica Lewinsky affair was made public by the House of Representatives on September 10, 1998. According to Starr, Clinton was guilty of several impeachable offenses, including perjury and obstruction of justice. The report set off a nationwide debate on morality and the appropriateness of prying into the private affairs of public officials. At the end of the year, the House of Representatives voted to bring three impeachment charges against Clinton, but none of the charges won even a simple majority in the Senate in early 1999.

Clinton consolidated his position on the international stage and as the leader of the only world superpower by making a number of overseas trips. At the beginning of 1998, he made an unprecedented presidential tour of Africa, demonstrating, by the countries he selected to visit, U.S. support for democratic, civilian regimes. In June he visited China, emphasizing support for its democratic political and economic development. In early 1999 he joined leaders of other Western powers to order massive air strikes against the Serbian government of Yugoslavia for its abuses of the rights of ethnic Albanians in its Kosovo province.

Summary

As a centrist and "New Democrat," Clinton positioned himself cautiously to the left or right of issues as political circumstances demanded. He thereby helped to salvage many of the liberal Democratic policies first instituted in the New Deal. These historic policies—and, therefore, the Clinton presidency—were sorely challenged by leaner economic conditions, diminishing federal budgets, and a conservative political and ideological environment.

Clinton demonstrated foresight and effort in regard to public policy and practices. He also demonstrated leadership in such diverse areas as international trade, education, and the environment and became an effective advocate for the poor and the elderly as well as for women and minorities. He notably failed, however, in one of his principal objectives, the creation of a national health-care system. Furthermore, he compromised one of his party's major tenets, financial assistance for the poor, by consenting to drastic cuts in federal welfare programs. Occasional episodes of political clumsiness and recurring questions about his ethics and personal charac-

ıded his government. Presiding over unprecedented national rity and world peace, he enjoyed consistently high approval ratings.

Throughout his political career, and in his life in general, Clinton has shown a clear tendency to lead through conciliation. As a boy and a young man, he worked to reconcile mother and stepfather, Protestant and Catholic traditions, upper and lower classes, and black and white in the Deep South. In dealing with political opponents, too, he has typically avoided confrontation. He also has developed policy in exceptionally substantive, thorough, and analytical terms, and conveyed it in an articulate manner. Like Thomas Jefferson, Abraham Lincoln, and John F. Kennedy before him—presidents he has deeply admired—he may prove to have been a president inadequately understood in his own time, yet out of office soberly respected for his foresight and diligence.

Bibliography

Allen, Charles F., and Jonathan Portis. *The Comeback Kid: The Life and Career of Bill Clinton*. New York: Carol Publishing Group, 1992. Issued on the eve of the 1992 presidential election, this book examines Clinton's previous elections and strategies for them. Emphasizes his political shrewdness, resolution, and resilience.

Carville, James, and Mary Matalin, with Peter Knobler. *All's Fair: Love, War, and Running for President*. New York: Random House, 1994. Carville was a principal strategist for the Clinton presidential campaign in 1992; he is married to Matalin, a Republican political consultant and strategist for President Bush. This book contains their varied, not necessarily opposing, views on the 1992 campaign.

Campbell, Colin, and Bert Rockman, eds. *The Clinton Presidency: First Appraisals*. Chatham, N.J.: Chatham House, 1996.

Clinton, Bill, and Al Gore, Jr. *Putting People First: How We Can All Change America*. New York: Times Books, 1992. Published during the 1992 presidential campaign. The authors explain their views on and strategies for dealing with issues such as arms control, children, education, the environment, health care, trade, and many other topics.

Drew, Elizabeth. *On the Edge: The Clinton Presidency*. New York: Simon & Schuster, 1994. A noted journalist's analysis of the early years of the Clinton presidency. Focuses on its unevenness and on questions about the president's character.

Maraniss, David. *First in His Class: A Biography of Bill Clinton*. New York: Simon & Schuster, 1995. Examines the complexity of Clinton's character in the context of the schools and social environment that molded him.

Oakley, Meredith L. *On the Make: The Rise of Bill Clinton*. New York: Regnery Publishing, 1994. An analysis of Bill and Hillary Clinton as an ambitious couple. Includes balanced and candid insights.

Renshon, Stanley A. *High Hopes: The Clinton Presidency and Politics of Ambition*. New York: New York University Press, 1996. Attempts a psychological analysis of Clinton, studying his presidency within the framework of his contradictions and accomplishments.

Stephanopoulos, George. *All Too Human: A Political Education*. Boston: Little, Brown, 1999. Revealing, often scandalous, look at Clinton's political life by a prominent former staff member who began working for him when he was governor of Arkansas.

Stewart, James B. *Blood Sport: The President and His Adversaries*. New York: Simon & Schuster, 1996. A temperate, even compassionate, analysis of the Whitewater affair.

Will, George F. *The Leveling Wind: Politics, the Culture, and Other News, 1990-1994*. New York: Viking, 1994. An anthology of articles by a noted conservative columnist. Describes the sociopolitical context in which Clinton assumed the presidency.

Woodward, Bob. *The Agenda: Inside the Clinton White House*. New York: Simon & Schuster, 1994. Woodward rose to prominence as an investigative reporter during the Watergate scandal; here he examines the early years of the Clinton presidency, focusing on the conflicts and dilemmas of the president and his core advisers.

__________. *The Choice*. New York: Simon & Schuster, 1996. Analyzes the 1996 presidential campaign. Based on interviews and primary sources.

Edward A. Riedinger

CALVIN COOLIDGE

Born: July 4, 1872; Plymouth, Vermont
Died: January 5, 1933; Northampton, Massachusetts

Practicing the virtues most Americans seemed to honor in absentia, Calvin Coolidge served as president of the United States during the central years of that extraordinary decade, the 1920's.

Early Life

John Calvin Coolidge was born in Plymouth, Vermont, on July 4, 1872. His father, Colonel John Calvin Coolidge (the rank was an honorary one bestowed for service on the governor's staff), was a prominent local figure who had served several terms in the state legislature. His mother, the former Victoria Josephine Moor, died when young Calvin was twelve. It was a painful loss to the boy, and his memories of his mother were precious to him. It was from her family that he inherited the dash of Indian blood which so charmed political pundits during his presidential years. His only sister, Abigail, who was three years younger than Calvin, died in her teens. Her death was another blow to the sensitive youth.

After a brief period spent teaching school, Coolidge entered Amherst College in 1891. There he joined the College Republican Club and, in his senior year, a social fraternity. He was one of three persons in his class chosen to speak at graduation. His was the task of presenting a humorous speech, which he completed with considerable wit and the approval of his class. In 1895, he moved to Northampton, Massachusetts, and began the study of law. At the age of twenty-five, he was admitted to the bar and settled into the quiet, sober, often dull, and always frugal life-style which he followed until his death.

Standing slightly over five feet eight inches tall, Coolidge was a slim, rather drab, and colorless figure. His once reddish hair became a sandy brown as he matured. With his broad forehead, cleft chin, and thin features, he lived up to the Washington description of him as one who was "weaned on a dill pickle." Well deserving the sobriquet "Silent Cal," Coolidge began his diligent climb through small-town politics. Always listening and working rather than talking—though he could speak effectively, with his dry, raspy voice and flat New England accent—Coolidge became a local Republican committeeman before he was thirty and not long thereafter was elected to the Republican Party's state committee. In addition, Coolidge served on the town council, was named vice president of a local savings bank, and, in 1900, was appointed city solicitor.

At the age of thirty-two, Coolidge courted and wed Grace Goodhue, a teacher at the local school for the deaf and dumb. Her charm and vivacious personality were a perfect foil to his lack of, and disregard for, the social graces. Theirs was a happy and contented marriage, each understanding and accepting the foibles of the other. They had two sons, John and Calvin, Jr., who completed the family.

In 1906, Coolidge was elected to the Massachusetts House of Representatives, where the same qualities that had served him so well in Northampton led to his slow but steady rise to leadership. Coolidge was elected mayor of Northampton in 1910; in 1912, he was elected to the state Senate; and two years later, was chosen president of the state Senate. The next logical step was the office of lieutenant governor, to which he was elected in 1916, and in 1918, he was elected governor of Massachusetts.

Life's Work

Events unfolded to make Governor Coolidge a national figure. The labor unrest which followed the end of World War I produced the Boston police strike in 1919. Though the strike was settled largely without the intervention of the governor, Coolidge captured the imagination of the country and the convictions of the time with a dramatic phrase in a telegram sent to American Federation of Labor president Samuel Gompers: "There is no right to strike against the public safety by anybody, anywhere, any time." This statement catapulted Coolidge into national prominence and made him the popular choice for vice president among the delegates to the Republican National Convention in 1920. Safely elected with President Warren G. Harding in the Republican return to "normalcy," Coolidge gave undistinguished service in an undistinguished office.

Calvin Coolidge had no part in the scandals pervading the Harding administration. He remained untouched by the revelations of bribery and misuse of high office. When he succeeded to the presidency upon the death of Warren G. Harding in 1923, he seemed to represent the incorruptible side of a tarnished Republican coin. As

Calvin Coolidge *(Library of Congress)*

if to symbolize his virtues, Coolidge, visiting his home in Vermont when he learned of Harding's death, was sworn in as president by his father (a notary public) in the light of a kerosene lamp. The rugged simplicity of the swearing in was in sharp contrast to the bright urban lights and fast-paced life that seemed more typical of the 1920's. Coolidge made no changes in Harding's cabinet. He came especially under the influence of Secretary of the Treasury Andrew W. Mellon, who represented the established wealth that was, to Coolidge, the result of success in America. Coolidge particularly identified his and the country's interests with the class represented by Mellon in his most often quoted statement that the "business of America is business."

Coolidge presided over a government largely retreating from the activism and reform of the Progressive Era and from the demands of victory in World War I. He was personally honest, loyal, and frugal—and he served as the keeper of America's conscience. While the nation indulged itself in an orgy of spendthrift frivolity, the silent approval of so austere a president seemed to make virtuous an otherwise hedonistic attitude toward life.

Coolidge was personally popular and was always an adroit politician, so it was with ease that he was nominated for president in his own right in 1924. These same factors, supported by an accelerating prosperity and aided by a seriously divided Democratic Party (whose nominating convention cast 103 ballots before deciding upon John W. Davis of West Virginia as their candidate), led to a Republican victory. The Coolidge years saw decreasing governmental activity and few legislative accomplishments. Coolidge vetoed one of the few major bills of the era, the McNary-Haugen bill, which was designed to bring stability to the farm market. He continued the traditional high tariff policy supported by the Republicans, and both his policy and his pronouncements encouraged the upward movement of the stock market that characterized his years as president.

Coolidge vigorously supported economy in the operation of the government. He believed that a reduction in government costs, while beneficial in its own right, would also make possible a reduction in taxes, particularly for the business classes. He mildly favored railroad consolidation in the interest of greater efficiency and was interested in a waterways project in the St. Lawrence area (though never the Mussel Shoals project proposed during his term, which formed the base of the future Tennessee Valley Authority). In spite of a growing reputation as "Silent Cal," Coolidge held frequent and often lengthy press conferences during his years as president.

In foreign policy, Coolidge, like his party, opposed American membership in the League of Nations. He did, however, unsuccessfully support American participation and membership in the World

Court. In line with his respect for business, Coolidge staunchly demanded that European nations repay to the United States their debts from World War I. He supported efforts to work out a schedule of payments (tied to the payment of German reparations), and he believed that the payment of the valid debts was necessary to provide worldwide economic stability. He was also a strong advocate of the Kellogg-Briand Pact and its effort to promote peace by outlawing the use of war as a national policy.

Coolidge's personal popularity, combined with the continuing prosperity of the nation during his administration, made him seem a logical candidate for renomination in 1928. Therefore, it was a stunning surprise when, while on vacation in 1927, he informed reporters that "I do not choose to run for president in 1928." It was a statement on which he never elaborated and from which he never deviated. Many contemporaries believed that he wanted another full term but wanted to be drafted by his party. Others believed that the decision stemmed from a reluctance to violate the two-term tradition (since he had already served the remainder of Harding's term). For others, it seemed that the death of his youngest son in the White House had taken much of the joy from public life, and he seemed tired of holding office. Whatever the reason, the decision was never effectively challenged, and the Republicans turned to Secretary of Commerce Herbert Hoover as their candidate in 1928.

Coolidge and his wife left the White House in the same quiet style which had always characterized their life. Coolidge refused many offers of employment, lest his name and former position be used to advertise a business. He and Grace returned to Northampton, where, for the first time in all of their years of marriage, Coolidge finally purchased a house. He kept busy writing his autobiography, as well as a number of magazine articles, and served on several committees. He died quietly and alone of a coronary thrombosis on January 5, 1933.

Summary

With the advent of the Great Depression in 1929, the Roaring Twenties, the Coolidge Era, came to an end. Coolidge was deeply concerned about the effect of the Depression, especially so for those whose losses were heavy. Yet he had always had a clear perception of credit as another form of debt and was, himself, largely untouched by the crash. Far more a Hamiltonian than a Jeffersonian in his philosophy of government, Coolidge supported the interests of property as necessary for the stability of the government. He believed that a healthy business environment was essential to the national well-being of the United States. Coolidge was personally frugal, always saving a part of his salary no matter how small, and he carried that same commitment to frugality with him into government.

Coolidge believed that government should not intrude in the daily lives of its citizens. It is one of the great ironies of American history that his years of inactivity at the head of the nation helped to pave the way for the enlarged role of government which the New Deal of President Franklin D. Roosevelt brought about in an effort to recover from the Depression.

The decade of the 1920's was unique in American history. Presiding over this boisterous era was an essentially shy little man; competent, respectable, cautious, loyal, and honest. These were qualities of character held in high regard by Americans even as they flouted them. Coolidge was always an intensely political person—a quality often overlooked as more flamboyant personalities strutted on center stage. He had a politician's sensitivity to the public's needs and wishes. He captured in himself those qualities Americans both desired and trusted—an island of stability and old-fashioned virtue in an ocean of new values.

Coolidge Prosperity was more than simply a campaign slogan. It was a real perception of cause and effect, and much of Coolidge's popularity stemmed from that perception. Coolidge was an enormously popular president—popular more as a symbol than as an individual whose idiosyncrasies and foibles were well known and well loved. He was precisely suited to the public temperament in the 1920's, and perhaps he could have succeeded in no other era. His personality and philosophy could not have provided effective leadership for either the surging reforms of the Progressive Era or the demands for an enlarged government under the New Deal. Rather, he provided a period of rest and retreat from government activity.

Calvin Coolidge was not a great president; neither was he a failure. He was a man unusually suited to an unusual time. More a symbol of an imagined past—in which simplicity, honesty, and frugality were cherished—than a reflection of the roaring rush of modernity that characterized the 1920's, Coolidge gave Americans what they wanted, though the lesson of history might suggest that he was not exactly what they needed.

Bibliography

Abels, Jules. *In the Time of Silent Cal.* New York: G. P. Putnam's Sons, 1969. Excellent brief survey of Coolidge, the man, and a useful analysis of the years in which he served the United States.

Booraem, Hendrik. *The Provincial: Calvin Coolidge and His World, 1885-1895.* Cranbury, N.J.: Associated University Presses, 1994.

Coolidge, Calvin. *The Autobiography of Calvin Coolidge.* New York: Cosmopolitan Book Corp., 1929. The length of this work certainly refutes the idea of an always "Silent Cal." It offers some insights into the mind and philosophy of this generally unknown president. Like most autobiographies, it must be read with caution and supplemented by other, more objective works.

Ferrell, Robert H. *The Presidency of Calvin Coolidge.* Lawrence: University Press of Kansas, 1998.

Fuess, Claude Moore. *Calvin Coolidge: The Man from Vermont.* Boston: Little, Brown, 1940. A lively, well-written account of a not-so-lively man. It is, however, partisan toward Coolidge and needs to be balanced by other works.

Hicks, John D. *Republican Ascendancy, 1921-1933.* New York: Harper and Row, Publishers, 1960. An excellent book for background on the 1920's from a governmental and political perspective.

McCoy, Donald R. *Calvin Coolidge: The Quiet President.* Lawrence: University Press of Kansas, 1988.

Moran, Philip R., ed. *Calvin Coolidge, 1872-1933: Chronology, Documents, Bibliographical Aids.* Dobbs Ferry, N.Y.: Oceana Publications, 1970.

Murray, Robert K. *The Politics of Normalcy: Governmental Theory and Practice in the Harding-Coolidge Era.* New York: W. W. Norton, 1973. Yet another excellent account of the 1920's, with an emphasis upon the part played by Coolidge. There are not many available biographies of Coolidge, and books such as this one on the 1920's are thus especially valuable to the student.

Silver, Thomas B. *Coolidge and the Historians.* Durham, N.C.: Carolina Academic Press, 1982.

White, William Allen. *A Puritan in Babylon: The Story of Calvin Coolidge.* New York: Macmillan, 1938. An excellent standard biography of Coolidge. White was well acquainted with Coolidge and admired him, so this book also should be balanced by a less admiring view. White's verbose style somewhat dates this book, but his talent and insight make it well worth reading.

Carlanna L. Hendrick

F. W. DE KLERK

Born: March 18, 1936; Johannesburg, Transvaal, South Africa

As president of South Africa, de Klerk initiated the process of dismantling the racist system of apartheid that had existed in his country since 1948. He was central in the negotiations that led to the first truly national elections in South African history.

Early Life

Frederik Willem de Klerk was one of two sons, and his parents quickly dubbed him "F. W." to distinguish him from his grandfather. Eight years younger than brother Willem, he was raised more like an only child. His father Jan, a teacher during de Klerk's youth, was gone most of the time, so the boy was brought up primarily by his mother, who instilled in him an appreciation for art. De Klerk's family had long been pillars of the Afrikaner community in South Africa, actively participating in two central institutions: the church and politics. De Klerk's parents belonged to a fundamentalist branch of the Dutch Reformed Church called the Doppers. Young de Klerk became a devout Dopper, and his Christian faith became central to his outlook.

In 1945 Jan left education to work for the National Party, which sought to protect Afrikaner culture from perceived threats such as communism, the English language, and nonwhite peoples who made up the vast majority of South Africa's population. Jan frequently brought his sons to political rallies, and their house was often the sight of lively debate. When the National Party triumphed in 1948, the youngest de Klerk helped count the ballots.

During the 1950's, the Nationalists established a system known as apartheid. Under this system, all South Africans were classified as white, black, coloured, or Indian. Blacks, who constituted about 75 percent of the population, were not allowed to vote. Furthermore, they were moved onto remote homelands and were not allowed to own land anywhere else. Black people were required to carry passes in order to travel. The Nationalist government used repression and violence to enforce apartheid, which quickly became notorious around the world.

De Klerk's family was intimately connected to the establishment of apartheid. His aunt was married to Johannes Strijdom, prime minister from 1954 to 1958. His father served in Strijdom's cabinet, which enacted many of the cornerstones of apartheid. Coming from such a family, it was fitting that de Klerk studied law and participated in student politics at Potchefstroom University, a Dopper institution. While at Potchefstroom he met Marike Willemse, who considered him a ladies' man. Indeed, despite a deformed nose broken in a hockey game, de Klerk was handsome. While he would later become a chain-smoker and suffer from migraines, he was healthy during his younger days. De Klerk graduated in 1958 and married Marike in 1959. They lived briefly in Pretoria then moved to Vereeniging, a mining town near Johannesburg, where de Klerk practiced law from 1961 until 1972. During this period they had three children, and de Klerk began participating in National Party politics.

Life's Work

In 1972, de Klerk was offered a position as a professor at Potchefstroom University. He was interested, but before he accepted it, the National Party leadership asked him to run for parliament. He consulted with his wife, who encouraged him to enter politics full time. He easily won a seat in the House of Assembly as Vereeniging's representative. He served in the House for six years, attracting little attention.

In 1978 Prime Minister John Vorster appointed de Klerk, then just forty-two years of age, as minister of posts and telecommunications. While in this position he oversaw the installation of South Africa's digital phone system in spite of the international sanctions that sought to prohibit such technology from reaching the apartheid regime. During the next several years, de Klerk held a variety of jobs in the cabinet of Prime Minister Pieter W. Botha, including minister of sports and minister of mines. As with his years in the House of Assembly, his work as a junior cabinet officer did not bring de Klerk widespread notoriety.

That began to change in 1984, however, when he took over as minister of national education. Opponents of apartheid criticized de Klerk because the only reform of education he would consider was to spend equal amounts on white, black, and coloured children. As de Klerk became well known outside of the government for his conservative approach to reforming education, he simultaneously gained more influence within the white ruling circles. In 1985 he became the chair of the ministers' council in the House of Assembly and in 1986 became the leader of the House.

Much of de Klerk's energy went into trying to block a massive exodus out of the National Party by the ultra-right wingers. In the early 1980's Botha had implemented a number of reforms, including the formation of a tricameral parliament that allowed Indians and coloured (mixed race) people to participate in politics. In response to these reforms, the most extreme members left the National Party and founded the Conservative Party. In order to prevent more defections, de Klerk directed the Education Ministry in a way that would appeal to conservative whites. He proposed limiting black enrollments in universities, expelling any students who took part in political protests, and basing funding for each university on its ability to prevent demonstrations on campus. His suggestions were not accepted, but they did earn him a reputation as a conservative.

In February of 1989, after suffering a mild stroke, Botha resigned from leadership of the National Party. The caucus chose de Klerk as the new party chief. However, Botha retained the presidency, a position that had become powerful with the reforms of 1984. Therefore, as long as Botha remained as president, de Klerk's power to initiate policy was limited. Between June and August, de Klerk visited heads of state in Great Britain, West Germany, Mozambique, and Zambia. His intention was not only to improve South Africa's international reputation but also to gain personal credibility and thus convince Botha to vacate the presidency.

On August 14, 1989, Botha resigned. On the following day, de Klerk was sworn in as acting president. In September de Klerk was elected in his own right to a five-year term as president. At his inauguration, he explained that he desired peace and would negotiate with anyone. Nelson Mandela, the leader of the African National Congress (ANC) who had been imprisoned since 1962, was impressed.

During October and November, de Klerk took several concrete steps that further impressed Mandela. He overturned the laws requiring racial segregation of public facilities. He disbanded the secret security apparatus that had crushed antiapartheid activism for decades. He released many political prisoners, including Mandela's close friend Walter Sisulu. In early December, he informed Mandela that their initial meeting would occur shortly.

On December 13, 1989, Mandela met de Klerk for the first time.

During a long discussion, Mandela was struck by de Klerk's willingness to listen. Mandela criticized the notion of "group rights," which de Klerk had recently been championing as a way to protect the rights of the white minority. Mandela explained that by defending "group rights," white people were actually holding on to apartheid. He insisted that apartheid must be eliminated, not just revised. Rather than argue, de Klerk listened carefully. Nothing was decided during this meeting, but Mandela concluded afterward that unlike his predecessors, de Klerk was sincere about ending apartheid.

De Klerk made his sincerity absolutely clear in his address to parliament on February 2, 1990. He announced that the bans against more than thirty political organizations, including the ANC, were lifted. Furthermore, de Klerk eased many aspects of the state of emergency that had held South Africa under virtual martial law since 1985. The political scene was opening up with amazing speed. Mandela was thrilled, particularly that the ANC was legal again after over thirty years as an outlaw group. He got more exciting news one week after the speech when government officials brought him once again to meet with de Klerk. The president informed Mandela that he would be set free the next day. The surprised Mandela asked if his release could be postponed for a week so the ANC could plan sufficiently to prevent chaos, but de Klerk insisted. Mandela eventually agreed, and the two drank a toast of whiskey to celebrate.

During the next two years, de Klerk was a central figure in the negotiations that brought white rule to an end. The process was difficult and on several occasions appeared to be on the verge of breaking down. Violence flared up among the Zulu people of Natal province, and Mandela blamed de Klerk for not stopping the killing. De Klerk also faced challenges from the white Conservatives, who won a shocking victory in Potchefstroom in February, 1992. In response, de Klerk held a national referendum among white voters, offering to resign if the voters rejected his policies. Over two-thirds of the white electorate approved of how he was proceeding, and so he carried on.

After another year of bitter negotiations, a breakthrough occurred on June 3, 1993. The twenty-seven participating parties agreed that multiracial national elections would be held on April 27, 1994. Voters, including, for the first time, black people, would elect a four-hundred-person assembly. The assembly, in turn, would select a president and draft a new constitution. Now that a date had been set, there was no going back. Mandela and de Klerk, who had been the central players in the drama, were named cowinners of the 1993 Nobel Peace Prize for their efforts.

As expected, the ANC triumphed in the April, 1994, elections, capturing 252 of the 400 seats in the National Assembly. On May 2, de Klerk conceded defeat. On May 10, he was sworn in as the second deputy president, and Thabo Mbeki was sworn in as first deputy president. Finally, Mandela was sworn in as president, officially ending some three hundred years of white rule in South Africa. Having dismantled apartheid, de Klerk would now attempt to help Mandela's Government of National Unity bring prosperity to their people.

Summary

F. W. de Klerk, as president of South Africa from 1989 to 1994, was instrumental in overturning apartheid and bringing democracy to South Africans of all races. Along with the collapse of the Soviet Union and the end of the Cold War, the demise of apartheid was among the most remarkable developments of the second half of the twentieth century. De Klerk came from a traditional Afrikaner family who had helped establish apartheid. After years in parliament and the cabinet, he brought a conservative reputation to the presidency. Few expected him to be the one to end white rule. Yet his conservative record probably helped, as a similar reputation had helped U.S. president Richard Nixon open relations with China.

De Klerk saw the writing on the wall and decided it was better to work for a peaceful transition than to wait for the violent explosion that was bound to come. Pragmatism probably motivated him more than any idealistic desire for racial equality. Regardless of his motives, though, his accomplishments make him one of the great leaders of the twentieth century. Like Mikhail Gorbachev, de Klerk initiated a reform process that ultimately ended his presidency but at the same time secured his place in history.

Bibliography

De Klerk, Willem. *F. W. de Klerk: The Man in His Time*. Johannesburg: Jonathan Ball, 1991. Written by de Klerk's brother, this biography contains valuable personal insights. However, it was published before the final events of apartheid's end.

Lauren, Paul Gordon. *Power and Prejudice: The Politics and Diplomacy of Racial Discrimination*. 2d ed. Boulder, Colo.: Westview,

1996. This classic work on international race relations contains a fine discussion of the end of apartheid in the final chapter. Includes photos, endnotes, and a bibliography.

Mandela, Nelson. *Long Walk to Freedom: The Autobiography of Nelson Mandela*. Boston: Little, Brown, 1994. Mandela's compelling story in his own words. Contains his insightful views on de Klerk's contribution to ending apartheid and many excellent photos.

Massie, Robert. *Loosing the Bonds: The United States and South Africa in the Apartheid Years*. New York: Doubleday, 1997. A thorough study of relations between the United States and South Africa, concluding with the end of apartheid. Includes an extensive discussion of de Klerk's role, photos, and nearly two hundred pages of notes and bibliography.

Ottoway, David. *Chained Together: Mandela, de Klerk, and the Struggle to Remake South Africa*. New York: Random House, 1993. This book is based mostly on interviews with principal participants in the story such as de Klerk's wife. No notes or bibliography.

Waldmeir, Patti. *Anatomy of a Miracle: The End of Apartheid and the Birth of the New South Africa*. New York: W. W. Norton, 1997.

Andrew J. DeRoche

DENG XIAOPING

Born: August 22, 1904; Paifang village, Xiexing township, Guang'an county, Sichuan province, China
Died: February 19, 1997; Beijing, China

Deng was a member of the central committee of the Chinese Communist Party until 1987, held various official titles from 1949 to 1989 (including deputy prime minister), and was China's de facto ruler from 1978 until his death in 1997. The rapid economic growth that China experienced after 1979 was largely the result of his economic policies.

Early Life

Deng Xiaoping, born Deng Xixien, came from a wealthy landlord family that owned about ten hectares of land and employed servants and farm laborers. They grew rice, wheat, sorghum, and other cereal crops, and harvested over thirteen tons of grains annually. His father Deng Wenming was a respected local leader whose wife (née Zhang) was childless. He then took three concubines; the first one (née Yen) bore him a daughter and three sons. Xixien was the eldest son; he took the name Xiaoping at age twenty when he joined the Chinese Communist Party. Deng attended the local elementary school and middle school in the county town.

In 1919 Deng enrolled in a special French-language school in Chongqing that prepared students for the Work-Study program in France (begun in 1912). He was one of over eighty Sichuan students who passed the qualifying exams in 1920; they set sail for France in the fall of that year. Deng remained in France until 1924, but he did not enroll in any schools for formal study. Instead, he spent his time working in various factories, studying French, and organizing activities. He and other Chinese students also interested in Marxism, most notably Chou En-lai and Li Lisan, founded the Chinese Communist Youth Corps in France in 1922. He was admitted to the Chinese Communist Party in 1924 and was sent to Moscow to the University of the Toilers of the East (later renamed Sun Yat-sen University) to study Marxism.

Deng returned to China in August, 1926, as a staff member of maverick warlord Marshal Feng Yu-hsiang, who was successively a Christian, a Marxist, and later a member of the Kuomintang. Deng served in Feng's army for one year until the Kuomintang-communist split, when Feng expelled all the communists on his staff.

Life's Work

Deng rose in the ranks of the Chinese Communist Party, working in the communist underground in Wuhan, Shanghai, and then at various positions in the guerrilla bases in Guangxi and Jiangxi provinces. He took part in the Long March to Yan'an while serving as the secretary-general of the central committee of the Chinese Communist Party. He was the deputy director of the general political department of the Eighth Route Army during the war against Japan (1937-1945) and also held other important positions during that war and the subsequent civil war against the Nationalist government (1946-1949). In 1954 Deng was appointed vice premier, vice chairman of the National Defense Council, and party general secretary.

In 1956 Mao Zedong launched the Hundred Flowers Campaign that allowed intellectuals to criticize the Communist Party. When the criticism became too sharp and bitter for Mao, he turned to Deng to clamp down and punish the critics for daring to speak out. Deng presided over a harsh crackdown. Between one-half to three-quarters of a million intellectuals and cadres were sent to the countryside to perform manual labor. When Mao's Great Leap Forward (which began in the late 1950's and included the building of hundreds of thousands of backyard furnaces to make steel and the introduction of communes) turned into disaster and a massive famine, Deng sided with Liu Shaoqi and other "pragmatists" in the Communist Party leadership to force Mao to relinquish the state chairmanship and retire from the day-to-day running of China's affairs. Together with Liu, who became state chairman, Deng (the party's general secretary) and other pragmatists repaired the enormous damages inflicted by the Great Leap Forward by dismantling the communes and restoring incentives.

In 1966 Mao launched the Great Proletarian Cultural Revolution to restore himself and his radical policies to power. Liu and Deng were the principal victims of the Cultural Revolution. They were dismissed from all posts and publicly humiliated. While Liu died in jail, Deng survived to be rehabilitated and appointed vice premier in 1973 by premier Chou En-lai. Stricken with cancer, Chou appeared to be grooming Deng as his successor, delegating to him the routine supervision of the administration.

Deng Xiaoping *(Archive Photos/AGIP)*

Deng's career met a major setback at the hands of Mao's ambitious wife, Jiang Qing, and her radical supporters when Chou died in January, 1976. While Hua Guofeng was appointed acting premier, Deng fled to Canton in southern China, to the protection of friendly colleagues there, and came under severe attack as a "capitalist roader" by the official newspaper, the *People's Daily*. Mao's death on September 9, 1976, was followed by a power struggle in which his widow Jiang Qing and her chief supporters (nicknamed the Gang of Four) were ousted from power by senior leaders of the Communist Party. Thus ended the decade-long chaos called the Cultural Revolution (1966-1976). By 1978 Hua Guofeng had also been edged out of power, and Deng was in control.

The Deng era (1978-1997) was characterized by the rehabilitation of the victims of the Cultural Revolution, punishment of the Gang of Four in nationally televised trials held in 1981, and ending of the radical policies and chaos of the last ten years of Mao's life. Mao was also taken off the pedestal on which he had placed himself. Deng instituted reforms called the "four modernizations" in agriculture, industry, science and technology, and the military. This entailed the opening of China to the outside world, including sending Chinese students to study abroad. Deng called his era one in which economics were in command, not politics and ideology as during the Maoist era. The goal was to make China a modern nation by the year 2000.

In agriculture, reforms meant the dismantling of collective farms under a "responsibility" system that, in effect, restored the private farm, although the farmers did not own the land they tilled as many had before the Communists took power. The restructuring of agriculture improved the livelihood of the majority of China's population and gave Deng a wide base of support. Industries were more difficult to restructure, and while small enterprises became privatized, major industries that employed large numbers of people remained state-owned and unprofitable. Deng left restructuring of this dangerous sector to his successors. Outside capital and know-how, in the form of joint enterprises, did, however, introduce many new industries to China.

Agricultural reforms and the partial restructuring of industry resulted in growing inequities in income between individuals and provinces. Unemployment, inflation, and rampant corruption by still-powerful Communist bureaucrats became major problems. Deng was, however, willing to tolerate these problems in the interest of overall improvements in the standard of living.

In modernizing the scientific and technological sector, China needed new schools, universities, and research institutions. Thousands of Chinese students and scholars were sent to the West to learn, and Western specialists were invited to China to teach and train the Chinese. Deng faced a particularly dangerous double-edged sword: the introduction of Western sciences and technologies as well as political ideas and social ideals through these contacts. Deng and other communist leaders referred to Western ideas and ways of life—from music and blue jeans to democracy—as "spiritual pollution." In 1979 human rights activist Wei Jingsheng demanded a fifth modernization—that of the political process—to accompany the other four modernizations. Deng had Wei and other prodemocracy activists tried and jailed on trumped-up charges.

In 1987 Deng cracked down on student protesters and dismissed his heir, party secretary Hu Yaobang, for being too sympathetic to the students. Deng and his hard-line allies' policies culminated in the mobilization of 300,000 troops in the bloody suppression of peaceful student demonstrators on June 4, 1989, in the Tiananmen Square massacre. In the process, Deng also dismissed his new heir, party secretary Zhao Ziyang, again for being too soft on the students. The massacre of students and their sympathizers in Beijing and many other cities became an indelible blot on Deng's record.

Modernization of the military entailed downsizing the army to emphasize better training and equipment. Up to 1989, the portion of the budget allotted to the military was reduced. However, in the wake of the Tiananmen massacre, and to ensure the loyalty of the military, Deng dramatically increased the military budget.

In 1984 Deng signed an agreement with Great Britain for the return of Hong Kong, controlled by Britain since 1841, to China in 1997. China agreed to allow Hong Kong to remain a special administrative region with its own laws and institutions for fifty years. The people of Hong Kong had no voice in negotiating, nor the right to reject the agreement. Since Great Britain had granted independence to hundreds of millions of former subjects across the globe decades before, this was hardly a triumph of China's might as Deng and the Chinese Communists wished to indicate. He had expressed a hope to live to see Hong Kong's return to China in 1997 but died that year before it happened.

Deng hoped that the agreement regarding Hong Kong would serve as a model to entice the Nationalist government and the people of Taiwan to accept a similar arrangement with China. However, even before the retrocession of Hong Kong, China began to renege on aspects of the agreement regarding the political rights of its people. The people of Taiwan, enjoying democratic rights and a First World standard of living, were unimpressed with Beijing's offer. Deng, like Mao before him, did not renounce China's right to use force to unify with Taiwan. Despite the general desire of Chinese people to be unified and continued dialogue between the two Chinas, the chances of reunification in the near future, while China remains under Communist rule, seem remote.

Deng was only partially successful in persuading the party elders to step down to ensure an orderly transfer of power. Despite his own "retirement" from all official positions in 1989, he retained ultimate power until his death; many other gerontocrats did likewise. He was succeeded by his last heir, Jiang Zemin.

Summary

Determining Deng's place in Chinese history will take much time. He was responsible for reversing the Maoist course after 1979 and for the economic miracle that swept China afterward. However, he refused to make political reforms and insisted on retaining the

Leninist dictatorship. Thus China remained stuck with a form of government that had clearly failed worldwide. Because political liberalization, or the fifth modernization, was yet unrealized, Deng's reforms remained partial, and China's transformation into a modern nation remained incomplete.

Bibliography

Chang, Maria Hsia. *The Labors of Sisyphus: The Economic Development of Communist China*. New Brunswick, N.J.: Transaction, 1998.

Deng, Maomao. *My Father Deng Xiaoping*. New York: Basic Books, 1995. A personal, uncritical biography by Deng's youngest daughter.

Evans, Richard. *Deng Xiaoping and the Making of Modern China*. Revised. New York: Penguin, 1997. One of many books published after Deng's death to assess and evaluate his historic role.

Goldman, David. *Deng Xiaoping and the Chinese Revolution*. London: Routledge, 1994. An evaluation of Deng's role in late twentieth century Chinese history.

Li Zhisui. *The Private Life of Chairman Mao*. Translated by Tai Hung-chao. New York: Random House, 1994. The story of Mao and the court that surrounded him, by Mao's personal physician. Includes accounts of Deng's ups and downs during Mao's last years.

Liberthal, Kenneth. *Governing China: From Revolution Through Reform*. New York: W. W. Norton, 1995. An important book on China since 1949, including Deng's role and his legacy.

Salisbury, Harrison. *The New Emperors: China in the Eras of Mao and Deng*. Boston: Little, Brown, 1992. Well-written and interesting discussions of the Chinese leadership since 1949.

Yang, Benjamin. *Deng: A Political Biography*. Armonck, N.Y.: M. E. Sharpe, 1998. An evaluation of the career of a many-faceted man.

Jiu-Hwa Lo Upshur

EAMON DE VALERA

Born: October 14, 1882; New York, New York
Died: August 29, 1975; Blackrock, near Dublin, Ireland

The leading Irish statesman of the twentieth century, de Valera embodied the Irish nationalist movement and served as leader of the independence movement and later as head of the Irish government for twenty-one years.

Early Life

Eamon de Valera was born in New York in 1882. His immigrant Irish mother, Catherine Coll, met a Spaniard, Vivion de Valera, and they were married in 1881. Of his parents he remembered little, for his father died in 1885 and he was sent to Ireland to be reared by his maternal grandmother and uncle. He attended the national school at his village of Bruree and later the Christian Brothers School at Charleville. His family was too poor to be able to afford his educational fees, but de Valera's aptitude at mathematics and general excellence in his studies earned for him a scholarship to Blackrock College in Dublin. In 1898, he began Blackrock and again earned scholarships which allowed him to continue at the University College Blackrock and to take a degree in mathematics. He then took a position at Rockwell College in Tipperary, teaching mathematics.

In 1908, de Valera joined the Gaelic League, which encouraged the study and preservation of the Irish language. De Valera was taught Irish at Leinster College by Sinead O'Flanagan, with whom he fell in love. They were married in 1910 in Dublin and had seven children. Tall and thin, de Valera looked more like an austere scholar than a charismatic politician.

The Gaelic League brought de Valera into contact with men who were active in the nationalist movement. A wide variety of groups were harnessed together by the home rule movement, which pressured the British Parliament to give Ireland governing autonomy. The opposition to home rule by the Protestant Unionists of Ulster prompted them to form the Ulster Volunteer Force in 1912. This force in turn prompted the formation of the Irish Volunteers in 1913 by the nationalist supporters of home rule. De Valera joined the Volunteers and rapidly became commandant of the Third Battalion of the Dublin Brigade.

The mainspring organization behind the militant nationalists and the Volunteers was the Irish Republican Brotherhood (IRB), a secret organization. De Valera joined the IRB, but reluctantly, as he opposed the secrecy of the group. The Brotherhood planned the 1916 Easter Rising, which played such an important role in the Irish nationalist movement. When that rising took place, de Valera and his brigade inflicted severe casualties on the British troops and for a week held out. De Valera was the last to surrender. De Valera, among the other leaders, was condemned to death, but he was reprieved and sent to prison in England. Among the prisoners, de Valera emerged as their leader. When he was released in May, 1917, de Valera, at age thirty-five, was to become a leader on a much larger stage.

Life's Work

When released from prison in 1917, de Valera and others of the 1916 rising were seen as heroes by the Irish people. In a 1917 election in Clare, de Valera was elected president of Sinn Féin (ourselves alone), the nationalist party, and also elected president of the Irish Volunteers. De Valera was then arrested. Running in the 1918 election, the members of Sinn Féin won an immense victory, including a seat won by de Valera while in prison. Sinn Féin set up a revolutionary parliament called Dáil Éireann, which declared Ireland an independent republic. After his dramatic escape from prison, Dáil Éireann elected Eamon de Valera president of the new republic. His first act as president was to return to the place of his birth, the United States, in order to raise money for the revolutionary government, organize Irish American support, and lobby for United States recognition of the new Irish Republic.

Upon his return to Ireland in 1920, de Valera found the country under martial law and the Irish Republican Army fighting a guerrilla war with the police and British paramilitary irregulars, the Black and Tans, brought to Ireland for the purpose of maintaining order.

The election of May, 1920, was an overwhelming victory for Sinn Féin, and David Lloyd George, the British prime minister, sought negotiations which culminated in a treaty in December, 1921. The treaty contains provisions which were unacceptable to de Valera and others, including the partition of Ireland and an oath to the Crown.

Eamon de Valera *(Library of Congress)*

In January of 1922, Sinn Féin was riven apart on the question of adopting the treaty. The split deteriorated into a civil war during 1922-1923, which found de Valera on the anti-treaty and losing side.

Arrested by the Irish government's troops in 1923, de Valera spent eleven months in detention. Upon his release, he assumed leadership of the antitreaty party, Sinn Féin. De Valera sought to enter the government of the Irish Free State and to this end founded a new political party, Fianna Fáil (soldiers of destiny), in 1926. The members of this party entered the Dáil in 1927, signing the oath but not taking the oath to the Crown.

In March of 1932, de Valera became president of the executive council when his party won enough seats to form a government. De Valera's objectives were clear, as he had been enunciating them since 1916. He began through legislation to dismantle the treaty arrangements and move Ireland to full sovereignty. The oath to the king was abolished, the payment of land annuities to London stopped, the status of governor-general diminished, and appeal to the Privy Council was abolished, all enjoying widespread popular support from the Irish people. In 1937, de Valera instituted a new constitution which incorporated Catholic elements as well as a claim to the North Ireland Partition since 1922. De Valera also played a part on the world stage serving as president of the League of Nations Assembly in 1938.

A number of pressing matters with London were dealt with in the 1938 Anglo-Irish Agreement, which settled the land annuities issue, among others, and set up favorable trade arrangements. The world was on the brink of war, however, and de Valera was thrust into the position of having to choose between Adolf Hitler and his Axis powers and Great Britain. He chose neither, and Ireland remained neutral during World War II. De Valera maintained that he could not put Ireland on the side of Great Britain while the partition of Ireland existed, but obviously would not support Germany against the United Kingdom. De Valera resisted enticements (such as a promise to end the partition) and threats in order to lead Ireland to the full exercise of her sovereignty.

De Valera remained in power until 1948, when his party was eclipsed by a coalition government, and after sixteen years of rule he became opposition leader again. He returned as prime minister from 1951 to 1954 and again from 1957 to 1959. In 1959, in his mid-seventies, he stepped down as prime minister upon his election as president of the Republic of Ireland. After two terms as president in 1973, he returned to private life after more than five decades of service as a public representative from the revolutionary Dáil Éireann to the presidency of the republic. He died on August 29, 1975, only seven months after the death of his wife.

Summary

In the view of his admirers, Eamon de Valera accomplished a catalog of achievements culminating in the full independence of Ireland. Among the most notable were his leadership of the independence movement Sinn Féin up to the civil war, his return from the political wilderness in 1926 with the creation of Fianna Fáil, his diplomatic skill and toughness in dealing with London, and his guidance of Ireland through the storms of neutrality. His detractors contend, however, that de Valera should be held responsible for a list of failures at least as long, including failure to lead the treaty delegation personally; actions and words that encouraged the civil war; failure to recover the Irish language; his lack of a social and economic vision, which left Ireland a poor, parochial corner of Europe; and a dictatorial style of leadership. All of his life, de Valera had tried to eliminate the partition of Ireland, instituted in 1922, and in his mind that was the one aspect of the treaty that was not eliminated.

While a balanced view would encompass both the positive and

the negative assessments of de Valera, his impact on Ireland goes beyond the specifics of particular policies: He came in his person, his actions, his speeches, and his convictions to symbolize charismatically the qualities of Irish nationalism and the quest for Irish independence. His power flowed from his Catholicism, his commitment to the Irish language, and his unrelenting visualization of the Irish nation, as well as his political skills and specific policies. De Valera once observed that when he wanted to know what the Irish people wanted, he had only to look into his own heart. Such a statement is bold, but it holds more than a little truth.

Bibliography

Bowman, John. *De Valera and the Ulster Question, 1917-1973*. Oxford: Clarendon Press, 1982. Focusing specifically on the question of partition, this book is one of the best on both de Valera and Northern Ireland.

Bromage, Mary C. *De Valera and the March of a Nation*. London: Hutchinson, 1956. Reprint. Westport, Conn.: Greenwood Press, 1975. Bromage is favorably disposed to de Valera and the Irish nationalist position.

Coogan, Tim Pat. *Eamon de Valera: The Man Who Was Ireland*. New York: HarperCollins, 1993.

De Valera, Eamon. *Speeches and Statements by Eamon de Valera, 1917-1973*. Edited by Maurice Moynihan. Dublin: Gill and Macmillan, 1980. An extensive collection, this book is indispensable for an insight into de Valera's positions.

Dwyer, T. Ryle. *Eamon de Valera*. Dublin: Gill and Macmillan, 1980. One of a series of shorter biographies. Dwyer captures de Valera well in this book.

Longford, Earl of, and Thomas P. O'Neill. *Eamon de Valera*. Boston: Houghton Mifflin, 1971. This biography is considered semiofficial in that the authors had the extensive cooperation of de Valera. Thus, this book is comprehensive but generous in its view of de Valera.

Moynihan, Maurice, ed. *Speeches and Statements by Eamon de Valera, 1917-1973*. New York: St. Martin's Press, 1990.

O'Carroll, John P., and John A. Murphy, eds. *De Valera and His Times*. Cork: Cork University Press, 1986. A collection of first-quality essays on de Valera covering various topics and offering diverse interpretations.

Richard B. Finnegan

ALEXANDER DUBČEK

Born: November 27, 1921; Uhrovec, Czechoslovakia
Died: November 7, 1992; Prague, Czechoslovakia

After becoming first secretary of the Czechoslovakian Communist Party on January 5, 1968, Dubček led the liberalization movement known as the Prague Spring. He attempted, unsuccessfully, to move Czechoslovakian politics and economy away from Stalinist notions of Marxist socialism.

Early Life

Alexander Dubček was born in Uhrovec, Czechoslovakia, on November 27, 1921. His father, Stefan, and his mother, Pavlina, had returned to Slovakia from Chicago only a few months before his birth. Although he had become a U.S. citizen in 1916 at age twenty-five, Stefan was disenchanted with the United States. In 1917, he joined the American Socialist Party, led by Eugene V. Debs, and shortly thereafter was imprisoned for eighteen months when he refused to honor a draft notice. Following his release, and with the encouragement of Pavlina, Stefan began to study the writings of Karl Marx. Their great dissatisfaction with the United States led Stefan and Pavlina to return to their homeland in 1921. By this time, West Slovakia was part of the new state of Czechoslovakia.

In March, 1925, the Dubčeks moved across the Soviet Union to Frunze, a village in Kirgiz Soviet Socialist Republic. Stefan and Pavlina, along with hundreds of other West Slovaks, were responding to an appeal from the Comintern for workers to help the Soviet Union in the construction of a communist state. Life was difficult in Kirgiz, and many Slovakian children succumbed to malaria in the first year. Alexander and his elder brother Julius (born in Chicago in 1920) escaped the disease. In 1933, the Dubčeks moved to Gorki, an industrial city some 250 miles east of Moscow. Neither Pavlina nor Stefan questioned the direction taken by the Communist Revolution under Joseph Stalin. At home and at school, Alexander was taught to believe that Stalin must do whatever was necessary to preserve the Revolution.

In 1938, Stalin forced all foreigners in the Soviet Union either to become Soviet citizens or to leave the country. This convinced Stefan that he should return with Alexander to Czechoslovakia. They were reunited there with Pavlina and Julius, who had returned in 1936 after Julius had become seriously ill. Although Stalin had forced their departure from the Soviet Union, Alexander retained his enthusiasm for the goals of the Communist Revolution. His thirteen years in Russia helped to shape his later political decisions.

In March, 1939, Slovakia became a puppet state for the Nazis after Adolf Hitler sent troops into Czechoslovakia. Alexander, following the example of his father, joined the illegal Communist Party of Slovakia. In August, 1944, Alexander participated in the Slovak national revolt against the Fascists and was twice wounded. His brother Julius was killed. In May, 1945, Czech and Slovak lands were liberated, and, in November, Alexander married Anna Ondrisova, whom he had known since his days in Russia. Despite his communist beliefs, the wedding was held in a church and, in a touch of considerable irony, was blessed by the pope.

The Communist Party assumed power in Czechoslovakia in February, 1948, and shortly thereafter Dubček was given a position in the party bureaucracy. He was one of fifteen junior secretaries in Trencín assigned to prepare the nationalization of the economy. Thus began Dubček's quiet rise to leadership in Czechoslovakia.

Life's Work

Between 1949 and 1955, Dubček held Slovak Communist Party posts in Trencín, Bratislava, and Banská Bystrica. In Banská Bystrica, Central Slovakia, Dubček served as regional secretary. His main responsibility was to increase agricultural production through socialist farming methods. Dubček appeared to be an unexceptional and unexciting party bureaucrat. He was completely loyal to party ideology. During these years, the Czechoslovak Communist Party, of which the Slovak Communist Party was a section, carried out a reign of terror similar to the Stalinist purges of the 1930's. Dubček remained on the fringes of the terror, never becoming a suspect and never becoming an accuser.

Early in 1955, the party selected Dubček to study at the Higher Party School in Moscow. He spent three years in the Soviet Union, learning the fine points of party management. In February, 1956, the Soviet Communist Party and the Higher Party School were thrown into confusion by Nikita Khrushchev's anti-Stalinist speech before the Twentieth Party Congress. Dubček completed his course of study, although the ideological certainties being taught when he entered the Higher Party School in 1955 now were shaken to the core. Upon his return from Moscow in 1958, Dubček was made regional secretary of the Bratislava Party. Over the next five years, Dubček rose so quickly in the communist ranks that, in 1963, he was selected by the Slovak Communist Party's central committee to succeed Karol Bacílek as first secretary of the Slovak Communist Party.

Dubček's position in the party brought him little public notice. He was, even in Slovakia, virtually unknown outside the bureaucracy. He was a notoriously poor orator with a benign personality. He may well have receded to total obscurity had it not been for economic and political circumstances that forced Antonín Novotný to resign as first secretary of the Czechoslovak Communist Party on January 5, 1968. Opposition to Novotný was particularly intense in Slovakia. Dubček not only permitted journalistic criticism of Novotný but also encouraged it by suggesting that Novotný, who also served as president of the Czechoslovakian Republic, treated Slovaks unfairly. The Czech president received little help from Leonid Ilich Brezhnev (the Soviet leader resented Novotný's long friendship with Khrushchev), and by the autumn of 1967 it was apparent, in party circles at least, that Novotný was finished.

Czechoslovaks were surprised by the announcement that Dubček had succeeded Novotný as first secretary of the Czechoslovak Communist Party. Dubček's selection owed much to the support he received from Slovakian members of the party's central committee and to the fact that potential Czech successors were tarnished by their association with Novotný. There is also reason to believe that Brezhnev may have assisted in the selection.

When he took control of the party in January, 1968, Dubček contended that Czechoslovakia was an "inseparable part of the world socialist system, firmly linked to the Soviet Union." He never thought the reform effort he was about to unleash would in any way subvert Czechoslovakia's relationship with Moscow. From the outset, Dubček let it be known that he would ease restrictions on the press and radio, that he would encourage political democratization, and that he would remove from party posts those who had been adamant against any changes.

On February 22, 1968, Dubček spoke to the nation from Prague, with Brezhnev present, and promised the "widest possible democratization of the entire socio-political system." Three weeks later,

Novotný, who had retained his presidency, resigned and was succeeded by Ludvík Svoboda. Svoboda was sympathetic to Dubček's policies. On April 9, the Action Program, which became the touchstone for the Prague Spring, was published. It called for personal freedoms, significant political reform, a new constitution for the Slovak peoples, and economic liberalization.

By this time, Brezhnev and Soviet Party leaders were concerned. Dubček tried to reassure Moscow that his efforts should not be seen as anti-Soviet, but suspicions in the Kremlin remained acute. Early in July, at the conclusion of the Warsaw Pact military maneuvers, the Soviet Union refused to withdraw its forces from Czechoslovakia. Two weeks later, Kremlin leaders demanded a meeting with Czech officials. The meeting was held at Cierna on July 29. Dubček again told Brezhnev that the Prague Spring was no threat to the Warsaw alliance. Brezhnev angrily responded that Dubček offered balm to "counter-revolutionaries" and "bourgeois-revisionists." The meeting ended unsatisfactorily for both sides.

On the night of August 20, 1968, some 300,000 troops from Hungary, Poland, East Germany, Bulgaria, and the Soviet Union entered Czechoslovakia. The Czechs, and the rest of the world, were taken by surprise. The next morning, Dubček and several other Czech officials were arrested and taken to Moscow. They were joined three days later by President Svoboda. Out of touch with the circumstances in Prague, where Warsaw forces met severe resistance, Dubček had no reason to doubt Brezhnev's threat to make Czechoslovakia another socialist republic of the Soviet Union. On August 27, Dubček tearfully spoke to his countrymen in a way that signaled the end of the Prague Spring. It would be necessary to reconcile the dreams of reform to the reality of Soviet dominance.

From September, 1968, until mid-April 1969, Dubček tried to salvage some of the Action Program by following a moderate course. He was caught between pressure from Moscow and from Czechoslovak liberals, who thought he was compromising the reform effort. Czech nationalists continued periodic demonstrations against the Soviet presence, with the worst rioting occurring in January, 1969, after a philosophy student, Jan Palach, set himself afire. In March, Dubček was forced to impose censorship on the press.

In mid-April, 1969, Dubček resigned to take the far less important post as president of the Federal Assembly. By this time, most of his reform-minded associates had been removed from their party positions. In January, 1970, Dubček was made ambassador to Turkey. He received this post, in part, because his great popularity in the country continued to embarrass party hard-liners. As long as he remained in the country, he was a lightning rod for the discontented. Six months after he arrived in Ankara, he was ordered to return to Czechoslovakia, and every effort was made to force him to admit that Soviet intervention was necessary. He refused. On June 27, 1970, it was announced that Dubček had been expelled from the party. He spent the next decade as a supervisor in the government's forestry department in Bratislava. He retired in 1981 but was kept under surveillance until 1987.

In 1989, Dubček returned to prominence when Czech reformers, inspired by Soviet leader Mikhail Gorbachev, revived the Prague Spring and threw out the party's old guard. Dubček once again spoke to the adoring masses in Prague and, in December, made himself available for the presidency of the Czechoslovakian republic. Although showing great respect for their onetime leader, the reformers stood behind Václav Havel, a stalwart reformer of more recent vintage, as their candidate for president. Dubček was instead elected as head of the parliament.

Dubček opposed the break-up of Czechoslovakia, but nevertheless was considered a front-runner for the presidential office in the new Slovak Republic. An automobile accident, however, ended the life of the popular reformer.

Summary

Alexander Dubček was an unlikely leader of the Prague Spring in 1968. He had no oratorical skills and his public personality lacked any semblance of charisma. On many occasions, he had averred his support for the Soviet Union as leader of the communist world. He never intended to do anything to weaken the ties between Moscow and Prague. His commitment to Marxist ideology (as interpreted by Vladimir Ilich Lenin) was firm and unshaken throughout his political career. He believed, however, that Marxist socialism was never incompatible with democratic principles. For Dubček, Stalinist repression was an aberration; it was not a true expression of how the communist system should function. When he became first secretary, he acted on what he believed. He assumed that the Brezhnev regime would accommodate his policies of greater personal, economic, and political freedom. He was shocked and embarrassed when the Kremlin turned on him and the country he led. Indignity was added to humiliation when Dubček, to save himself and his countrymen from further repression, severely moderated his stand on reform. Although he remained a popular hero to most in Czechoslovakia, Dubček suffered a precipitous political demise in 1968.

For fifteen years after 1968, the Prague Spring appeared to be nothing more than a brilliant, but brief and failed, attempt to establish an independent communism. In the mid-1980's, however, the Prague Spring took on a new significance. When Mikhail Gorbachev succeeded Konstantin Chernenko as Soviet communist leader in 1985, he initiated a reform effort that emulated the Action Program of the Prague Spring. Like Dubček, Gorbachev saw no conflict between Marxism-Leninism and greater personal, political, and economic freedom for all who live in the communist world. No wonder Dubček, in 1988, heartily endorsed Gorbachev's call for opening political discussion (*glasnost*) and for restructuring (*perestroika*) on all matters important to the Warsaw Pact countries.

Bibliography

Dubček, Alexander. *Czechoslovakia's Blueprint for "Freedom": The Original and Official Documents Leading to the Conflict of August, 1968.* Introduction and analysis by Paul Ello. Washington, D.C.: Acropolis Books, 1968. A collection of speeches, proclamations, and other statements by Dubček. The "analysis" by Ello is thin and lacks perspective. The book is unattractively printed and difficult to follow.

__________. *Dubček Speaks.* New York: Tauris, 1990.

__________. *Hope Dies Last: The Autobiography of Alexander Dubček.* Edited and translated by Jiri Hochman. New York: Kodansha International, 1993.

James, Robert Thodes, ed. *The Czechoslovak Crisis, 1968.* London: Wiedenfeld & Nicolson, 1969. This excellent book provides, from a variety of perspectives, a thorough discussion of Novotný's fall and Dubček's struggles with Moscow.

Kusin, Vladimir V. *Political Grouping in the Czechoslovak Reform Movement.* New York: Columbia University Press, 1972. This is an account of the creation of reform political organizations from the post-World War II era through 1968. It is essential background information for understanding the Prague Spring.

Littell, Robert. *The Czech Blackbook.* New York: Frederick Praeger, 1969. Littell provides a superb introduction to the events of 1968. Contains a highly useful day-by-day account of the happenings from August 20 to 27, 1968.

Navazelskis, Ina. *Alexander Dubček.* New York: Chelsea House Publications, 1991. Entry in the publisher's World Leaders Past and Present series, edited by Arthur M. Schlesinger, for younger readers.

Shawcross, William. *Dubček.* New York: Simon & Schuster, 1970. This is the principal biography of Dubček in the English language. Shawcross, a journalist, has produced a detailed and surprisingly balanced study of Dubček's political career. Written within two years of the main events in Dubček's life, the biography lacks the necessary perspective and cannot be considered definitive. It is, however, well written and informative.

Skilling, H. Gordon. *Czechoslovakia's Interrupted Revolution.* Princeton, N.J.: Princeton University Press, 1976. Skilling's work provides the best account of all aspects of the Prague Spring. The book gives superb insights into Dubček's behavior during 1968. There is, as well, an excellent discussion of relevant scholarship on the events of 1968 published in the early 1970's.

Valenta, Jiri. *Soviet Intervention in Czechoslovakia, 1968: Anatomy of a Decision.* Rev. ed. Baltimore: Johns Hopkins University Press, 1991. Influential assessment of the Soviet Union's occupation of Czechoslovakia in 1968, with comparisons of the Soviet Union's more tolerant policies toward its Central and Eastern European allies on the eve of its own breakup.

Ron Huch

FÉLIX ÉBOUÉ

Born: December 26, 1884; Cayenne, French Guiana
Died: May 17, 1944; Cairo, Egypt

Éboué rose from the lower ranks of the French colonial service to become the first black governor of Guadeloupe, the first black governor of Chad, and the first black governor-general in French-speaking Africa when he was appointed to head former French Equatorial Africa in 1941.

Early Life

Adolphe-Félix-Sylvestre Éboué was born at Cayenne, French Guiana, on December 26, 1884, of Yves Éboué and Aurélie Leveilles. He was the youngest of four brothers and one sister. (*Éboué*, a West African word, was the name of his paternal slave great grandfather.) Félix's mother, a devout Catholic, was a homemaker but eventually owned and ran a candy store to sustain the family. His father was a gold searcher who died in 1898. Félix's three brothers died either from drowning in rivers while searching for gold or from disease, before even having the chance to marry. As a result, young Félix had to help his mother at home, even to the point of cooking meals after school, while Madame Éboué took care of the store. She was determined, however, to sacrifice all of her savings to ensure that young Félix would be educated in France and become prominent in Guianese society.

In elementary and secondary school (at the Collège de Cayenne), Éboué distinguished himself in French and music. In 1901, he graduated from the first years of secondary school and received a teaching certificate and immediately received a government scholarship to complete his high school at the Lycée Montaigne in Bordeaux, France. He received his *baccalaureate* in 1905 and was accepted at the Colonial School in Paris, as he chose to become a career civil servant.

At both schools, however, Éboué had been a mediocre student, still loving French and music but doing poorly in military-related courses. He was heavily involved in extracurricular activities, is said to have had an Italian mistress, played bridge constantly, and was a chain-smoker. While at the Lycée Montaigne, he was exposed to and embraced the Stoic and Pythagorean philosophy that would mold his outlook on life after he repudiated Catholicism. At both schools, he had had several classmates, such as novelist René Maran, who later became important friends and supporters.

Also at the Colonial School, Éboué studied under Africanist historian and ethnographer Maurice Delafosse, who interested him in ethnography and linguistics and helped him to appreciate the culture of the African peoples. In spite of his mediocre performance, Éboué graduated from the Colonial School and was assigned to work in Madagascar. Eventually, the colonial office changed his assignment and sent him instead to Brazzaville, Congo, where he arrived on January 21, 1909. Éboué disliked Brazzaville and requested to be posted in Oubangui-Chari (later the Central African Republic), where René Maran's father and the former governor of French Guiana, Émile Merwart (who had approved his scholarship to France), worked. Merwart was the governor there. Éboué's request was accepted, and he moved on to Bangui, the capital of Oubangui-Chari. He felt mentally prepared and adequately trained to work in Africa rather than in his preferred Antilles.

Life's Work

In Oubangui-Chari in 1909, Éboué, twenty-five years old then, was posted to Bouca, capital of the Ouam circumscription, as a cadet administrator and as an assistant treasurer. He had decided that, wherever he worked, his first task would be to learn about the people and familiarize himself with this large circumscription of Oubangui-Chari. He took a Mandja girl as his companion (she bore him a son, Henri-Yves-Félix Éboué, in 1912). In 1910, Éboué was promoted to deputy administrator third class. (At Bouca, he was joined by his best friend René Maran, who was posted there in 1910.) It was there that Éboué showed his incipient administrative skills. He opened schools (at some of which he himself taught when he had the time), built roads, and urged the people to work for the development of their territory. Whenever they refused, however, he did not hesitate to use force to make them do so, as this was part of the colonial system. He learned the local language, befriended the African chiefs, and began a systematic study of the peoples' customs and traditions as well as of their music. His superiors were impressed with his achievements.

Following a six-month vacation in France and Guiana in 1912, Éboué returned to Oubangui-Chari but was transferred as deputy administrator (1913-1914) to Ombello-Mondjo, where he gained the unflattering reputation of being the imprisoner of many Africans who attempted to migrate to the Belgian Congo to escape forced labor and taxes. As usual, he maintained his friendship with and

Félix Éboué (left) welcoming Charles de Gaulle to Chad during World War II
(Library of Congress)

respect for the African local authorities, on whom he often relied for the enforcement of his orders. Well known then for his administrative abilities, Éboué was asked to pacify the restless populations of Kouango, a task he did brilliantly in 1914-1917.

Under local custom, Éboué took for his companion a chief's relative, who bore him a second son, Robert Max Éboué, in 1919. In recognition of his successful efforts in the pacification of his area, the colonial authorities promoted him to full third class administrator in 1917. As a mature civil servant, Éboué began seriously questioning the validity of the assimilation policy for Africans and shifted emphasis in his area from rubber collection to the cultivation of food and cash crops such as peanuts and cotton. He was convinced, however, that, if the colony and the Africans were to advance economically, forced labor and taxes were a necessity, as long as the Africans were treated humanely and the market price of their crops (such as cotton) was fair.

In 1917-1918, Éboué went on vacation to Paris and Cayenne but returned once again to Oubangui-Chari in 1919 as a full administrator at Bambari and continued his economic emphasis on peanuts, cassava, rice, sesame, and other crops; he encouraged the prospecting of mineral resources and opened a major road between Bambari and Bangui, the colonial capital. He created health-care centers and spearheaded the eradication of epidemic diseases (sleeping sickness, cerebrospinal meningitis, malaria, yellow fever, and cholera), an effort that made him a recipient of the Médaille des Épidémies from the authorities in 1919, the same year in which he was promoted to administrator second class. His first serious administrative troubles began there, when Governor-General Augagneur accused him of abusing the *indigenat*, which allowed the authorities to imprison him for two weeks and fine him without trial. Éboué subsequently cleared his name but decided to request a leave and went to Cayenne, where he married Eugénie Telles in 1922 and became a Freemason, as was customary among the educated and the wealthy of the islands (who did not necessarily repudiate Catholicism).

It would appear, however, that Oubangui-Chari was tied to Éboué's fate, for, in 1923, the colonial office asked him to return to the territory, after promoting him to administrator first class of Bas Mbomou. There he introduced a systematic cultivation of cotton, which reached a record amount of five hundred tons in 1926. Although he and Eugénie were happily married and had a daughter (Ginette), born in 1923, and a son (Charles Eboué), born in 1924,

Éboué's intermittent earaches and bouts of pulmonary congestion preoccupied the family. The young administrator, however, was determined to fulfill his administrative duties competently, regardless of his health, with an eye to an important promotion, which came in 1930 when he was appointed administrator in chief after a brief period of service at Fort Sibut in Kemo-Gribingui, Ouaka, and Bambari. Exhausted and interested in maintaining contact with important personalities in France, Éboué left for Paris on vacation on March 31, 1931.

By 1932, indications were that Éboué's career would shift from Africa (which he called the "land of his ancestors") to the Antilles, his birthplace. His Senegalese friend, Blaise Diagne, who served as the undersecretary of state for colonies, used his influence to have Éboué appointed secretary-general of Martinique, a position he gladly assumed on February 23, 1932. As secretary-general, Éboué had a wide range of executive responsibilities within the governor's domain. On July 15, 1932, Éboué was named acting governor of Martinique. This appointment brought him a great sense of pride and vindicated his abilities. However, he had no sooner been appointed than he had to step down on August 23, when the governor returned from the metropolis. He became interim governor of Martinique on June 4, 1933, the same year that he published his book *Les Peuples de l'Oubangui-Chari*, as he continued to aspire to be an administrator-scholar. His position as governor was short-lived, as it lasted only until April 19, 1934.

Éboué was reassigned to Africa but to French Sudan (later Mali), first as secretary-general (May 23, 1934) and then as acting governor (December 12, 1934, to November 20, 1935). Éboué was disappointed with this assignment because of his unfamiliarity with the location and became disillusioned when he was not appointed permanent governor.

While in French Sudan, Éboué experienced racism from white administrators and encountered problems with the Muslim populations and the nomads, with whom he had never dealt before, in his constant effort to submit them to colonial rule and to forced labor and taxation. He still maintained his belief that some attention should be paid to African local authorities if colonization were to succeed. His assignment in French Sudan was short-lived also. The colonial office reassigned him to Martinique as interim governor on September 29, 1936, and then as governor third class on November 25, 1936.

This assignment was a great honor for him, but he encountered racism there too and was a victim of local politics, worsened by a strike of dock-workers and masons. He fought without success the introduction of a forty-hour work week, the adoption of paid vacation for civil servants, and the acceptance of the principle of collective bargaining. Removed as governor in July, 1938, Éboué was asked to go to Chad as governor second class. Although this was a promotion in rank, Éboué was quite unhappy with the assignment because of the territory's backwardness and the fact that all colonial officers viewed a posting to Chad as a demotion. It was this posting, however, that would finally bring him the most fame. As soon as he arrived at Fort-Lamy (later N'Djamena), the capital of Chad, on January 24, 1939, he began to apply his principles of colonization, which included rapid improvement of communication and transportation networks, cultivation of cash and food crops, preservation of local authorities, enforcement of work laws and taxation, and administrative decentralization.

However, the fall of France to Nazi Germany in June, 1940, dashed Éboué's hopes of implementing his grand colonial designs. In a courageous stand, he refused to follow orders from the Vichy government and rallied Chad to General Charles de Gaulle in August, 1940, and urged the other African colonies to follow suit. His effort was so successful in Africa and so gratifying to de Gaulle that on November 12, 1940, the latter named Éboué provisional governor-general of French Equatorial Africa. Éboué was totally surprised and happy with his new appointment, which became a permanent one on July 15, 1941. That August, during a visit to French West and Equatorial Africa, de Gaulle bestowed upon Éboué the Croix de la Compagne de la Libération in recognition of his war effort in Equatorial Africa on behalf of the French Resistance.

As a permanent governor-general, Éboué now had the opportunity to implement his colonial philosophy, which became known as *la nouvelle politique africaine.* De Gaulle listened to him and urged the acceptance of Éboué's colonial policies. To show his trust and gratitude to Éboué, de Gaulle held in Brazzaville the Governors' Conference of January, 1944. De Gaulle made an emotional speech at the soccer stadium, praising Éboué as one of the most able governors-general and one of the greatest patriots France had ever seen.

With his reputation high in French colonial circles, Éboué's philosophy triumphed after Brazzaville, eventually leading to the abolition of the *indigenat* and to the establishment of special schools and the communes he had advocated. Happy but tired and wishing to see Egypt and the Middle East, Éboué left Chad on March 18, 1944, on a three-month vacation with his family. While in Cairo, he fell sick from pneumonia. Doctors administered to him the most modern medicine then available. Although everyone expected him to recover quickly, Éboué's health suddenly deteriorated. He died in the hospital on May 17, 1944.

Éboué was buried two days later in Egypt after funeral ceremonies at the Roman Catholic Church of Saint Mark de Choubrah. De Gaulle was unable to attend the funeral but sent a message, and René Pleven, the national commissioner for economy, finances, and colonies in the Comité National Français (and de Gaulle's number one man), gave the eulogy and promised that a proper burial for the governor would be found after the war. Several British and French governors also attended the ceremonies. Finally, in 1949, Éboué's coffin was shipped to France, and, with full honors, it was placed in the Panthéon on May 20, 1949. Thus ended prematurely the life and career of one of the most prominent black civil servants of the French colonial empire.

Summary

Félix Éboué's ambition in life was to advance to the highest rank of the colonial civil service ladder. As a black man, he never overlooked the problems that lay ahead of him. Through sheer determination, favorable circumstances beyond his control (which some would call luck), his friendships, the crucial connections he had forged in the colonial office in France and overseas, and his own administrative talent, Éboué achieved his goal in life in 1941 when he became governor-general of French Equatorial Africa. However, his somewhat premature death at the age of fifty-nine prevented him from implementing to the fullest extent his colonial philosophy. A Stoic and Pythagorean, a Freemason, and a man of great respect for human values and human dignity, Éboué faced his administrative tasks with the vision of a better France and a better colonial empire for all, where fairness, brotherhood, and justice would be the guiding principles.

Throughout his career and after his death, Éboué continued to be a symbol of success and an inspiration for all black people within the French Empire. In Africa, however, his task was made more difficult by the fact that he had to enforce the colonial policies that were designed to coerce the Africans to become part of the empire through the *indigenat*, forced labor, taxation, and the abandonment of their nationalistic aspirations. From this perspective, therefore, he was seen not only as a black "foreigner" from the Antilles but also as a colonial administrator and even as an oppressor masked in a black skin.

Perceptive Africans were able to view Éboué also in a more positive role—as one who fought colonial abuses, who created schools and hospitals, and who encouraged the preservation of certain elements of African tradition, convinced that French assimilation and citizenship for Africans were unrealistic. He preferred association and would have liked to see educated Africans given a special status in the colonial empire—that of *notables évolués*—and the establishment of urban and local communes with certain voting and political rights, which would lead, however, not to nationalistic aspirations but to a colorful diversity within a unified French Empire.

Bibliography

Azevedo, Mario. *Sara Demographic Instability as a Consequence of French Colonial Policy in Chad (1890-1940)*. Ann Arbor: University Microfilms, 1977. Despite the title's reference to demography, this work discusses all aspects of French colonial policy in Chad and reveals the social, economic, and political environment in which Éboué had to work as an administrator.

Betts, Raymond F. *Assimilation and Association in French Colonial Theory, 1890-1914*. New York: Columbia University Press, 1961. An essential work for any English reader interested in the debate over assimilation and association, of which Éboué chose the latter, at least insofar as the Africans were concerned.

La Roche, Jean de. *Le Gouverneur Général Félix Éboué, 1884-1944*. Paris: Hachette, 1957. Weinstein calls this work Éboué's best biography in French but adds that it focuses mostly on his life as a statesman. This biography, written by one of his friends, is sympathetic to the governor but is not as extensive in its sources as Brian Weinstein's work.

O'Toole, Thomas. *The Central African Republic*. Boulder, Colo.: Westview Press, 1986. For a better understanding of Éboué's times and the milieu in which he worked during the first four decades of the twentieth century, O'Toole's book constitutes an important source of information and historical interpretation.

Weinstein, Brian. *Éboué*. New York: Oxford University Press, 1972. This is the most complete and objectively written biography of Éboué. Professor of political science at Howard University at the time he wrote it, Weinstein has made extensive use of primary sources, written and oral, on the governor, making the work a true study of Éboué's life and times. This essay would have been incomplete without Weinstein's work.

White, Dorothy S. *Black Africa and de Gaulle: From the French Empire to Independence*. University Park: Pennsylvania State University Press, 1979.

Mario Azevedo

ANTHONY EDEN

Born: June 12, 1897; Windlestone Hall, near Bishop Auckland, Durham, England
Died: January 14, 1977; Alvediston, Wiltshire, England

Although his three appointments as foreign secretary, during 1935-1938, 1940-1945, and 1951-1955, brought Eden a high reputation for firmness and diplomatic adroitness, his tenure as prime minister, between 1955 and 1957, ended in humiliation and resignation for his part in the ill-starred invasion of Egypt which brought the Suez crisis to a head.

Early Life

The fourth of five children, Robert Anthony Eden was born on June 12, 1897, on his family's estate near Bishop Auckland in county Durham. His father's lineage, through local nobility, could be traced back at least to the fifteenth century; among others, Sir William Eden could claim descent from royal governors of Maryland and North Carolina. Lady Sybil Frances Grey Eden, Eden's mother, was partly of Danish ancestry, although one side of her family was related to that of Sir Edward Grey, Great Britain's foreign secretary immediately before and during World War I. Young Anthony (he eventually preferred the middle to his original given name) was educated in part by tutors during his early years. For a time, he was taught by a German governess, from whom he evidently received more thorough instruction in French than in her native language. At the age of thirteen, he entered Eton, where he was regarded as promising and intelligent but not notably distinguished.

Before Eden could consider further studies, World War I broke out, and late in 1914, John Eden, his eldest brother, was killed while on active duty in France. Another brother, Timothy, was captured and held in Germany as a prisoner of war. Nevertheless, in September, 1915, Eden enlisted in the infantry and was commissioned a lieutenant. He was to spend more than three years on the Western Front, chiefly at Ypres and on the Somme. He was appalled at the carnage and suffering of war as it affected those around him. He learned as well that his younger brother, William Nicholas, a midshipman, had perished in 1916 at the Battle of Jutland. Eden nevertheless performed his duties loyally and with conspicuous gallantry. In June, 1917, he was awarded the Military Cross for bringing a wounded sergeant back to safety while under German machine-gun fire. Early in the spring of the following year, he was promoted to brigade-major.

Upon his return to civilian life, Eden entered Oxford University. Enlarging upon the example of one of his neighbors from Durham, a former diplomatic official who had taught him some elements of Turkish, Eden decided to read for a degree in Oriental languages; he concentrated upon Persian, with some attention also to Arabic. When he completed his studies, he obtained first-class honors. Rather than take up a diplomatic calling, however, the lure of political challenge led him to stand as a Conservative candidate for Parliament.

Although the first time, in November, 1922, he was defeated in a district where the Labour Party had a preponderant following, he was later nominated in a neighboring area, around Warwick and Leamington. Eden, espousing conventional party doctrines, campaigned diligently, and he was elected handily in December, 1923. Not long beforehand a major event took place in his personal life: He was married to Beatrice Beckett, the daughter of a Conservative member of Parliament who was the chairman of the *Yorkshire Post*. To the young couple two sons, Simon and Nicholas, were born during the next seven years.

Life's Work

Eden's first speech before the House of Commons warned of the need, not merely for air defense, but also for the means to develop offensive capabilities which then might deter any would-be attacker. Other statements, on economic concerns, recorded his beliefs that the working and lower classes had interests in social stability to the extent that they might also become property holders. Eden seemed more comfortable dealing with matters of international concern. He spoke out on issues such as imperial defense, relations with Turkey, and disarmament proposals. After a wide-ranging foreign tour he produced his first book, *Places in the Sun* (1926), which made little impression and was regarded by critics as platitudinous.

As his political career developed, Eden became increasingly

Anthony Eden *(Library of Congress)*

known, by supporters and detractors alike, for his appearance and bearing. To his admirers, he was the embodiment of self-assurance and polished ease, a tall, trim figure, impeccably tailored, who gave the impression of strength and dignity. Later cartoonists and critics found his personality symbolized by his bushy eyebrows and the thick overhanging mustache that he had cultivated since his army days; his protruding front teeth contrasted with a somewhat weak chin to produce an effect of awkward irresolution. On the radio, his voice seemed thin and reedy to many, though his later television appearances produced somewhat more favorable impressions.

Eden's growing expertise in diplomatic matters was widely recognized, and in 1931, he became undersecretary of state for foreign affairs. For some time, he represented Great Britain at the World Disarmament Conference in Geneva and later dealt with the crisis of October, 1934, when Italy and Hungary were suspected of complicity in the assassination of Yugoslavia's king Alexander. In January, 1935, he endorsed the return of the Saar to Germany when this measure was approved by a local plebiscite. In the course of his diplomatic work, Eden met with Italy's Benito Mussolini, Chancellor Adolf Hitler of Germany, and leading French statesmen. In April, 1935, he was received at the Kremlin by Soviet premier Joseph Stalin. During that summer, Eden was appointed to a cabinet-level position: minister for League of Nations affairs.

At times, Eden seemed poised between conciliatory overtures and more forthright assertions of resistance to the minatory policies of European dictators. When Italy went to war in order to subjugate Ethiopia, in October, 1935, Eden urged that all measures short of actual military involvement should be used to oppose Mussolini's imperial designs. Eden became foreign secretary in December of that year, after Sir Samuel Hoare, his predecessor, was forced to concede that efforts to find a solution through diplomatic concessions had failed.

While the Ethiopian issue remained unsettled, further problems were posed by Germany's introduction of troops into the Rhineland in March, 1936, in pointed defiance of the Treaty of Versailles. In July, 1936, civil war broke out in Spain, and it was not long before Nationalist forces received active assistance from Germany and Italy. Eden sternly contended that all powers should follow a policy of nonintervention in the Spanish conflict. It would appear that during this period, Eden was at least as much concerned with Italian as with German challenges to peace, and his position began to diverge from those of others in the government.

Neville Chamberlain, who became prime minister in May, 1937, clashed with Eden on certain points. His efforts to secure an understanding with Italy, in the absence of preconditions which Eden insisted were essential, were followed by secret meetings with Italian diplomats. Rather abruptly, in February, 1938, Eden resigned from the Foreign Office, though he avoided any outward recriminations that might have proved embarrassing to the Conservative government.

Subsequently, Eden's standpoint seemed amply vindicated by events, as the Fascist dictators became even more intractable, although it is not clear the extent to which principled prescience guided his decisions. In September, 1938, the prime minister took part in the Munich accords, which consigned part of Czechoslovakia to the Third Reich. In the wake of this agreement, Eden spoke from his seat in the Commons, expressing reservations about Chamberlain's diplomacy without venturing to judge its ultimate results.

After Great Britain declared war on Germany, in September, 1939, Eden became secretary of state for the Dominions; in May, 1940, with Winston S. Churchill as prime minister, he was appointed secretary of state for war. That December, he again was made foreign secretary. On some matters, Eden differed sharply with Churchill; for some time he favored firmer support for General

Charles de Gaulle's French Committee of National Liberation.

On some occasions, Eden believed that the prime minister's treatment of him was high-handed. Particularly troubling questions arose in the course of Great Britain's alliance with the Soviet Union. While Eden had earlier acquiesced in Soviet territorial claims, during the later stages of the war he was distinctly wary of Stalin's intentions. In particular, he insisted that after the liberation of Greece from the Germans, in October, 1944, British forces stationed there should act to preclude a communist seizure of power. Somewhat uncomfortably, Eden did agree to the repatriation of Soviet nationals found among the German troops that British forces captured in Central Europe. In carrying out this decision of the war cabinet, however, his aim was to avoid further difficulties with the Soviets over the Balkans and to assure the return of British prisoners of war who had been liberated by the Red Army.

In July, 1945, Eden was informed that his elder son, Simon, a pilot, had died over Burma. Shortly thereafter, the electorate turned the Conservative Party out of office. Late in 1946, during a visit to the United States, Eden's wife finally wearied of her husband's political commitments and remained behind in New York. Their marriage was formally dissolved in 1950. When after the general election of 1951 the Conservatives again formed a government, Eden once more became Churchill's foreign secretary, though some observers detected a growing impatience on his part to succeed the older man. Eden's personal life took a turn for the better in 1952 when he married Anne Clarissa Spencer Churchill, the prime minister's niece, who was twenty-three years his junior.

In spite of Great Britain's difficulties in adjusting to its loss of influence abroad after World War II, Eden's third term as foreign secretary was distinguished by the settlement through negotiation of several troublesome issues. At Geneva in 1954, Eden was instrumental in arranging accords which brought an end to France's prolonged war against local insurgents in Indochina; it seemed unavoidable that communist advances there would lead to the division of Vietnam. Eden also assisted in the resolution of territorial differences in Europe, whereby Italy received Trieste and Yugoslavia was awarded much of the region east of the city.

Perhaps Eden's most notable achievement from this period was the conclusion of an agreement facilitating the entry of the Federal Republic of Germany into the North Atlantic Treaty Organization (NATO). To counter objections, especially from French leaders who feared German rearmament, Eden offered a continuing pledge to maintain British forces on the Continent. After this measure was accepted, in October, 1954, proposals for supranational military structures were replaced by more definite commitments within the Atlantic Alliance. For this action, Eden was formally knighted by the British Crown.

In April, 1955, Churchill retired and Eden duly became prime minister. In a bold gesture, he called for general elections the next month, to which the country responded by voting in a larger Conservative majority. Although henceforth economic issues, notably deflationary measures which would require fiscal austerity, troubled him in an area where he had little real expertise, Eden devoted most of his attention to diplomatic concerns.

After a summit conference where they met Western leaders in Geneva, in July, 1955, Soviet leaders Nikita Khrushchev and Nikolai Bulganin came to Great Britain the following April for a state visit. Middle Eastern problems, however, soon became a virtual preoccupation. Efforts to form military alliances with Arab countries led to an agreement with Iraq, but President Gamal Abdel Nasser of Egypt denounced such undertakings and turned to Czechoslovakia and the Soviet Union for aircraft and other modern weapons.

In March, 1956, King Hussein of Jordan dismissed General John Bagot Glubb, the British commander of that country's Arab Legion. Eden suspected that Nasser had instigated this measure. In July, the American secretary of state, John Foster Dulles, wary of mounting Soviet influence in Egypt, abruptly cancelled a proposed offer for a loan to finance the Aswan Dam. Within one week, Nasser retaliated by announcing the nationalization of the Suez Canal Company.

Eden regarded this act as a severe blow to Great Britain's vital interests. In discussions with the French premier, Guy Mollet, the use of force was considered repeatedly, but at the outset of the crisis it was realized that additional time was required to make preparations from bases in the Mediterranean. Other measures, such as collective negotiations among nations using the canal, which Dulles favored, seemed both prolonged and inconclusive. By the middle of October, military alternatives, to which Eden invariably had attached great importance, were decided upon in more definite terms. It is probably just as well that British leaders became involved in concurrent planning between French and Israeli commanders. Toward the end of the month, Israel invaded the Sinai peninsula;

ostensibly to separate the combatants and to establish international control of the canal, an Anglo-French ultimatum was delivered to Egypt. British warplanes based on Cyprus then attacked Egyptian air bases. By the first week of November, British and French troops had landed at Port Said and advanced alongside the waterway.

The Suez expedition met with wide condemnation from many nations of the world. The pretexts under which it had been launched—to maintain access to the canal and to keep Israeli and Egyptian forces apart—were generally regarded as specious. Eden's veracity was called into question and there were widespread charges of multilateral collusion in the surprise attack on Egypt. American diplomats openly called for the withdrawal of British and French troops. International speculation threatened the exchange value of the British pound. Moreover, vague Soviet threats of rocket attacks on London and Paris further complicated matters. The British and French governments were forced to agree first to suspend operations against Egypt and then to withdraw their forces to make way for United Nations troops that were dispatched to the area. At one stroke, Eden's political stature had fallen catastrophically.

Over the years, Eden had suffered repeatedly from poor health: Early in his career at the Foreign Office heart strain was diagnosed, while on other occasions he was treated for a duodenal ulcer. Jaundice and gastric complaints had also troubled him. During the later stages of the Suez crisis, he was stricken with an abnormally high fever. Accordingly, without referring to the disturbing questions that had arisen about his political judgment, he cited medical concerns on January 9, 1957, when he tendered his resignation from the prime ministry to Queen Elizabeth II.

During his retirement, Eden did not much involve himself in political concerns, though as a former prime minister he accepted elevation to the peerage and became the earl of Avon in 1961. He wrote four volumes of memoirs, which did not appear in a chronological sequence and were considered of uneven quality. He also composed a brief treatise, *Towards Peace in Indo-China* (1966), which drew upon his experience in negotiating the accords of 1954 and proposed that through international agencies the United States should work for a compromise settlement of the Vietnam War. Otherwise, Eden receded from public view. After struggles with cancer, Eden died finally at Alvediston, his farm home in Wiltshire, on January 14, 1977.

Summary

For a diplomat who had long been regarded as fortune's favorite, the obloquy that attached to Anthony Eden's name after the crisis of 1956 was particularly ironic: In many quarters it was thought that he had invariably come down on the right side of major questions before the Suez conflict. Some subsequent historians have regarded this verdict as simplistic; inconsistencies and moments of naïveté have been discerned in positions he adopted preceding World War II. Some have castigated Eden for his wartime dealings with the Soviet Union. Others have insisted that the national interests of his own country were paramount to him. It is arguable that Eden followed no single guiding principle but, rather, aimed to preserve order and safeguard peace. He was in no sense a great writer or orator, but for most of his career he displayed great skill as a diplomatic tactician. Against his later critics it may be contended that a lesser man would have fallen by the wayside during the 1930's debate on appeasement or would have been daunted by the multiple concerns of Great Britain's international role during the first decade of the Cold War.

That Eden suffered a fatal lapse of judgment in Middle Eastern concerns, an area where he was thought to be particularly knowledgeable, points up perhaps some of the conclusions that may be drawn from the tragic denouement of his public life. For one thing, it was difficult for him to act both to negotiate and to resolve upon sterner measures. After a career in which difficult decisions had frequently arisen, he erred finally on the side of using force. Almost certainly, he mistook the actual trend of political events in the Middle East; his vision was derived too much from a simpler era, when Great Britain's overseas requirements could more easily be accommodated. Finally, it seems likely that he did not readily grasp the implications of declining British power during the era following World War II. That these shortcomings should have been exhibited all at once during the single major crisis of his prime ministry suggests as well the unhappy vicissitudes of international politics, where certain tragic flaws combined to cut short a career which otherwise had offered much.

Bibliography

Aster, Sidney. *Anthony Eden*. New York: St. Martin's Press, 1976. Brisk, popular narrative which weighs the achievements of Eden's diplomatic work against the tragic miscalculations over Suez which brought his political career to an end.

Barker, Elisabeth. *Churchill and Eden at War*. New York: St. Martin's Press, 1978. This extensive and fair-minded study of Eden's relationship with the prime minister during World War II is based largely upon cabinet papers, Foreign Office records, and other archival materials. The author systematically traces the actual differences that existed between the two British statesmen while warning against exaggerated claims of discord or strife.

Carlton, David. *Anthony Eden: A Biography*. London: Allen Lane, 1981. This lengthy critical study, based upon many American as well as British diplomatic documents, is rather more critical of Eden's positions during the 1930's and World War II than other major works; on the other hand, some subsequent difficulties are traced to underlying problems of Great Britain's declining position relative to the United States and the Soviet Union. This work is important as a kind of revisionist treatment of the British statesman's political career.

Dutton, David. *Anthony Eden: A Life and Reputation*. New York: Arnold, 1997.

Eden, Anthony. *Full Circle*. London: Cassell, 1960. The author's first volume of memoirs, covering his service between 1951 and 1957 as foreign secretary and prime minister, is persistently marred by his tone of injured self-justification. Although somewhat more dispassionate on other issues, the last section, dealing with the crisis of 1956, contains unfortunate displays of rhetorical excess and special pleading.

__________. *Facing the Dictators*. London: Cassell, 1962. Although some episodes are treated at greater length than others, and there are some rather curious omissions, this work both traces the development of Eden's political career and comments on diplomatic problems from 1931 to 1938. There is some reasoning from hindsight, but probably no more than in other memoirs from this period.

__________. *The Reckoning*. London: Cassell, 1965. Eden's memoirs from World War II reveal some of the difficulties that Great Britain encountered in its diplomatic relations with the Soviet Union and the United States. The author is not inclined to dwell upon problems in dealing with Churchill or other leaders from his own country.

__________. *Another World, 1897-1917*. London: Allen Lane, 1976. This slender volume combines bittersweet recollections of the author's early years with poignant, haunting sketches from his military service on the Western Front. The later portions furnish grim evidence of the impact World War I had on Eden's family and on his political outlook.

James, Robert Rhodes. *Anthony Eden*. London: Weidenfeld & Nicolson, 1986.

Peters, Anthony R. *Anthony Eden at the Foreign Office, 1931-1938*. New York: St. Martin's Press, 1986. This well-documented monograph carefully assesses the various approaches—through international organizations, negotiation with individual states, and forthright opposition to Fascism—that Eden employed during his early diplomatic career. The author provides some rather persuasive explanations for Eden's resignation as foreign secretary during the fateful year 1938.

Trukhanovskii, Vladimir Grigor'evich. *Anthony Eden*. Translated by R. English. Moscow: Progress Publishers, 1985. Based on an original version published in 1976, this Soviet biography provides a curious riposte to certain Western writers: Trukhanovskii contends that in various ways Eden's anticommunist and anti-Soviet views impeded his dealings with Moscow and that his neocolonialist outlook led finally to the Suez fiasco. From this standpoint, the author, who has also published works on Churchill and on the problems of modern British diplomacy, considers the particular circumstances surrounding Eden's rise and fall.

J. R. Broadus

DWIGHT D. EISENHOWER

Born: October 14, 1890; Denison, Texas
Died: March 28, 1969; Washington, D.C.

During World War II, Eisenhower served with distinction as Allied Commander for the invasions of North Africa, Italy, and France. He won the presidential elections of 1952 and 1956 and guided the country through eight years of peace and prosperity.

Early Life

Although born in Texas, where his parents lived briefly, Dwight David Eisenhower grew up in the small town of Abilene, Kansas. The Eisenhowers were a close-knit family and belonged to the Brethren Church, part of the heritage of ancestors who had immigrated to Pennsylvania from Germany during the eighteenth century. The third of seven sons (one of whom died as an infant), Dwight Eisenhower enjoyed a secure childhood, completed high school, and worked in a creamery for two years before entering West Point on the basis of a competitive examination. West Point appealed to him because it offered a free college education.

As a cadet, Eisenhower excelled briefly at football until a knee injury ended that career. He proved a conscientious but not exceptional student and graduated sixty-first in a class of 164. At graduation in 1915, he stood five feet, eleven inches tall and weighed 170 pounds. His classmates remembered and respected "Ike," as did his boyhood friends, as likable, honest, and confident, a person with a quick temper but a quicker infectious grin. He had an expressive face, blue eyes, and light brown hair that thinned and receded when he was a young man.

Eisenhower's early military years were uneventful except for his marriage in 1916 to Mamie Geneva Doud of Denver, Colorado. The two had met in Texas during his first assignment at Fort Sam Houston. They became parents of two sons, the first of whom died as a child.

Dwight D. Eisenhower *(Library of Congress)*

Life's Work

During the 1920's and 1930's, Eisenhower demonstrated exceptional organizational skill and an ability to work with others. In 1926, Eisenhower, who had been merely an average student at West Point, finished first among 275 in his class at the army's elite

Command and General Staff School. When General Douglas MacArthur served as the army's chief of staff, Eisenhower assisted him, and then served as his senior assistant in the Philippines. MacArthur once evaluated Eisenhower as the most capable officer in the army.

Eisenhower's personality and his performance during maneuvers in the summer of 1941 impressed the army's chief of staff, General George C. Marshall. Both in 1941 and in 1942, Eisenhower won two promotions, jumping from lieutenant colonel to lieutenant general. In June, 1942, Marshall appointed Eisenhower European Theater Commander. The next year, as general, Eisenhower became Supreme Allied Commander and won fame as the leader of the multinational invasion of Europe in June, 1944.

After accepting Germany's surrender, Eisenhower served as the army's chief of staff. He retired in 1948 and became president of Columbia University. His book *Crusade in Europe*, published the same year, sold millions of copies and gave him financial security. Two years later, President Harry S Truman recalled Eisenhower to active duty as Supreme Commander of the North Atlantic Treaty Organization (NATO) forces.

In May, 1952, Eisenhower retired from the army to seek the Republican Party's nomination for president, an office leaders in both parties had urged upon him for years. With his decisive victory in the November election, Eisenhower embarked upon a second career, one even more important than the first.

As president, Eisenhower set his primary foreign policy objective as maintaining the international role the United States had assumed during the previous decade. More specifically, he intended to end the fighting in Korea, reduce military spending, and lessen the intensity of the Cold War while still adhering to the policy of containment. Militarily, Eisenhower pursued a policy of strategic sufficiency rather than superiority. This policy, as well as a reduction of the capacity to fight limited wars, made possible cuts in the defense budget.

In 1953, Eisenhower approved an armistice in the Korean War and the next year rejected the advice of his secretary of state and the chairman of the Joint Chiefs of Staff, among others, and refused to intervene in the French war in Indochina. The United States took the lead, however, in establishing the Southeast Asia Treaty Organization as an attempt to accomplish in a region of Asia what the North Atlantic Treaty Organization had accomplished in Europe.

During this same period, Eisenhower also approved Central Intelligence Agency covert activity that helped overthrow the governments of Iran and Guatemala and thereby contributed to the growing acceptance of undemocratic action in the name of freedom.

In 1955, he helped terminate the post-World War II occupation of Austria and then, at Geneva, Switzerland, became the first president to meet with Soviet leaders in a decade. That same year and again in 1956, Eisenhower reacted to crises in the coastal waters of the People's Republic of China, in Hungary, and in Suez in a manner that helped prevent these crises from escalating into greater violence.

On the domestic side, Eisenhower followed a moderate path. He accepted the New Deal programs and even expanded those covering labor, Social Security, and agriculture. Although he cut the budget of the Tennessee Valley Authority and reduced federal activity and regulations regarding natural resources, Eisenhower championed the nation's largest road-building project (the Federal Aid Highway Act of 1956) and federal development of the Saint Lawrence Seaway. He also approved spending increases in health care. Fiscally, Eisenhower cut taxes and controls, and each year balanced or nearly balanced the budget. The nation's gross national product, personal income, and house purchases all climbed. Inflation proved negligible, averaging 1.5 percent per year. Fundamental to Eisenhower's public philosophy was his belief that only a sound economy could sustain a credible, effective foreign policy.

In the presidential election of 1956, Americans gave Eisenhower a second, even greater, landslide victory over his Democratic opponent Adlai E. Stevenson, despite having a major heart attack in 1955 and an operation for ileitis in 1956. Voters approved his moderate policies and, like the friends of his youth and the military personnel with whom he worked, responded positively to his famous grin. His dislike of politics and his lifelong refusal to discuss personalities in public also struck responsive chords. Even his hobbies of golf, fishing and hunting, bridge and poker, and cookouts embodied widespread American values.

Eisenhower's second term continued the basic policies and themes of the first. He steadfastly resisted demands from Democrats and from conservative Republicans to increase defense spending, although he expanded the ballistic missile program after the Soviets launched the world's first human-made earth-orbiting satellite (*Sputnik*) in 1957. In 1958 (in Quemoy) and in 1958-1959 (in

Berlin), Eisenhower again handled crises with deliberation. After he hosted the visit of Soviet leader Nikita Khrushchev, Eisenhower looked forward to a Paris summit meeting in May, 1960, and to a visit to the Soviet Union as his final contribution to promoting peace. On the eve of the conference, the Soviets shot down an American spy plane over Soviet territory. The U-2 incident, named after the plane, ruined the conference, canceled Eisenhower's planned visit to the Soviet Union, and dashed his hopes to improve relations between the two superpowers.

Domestic highlights of Eisenhower's second term included his ordering troops to Little Rock, Arkansas, to maintain order while the high school racially integrated its classes. In the same year, 1957, Eisenhower signed the first civil rights act in eighty-two years. Important symbolically, the act produced little change in the lives of African Americans. The same proved true of another civil rights act in 1960. In response to Sputnik, Eisenhower established the National Aeronautics and Space Administration (NASA) and approved the National Defense Education Act, providing the first substantial federal aid to higher education in almost a century.

Criticism of Eisenhower dealt mostly with three subjects. First, he refused to exercise any public leadership in response to Senator Joseph McCarthy's excessive unsubstantiated accusations of disloyalty directed against numerous Americans, including General George C. Marshall. Second, after the Supreme Court ruled in *Brown v. Board of Education* in 1954 that separate-but-equal facilities were unconstitutional, Eisenhower refrained from lending his moral or political support for implementation of the ruling or for promotion of civil rights in general. The third area of criticism concerned his sparse defense budget and the limited range of responses it permitted in time of crisis. Eisenhower's confidence and public support, however, kept him from altering his positions because of such criticism.

In his presidential farewell address, Eisenhower warned the nation of the threat to democracy from the influence of the military-industrial complex, which benefited from massive military budgets. He retired to his Gettysburg, Pennsylvania, farm and wrote his memoirs. Most contemporary observers agreed that, had the Constitution permitted and had he been willing to run, Eisenhower easily would have won a third term.

Summary

Eisenhower, the career military officer, curtailed defense spending, pursued a foreign policy that emphasized conciliation rather than conflict, and presided over eight years of peace. An advocate of gradual domestic change, Eisenhower watched his most prominent appointee, Chief Justice Earl Warren, use his position and influence to bring sweeping changes to society. As a Republican president, Eisenhower, who disliked politics and favored limitations on the terms of senators and representatives, proved the most able politician of his generation. He adhered to definite policies, faced a Democratic Congress for six of his eight years in the White House, and suffered domestic and foreign setbacks, yet he gave the country eight years of economic growth and prosperity and left office with undiminished popularity.

Eisenhower obviously was a capable, complex man, but the key to his success seems to have been his ability to radiate straightforward honesty and uncomplicated common sense. The events of the decades following his presidency—the international arms race, war, riots, Watergate, inflation, declining standard of living, and uncontrollable budget deficits—have greatly enhanced respect for Eisenhower's accomplishments. Indeed, according to many, he has joined the ranks of the nation's great presidents.

Bibliography

Ambrose, Stephen E. *Eisenhower: Soldier, General of the Army, President-Elect, 1890-1952*. New York: Simon and Schuster, 1983. The most comprehensive book covering Eisenhower's life and career before he entered the White House. Based on an unequaled mastery of archival material, Ambrose provides an insightful and readable narrative. The book is especially strong on the influences that shaped Eisenhower's personality and career. The book's highlight is Eisenhower's tenure as Supreme Allied Commander during World War II.

__________. *Eisenhower: Soldier and President*. New York: Simon and Schuster, 1990. Condensed version of Ambrose's 1983 work.

__________. *Eisenhower: The President*. New York: Simon and Schuster, 1984. This authoritative volume presents a detailed chronology of Eisenhower's presidency. The coverage of personalities and events, both foreign and domestic, is broad. Ambrose, the leading Eisenhower scholar, concludes with a favorable assessment of his subject, awarding higher grades in foreign than in domestic affairs.

Bischof, Gunter, and Stephen E. Ambrose, eds. *Eisenhower: A Centenary Assessment*. Baton Rouge: Louisiana State University Press, 1995.

Burk, Robert F. *The Eisenhower Administration and Black Civil Rights*. Knoxville: University of Tennessee Press, 1984. The most important book about Eisenhower and civil rights. Although Burk concentrates on events, he also discusses Eisenhower's attitudes and beliefs. The bibliographical essay is especially valuable.

Divine, Robert A. *Eisenhower and the Cold War*. New York: Oxford University Press, 1981. A clear, brief summary of several problems and themes in Eisenhower's foreign policy. In four essays (dealing with the presidency, Asia and massive retaliation, the Middle East, and Russians), Divine offers a favorable view of Eisenhower and of his handling of international crises.

Eisenhower, David. *Eisenhower: At War, 1943-1945*. New York: Random House, 1986. This massive study (nearly a thousand pages long) provides an indispensable account of Eisenhower's wartime leadership. The author (who is the grandson of his subject) emphasizes Eisenhower's awareness of long-range strategic considerations that would shape the postwar era.

Eisenhower, Dwight D. *The Eisenhower Diaries*. Edited by Robert H. Farrell. New York: W. W. Norton, 1981. This 445-page volume presents the diary that Eisenhower started in 1935 and continued sporadically until late in life. Among other things, the diary records Eisenhower's frustration with individuals whom, as a matter of policy, he refrained from criticizing publicly. Farrell's introduction is excellent.

Greenstein, Fred I. *The Hidden-Hand Presidency: Eisenhower as Leader*. New York: Basic Books, 1982. This influential revisionist book examines Eisenhower's leadership techniques. Drawing heavily from the files of the president's personal secretary, political scientist Greenstein explains Eisenhower's behind-the-scenes domination of his administration. In doing so, he also reveals much about Eisenhower's personality.

Griffith, Robert. "Dwight D. Eisenhower and the Corporate Commonwealth." *American Historical Review* 87 (February, 1982): 87-122. A long, interpretative article that analyzes and synthesizes the components of Eisenhower's political philosophy (view of society, responsibility of government, role of economics) and the influence of this philosophy on his domestic and foreign policies. Griffith also describes the influences that shaped Eisenhower's philosophy.

Mayer, Michael S. "With Much Deliberation and Some Speed: Eisenhower and the Brown Decision." *The Journal of Southern History* 52 (February, 1986): 43-76. An assessment that portrays Eisenhower's civil rights record as more complex and, at times, more ambiguous than previous scholars have judged it to be. This article is broader in its concerns than the title suggests and is valuable for its account of Eisenhower's view of equality and blacks.

Pickett, William B. *Dwight David Eisenhower and American Power*. Wheeling, Ill.: Harlan Davidson, 1995.

Reichard, Gary. *The Reaffirmation of Republicanism: Eisenhower and the Eighty-third Congress*. Knoxville: University of Tennessee Press, 1975. A careful study of Eisenhower's relationship with Republicans in Congress during his first two years in office, the only period of his presidency during which the Republicans controlled Congress. By focusing on key domestic and foreign policy issues, Reichard evaluates Eisenhower as a party leader and as a Republican.

Keith W. Olson

ELIZABETH II

Born: April 21, 1926; London, England

Dignified and regal, yet down-to-earth and accessible, Elizabeth II has embodied the continuing vitality of the British monarchy. The popularity and esteem in which she is held make her an ideal head of state.

Early Life

Elizabeth Alexandra Mary was born on April 21, 1926, the first child of Prince Albert, duke of York, and Elizabeth, the duchess of York. Her father, the future George VI, was the second son of George V, and the Duchess of York, formerly Lady Elizabeth Bowes-Lyon, came from a distinguished Scottish family. A second daughter, Margaret, was born four years later.

A major influence on the first ten years of Elizabeth's life, until his death in 1936, was that of her grandfather, George V. His was the dominant voice in the family, and he inculcated in his granddaughter a strong sense of duty and self-sacrifice, and a willingness to undertake hard, and not always glamorous, work. Elizabeth was also strongly influenced by the gaiety and fun of the social life she enjoyed every summer as a child with her mother's family at Glamis, just north of Dundee in Scotland.

At her birth, Elizabeth was not in the direct line of succession to the throne. The major event which was to shape her destiny came in 1936, when her uncle, Prince Edward, succeeded to the throne as Edward VIII. Several months later, he abdicated because he wished to marry a divorced woman whom the family and the country thought unsuitable to become queen. Elizabeth's father, as the next in line to the throne, thus became George VI, and Elizabeth, at the age of ten, became the heir presumptive. She led a somewhat sheltered and secluded childhood, not unusual for royal children, and was educated privately. A conscientious, serious-minded, and fairly placid child, she was developing qualities which she would put to full use in her future role as queen.

In July, 1939, Elizabeth first met Prince Philip of Greece, five years her senior, who was about to embark on a naval career. The capable and handsome young prince made a deep impression on her but at the time the princess was only thirteen, and the outbreak of World War II in September prevented any immediate flowering of the friendship. For the duration of the war, Elizabeth was moved to Windsor Castle, near London, where she was to spend the remainder of her childhood. In 1940, at the age of fourteen, she gave a radio address which was broadcast throughout the British Empire. The young princess, who was quite small in stature, with very blue eyes and a quick, engagingly warm smile, accepted her opportunity with poise and confidence.

After the end of the war, the incipient romance between Elizabeth and Prince Philip (by then known as Lieutenant Philip Mountbatten) moved quickly. They became engaged in July, 1947, and were married in November. A year later, Elizabeth gave birth to a son, Charles; a baby girl, Anne, followed in 1950. At this time Elizabeth might reasonably have expected a decade or so to devote herself to rearing her children before inheriting her weightier responsibilities, but in February, 1952, George VI died prematurely at the age of fifty-six. Elizabeth, who was touring with her husband in East Africa, found herself, at the age of twenty-six, queen of Great Britain and her Dominions.

Life's Work

The coronation took place in June, 1953, and was celebrated, it was estimated, by a quarter of the entire population of the world. Within a month the new queen faced one of her most difficult decisions. Her sister Margaret wished to marry Group Captain Peter Townsend, a war hero who was at the time comptroller of the Queen Mother's household. However, Townsend was in the process of divorcing his wife and was on that account considered to be an unsuitable husband for royalty. Under the Royal Marriages Act of 1772, members of the royal family who are in line of succession to the throne and who are under twenty-five years old must have the sovereign's permission to marry. Elizabeth was sympathetic to the couple, but she felt compelled to act on the advice of her prime minister, Sir Winston S. Churchill, and the marriage did not take place. The issue resurfaced two years later, however, when Margaret became twenty-five. Amid public controversy, Elizabeth left the decision to Margaret, who decided that she would not marry Townsend.

In the winter of 1953-1954, the queen went on a tour of the

British Commonwealth, the first reigning British monarch to travel around the world. She would later become the most traveled monarch in British history, having visited well over one hundred different countries.

In the years following her return, she established the daily routine that she continued to follow. One of her most important tasks is her daily perusal of the "boxes," parliamentary papers which are delivered to her for signature. As the head of state, all government is conducted in her name. Although the signing is a formality, the queen takes her responsibility seriously. Many of her prime ministers can testify to her careful reading, and to the shrewdness of her questions and comments on government business.

Approximately once a month she holds an investiture at Buckingham Palace, in which she personally hands out honors to public servants and other outstanding individuals. Her other duties are many. She may spend an afternoon inspecting a factory or visiting a hospital ward, attending an exhibition or a major sporting event. On such occasions, practice has made her always imperturbable and dignified, interested and alert, however many eager hands there may be to shake.

Elizabeth II *(Library of Congress)*

On several occasions Elizabeth II has become involved in political controversy centering on the royal prerogative to appoint prime ministers. In 1957, the prime minister, Anthony Eden, resigned because of ill health. The ruling Conservative Party had no clearly defined system of electing a leader, but it was widely believed in the country that Eden would be succeeded by Richard Austen Butler. The queen, however, acting on the advice of Lord Salisbury, who had determined that a majority of Conservative members of Parliament favored Harold Macmillan, duly appointed Macmillan as prime minister. As a result, Elizabeth found herself open to the accusation that she had allowed herself to be manipulated by the elder statesmen of the party, who represented its aristocratic wing, and that she had not consulted widely enough before making her decision.

A similar but more serious controversy took place in 1963, when Macmillan resigned. Acting solely on his advice, the queen appointed the earl of Home as prime minister. This was quite unexpected by the country at large, there being at least four other strong candidates. Whereas the queen's instincts have always been to avoid political involvement, on this occasion her attempt to avoid politics had the opposite effect, making her seem less than impartial and independent.

Meanwhile, the royal family continued to grow. In 1960, Queen Elizabeth gave birth to a third child, Andrew, and a fourth, Edward, followed in 1964. In the next decade, the occasion of the queen's Silver Jubilee in 1977 gave the nation an opportunity for prolonged celebration which it had not known since the coronation. The occasion clearly showed, to anyone who doubted, the spontaneous affection and enthusiasm with which the British people regard their queen.

Summary

During the reign of Elizabeth II, the monarchy achieved an unprecedented popularity among the British people. Much of this is the result of the personal qualities of the queen: her sense of duty, her dignity and seriousness of manner, her desire to uphold the ideals of family life. She has weathered a number of storms, from widespread criticism of her supposedly stuffy and incompetent advisers in the 1950's to the simmering political row over royal finances in the inflation-riddled days of the 1970's.

In the 1990's the British public's appreciation of the royal family was sorely tested as two princes, Charles and Andrew, were married and divorced amid a variety of scandals. Elizabeth herself managed to emerge from it all relatively unscathed, although public reaction following the 1997 death of the immensely popular Diana, Princess of Wales, included open criticism of the queen's perceived coldness and impassivity in the face of the tragedy.

Elizabeth has had the intelligence and skill to adapt the monarchy successfully to a changing era. She has made it accessible without diminishing its grandeur or mystique. When in the 1970's she allowed television cameras into Buckingham Palace for the making of the film *Royal Family*, for example, she achieved a public relations breakthrough. The glimpse into the private life of the royal family fascinated the nation.

Elizabeth II has also presided with dignity over a difficult period in British history, marked by the steady decline in the nation's worldwide influence and prestige. Nevertheless, the transformation of the British Empire into the British Commonwealth, a voluntary association of equal and independent nations, has in many ways been a productive and useful change. As head of the Commonwealth, the queen is known to cherish its ideals of freedom and friendly cooperation between nations.

Her address to the Australian Parliament in 1954, shortly after her accession, remains an appropriate comment on her life: "It is my resolve that under God I shall not only rule but serve. This is not only the tradition of my family; it describes, I believe, the modern character of the British Crown." Inspired by her example, the house of Windsor has become a model of how a constitutional monarchy can flourish in a democratic and turbulent era.

Bibliography

Bradford, Sarah. *Elizabeth: A Biography of Britain's Queen*. New York: Riverhead Books, 1996.

Crawford, Marion. *The Little Princesses*. London: Cassell, 1950. Crawford was governess to Elizabeth and Margaret for more than twelve years and was in royal service for seventeen years. She horrified the royal family afterward by breaking the unwritten code of secrecy and writing books and articles about her experiences. The book, however, is interesting and authentic, presenting an attractive picture of the young princesses.

Keay, Douglas. *Elizabeth II: Portrait of a Monarch*. London: Century, 1991.

Lacey, Robert. *Majesty: Elizabeth II and the House of Windsor*. New York: Harcourt Brace Jovanovich, 1977. The best biography. Tasteful and sympathetic, balanced in judgment, yet avoids hagiography. Ranges over the great issues of the day with which the queen has been involved, and includes just enough trivia and gossip to keep the reader entertained.

Longford, Elizabeth. *The Queen: The Life of Elizabeth II*. New York: Alfred A. Knopf, 1983. Readable, anecdotal, sympathetic, but with a tendency toward hagiography. The queen declined to be interviewed, but many others who know her cooperated, including Princess Margaret and the Queen Mother. Gives insight into the role of the monarchy in the modern British constitution.

Morrow, Ann. *The Queen*. New York: William Morrow, 1983. Morrow was for many years the court correspondent of the London *Daily Telegraph*, and went on many royal tours. She gives a lively, anecdotal account of the queen's life at home and on official journeys abroad.

Packard, Jerrold M. *The Queen and Her Court: A Guide to the British Monarchy Today*. New York: Charles Scribner's Sons, 1981. Explains in detail how the British court functions. Discusses laws of succession, finances, titles and ranks, and protocol and procedures, and gives a brief history of the present royal family.

White, Ralph M., and Graham Fisher. *The Royal Family: A Personal Portrait*. New York: David McKay, 1969. White was Elizabeth's personal footman for eight years, and also served her father, George VI. His portrait of life in the royal household includes the daily duties of every member of the royal family and a host of other tiny details.

Ziegler, Philip. *Crown and People*. New York: Alfred A. Knopf, 1978. Using the archives of Mass Observation, the pioneer public opinion survey established in 1937, Ziegler gives a commentary on the attitude of the British public toward monarchy, from George V's jubilee in 1935 to Elizabeth's in 1977. Finds that nine out of ten people have consistently supported the monarchy.

Bryan Aubrey

FAHD

Born: 1922 or 1923; Riyadh, Arabia (later Saudi Arabia)

Continuing the reign of the al-Saud family, Fahd has led Saudi Arabia through two decades of development and has become a major force in the political and economic affairs of the Arab and Western worlds.

Early Life

King Fahd was born Fahd ibn Abd al-Aziz al Saud (Fahd son of Abd al-Aziz of the House of Saud). Sources vary as to his date of birth. His father was Abd al-Aziz ibn Abd al-Rahman (known as King Saud or Ibn Saud in the West), the first king of the modern state of Saudi Arabia. His mother was Hassa bint Ahmad al-Sudayri. Fahd is the eldest of seven sons by Saud and this wife.

Fahd belongs to the al-Saud family, which is one of the country's families of royal lineage. His six full brothers are Sultan (minister of defense), Nayif (minister of the interior), Ahmad (vice minister of the interior), Salman (governor of Riyadh), Turki (former vice minister of defense), and Abd al-Rahman. The seven brothers are known collectively as the Sudayri Seven in the West and as Al Fahd (house of Fahd) in Saudi Arabia. Fahd's father had forty-five sons, about half of whom are still alive, by various wives.

Fahd received the traditional schooling for princes at the Princes' School in Riyadh. In 1945, he accompanied his half-brother Faisal (later King Faisal) to San Francisco, California, for the convening of the United Nations. In 1953 he headed the Saudi delegation to the coronation of Queen Elizabeth II in England and in the same year also became the country's first minister of education. In 1962, under newly appointed King Faisal, Fahd was appointed minister of the interior. He also became second deputy prime minister and second in line for the kingship. In 1975, half-brother Khālid became king and appointed Fahd first deputy prime minister and crown prince (next in line for kingship). As Khālid's health deteriorated, Fahd gradually assumed more activity and became the major spokesperson for the country, gaining more experience in national and international affairs. He gained a reputation as an effective leader though he was also known as a playboy who enjoyed gambling and other such pursuits. When Khālid died in 1982, Fahd was named king and prime minister. His half-brother Abdallah was named first deputy prime minister and crown prince.

Life's Work

After becoming prime minister, Fahd strengthened ties with allied countries inside and outside the Arab world and became one of the most important figures in Arab affairs. He began courting the United States to build close economic and strategic relations. Saudi Arabia became a leading supplier of oil for the United States, and the United States provided Saudi Arabia with military training and equipment. Under a mutual defense assistance agreement, the United States also had a military training mission in the country. Relations between Saudi Arabia and the United States, and between Saudi Arabia and the Arab world, have at times been strained because of U.S. support of Israel.

Fahd wielded great influence in the Arab world, however, and became a key player in mediating conflicts. A well-known idea proposed by Fahd was the Fez Plan, also known as the Fahd Plan. This was a Middle East peace plan devised by then-crown prince Fahd in 1981. Its goal was the peaceful coexistence of all nations in the region and resolution of the Arab-Israeli conflict. The eight-point plan called for Arab recognition of Israel's legitimacy as a state and, in turn, Israel's withdrawal from the Arab areas it occupied in 1967. It also endorsed the founding of a Palestinian state. The plan was presented at the Arab Summit in Fez, Morocco, in November, 1981, and was accepted by the Palestine Liberation Organization (PLO) but rejected by other Arab groups and countries, some of whom refused to accept Israel's status as a state. Though not accepted, the Fahd Plan helped further Fahd's position as a mediator in Arab affairs. He reestablished various diplomatic relations between Saudi Arabia and other nations: Egypt in 1989 and Iran in 1991.

Fahd was a key player in the Iraq-Kuwait skirmish in 1990. In August of that year, tensions were high between Iraq and Kuwait. Iraq was angry because Kuwait refused to limit its oil production to meet Organization of Petroleum Exporting Countries (OPEC) standards, the oil was being taken from an area whose border had been disputed for centuries, and Kuwait was pressing Iraq for immediate debt repayments from the Iran-Iraq war. After several unproductive attempts at mediation, Iraq invaded Kuwait on August 2.

King Fahd, along with other rich oil countries who saw Iraqi leader Saddam Hussein as a threat, supported Kuwait. Because of his economic and political power in the Arab and Western worlds, the fate of the Kuwaiti invasion rested heavily on Fahd. However, he remained relatively quiet until the invasion. A few days after the attack, Fahd met with U.S. secretary of defense Dick Cheney, and it was decided that Fahd would invite U.S. troops to Saudi Arabia to demand Iraq's withdrawal from Kuwait. At the same time, Fahd tried to dispel the view of Saudi Arabia as an instrument of U.S. strategy by involving other countries in the defensive force against Iraq. About thirty countries offered aircraft, ships, and troops, led by the United States and Saudi Arabia. Attempts at United Nations (U.N.) mediation during this time were unsuccessful, and in January, 1991, a military plan called Operation Desert Storm began, with the goal of liberating Kuwait from Iraq. Fighting continued for over one month, resulting in casualties and much environmental damage, mostly from oil released by Iraqi bombers into the gulf. During the war, Fahd provided temporary headquarters for the Kuwaiti government.

After the liberation, Kuwait's leaders returned home, and foreign troops gradually withdrew from Saudi Arabia. Saudi Arabia returned thousands of Iraqi political prisoners of war and gave refuge to Iraqi political dissidents who had recently attempted an unsuccessful coup against Hussein. Fahd and seven other Arab leaders joined forces to create a peace-keeping coalition in the area.

The war resulted in great costs to Saudi Arabia: The costs of hosting troops as well as having to replace military supplies was high. Although a leading supplier of oil, the country had run a budget deficit for almost two decades by the late 1990's, when it faced a mounting external debt. Apart from war debt and great dependence on oil income, the country's treasury supports the royal family, which numbers in the tens of thousands, by means of salaries and benefits. These benefits may be given as quantities of oil to sell on the open market or large commissions from telecommunications deals, for example.

Critics also point to Fahd's personal spending habits as a drain on the economy: He is the second richest person in the world with an estimated personal wealth of twenty-five billion dollars. These critics believe that Fahd and the royal family see the country's wealth as synonymous with their own pocketbook. Furthermore, Saudi Arabia has at times offered aid and oil to needy countries in return for political alliance. Finally, Fahd has tried to keep standards of living high for Saudis, continuing the tradition begun in the 1970's of providing Saudi citizens with highly subsidized social services.

Fahd also faces continuing fluctuation of oil prices. In the early 1980's, changes in OPEC's policy led to declining prices. Fahd's oil policy made Saudi Arabia the "swing producer," or the producer that decreased production when there was less demand for oil and increased production when demand was high. The policy resulted in economic troubles and was abandoned in 1986. The Asian crisis of early 1998 affected world oil prices, as did the recession in Japan, one of Saudi Arabia's biggest oil customers. In addition, it must compete in the oil market against Mexico and Venezuela, two other large oil producers. Finally, the reintroduction of Iraq into OPEC in the late 1990's proved difficult for Saudi Arabia, as it accounted for much of the oil needed when Iraq was under an oil embargo.

Though Fahd is commonly known as a king, his official title is "custodian of the two holy mosques." This title bears great religious significance within the Arab world because it deems Fahd spiritual custodian of Mecca, the largest Muslim pilgrimage site. He plays a crucial role in all governmental decisions, and although Islamic law dictates that decisions must be made by consensus, Fahd ultimately maintains power over all branches of Saudi government and makes all final decisions. In 1992 Fahd introduced a new Basic Law system of governing based on Shari'ah law of the Wahhabi branch of Islam. The king and Council of Ministers hold executive power, while a Consultative Council of sixty members and a chairman, all appointed by Fahd, can make recommendations, although they have no legislative power.

Fahd's council is seen by some as a move toward democracy, though others maintain that anyone proposing ideas contrary to Fahd's risks severe repercussions. Fahd draws criticism from human rights groups such as Amnesty International for repressive policies limiting freedom of speech and religion; political prisoners and common law criminals have been tortured and forced to confess to crimes, resulting in flogging, amputation, imprisonment, beheading, or death by firing squad. Although a 1975 judicial law in Saudi Arabia guaranteed a free and public hearing by an impartial and independent tribunal, Fahd continued to wield ultimate authority over deciding individual cases as well as appointing and firing judges.

Summary

Fahd attempted to continue the process of modernization while retaining the strict religious laws of Saudi Arabia's sect of Islam, Wahhabi. His major influences were Islam, Arab nationalism, and the security of Saudi Arabia and surrounding countries. These influences often conflicted with each other: Fahd's alliance with the United States, for example, made anti-Israel Arab countries unhappy. Internally, conservative religious leaders and their followers disliked the influence of foreign business on Saudi culture and also complained of not having enough control of the moral and religious conduct of Saudi citizens. In addition, the middle-class elites were another force that, while not showing direct opposition for fear of punishment, posed some threat to Fahd. To balance these forces, Fahd tried to grant concessions to each group, keep social services high, and strike some sort of balance between forces to keep his brand of economic progress in motion. In keeping with the al-Saud leaders before him, Fahd created an international presence for himself, becoming a leader with strong economic and political power in the Arab and outside worlds. In the late 1990's, Fahd's health began deteriorating—he suffered from diabetes and a heart condition—and many of his duties were taken on by his appointed successor, Abdallah.

Bibliography

Abir, Mordechai. *Saudi Arabia: Government, Society, and the Gulf Crisis*. London: Routledge, 1993. The chapter on Fahd provides an excellent overview of Fahd's reign, focusing on the early to mid-1980's. Covers economic changes, the 1980's oil crisis, opposition to the king, and internal challenges.

__________. *Saudi Arabia in the Oil Era*. Boulder, Colo.: Westview Press, 1988. Discusses in detail the power struggles between Fahd and within the family, Fahd's relationship to Saudi Arabia's Wahhabi sect of Islam, issues of militant opposition, and the changing power of the middle-class elites.

Aburish, Said K. *The Rise, Corruption, and Coming Fall of the House of Saud*. New York: St. Martin's Press, 1996. A well-researched, critical account of the current state of Fahd and his reign, with emphasis on economic and foreign affairs. Contains many insider details about Fahd.

Chapin Metz, Helen, ed. *Saudi Arabia: A Country Study*. Lanham, Md.: Bernan Press, 1993. Perhaps the most exhaustive source of information on Saudi Arabia, this book features a chapter on Fahd and many references to him with respect to economics, religion, policy, defense, and media.

Lacey, Robert. *The Kingdom: Arabia and the House of Saud*. New York: Avon Books, 1983. Though not the most up-to-date source, this book's chapter on Fahd lends insight into the personal life and thinking of the man.

Minnesota Lawyers International Human Rights Committee. *Shame in the House of Saud—Contempt for Human Rights in the Kingdom of Saudi Arabia: A Report by the Minnesota Lawyers International Human Rights Committee*. Minneapolis, Minn.: The Committee, 1992. Details human rights abuses in Saudi Arabia and Fahd's role in judicial matters. Excellent source for understanding how the judicial system works and the king's power over the system.

Mortimer Snell

FAISAL

Born: c. 1905; Riyadh, Arabia
Died: March 25, 1975; Riyadh, Saudi Arabia

As crown prince and eventually as king of Saudi Arabia, Faisal led his country to its status as a world power through his participation in the Arab oil embargo and the formation of the United Arab Emirates and OPEC. He also advanced many domestic reforms.

Early Life

Faisal ibn Abdul Aziz was the third son of the founder of the modern Saudi state, Ibn Sa'ud. His mother was Tarfa, a descendant of the founder of the Wahhābi sect. Faisal was reared in the home of his maternal grandmother as a devout Muslim. He learned to recite from the Koran by age ten. His father made it clear that in addition to book learning, he wanted his son to learn the ways of the Bedouin. Faisal was trained to ride horseback, walk barefoot, eat modestly, and rise two hours before dawn. His personal life was unpretentious, even ascetic according to many who knew him. He prayed five times a day, as is customary among devout Muslims, and avoided smoking, drinking, and gambling. Faisal was known to possess an inner puritanism and great integrity. Known as a hard worker, he attended to business of state on a rigorous schedule.

Faisal studied Western technology and politics and spoke fluent English and French. Most of his own children (seven of eight) studied at the Hun School in Princeton, New Jersey, and then went on to colleges in the United States or the United Kingdom. Faisal became known in the 1930's as a poet whose works were published in Europe. Politically, he was often considered enigmatic, replying to questions in parables rather than straight answers. Faisal's explanation of such behavior to Yasir Arafat was: "If I say the wrong thing, or if I say the right thing in the wrong way, the Middle East will go up in flames."

Faisal married three times. His first wife bore him one son; his second, two sons; and his third, five sons. Faisal sent his third wife to Turkey in 1940, because of his displeasure with her feminism. Faisal was also believed to have had at least five daughters.

Life's Work

After the premature death of one of his elder brothers, Turki, in 1918, Faisal became an important component of his father's politics. Along with a group of advisers, the fourteen-year-old Faisal was sent to London in October and November, 1919, as part of the Central Arabian Mission. This was the first foreign trip by any member of the family. When he returned to Arabia, Faisal was put in charge of an operation against the Idrisi tribe of Asir, near Yemen. The Idrisi, allies of the British against the Turks, were trying to extend their power over the Aidh clan in the city of Abha. The Aidh appealed for help from Ibn Sa'ud. The Idrisis were pushed back by Faisal. He returned to the region again in 1924 to put down an uprising of the Aidh people fomented by Sherif Hussein, who had been ousted by the Saudis from the Hejaz. In 1925, Faisal commanded one of the armies of the besieged Jeddah. In 1926, his maneuvers led to the fall of Mecca and Medina to the Saudis. Saudi Arabia was officially proclaimed in 1932, although power over most of the kingdom had been secured by 1926. Faisal became viceroy of the Hejaz and secretary of state for foreign affairs. He lived most of his life in Mecca, rather than Riyadh, until his accession to the throne.

Faisal was a frequent traveler to the West. He visited Western Europe again in 1926 and the Soviet Union in 1932 and was apparently impressed by Soviet oil production in Baku and along the Caspian Sea. During March, 1934, a dispute broke out between Ibn Sa'ud and the rulers of Yemen, who belonged to a rival Zeidi sect of Islam. Faisal captured the port of Hodeida, but the Saudis withdrew quickly under pressure from the great powers. In 1939, Faisal was Saudi Arabia's representative to the Conference on Palestine in London. The conference ended with the Arabs refusing to sit in the same room with the Zionists. In 1943, Faisal made a state visit to the United States, accompanied by his younger brother Khālid. In 1945, Faisal represented Saudi Arabia at the San Francisco conference that created the United Nations. Although he objected to the great power veto, he approved the texture of the future direction of the United Nations.

After World War II, Faisal frequently spoke out against Zionism and later Israel. In 1948, he accused Zionists of practicing "Nazi-like tactics," a charge that would later be repeated in Middle East debates. He was visibly disturbed by the change in American policy during 1947 to support the partition of Palestine, so much so that he urged breaking relations with the United States. Faisal became crown prince and premier in 1953, when his father named Saud, another elder brother, as heir. Faisal was at first seen as apathetic to the changes that were going on within the Saudi government. He soon became the actual governor of the country because of Saud's propensity for sensual pleasure over interests of state. Faisal began processes of modernization, balancing respect for the integrity of religion against the demands of technology.

Faisal sought internal reform as a means of making Saudi Arabia survive. He introduced education for both sexes, prohibited the importation of slaves (1959), and emancipated the slaves within the country in 1962. The slavery question was part of his "ten-point reform program" of November, 1962. Traditionalists within the country objected to the reform, and informal forms of slavery continued. Other reforms of an administrative nature, however, including increased public investment, rational planning, protection of workers against unemployment, and establishment of provincial government, continued.

When Ibn Sa'ud died on November 8, 1953, some analysts believed that Faisal might take power. Any thought of this was dispelled quickly as Faisal swore allegiance to his brother Saud, who in turn made Faisal crown prince and heir apparent. In 1957, Faisal had a serious stomach problem in the form of a nonmalignant tumor, which was treated in the United States. He returned home in early 1958, after a stop in Cairo for discussions and reconciliation with President Gamal Abdel Nasser, to find most of the country's wealth dissipated by Saud's excesses. As a result, on March 22, 1958, power was handed over to Faisal, who immediately started to cut spending to alleviate a major crisis in Saudi finances. Faisal retired part of the debt, increased oil production, and limited payments to the king. Saud, however, reasserted his kingly powers in December, 1960, and Faisal resigned his posts. Liberal Saudis hoped that Saud's reassertion of power would lead to a constitutional monarchy.

The process of reconciliation of the two brothers, Saud and Faisal, began in August, 1961. After accommodation worked out by his other brothers, Faisal became prime minister in 1962. On March 28, 1964, Faisal took full power as viceroy, premier, and commander in chief of the armed forces. From March until November, Saud remained a figurehead and was formally deposed on November 2. Faisal appointed his brother Khālid as crown prince in March, 1965.

Nasser and Faisal drifted apart after the 1958 coup in Baghdad. Nasser was later seen as a menace to Saudi Arabia when he began interfering in the affairs of Yemen in 1962. On September 26, 1962, local revolutionaries backed by Nasser overthrew and killed Imam Mohammed al-Badr, the ruler of Yemen. The Saudis subsequently supported the royalists. The result was a near-war situation with Egypt over the Yemen question, with Faisal attempting to establish a closer relationship with the United States. There were Egyptian air raids on Saudi towns near Yemen during 1963. On August 24, 1965, Nasser and Faisal signed the Jeddah Agreement, which promised a withdrawal of Egyptian forces within a year. At the same time, Nasser tried to destabilize the Saudi government by supporting terrorist and dissident groups. The Yemen war wound down only after Nasser's 1967 defeat at the hands of Israel, and the remaining troops were withdrawn after his death in 1970.

Faisal generally had support from the more moderate Islamic states, such as Jordan and Iran, for solving regional disputes. Faisal reconciled himself with the new president of Egypt, Anwar Sadat, in June, 1971, during a week-long visit to Cairo. Sadat's strategy, of which the king approved, was to remove Soviet influence, seek rapprochement with the United States, and confront Israel if no peaceful solution could be found to the issue of Israeli-held territories. In 1971, Faisal established more cordial relations with the Baathist regime in Syria.

During 1971, Faisal sought to promote a confederation of Saudi Arabia, Kuwait, and the nine Persian Gulf emirates. This plan, however, was complicated by Saudi political claims on the territory of Kuwait and Abu Dhabi, as well as family disputes between the Saudis and rival families. Most of the remaining emirates were formed into a new state, the United Arab Emirates. Common frontiers were recognized in 1974.

During 1960, Faisal was one of the founders of the Organization of Petroleum Exporting Countries (OPEC). While oil shipments to the United States and the United Kingdom were halted for a short time in 1967, it was in 1973, at the time of the October War, that an oil boycott was used as a serious weapon in the Arab-Israeli conflict. Faisal, through his petroleum minister, Sheik Ahmed Zaki Yamani, also engineered participation-type agreements with the foreign oil companies that were active in the region. The General Agreement on Participation of October 5, 1972, gave a 25 percent share of operations to the Saudis. As oil revenues rose, Faisal committed the kingdom to spreading the wealth among its citizens through development of educational, technological, and modernization projects.

As king, Faisal's aim was to steer Saudi Arabia into a stable type of middling politics within the Arab world. He sought to please all ideologies, except Zionism and communism, both of which he detested. Faisal was a prime supporter of Egypt, Syria, Jordan, and the Palestine Liberation Organization (PLO) against Israel, providing Saudi funding for arms and other purposes. Al-Fatah, led by Yasir Arafat, was the prime beneficiary of Saudi money during the 1960's and early 1970's. At the same time, however, Faisal was fearful of the more radical elements within the PLO, such as the Popular Front for the Liberation of Palestine (PFLP), which sought to solve the problem of Palestine by replacing all traditional regimes in the region with socialist states. Faisal attended the Rabat Summit Conference in September, 1969, which recognized the PLO as the "sole, legitimate representative of the Palestinian people." In all the peace proposals that emerged during the early 1970's, Faisal indicated his special interest in returning the Muslim Holy Places in Jerusalem, the al-Aqsa Mosque and the Dome of the Rock, to Islamic control. This was, in his view, a Muslim obligation in addition to a political question.

From July through October, 1973, Faisal was one of the principal architects of the Arab oil embargo against the United States and other countries that supported Israel. Warnings of the changes in Faisal's policy began in early July when the king called for a more evenhanded approach by the United States to the Arab-Israeli conflict. Faisal encouraged the price rises, which led to a tenfold increase in Saudi oil revenues between 1973 and 1975. The international frenzy that surrounded the oil boycott and rise in prices made Saudi Arabia a major player in not only the Middle East but also world politics.

In November, 1973, Faisal met with U.S. secretary of state Henry Kissinger, an encounter that was tense on both sides, since Kissinger was a Jew. The discussions regarding Saudi and American interests were frank. Kissinger later described Faisal as a religious fanatic who had little interest in the Palestinians; he apparently failed to understand the level of Faisal's commitment to Arab causes. During 1974, however, a special relationship developed between the United States and Saudi Arabia, which saw future Crown Prince Fahd visit Washington and a return visit to Riyadh by

President Richard Nixon. American arms sales to Saudi Arabia increased.

Faisal possessed a great interest in the spread of Islam beyond the Arab world. To achieve this goal, he visited non-Arab Islamic countries in 1970, journeying to Afghanistan, Indonesia, and Malaysia, as well as Algeria. The wealth of Saudi Arabia was enhanced through rises in international oil prices during the 1970's, which, when connected with more sophisticated planning, secured a favorable financial situation for the Saudi government.

Faisal's reign ended abruptly on March 25, 1975, when he was shot and killed by a nephew who was described as deranged. The assassination took place on the anniversary of the birth of the prophet Muhammad. Faisal himself believed that events such as birth and death were preordained and permitted security to lapse. The assassin, who had been educated in the United States and had been involved in several drug-related incidents, was later beheaded. Faisal was succeeded by his brother, Khālid. Real power was subsequently exercised by Crown Prince Fahd.

Summary

King Faisal left a definite mark on the history of Saudi Arabia and may be regarded as having saved the kingdom from destruction from within. His deft handling of the politics surrounding his irresponsible brother Saud led him to become king with a broad consensus. On an international level, Faisal had been recognized early in his career as a responsible and capable diplomat well before he received the throne. While Faisal possessed a strong understanding of Saudi Arabia's problems, his personal outlook and puritanical attitudes led him to resist extreme change and compromise where religious principles were involved. In the long run, this may have been the correct policy, as it has been observed that developing countries with traditional regimes that undergo rapid modernization are often susceptible to revolution. In his later years, Faisal became more autocratic and fearful about the future of Saudi Arabia. Corruption in the form of bribes at the top became rampant, largely because of the lack of educated administrators in top positions. The Saudis felt continually threatened by nationalist and radical forces within the Arab nations.

Faisal was genuinely loved by his people, partly because of the way that he moved Saudi Arabia onto the world scene and partly because of his attempts to distribute wealth among the bulk of the population. In Western eyes, however, particularly as a result of his position on the Arab-Israeli conflict and his role in the 1973 oil embargo, Faisal was considered no friend of the West and, in fact, someone who had inflicted great harm. At the time of Faisal's death, many Saudis believed that the assassination may have been a plot by foreign intelligence services, American or Soviet, to replace him. In this respect, Faisal was an interesting figure, because he was disliked by both American and Soviet politicians. The shooting, however, was undoubtedly the work of a single man.

Bibliography

Aburish, Said K. *The Rise, Corruption, and Coming Fall of the House of Saud*. New York: St. Martin's Press, 1996.

Beiling, William A., ed. *King Faisal and the Modernization of Saudi Arabia*. London: Croom Helm, 1980. A useful book of articles that deals with various dimensions of the modernization process that Saudi Arabia underwent during the Faisal era.

De Gaury, Gerhard. *Faisal: King of Saudi Arabia*. London: Arthur Barker, 1966. An early but detailed biography of Faisal, useful more for his early life than later. It does not cover the critical period of the 1967 Arab-Israeli War through the Arab oil embargo of 1973.

Hart, Alan. *Arafat: Terrorist or Peacemaker?* London: Sidgwick and Jackson, 1985. Hart's biography of PLO leader Arafat contains significant information on Faisal's relationship with the Palestinians.

Holden, David, and Richard Johns. *The House of Saud*. New York: Holt, Rinehart and Winston, 1981. This is an exceptionally comprehensive and detailed history of the Saudi monarchy and state, with substantial details of the life and activities of Faisal. One of the authors, Holden, was murdered in Cairo in 1977.

Lacey, Peter. *The Kingdom: Arabia and the House of Saud*. New York: Avon Books, 1981. A sympathetic yet sensitive and sometimes critical account of the history of Saudi Arabia, with extensive information on Faisal, who was perhaps the most controversial Saudi ruler because of his preconceptions about Jews and his dualistic attitude toward the United States.

Mackey, Sandra. *The Saudis*. Boston: Houghton Mifflin, 1987. This is a journalistic account and memoir written by a *Christian Science Monitor* reporter who lived in Riyadh in various disguised professions other than journalist. The work contains many perceptive views of daily life in Saudi Arabia.

Powell, William. *Saudi Arabia and Its Royal Family*. Secaucus, N.J.: Lyle Stuart, 1982.

Sampson, Anthony. *The Seven Sisters*. New York: Viking Press, 1975. An account of the rise of the oil companies in the Middle East and their importance in global politics. The work includes significant information on the 1973 Arab oil embargo.

Stephen C. Feinstein

GERALD R. FORD

Born: July 14, 1913; Omaha, Nebraska

Becoming president after Richard M. Nixon's resignation in disgrace, Ford restored integrity to the office of president of the United States and a sense of decency and unity to the nation.

Early Life

Gerald Rudolph Ford, Jr., was born July 14, 1913, in Omaha, Nebraska, the son of Leslie and Dorothy King. When he was two, his parents divorced. His mother soon married Gerald R. Ford, Sr., who adopted her son as his own. Jerry Ford grew up in the conservative environment of Grand Rapids, Michigan, in a warm family in which the emphasis was on integrity and hard work. These traits helped Ford, Sr., to maintain his paint manufacturing business through the Depression of the 1930's, which must have been a lesson for his sons. A good student in high school, Jerry was also an exceptional athlete both in high school and at the University of Michigan, where he earned a B.A. degree in 1935 with a B average. He then enrolled in the Yale Law School, also working full-time at Yale as a football and boxing coach. He earned his law degree in 1941, also with a B average, despite his full-time work. By this time he was more than six feet tall, powerfully built, with ruggedly handsome features which allowed him to model sports clothing in Look magazine. As years passed, his full blond hair slowly receded from his forehead.

Admitted to the Michigan bar in 1941, Ford and a friend founded their own law firm. Ford specialized in labor cases, always important in Michigan. When the United States entered World War II, he entered the navy as an ensign, on April 20, 1942. After a year of giving aviation cadets physical training, he went first to gunnery school and then to the *Monterey*, a new, small aircraft carrier in the Pacific. He received the highest ratings possible for an officer while serving in ten battles and through one of the worst typhoons in history, his commander describing him as an "excellent leader . . . steady, reliable, resourceful." He was released from active duty early in 1946 with the rank of lieutenant commander and returned to Grand Rapids.

During the war, Gerald Ford, Sr., had become Republican Party chairman for Kent County, elected by reformers who wanted to clean up the local political machine. There, too, was Republican senator Arthur Vandenberg, a leader of the Senate's internationalists and a believer in a bipartisan foreign policy. Young Ford's military experience had convinced him that prewar isolationism had been disastrous. He also believed in honest government and ran for the local seat in the U.S. House of Representatives in 1948, campaigning hard and winning the Republican nomination with 62.2 percent of the vote, and the general election with 60.5 percent. The same year, on October 15, he married Elizabeth "Betty" Bloomer; they had three sons and a daughter.

Life's Work

Gerald Ford represented Michigan's Fifth District for more than twenty-four years, never winning less than 60.3 percent of the vote in general elections and usually winning far more. In the House, he served on the Central Intelligence Agency and Foreign Aid subcommittees of the Committee on Appropriations and was soon regarded as an expert on drafting defense budgets. Such budgets are infinitely complex; his expertise made him one of the significant members among the 435 representatives. Hoping to become Speaker of the House one day, he turned down chances to run for the Senate or for governor of Michigan.

With the election of Dwight D. Eisenhower to the presidency in 1952, there seemed a chance of an era of Republican control of government, but Eisenhower's popularity did not have enough impact on congressional elections. Apart from 1953-1955, Ford always served in a Congress with Democratic Party majorities. His record was one of enlightened conservatism with some liberal tendencies, supporting foreign aid and military appropriations, the reform of House rules, civil rights bills, and caution in government spending. In 1966, Americans for Democratic Action rated his voting record liberal 67 percent of the time. By the 1960's, he was making hundreds of speeches each year to raise money for Republican candidates.

He also began to have formal leadership roles, being elected chairman of the Republican caucus in the House in 1963 and serving on the Warren Commission to investigate the assassination

Gerald R. Ford *(Library of Congress)*

of President John F. Kennedy. In 1965, he was the House Republicans' choice to become the new minority leader, replacing the older, more conservative, and less effective Charles Halleck of Indiana. This meant that if the Republicans had won control of the House, Ford would have become the Speaker. As minority leader, Ford listened to the views of congressmen of all opinions, respected others' principles, accepted differences, and tried to avoid enforcing party loyalty on every vote. He helped to shape legislation in fields ranging from education to crime control. He became a national figure and a leading spokesman for his party on major issues. He continued to support civil rights legislation, tried to keep government spending down in President Lyndon B. Johnson's Great Society programs, and supported Johnson's actions in Vietnam.

Ford had first visited Vietnam in 1953, becoming a "hawk" in his support for American intervention. In the 1960's he urged more effort to win the war, not less, telling a group of Nixon campaign strategists in 1968 that the proper response to that year's Tet offensive was to Americanize the war. He later defended Nixon's bombing of Cambodia and served as a channel to the House for the views of the administration. Critics accused him of being an unthinking "hawk" who merely reacted patriotically rather than analyzing the problem.

His loyalty to an administration already haunted by the Watergate scandal probably made Ford Nixon's choice for vice president under the Twenty-fifth Amendment when Spiro T. Agnew, under indictment, resigned the office. Allegedly, Nixon's first choice had been John Connally, a recent convert from the Democratic Party, but the Texan was too controversial to win congressional confirmation. The Senate confirmed Ford by a vote of 92 to 3; the House, by 385 to 35. As vice president, Ford remained doggedly loyal to Nixon while the Watergate cover-up became ever more obvious, but with the House Judiciary Committee about to vote articles of impeachment, the president resigned. On August 9, 1974, Gerald Ford became president, an office he had never even contemplated seeking.

Ford's presidency was made difficult by the lack of time for a proper transition, such as occurs after an election, and by the presence in the White House of many Nixon men whose loyalty remained to their old leader. Some critics and even some friends asserted that Ford was not really in command of his administration. Moreover, he inherited an economy caught in the grip of "stagflation" (recession accompanied by inflation, supposedly an impossible combination) and the aftermath of both the Vietnam War and the Watergate scandal. Ford did have widespread public approval, but that dropped from 71 to 50 percent, according to the Gallup poll, after he gave Nixon a pardon. Yet, this was something that Ford believed he "must" do in mercy to Nixon and his family and to end a "nightmare" for the country. He also divided his own party by naming the often controversial Nelson Rockefeller, governor of New York for several terms, as vice president.

The Ford administration was unable to end either the recession or inflation, in part because of a difficult global economic situation and in part because of advisers' belief that "tight money" and a "slump" would soon end inflation. The slogan Whip Inflation Now (WIN) and presidential exhortations became subjects of ridicule. Ignorant of foreign policy matters, Ford was virtually the captive of the able but egocentric Henry A. Kissinger, who served as both secretary of state and presidential adviser. Ford's "summits" with Soviet leaders accomplished little but to associate the United States with the Helsinki Accords on human rights and Eastern Europe, which left that region under Soviet control without ending Soviet human rights violations. Worse, the South Vietnamese government fell to North Vietnam during Ford's time in office, its impending collapse leading him to ask Congress for massive aid for the Saigon regime, using such 1960's rhetoric as South Vietnam's "fighting for freedom." He was bothered by congressional refusal, apparently not grasping the Vietnam War's impact on the country, which included widespread distrust of Saigon.

In 1976, Ford was defeated for reelection by Democrat Jimmy Carter, former governor of Georgia. Probable reasons include Carter's imaginative and relentless campaigning, Ford's choice of the capable but then acid-tongued Senator Robert J. Dole of Kansas as his running mate, and voters' perception of Ford himself as a good man but an inept one. Retiring from the presidency on January 20, 1977, Ford wrote his memoirs. In 1981 he represented the United States at the funeral of assassinated Egyptian president Anwar Sadat, along with fellow former presidents Nixon and Carter, and later joined Carter in sponsoring conferences for serious discussion of major international issues.

Summary

Gerald Ford's presidency was that of a man of integrity, character, and modesty, in important contrast to his imperious predecessors of questionable honor, Lyndon B. Johnson and Richard M. Nixon. Johnson and Nixon had divided the nation; Ford sought to heal it and to some extent succeeded. Americans were relieved to find an honest man in the highest office and also to find that the "imperial presidency" of Johnson and Nixon was not permanent. Ford thus redressed the balance in American public life, making the president once more a part of the federal government rather than its tyrant. Voters also, however, perceived him as less than imaginative and forceful in a time of economic trouble; at such times Americans have customarily demanded strong leadership. Ford's speaking style, adapted to pretelevision party rallies, made him seem inarticulate, even fumbling, when exposed to the new medium nationwide and to comparison with anchormen and actors. The length of his presidency and his impact on the country were thus limited by his own characteristics.

Bibliography

Cannon, James M. *Time and Chance: Gerald Ford's Appointment with History*. New York: HarperCollins, 1994.

Ford, Gerald R. *A Time to Heal: The Autobiography of Gerald R. Ford*. New York: Harper and Row, 1979. Like the man himself, calm, unpretentious, straightforward; the honesty contrasts sharply with memoirs of Lyndon Johnson and Richard Nixon. Ford admits some mistakes but does not go beneath the surface to analyze his motives and decisions.

Greene, John Robert. *The Presidency of Gerald R. Ford*. Lawrence: University Press of Kansas, 1995.

Hartmann, Jerry. *Palace Politics: An Inside Account of the Ford Years*. New York: McGraw-Hill, 1980. Ford's chief of staff's revealing if egocentric account, emphasizing the interplay of personalities between the Ford men and the Nixon men. Blames the failures of Ford's presidency on the held-over Nixon staff members.

Hersey, John. *The President*. New York: Alfred A. Knopf, 1975. A brilliant writer's diary of a week in Ford's presidency, well illustrated, but useful mostly for personal glimpses of Ford interacting with others. Avoids policy issues.

Mollenhoff, Clark R. *The Man Who Pardoned Nixon*. New York: St. Martin's Press, 1976. An investigative reporter's harshly critical account, accusing Ford of deception behind his promises of openness. Includes attacks on Ford's appointments, policies, and use of executive privilege.

Reeves, Richard. *A Ford, Not a Lincoln*. New York: Harcourt Brace Jovanovich, 1975. The most informative critical book, analyzing Ford's personality and political techniques, including the best explanation of the Nixon pardon. Reeves finds Ford decent but ignorant, overdependent on his staff, not really a leader.

Sidey, Hugh. *Portrait of a President*. New York: Harper and Row, 1975. Evocative of the "feel" of the Ford presidency through pictures and tales of Ford's dealing with his staff and with congressmen, voters, and chiefs of state.

Vestal, Bud. *Jerry Ford, Up Close: An Investigative Biography*. New York: Coward, McCann and Geoghegan, 1974. A friendly account of Ford's early years, family, schooling, navy service, years in Congress, and the vice presidency. One can see emerging the kind of president Ford would be.

Robert W. Sellen

FRANCISCO FRANCO

Born: December 4, 1892; El Ferrol, Spain
Died: November 20, 1975; Madrid, Spain

Franco led the Nationalist forces to victory in the Spanish Civil War (1936-1939), established a stable, although authoritarian, government, kept Spain neutral in World War II, associated Spain with the West in the Cold War, and provided for a smooth transition of power upon his death.

Early Life

Francisco Franco was born Francisco Paulino Hermenegildo Teódulo Franco y Bahamonde on December 4, 1892, in El Ferrol, a town in northwestern Spain. His father, Nicolas Franco, was an officer in the Spanish Naval Administrative Corps. His mother, Pilar Bahamonde Franco, was a pious and conservative-minded Catholic woman from an upper-middle-class family. The youthful Franco obtained his elementary education in El Ferrol's Roman Catholic School of the Sacred Heart. He was destined to follow the family tradition and pursue a career in the navy, but fate intervened. Admissions to the Academia de Marina (Naval Academy) were temporarily halted in 1907. Thus Franco entered the Academia de Infantería (infantry academy) in Toledo. Three years later, he graduated and was commissioned a second lieutenant in the army at only seventeen years of age.

Franco began active duty in Spanish Morocco in 1912. The following year he was promoted to first lieutenant. It was the first of a rapid succession of promotions in a meteoric career that found him a national hero and brigadier general in 1926, at only thirty-three years of age. Franco's career was interrupted in 1931. In that year, King Alfonso XIII was ousted from power, and a republic was established. Franco, a monarchist, was sent into semiretirement as captain general of the Baleric Islands. With the coming to power of conservative forces, Franco was called back to Spain in 1933.

In an incident reminiscent of the early career of the great Napoleon I, Franco used military force to suppress a rising of Asturian miners in 1934. The miners rose in opposition to the newly elected conservative government. Franco's swift but brutal action won for him new recognition from the Right and the nickname the "Butcher" among leftists. He was promptly promoted to major general and appointed chief of the army's general staff. He immediately set about restoring discipline in the army, seriously weakened by the antimilitaristic policies of the early republican government.

The rightist National Bloc suffered defeat in the elections of February, 1936. A new leftist Popular Front government was formed. Social disorder and economic decline followed. Franco, himself, did not associate with any political faction. Believing that anarchy was the greatest threat to Spain, he urged the government to proclaim a state of emergency in order to assure law and order. The government, perhaps fearing Franco's popularity within the army, removed him from the general staff and sent him to the Canary Islands as commander and chief. Loyal to the state, Franco did not protest what amounted to a sentence of exile.

As the political situation in Spain deteriorated during the summer of 1936, an antigovernment plot began to take shape among right-wing army officers. Franco did not join the conspiracy until after the political situation worsened to the point at which anarchy threatened to engulf the nation. The assassination of Calvo Sotelo, a prominent rightist politician, in which government security forces were involved, pushed the army into open revolt. The revolt began in Morocco, on July 17, 1936, and soon spread to army garrisons in Spain.

On July 18, 1936, Franco broadcast from the Canary Islands a manifesto proclaiming the revolution. The following day, he flew to Morocco and assumed command of the army in revolt. Franco led the army in a march on Madrid, the capital. On October 1, 1936, as the army halted outside Madrid in preparation for the final assault, Franco was proclaimed head of state and generalissimo of the army by the Nationalists. It was the beginning of almost three years of bloody civil war in Spain.

Life's Work

The outcome of the civil war could not have been in doubt from the beginning. All the advantages were on the side of General Franco and the Nationalist forces. Whereas the Republican armed forces were a mélange of disunited, poorly led, and ill-equipped militiamen, Franco's armies were well trained and led by competent senior

Francisco Franco *(Library of Congress)*

and junior officers. Of significance was the aid given to the Nationalists by Germany and Italy and the lack of any decisive aid for the Republican forces. Franco appealed to Adolf Hitler and Benito Mussolini for military assistance. Both responded favorably, perhaps seeing an opportunity to test weapons, gain combat experience for officers, and expand their anticommunist Fascist alliance. Both sent aircraft, tanks, and artillery. Germany sent an air force of one hundred combat planes, known as the Condor Legion. Italy sent infantry soldiers.

The Republicans were never able to muster any meaningful international support. Both Great Britain and France, deeply divided at home and pursuing foreign policies of appeasement, announced that they favored nonintervention. They refused to supply either arms or soldiers. The only power that assisted the Republican forces was the Soviet Union. The Soviets sent military supplies, and the communist International, under Soviet leadership, recruited the International Brigades to serve in Spain. Yet Soviet support waned in 1938, as the war turned decisively in favor of the Nationalists.

By late fall, 1937, Franco's forces had captured the nation's key industrial area in the north. As Franco pressed the attack during the winter and spring of 1938, discipline among the Republican forces broke down. Divisions within the Republican government came to the forefront, and on March 7, 1939, civil war between communists and anticommunists broke out in the Republican capital of Madrid. On March 28, Madrid fell to the Nationalists. By April 1, the Nationalists under Franco's leadership had secured an unconditional victory in the civil war.

Perhaps resigning themselves to the inevitable, both France and Great Britain recognized Franco's government in February, 1939. The United States hesitated to do so until after the final victory in April. Franco gave evidence of the fact that his sympathies lay clearly with the Axis (Germany and Italy) when he hastened to sign the Anti-Comintern Pact in April, 1939. Within five months, Franco was shocked by Germany's unprovoked attack upon Catholic Poland.

It was during World War II that Franco proved himself a capable leader and diplomat. Spain was exhausted by the civil war. The economy was in ruins. What the nation needed most of all was peace. Franco skillfully resisted Hitler's persistent wooing. He declared Spain's neutrality in 1939, while remaining on friendly terms with the Axis, even allowing the Germans to recruit soldiers in Spain to serve on the Russian front as the Spanish Blue Division. He refused Hitler's demand to allow German military aircraft to fly through Spain to North Africa in 1941.

Although Franco never made any real commitments to the Axis, it is generally believed that, had the Axis been able to win a swift and decisive victory in the war, Franco would have joined them. To what extent his moral support for the Axis seemed to stem from sincere sympathies for German national socialism and Italian Fascism, or gratitude for their active aid during civil war, or, what is more likely, his consistent anticommunism is impossible to discern. In 1943, when Germany's defeat was imminent, Franco attempted to negotiate an end to the war in order to unite the West against what he regarded as the real enemy, the Soviet Union.

When World War II ended in 1945, the victorious Allies sought to isolate Spain and force the downfall of Franco's government. The United Nations refused to admit Spain to membership, regarding Franco as the last Fascist dictator. Responding to a U.N. General Assembly resolution of December 12, 1946, the United States withdrew its ambassador from Spain. Other nations followed the U.S. example and called their ambassadors home.

Franco responded to various efforts to foment revolution by issuing a Charter of Rights in July, 1945, strengthening his ties with the Roman Catholic church and diminishing the role of the Falange (Fascist) Party. Franco was able to use such external opposition to unite Spain behind his government. He seemed to sense all along that time was on his side. As the rift between the wartime Allies widened and the Cold War deepened, it was inevitable that the Western alliance would court the longtime foe of communism.

The restoration of Franco was not long in coming. By 1948, he was regarded once again as a leading anticommunist statesman. In November, 1950, the United States voted to end Spain's diplomatic isolation. American loans to the Spanish economy followed in 1950. In 1951, a new American ambassador arrived in Spain, and negotiations began for an American-Spanish defensive alliance. In 1953, the United States was granted four air and naval bases in Spain in exchange for significant economic aid. Throughout the 1950's, 1960's, and 1970's, the Spanish economy enjoyed increasing prosperity from its integration into the Western alliance system. In 1972, Spain signed a trade agreement with the Soviet Union.

Franco's skill as a leader was also evident in his domestic policies. His rule was always authoritarian and at times brutal. According to some sources, "tens of thousands" were executed during the civil war and the immediate years following its conclusion. Unlike most dictators, however, Franco took steps early in his rule to ensure that there would be a smooth transition of power upon his death. In 1947, an official referendum resulted in Spain's being designated as a monarchy with Franco as regent for life.

In 1969, Franco named Prince Juan Carlos, the eldest son of the pretender to the Spanish throne and grandson of its last king, Alfonso XIII, as his legal heir and future king of Spain. Franco, in failing health during the summer of 1974, delegated his constitutional powers to Juan Carlos. Franco, Europe's last Fascist dictator, died in Madrid on November 20, 1975.

Summary

It is not easy to assess the career of Francisco Franco. One's perspective is likely to be influenced by one's view of the Spanish Civil War and the fact that Franco's Nationalists were openly supported by Nazi Germany and Fascist Italy. Franco's association with, even admiration for, Hitler, one of history's most infamous characters, makes it difficult to evaluate him on his merits as a statesman.

Franco remained a monarchist throughout his life, a fact which is evidenced in his provision for the restoration of the monarchy upon his death. In so doing he attempted to see through his commitment to maintaining law and order in Spain. Franco, the young army officer, remained loyal to the republic until it became evident that the Republican government was leading Spain down the road to anarchy.

Franco's regime was never popular among the masses. Yet, after he successfully integrated Spain into the Western alliance, the economic prosperity that came to Spain as a result, and his efforts at liberalizing an admittedly authoritarian government, did much to eliminate all direct opposition to his rule. During the 1960's, he successfully courted the image of an elder statesman.

Outside Spain, Franco's image improved as the Cold War demonstrated the strategic importance of Spain to the Western alliance. Western leaders, who themselves fought a world war in alliance with the Soviet Union, preferred to forget Franco's flirtation with the Axis and remember instead his consistent anticommunism. Since Franco's death and the transfer of power to a constitutional monarchy, democratic institutions have continued to develop in Spain. Perhaps therein lies his legacy.

Bibliography

Amodia, José. *Franco's Political Legacy.* Totowa, N.J.: Rowman & Littlefield, 1977. This is a useful reference book and introduction to how Spain was governed under Franco. Amodia believes that Franco never intended to give Spain a democratic government.

Crozier, Brian. *Franco: A Biographical History.* Boston: Little, Brown, 1967. This is a balanced, well-researched, and very readable study by a journalist. Crozier assesses Franco's importance in world history, while discounting myths of both Right and Left.

Ellwood, Sheelagh M. *Franco.* London: Longman, 1993.

Hills, George. *Franco: The Man and His Nation.* New York: Macmillan, 1967. Intended for the general reader with some knowledge of modern Spain, Hills's biography of Franco is based on official army documents and conversations with Franco and associates of his from various stages of his career.

Jackson, Gabriel. *The Spanish Republic and the Civil War, 1931-1939.* Princeton, N.J.: Princeton University Press, 1965. Jackson attempts to view the civil war from within Spain. It is a clear and scholarly account, although sympathetic to the Republican cause.

Payne, Stanley G. *The Franco Regime: 1936-1975*. Madison: University of Wisconsin Press, 1987.

Preston, Paul. *Franco*. New York: Basic Books, 1994.

Thomas, Hugh. *The Spanish Civil War.* New York: Harper & Row, 1961, rev. ed. 1977. This is the classic history of the civil war in Spain. Thomas concentrates on the military, political, and diplomatic history of Spain from the 1920's to 1939. Extensively researched, it is the most balanced account.

Trythall, J. W. D. *El Caudillo: A Political Biography of Franco.* New York: McGraw-Hill, 1970. Packed with factual detail, yet easy to read, this work focuses on Franco's career from the origins of the civil war to 1969. It is respected as an objective account.

Paul R. Waibel

INDIRA GANDHI

Born: November 19, 1917; Allahabad, India
Died: October 31, 1984; Delhi, India

By serving as prime minister of India for almost two decades, Gandhi carried on a family tradition of political leadership, maintained her country's nonaligned status, and attempted to enact social reforms to eliminate poverty and hunger in her Third World democracy.

Early Life

On November 19, 1917, a daughter was born to Jawaharlal and Kamala Nehru in Allahabad, India. As she grew up in her grandfather Nehru's home, Indira Gandhi enjoyed the privileges of the Brahman class, but the home was periodically invaded by police and her parents and grandparents arrested for their involvement in the nationalist movement against British colonial power. Such a disruptive childhood probably explains the reserve and aloofness Indira exhibited throughout her life. It certainly explains the sporadic nature of her early education. Indira's father attempted to supplement that education by writing her letters from prison, later published as *Glimpses of World History* (1934-1935). Combined with knowledge gleaned from the conversations of relatives and their political friends such as Mohandas Gandhi, these history lessons served as the foundation for Indira's work.

After the death of her mother, whom she admired greatly, in 1936, Indira continued to study in England for a time. She believed that her father needed her at home, however, since he had been elected president of the Congress Party and was moving rapidly to the forefront of the Indian independence movement alongside Gandhi. Indira left Somerville College of Oxford without completing a degree and returned to India in 1941. While she had been away, she had fallen in love with Feroze Gandhi, a young, lower-class Indian nationalist. At first Nehru objected to the union but eventually accepted it, partially because Mohandas Gandhi, though not related to Feroze, had given the couple his blessing.

Indira Nehru became a Gandhi on March 26, 1942. Before the

end of the year, she and her husband were imprisoned for their defiance of British rule. When Indira was released early because of ill health, she returned to her father's home. Feroze joined her there, and soon their first son, Rajiv, was born. Two years later they had another son, Sanjay.

Like her mother, Indira did not allow domestic duties to impede her political support for a free India. When Nehru became prime minister, Indira decided her duty to her country and to her father were one and the same. Since her husband and father seemed incompatible, Indira chose to remain with her father as his hostess, while Feroze left to pursue his own political career. The couple did not divorce and appear to have been reconciled years later.

Life's Work

From August, 1947, when India gained its independence, to 1964, Indira Gandhi learned from her father how to be a successful politician in a democracy. She traveled abroad with him and met the world's leaders. As Nehru's daughter, she commanded respect which, in turn, gave her confidence in her own abilities. She became active in the Congress Party and served as president in 1959-1960.

When Nehru died in 1964, more important to Gandhi than her own tragic loss was the fate of Indian democracy, which seemed threatened by corruption and party dissension. Although Nehru had not intended for his daughter to succeed him, the new prime minister, Lal Bahadur Shastri, recognized her popularity and appointed her to the cabinet as minister of information and broadcasting. When Shastri died suddenly, Gandhi was asked to enter the contest for Congress Party leadership and thus the office of prime minister. Her subsequent election in 1966 portended several things: the continuation of a family tradition of leadership, world recognition of women's abilities, and the beginning of a new era in Indian politics.

When Gandhi took office, she did so with firmness and resolve. Although the party leadership expected to manipulate her, they could not. Those who questioned her leadership lost their political offices as she consolidated her power, primarily by projecting herself as "Mother Indira." As she explained in 1967,

> Scores of my family members are poverty-stricken and I have to look after them. Since they belong to different castes and creeds, they sometimes fight among themselves, and I have to intervene, especially to look after the weaker members of my family, so that the stronger ones do not take advantage of them.

This statement was the core of Gandhi's political philosophy. In Indian politics, a multitude of parties including extremists on the Left and Right, compete for power. The dissension between Hindus and Muslims and the communalism of many Indians adds to the volatility of Indian democracy. Gandhi saw herself and the Congress

Indira Gandhi *(Library of Congress)*

Party—whose ideals were secularism, socialism, and nonviolent, constitutional reform—as the center. Therefore, her political aim was what she called balance.

Maintaining political balance and thereby retaining democracy in a heterogeneous society was a difficult challenge that Gandhi accepted as a personal one. In 1969, when members of her own party leaned to the Right, simultaneously accusing her of leftist tendencies, she consolidated her political authority, won the backing of the masses, and effectively split her own party. When the right wing became more solidified in 1971 and adopted a campaign to "Remove Indira," she countered with the slogan "Remove Poverty," which became the reform program that gave her the greatest popular election mandate of her reign.

In the same year, she cautiously, briefly departed from the international corollary to her domestic policy—India's nonalignment position. Balance in foreign affairs meant neutrality. Yet when Pakistan made war against Bangladesh and millions of refugees poured into India, she shifted her priorities. Once the sympathies of the Indian people and most of the world favored the Bengali, she made her swift, decisive attack—one of the most substantial victories of her career.

The spell of victory faded, however, as the country woke to a devastating drought, spiraling poverty and hunger, and escalating corruption in business and political administration, including her own. Gandhi's quest for balance in the political arena and for a better life for her large, diverse family was failing. She tried to implement more economic reforms, but working-class strikes and violence grew. Gandhi's abhorrence of violent means to achieve change ironically led in 1975 to a proclamation of a state of emergency, under which she accrued dictatorial powers. Yet, she initially acted within the Indian constitutional system and with the support of the majority of Congress and capitalists at home and abroad. Nevertheless, charges against her mounted: thwarting her party's interests, repressing criticism, damaging the structure of the federal judiciary and bureaucracy, politicizing the army, trying to establish a family dynasty, and failing to solve the country's economic problems despite her broad powers.

In 1977, Gandhi decided to end the state of emergency and hold elections in which she confidently expected to receive a mandate to continue her reforms. Instead, the people revealed that they were unwilling to follow anyone—even Mother Indira—blindly and that democracy would prevail. The Congress Party was ousted from power along with Gandhi and her son Sanjay. For anyone but Gandhi that humiliating defeat would have meant the end of her career, but Gandhi could not abandon her family and her life's work. When the opposition proved to be corrupt and incompetent, Gandhi regained a seat in Parliament and ultimately was restored to the office of prime minister in 1980.

Gandhi's India was beset by more crises in 1980 than she had ever faced. Added to the persistent economic and political exigencies was a strong religious movement of the far Right. In 1982, Sikh fundamentalists occupied the Golden Temple, a Hindu shrine, and used it as a base for terrorist activities. Two years later, when she had amassed the support of the Indian people, Gandhi ordered the Indian army to take the shrine—a successful, though costly, assault. In October, 1984, Gandhi was assassinated by her own Sikh security guards, who, like many Indians, placed their religious beliefs above their personal loyalties.

Summary

Indira Gandhi's accomplishments during her years as India's prime minister were possible because the majority of the Indian people believed in her. Gandhi possessed two major attributes of effective leadership—courage and commitment. In the midst of numerous tragedies—the loss of parents, husband, and son Sanjay—Gandhi exhibited great personal courage. She courageously faced her enemies whether military or political, and determinedly fought her battles, even those she could not win. Not only Indians but also people all over the world admired this type of fortitude, especially in a woman.

Gandhi's commitment to India was never questioned, probably because she refused to be a political observer. Her commitment entailed positive action to achieve a better India—one without major social problems like poverty and hunger. Most of her fellow citizens believed that Gandhi could accomplish her goals and achieve unity through a balance of political perspectives, policies, and institutions. They viewed her international diplomacy as an overall success. Even when she leaned too far in one direction, they did not entirely lose their faith in her ability to restore balance, as evidenced by her 1980 reelection.

In the minds of the Indian people, despite her flaws, Gandhi was the mother of India. Her death did not alter that perception. Her dream for a united, prosperous, and peaceful India lived on in her son Rajiv, who became prime minister after his mother's assassination. Addressing his countrymen, Rajiv Gandhi remarked, the "foremost need now is to maintain our balance."

Bibliography

Ali, Tariq. *An Indian Dynasty: The Story of the Nehru-Gandhi Family.* New York: G. P. Putnam's Sons, 1985. This well-written family history begins with Nehru, devotes a significant portion to Gandhi, and includes information on her sons, Rajiv and Sanjay. Its primary flaw is lack of documentation.

Bhatia, Krishan. *Indira: A Biography of Prime Minister Gandhi.* New York: Praeger, 1974. This is a sympathetic biography for the general reader. The author is an Indian journalist who had been acquainted with the Nehru family since the 1940's. A bibliography and index are included.

Gandhi, Indira. *Indira Gandhi: Letters to an American Friend, 1950-1984.* Selected from correspondence with Dorothy Norman. San Diego: Harcourt Brace Jovanovich, 1985. Since Gandhi is most often studied as a political figure, these personal letters provide essential insights into the private woman. Photographs and commentary are also provided.

Gupte, Pranay. *Vengeance: India After the Assassination of Indira Gandhi.* New York: W. W. Norton, 1985. Written by an Indian journalist, this examination of contemporary India begins with a detailed account of Gandhi's assassination and the events surrounding her death. It provides firsthand information and analyzes Rajiv's leadership potential.

Jaykar, Pupul. *Indira Gandhi: A Biography.* New York: Viking, 1993.

Lamb, Beatrice Pitney. *The Nehrus of India.* New York: Macmillan, 1967. This collective biography provides information on Gandhi's early life and her years spent as "First Lady" for her father, during which period she developed her political abilities. It is written for juveniles and has notes and a suggested reading list.

Malhotra, Inder. *Indira Gandhi: A Personal and Political Biography.* Boston: Northeastern University Press, 1991.

Masani, Zareer. *Indira Gandhi: A Biography.* New York: Thomas Y. Crowell, 1976. The author's insight into Gandhi's life and Indian politics comes from extensive research using primary and secondary sources. The last chapter, written during the state of emergency, predicts her fall from power. Notes and photographs are included.

Moraes, Dom. *Indira Gandhi.* Boston: Little, Brown, 1980. The strength and weakness of this biography is that it is based primarily on personal interviews and the author's changing relationship with Gandhi. Although he criticizes her flaws, he remains a sympathetic admirer. Photographs and an index are provided.

Vasudev, Uma. *Indira Gandhi: Revolution in Restraint.* Delhi, India: Vikas, 1974. This thoroughly researched biography synthesizes the private and public aspects of Gandhi's life within the context of political history. Unfortunately for the reader, it ends with the early 1970's. Documentation includes notes, an index, a glossary, and fifty-six pages of photographs.

Alice F. Taylor

MOHANDAS GANDHI

Born: October 2, 1869; Porbandar, India
Died: January 30, 1948; New Delhi, India

Gandhi, as one of the main figures of the Indian independence movement, pioneered the use of nonviolent protest; the strategies and tactics he employed have been adapted by many groups struggling to achieve justice, including the Civil Rights movement in the United States. Gandhi also worked to reform traditional Indian society, speaking out for women's rights and for the group known as the untouchables.

Early Life

Mohandas Karamchand Gandhi was the fourth child of the prime minister of the tiny city-state of Porbandar, about halfway between the major cities of Bombay and Karachi. Gandhi received the normal education for a boy of his family's position. His family married him at age thirteen to a girl from another locally important family; Kasturba would remain his wife until her death in 1944. After the death of Gandhi's father in 1885, the extended family decided that Mohandas should go to Great Britain and study law, with the hope that he might enter the civil service of local Indian princes.

Gandhi finally left for Great Britain in 1888. He did not study hard and apparently spent much of his time trying to maintain a strict vegetarian diet (the start of a lifetime interest in diet) and studying comparative religion, including his first serious research into his own Hindu culture.

Gandhi returned to India in 1891 to open a legal practice. For a variety of reasons, especially his own shyness and diffidence, the practice was a failure, first in his native region and then in Bombay. In 1893, a case required him to go to South Africa. He ended up staying, with only a few short trips back to India and Great Britain, until 1914.

On the train from the port to Pretoria his first evening in South Africa, Gandhi was literally kicked off for trying to sit in the first-class compartment when a white passenger objected to his presence. This event catalyzed Gandhi's energies. A week later, overcoming his shyness, he began speaking at meetings, and then started organizing his own. At first, his goal was to protect Indian workers and traders in South Africa and then to expand their rights. Because there were Indians from all over Britain's Indian empire working together in South Africa, news of Gandhi's work was sent back throughout the subcontinent. When he left in 1914, he was already one of the best-known Indians alive.

Mohandas Gandhi (left) spinning cotton at a political rally in 1925. *(Library of Congress)*

Life's Work

When Gandhi returned to India to stay, he found himself already being proclaimed a mahatma, a term in the Hindu religion meaning "great soul"; some went even further, believing him to be a reincarnation of Vishnu. More practically, Gandhi became one of the leaders of the Indian independence movement. From the 1920's through the early 1930's, he was the movement's leading planner, and throughout the interwar period he served as a bridge between rival religious factions, the various Hindu castes, the growing Westernized upper-middle class, and the masses working in the fields.

While in South Africa, Gandhi had developed his philosophy of nonviolent protest, which he called *satyagraha* (soul force). In India, he brought that vision to fruition. At times he might organize a section of the country to hold a general work stoppage or bring the entire Indian empire to a halt as he fasted for an end to the terrible conditions of the so-called untouchables, rioting, or other problems besetting the country as a whole. In short, Gandhi evolved from an important political and cultural leader to the conscience of the Indian empire and all of its people.

It was Gandhi's belief that *satyagraha* was the only way to win independence from Britain honorably, for if a free India was born in violence, it might never recover. Therefore, Gandhi had to spend almost as much time establishing, and then maintaining, as strict a control over his own people as was possible as he did in winning independence from the British. The first was harder than the second, since the British could use the internal quarrels of the various Indian groups as an excuse to keep ultimate power in their own hands, no matter what reforms they might offer. Therefore, as the 1930's ended, the independence movement had not really come much closer to its goal after two decades of struggle. Gandhi had staged impressive demonstrations such as the march to protest the salt tax in March and April of 1930, started numerous publications, written scores of articles, unified the various factions, and won concessions from the British after some bloody riots and reprisals, but India was not independent.

Gandhi also had trouble keeping control of day-to-day events, in part because of the sheer scope of the unrest affecting the huge subcontinent, but also because of the amount of time he spent in prison. Between 1922 and 1944, Gandhi spent nearly six years (2,089 days) in jail, mostly during the 1930's and in the latter part of World War II.

World War II would prove decisive for the fate of India. While Gandhi and his followers preferred the British and the Americans to the Nazis and Japanese, for the most part they refused to cooperate with the Allies unless India was given its independence. Gandhi and many of his closest followers spent most of the war in custody. Mohammed Ali Jinnah, the leader of the Moslem League and a former follower of Gandhi, used the war to make the Moslem

League independent of Gandhi and the Indian National Congress (the umbrella organization for most of the pro-independence organizations). By backing the Allies when most Indian groups refused, Jinnah was setting the stage to proclaim a separate Muslim state whenever India was granted independence.

When World War II was over, the Labour Party under Clement Attlee came to power in Great Britain. One of their goals was to establish the Indian Empire as an independent dominion within the British Commonwealth. The divisions that Gandhi had managed to unite within the Indian independence movement now came forward as the probability of independence came closer.

Gandhi was committed to a united India, but the Muslims, the rulers of most of Northern India before the British came but an overall minority, were inspired by Jinnah to seek a separate country for those areas with a Muslim majority. Although the British offered a plan for a confederated India that might have satisfied Muslim demands while maintaining a united Indian government, few Indian leaders of either side, including Gandhi, were willing to trust the British plan in 1946. The result was an India divided on religious lines, India and Pakistan becoming independent dominions in 1947.

When a divided India became inevitable, Gandhi basically kept silent on the plan, devoting the rest of his life to quelling the religious unrest which welled up in 1947 and 1948, as Muslim and non-Muslims (many of them unwillingly) left their homes and made their way to areas where they would be in the majority. Hundreds of thousands of people died from violence, disease, and malnutrition during the riots and forced marches and in the relocation camps. Gandhi made his way to some of the worst scenes of conflict, pleading, arguing, and fasting to bring the violence to an end. Although he nearly died from the fasting and was often threatened by mobs, he was finally able to bring the worst of the violence to an end by the beginning of 1948. Religious and ethnic tensions remained, but there was, in general, peace between Hindus, Sikhs, Muslims, and the other groups.

On January 30, 1948, Nathuram Godse, a thirty-five-year-old high-caste Hindu newspaper editor and a refugee from Muslim violence, bowed in respect before Gandhi, who was on his way to a prayer meeting, and shot him three times, killing him almost instantly. This was the only way Godse and his fellow conspirators could deal with Gandhi's message of peace for all Indians.

Summary

Mohandas Gandhi was not fully successful in his work in South Africa. When he left, Indians were treated as second-class citizens, looked down on by the whites who controlled the country. They were, however, treated as citizens with some rights, a vast improvement over the system that had been slowly taking hold since the late 1880's, which was becoming tantamount to slavery. More important, Gandhi had found his life's work and had won respect for himself and his ideals of nonviolence.

Gandhi also failed in much of what he tried to accomplish for India. While he was able to modify the caste system and many of the social taboos which went with it, they were still in effect in much of the country as the twentieth century drew to a close. While he succeeded in freeing India from British rule, colonial India was split between India and Pakistan (as Pakistan itself was later split between Pakistan and Bangladesh), and religious and class strife is still rampant throughout the former Indian empire. The small, self-sufficient, self-governing villages that Gandhi hoped would be the center of Indian cultural and political life remain largely a dream in an India troubled by chronic poverty and political unrest. Gandhi nevertheless succeeded in giving the people of the subcontinent an example of the best their culture had to offer, in promoting an ideal that they—and people throughout the world—could strive to achieve.

Bibliography

Datta, Dhirendra Mohan. *The Philosophy of Mahatma Gandhi.* Madison: University of Wisconsin Press, 1953. Datta traces Gandhi's basic philosophical ideals to their Indian and European roots in traditional philosophy and religion. He accomplishes this concisely and in easily understood terms. Datta was one of the many students who followed Gandhi's call to go and teach in the villages during the early 1920's before returning to higher academics and so was able to study the practical results of Gandhi's message as well as the abstract principles.

Easwaran, Eknath. *Gandhi the Man: The Story of His Transformation*. Tomales, Calif.: Nilgiri Press, 1997.

Fischer, Louis. *Gandhi: His Life and Message for the World.* New York: New American Library, 1954. A concise, readily available biography, written by a foreign correspondent who interviewed Gandhi twice in the 1940's. Fischer presents not only a full view of Gandhi's life, but the early myths and criticisms as well.

Gandhi, Mohandas K. *All Men Are Brothers: Life and Thoughts of Mahatma Gandhi as Told in His Own Words.* Paris: UNESCO, 1958. This selection of Gandhi's writings and speeches covers topics in politics, economics, education, and religion.

_________. *An Autobiography.* Translated by Mahadev Desai. Boston: Beacon Press, 1957. Written by Gandhi during the late 1920's in his native language, Gujarati, this autobiography was quickly translated into English to reach a wider audience in India as well as the British Empire. Much of the work concerns Gandhi's years in South Africa, although earlier recollections and the first years after his return to India are covered as well.

_________. *Gandhi's Letters to a Disciple.* London: Victor Gollancz, 1950. Madeleine Slade, known as Mira, the daughter of a British admiral, became one of Gandhi's most famous disciples in the early 1920's. In effect, Mira became a spiritual daughter of Gandhi, whom she called *Bapu* (father), like most of the common people in India. When she and Gandhi were separated, usually when Gandhi was traveling or in prison, they would exchange letters. The letters rarely touch on the major political and social battles of the times; instead, they focus on everyday events in the lives of the people surrounding Gandhi.

Huttenback, Robert A. *Gandhi in South Africa.* Ithaca, N.Y.: Cornell University Press, 1971. This is a detailed monograph on Gandhi's years in South Africa. Huttenback traces the origins of the problems Gandhi faced and details the solutions, and attempted solutions, for which Gandhi worked.

Iyer, Raghavan. *The Moral and Political Thought of Mahatma Gandhi.* New York: Oxford University Press, 1973. In this highly detailed work, Raghavan explores the conceptual foundations of Gandhi's religious, moral, and political ideologies and their interconnections. He is also interested in showing how much deeper Gandhi's philosophy was than the applications of most of his followers (especially his political followers) might suggest.

Nehru, Jawaharlal. *Nehru on Gandhi.* New York: John Day, 1948. Nehru became Gandhi's political heir in the late 1930's, even though the two men often differed on means to achieve Indian independence. Nehru became the first leader of independent India, and, with his daughter and grandson, Indira and Rajiv Gandhi, established a politically powerful dynasty over the next generations. This work, which contains Nehru's opinions and writings on his mentor, drawn from a wide range of sources, helps to show the connections between two of the most powerful voices of twentieth century India.

Parekh, Bhiku. *Gandhi*. New York: Oxford University Press, 1997.

Prasad, Bimal. *Gandhi, Nehru, and J. P.: Studies in Leadership.* Delhi: Chanakya, 1985. Prasad's work studies political and social leaders in three successive generations, starting with Gandhi and ending with Jayaprakash Narayan (popularly known as J. P., 1902-1979). The author traces Gandhi's influences on the other two and the ways in which they interpreted, changed, and added to Gandhi's message over time. This study provides a valuable perspective on Gandhi's legacy.

Severance, John B. *Gandhi: Great Soul*. New York: Clarion Books, 1997.

Terrance L. Lewis

CHARLES DE GAULLE

Born: November 22, 1890; Lille, France
Died: November 9, 1970; Colombey-les-Deux-Églises, France

Beginning from exile in 1940, de Gaulle became the leader of France against Germany in World War II. In 1958, he was recalled to power, created the Fifth French Republic, extricated France from Algeria and the rest of its overseas empire, and led France into a more independent foreign policy in Europe and the world.

Early Life

Charles André Joseph Marie de Gaulle was born in the northern French city of Lille on November 22, 1890. Over several centuries, his family had played many roles in the history of France, and his father, Henri, was wounded during the French defeat in the Franco-Prussian War. Henri later turned to teaching and instilled in his children, including Charles, the second child, a deep love for France. The de Gaulle household was traditional, conservative, patriotic, and Catholic.

Choosing a military career, de Gaulle enlisted in the French army in 1909. The following year he entered the prestigious military school of Saint-Cyr, where his great height—six feet, five inches—and large nose led to the nicknames of the "Great Asparagus" and "Cyrano." In 1912, he was assigned to an infantry regiment led by Philippe Pétain, a French hero in World War I who turned collaborator with Germany in World War II. During World War I, de Gaulle was wounded three times, captured by the Germans on the third occasion, and imprisoned for the duration of the war.

During the 1920's, while still a junior officer, de Gaulle developed his philosophy of military leadership, arguing that the successful leader must personify national grandeur and increase his power and prestige by distancing himself from the people. In 1932, he presaged his own later leadership in *Le Fil de l'épée* (*The Edge of the Sword*, 1960). In addition, de Gaulle disagreed with the prevailing military philosophy of the French high command, whose static defense posture culminated in the Maginot Line. De Gaulle, on the other hand, preached the virtues of the tank, with its more mobile possibilities. To publicize his ideas, in 1934 he wrote *Vers l'armée de métier* (*The Army of the Future*, 1940). Not the first nor necessarily the most important prophet of the tank—there were others in Germany and Great Britain—he remained an outspoken advocate of its use and a consistent critic of the army's policies. His influence was minimal, however, in part because of his own austerity and aloofness but more so because of the defeatism, apathy, and lack of vision of the leading politicians and generals of the Third French Republic.

Life's Work

It was only in the spring of 1940, with Germany's invasion of France, that de Gaulle was allowed to put into practice his theories of mobile defense. Yet his small successes proved insufficient, and the Third Republic crumbled. A minor member of the cabinet after having finally received the rank of general, de Gaulle alone among the government chose to flee France rather than capitulate to the Germans. After his escape to London, he addressed France over the British Broadcasting Company; his first speech was short and probably few heard him, but his message—resistance to Germany must continue—was the one he reiterated throughout the war. De Gaulle had supreme confidence in himself, but his emergence as the military and political leader of the French resistance was also the result of the lack of alternatives—the leading politicians and military figures remained loyal to the collaborationist regime of Marshal Philippe Pétain, de Gaulle's former mentor.

The position of the obscure general was precarious. Few in France or elsewhere had heard of de Gaulle; he had no resources and depended upon the generosity and the decisions of the British government. Winston S. Churchill admired de Gaulle, and the two men agreed on the necessity for continued French resistance, but their relationship remained difficult and often stormy. De Gaulle was a formidable figure, personally and physically, and his single goal was to restore what he envisioned as France's former glory and power. This restoration meant the defeat of Germany, but it also caused de Gaulle to frequently distrust the means and ends of Churchill's Great Britain and Franklin D. Roosevelt's United States. Having nothing, de Gaulle believed that he must demand everything for France. He was not an easy cross for Churchill to bear.

Charles de Gaulle *(Library of Congress)*

In addition to resistance to the German occupation within France, de Gaulle relied upon the resources and backing of the French overseas empire, sometimes to the opposition and chagrin of the British and American governments. Roosevelt particularly disliked the difficult Frenchman, and he underestimated de Gaulle throughout the war, treating him with petty disdain. Even as late as the Allied invasion of France in June, 1944, Roosevelt was still unwilling to recognize de Gaulle fully. Churchill was far more supportive, but Great Britain's need for American support caused him to defer to Roosevelt. De Gaulle never forgot the seeming inferiority accorded to himself and France by his American and British allies.

Perhaps the greatest moment for de Gaulle was the triumphal procession down Paris' Champs-Élysées to Notre Dame Cathedral on August 26, 1944. The Germans had withdrawn and the Allies, including French troops, had taken over the city. It was both de Gaulle's personal vindication and that of his country. He quickly moved to incorporate the French resistance forces into the regular French army, in part because he feared the revolutionary aims of communists within the resistance movement. In spite of French participation in the final battles of World War II, de Gaulle was not invited to attend the crucial Yalta Conference. Still, partially because of Churchill's influence, France was given an occupation zone in Germany at the war's end.

De Gaulle long believed that the weakness of the Third Republic was the predominance of politicians and parties and the excessive power of the national assembly. France needed a strong executive. In the months after the war concluded, de Gaulle, as head of the interim government, found himself frustrated by the revival of the claims of the assembly and the rivalries among the politicians. Fearing that the evils of the Third Republic had returned, in January, 1946, he suddenly resigned. The following year, he and his supporters formed the Rassemblement du Peuple Français (Rally of the French People), an overtly nationalistic and ostensibly antiparty movement, but, despite considerable initial success, after the creation of the Fourth Republic, it dwindled away. Critics claimed that de Gaulle had become too much the demagogue and was a potential dictator. Finally, in 1953 he retired to his country home at Colombey-les-Deux-Églises and in three volumes wrote his account of World War II.

Although he had withdrawn from public life, de Gaulle continued to believe that the Fourth Republic with its many governments and changing premiers would ultimately fail. The civil war in Algeria brought him back to power. Algeria had been a part of France since the mid-nineteenth century, but anticolonial and nationalistic elements demanded independence, and violence broke out in 1954. The military was committed to French rule, and the politicians of the Fourth Republic unenthusiastically followed the lead of the generals. By May 1958, it seemed likely that a military coup would result. De Gaulle appeared to be the only alternative, and he thus became the last premier of the Fourth Republic.

He received extraordinary powers. When the assembly once again reassembled the Fourth Republic was no more. A new constitution was written under de Gaulle's guidance, and he became the first president of the Fifth Republic. In it, the balance of power was shifted from the national assembly to the president, an increase in executive authority de Gaulle had long advocated. As always he remained concerned with restoring the power and the glory of France. To do so he came to the conclusion that the vast French colonial empire must be given the opportunity for more freedom. He had hoped that the colonies would accept some sort of community dominated by France, but, when most of them preferred independence, de Gaulle, and France, settled for influence instead of authority. The Algerian affair took longer to resolve. European settlers and the French army were adamantly opposed to Algerian independence; rumors of military coups continued, and there were several assassination attempts against de Gaulle. It was not until 1962 that de Gaulle and France were able to escape from the North African morass.

Although de Gaulle was one of the major public figures of the twentieth century, he was a very private man. His personal life was kept rigorously separate from his public career. He married Yvonne Vendroux in 1921, and she, always supportive of her husband, generally remained out of public view. They had three children. De Gaulle had few friendships outside his family and was loath to become too familiar with either his colleagues or his subordinates. His sense of humor, such as it was, was dry and satirical.

He remained more concerned with the image and position of France in the world than domestic life in France itself. Toward the end of the 1960's, the economy stagnated. Student unrest and labor demands led to demonstrations and violence in the spring of 1968. With some difficulty, de Gaulle and his regime survived. He resigned the following year, however, after the voters turned down a minor constitutional change that he had proposed. He retired once again to his country home, where he died shortly before his eightieth birthday.

Summary

It was said that Charles de Gaulle loved France but not the French. He distrusted most politicians, feared the excesses and irresponsibility of most parliamentary bodies, and was consistent in demanding a strong executive. Nevertheless, if he had doubts in the efficacy of many democratic institutions and practices, he himself was a superb communicator in a democratic age. A writer of considerable ability and accomplishment, he could also be a masterful public speaker. In particular, de Gaulle was a brilliant television performer, both in his news conferences and in more formal speeches. His physical appearance somehow conveyed grandeur, commitment, and ability.

De Gaulle's most controversial legacy was his foreign policy. Although distrustful of French communists, he was generally most difficult in his relations with his Western allies. After returning to power in 1958, he supported France's development of nuclear weapons. A strong nationalist, he only reluctantly participated in any political integration of the European Common Market: De Gaulle preferred a federal system in which the nations of Europe continued to maintain their unique identities. At the height of the Cold War, he opposed the continuing division of the world into two armed camps and withdrew France from the North Atlantic Treaty Organization. De Gaulle also vetoed Britain's application to join the common market: He argued that the British government was too subject to U.S. policies. He publicly objected to American involvement in Vietnam and gave diplomatic recognition to the communist regime in China. He wanted a Europe for the Europeans, even Germans, and, within that Europe, France was to play its traditional major role. His goals appeared quixotic at the time, but he had a consistent vision of a revived Europe, no longer dominated by the superpowers and their Cold War concerns.

Bibliography

Cogan, Charles G. *Charles de Gaulle: A Brief Biography with Documents*. Boston: Bedford Books, 1996.

Cook, Don. *Charles de Gaulle, a Biography.* New York: G. P. Putnam's Sons, 1983. Cook, a journalist who covered French politics for many years, has written a readable biography of de Gaulle. An American, the author particularly stresses the often difficult relations between de Gaulle and American presidents from Franklin Roosevelt to Richard Nixon.

Gough, Hugh, and John Home, eds. *De Gaulle and Twentieth Century France*. London: Edward Arnold, 1994.

Horne, Alistair. *A Savage War of Peace.* New York: The Viking Press, 1978. Horne, a British historian, writes brilliantly about the French-Algerian civil war, the conflict that brought de Gaulle back to power in 1958 and continued to be his major concern until it was finally resolved in 1962.

Kersaudy, François. *Churchill and De Gaulle.* New York: Atheneum, 1982. The author presents in a comprehensive manner and readable style the fascinating love-hate relationship between two of the major political figures of the twentieth century. Both were representative of their countries but both were also unique personalities.

Lacouture, Jean. *De Gaulle*. 2 vols. Translated by Patrick O'Brian (vol. 1) and Alan Sheridan (vol. 2). New York: Simon and Schuster, 1991-1992.

Ledwidge, Bernard. *DeGaulle.* New York: St. Martin's Press, 1982. The author, a British diplomat, served in Paris during the latter years of de Gaulle's last administration. Sympathetic to de Gaulle as a statesman and politician, Ledwidge is particularly interested in de Gaulle's foreign policies.

Shennan, Andrew. *De Gaulle*. London: Longman, 1993.

Werth, Alexander. *De Gaulle.* New York: Simon & Schuster, 1966. Subtitled a political biography, this volume was written before de Gaulle's final retirement in 1969. Nevertheless, Werth, a historian of modern French history, has many useful insights about the persona and accomplishments of de Gaulle.

Eugene S. Larson

MIKHAIL GORBACHEV

Born: March 2, 1931; Privolnoye, Soviet Union

Gorbachev, as general secretary of the Communist Party and also president of the Soviet Union, made efforts to implement major improvements in the economy and society, underscoring his genuine belief in the need for long-overdue reforms. The revisions and adjustments in Soviet foreign policy that occurred during the Gorbachev era are noteworthy.

Early Life

Mikhail Sergeyevich Gorbachev was born on March 2, 1931, in the village of Privolnoye, in the Stavropol Territory of the Soviet Union. This agricultural region, located north of the Caucasus Mountains, lies between the Black and Caspian Seas. Gorbachev came from several generations of farmers. He was baptized in the Orthodox Church but is not a Christian. During World War II, the area where he lived was occupied by Nazi military forces. Following the war, he continued his education and worked summers (1946-1950) in local farming. He was awarded the Order of the Red Banner of Labor (1949) at age eighteen and graduated second in his high school class.

Gorbachev entered Moscow State University in the fall of 1950, graduating with a degree in law in 1955. During this period, he joined the Communist Party (1952) and married Raisa Maximovna Titorenko (1954). Following graduation, he returned to the Stavropol area where he spent the next twenty-three years in Communist Party service.

Gorbachev's initial responsibilities were in the Komsomol (Young Communist League). He became first secretary of the Stavropol City Komsomol organization in 1956, holding this position until 1958. Between 1958 and 1962, he worked in the Komsomol Committee for the Stavropol Territory (Krai) and eventually became first secretary of the group. By 1962, he was responsible for choosing party members for promotion, and also headed a production board supervising collective and state farms. In 1963, Gorbachev became head of the agricultural department for the entire Stavropol region.

In 1966, Gorbachev moved into full-time party administration as first secretary of the Stavropol City Communist Party Committee. Two years later, in August, 1968, he became second secretary of the Stavropol Territory Communist Party Committee. In April, 1970, at age thirty-nine, Gorbachev was selected as first secretary of the Stavropol Territory Communist Party Committee and held this post until 1978. During these years he officially visited East Germany (1966), Belgium (1972), West Germany (1975), and France (1976). He also was elected to membership in the central committee of the Communist Party in 1971.

Life's Work

Gorbachev's competence, honesty, and effective administration, as well as the support given by party leaders (Yuri Andropov and Mikhail Suslov), eventually brought him to national attention. A front-page interview in *Pravda* (1977) and a brief meeting with General Secretary Leonid Ilich Brezhnev in September, 1978, culminated in his assignment in November, 1978, to Moscow as the party's agricultural expert in the secretariat. He held this position from 1978 to 1983. Although Gorbachev was known for his administrative skills and agricultural expertise, Soviet agriculture did not improve during his tenure. Gorbachev was elected in 1979 to the party's ruling Politburo as a candidate member and was raised to full membership in October, 1980. At the age of forty-nine, Gorbachev was the youngest member of a powerful group dominated by very senior party leaders.

Yuri Andropov succeeded Brezhnev in November, 1982, and shifted Gorbachev's responsibilities to personnel evaluation and selection. Upon Andropov's death in early 1984, Gorbachev nominated Konstantin Chernenko as general secretary. During the brief Chernenko interlude, Gorbachev provided important party leadership and gained stature among his colleagues. During the post-Brezhnev period, he also led Soviet delegations to Canada (1983) and Britain (1984). In April, 1984, he became chairman of the Foreign Affairs Commission in the Supreme Soviet of the Soviet Union. With Chernenko's death on March 10, 1985, the party elite immediately elected Gorbachev as general secretary.

A priority for Gorbachev was to replace government and party personnel at all levels. New appointments to the ruling party Politburo started in April, 1985, with other major changes in 1987 and

1988. More than half of the regional party secretaries and the Council of Ministers were replaced. A new prime minister was selected in 1985, as well as a new foreign minister. Andrei Gromyko was named president in 1985 and served in that role until Gorbachev replaced him in the fall of 1988 by taking that office himself. The Congress of People's Deputies, under the revised parliamentary system, elected Gorbachev chairman of the Supreme Soviet in May, 1989. Extensive changes in the central committee occurred in April,

Mikhail Gorbachev *(Reuters/Frederiqu Lengaigen/Archive Photos)*

1989, as senior members were replaced. Gorbachev showed effective control and leadership of major party and government meetings, especially the Twenty-seventh Communist Party Congress (1986), the Nineteenth Communist Party Conference (1988), and the Congress of People's Deputies (1989).

The Soviet economy was recognized as a problem for years in its lack of productivity, cumbersome bureaucracy, waste, poor growth rates, supply bottlenecks, and reduced worker output. Improving the economy was seen as the fundamental key to Gorbachev's ultimate success or failure. His calls for greater labor effort, reduction of alcohol abuse among workers, and more flexibility of economic planning yielded mixed results. Some new experiments promised the potential for improvement, but productivity remained low. New policies introduced to spur the economy included the cooperative system (some limited free enterprise), economic accountability (enterprises must make a profit or face closure), and provision for private ownership or long-term leases in agriculture.

These steps were part of Gorbachev's policy known as perestroika (restructuring). The results proved to be initially inadequate, and Gorbachev's economic advisers publicly predicted no substantial improvement of the economy from the implementation of these policies until 1992 at the earliest. Unemployment was expected to rise, creating further problems. Consumer goods, promised regularly, were in even shorter supply for many in 1989. Some food rationing was invoked. Ideology and reform blended in Gorbachev's Marxist orientation and his efforts to make improvements. He rejected changing the fundamental organizations and institutions of the nation and opposed a multiparty political system. Nevertheless, he called on the Communist Party and the public to be more efficient and active. Several constitutional changes occurred, altering the national government's structure and powers. Gorbachev's economic reforms cut sharply at the ideological patterns of seven decades.

Foreign policy during the Gorbachev era reflected more flexibility in meeting Soviet defense needs and addressing competition with the United States and other states. Gorbachev and U.S. president Ronald Reagan met in five summits (1985, 1986, 1987, and two in 1988). Some arms control agreements were reached (notably the INF Treaty of 1987), and others were negotiated.

Gorbachev undertook a nuclear testing moratorium for a lengthy period, called for the end of nuclear weapons by the year 2000, and, in December, 1988, made a significant address to the United Nations. His trips to other nations were remarkable for their effects and implications. Major trips in 1989 included West Germany, France, and China. Improvements in relations with allies and opponents became a prominent aspect of the Gorbachev years. The Soviet military leadership was extensively revised after Gorbachev came to power (from the chief of the general staff and the minister of defense down), and the Soviet Union's extensive participation in the Afghanistan war, starting in 1979, ended in early 1989 with the withdrawal of Soviet combat forces.

While Gorbachev's international popularity was at its height, however, his reputation at home was rapidly deteriorating. His policies resulted in both political openness and polarity, and his economic reforms were disastrous. Serious and substantial problems broke into the open in 1988 and 1989. Nationality discontent expanded to affect at least half of the nation's fifteen republics. Violent outbursts led to increasing deaths and injuries. Political activists, charging that Gorbachev was moving too slowly, attempted to create alternative political reform agendas and even called for a multiparty political system. Growing labor unrest, especially among striking Soviet coal miners in the summer of 1989, threatened economic stability. Anti-Semitism and ethnic antipathies, suppressed under previous regimes, re-erupted, and both the Soviet bloc countries and Soviet republics began breaking away. In 1989, the Soviet Union collapsed, and Gorbachev was soon succeeded by his protégé Boris Yeltsin. Gorbachev formed a research foundation and remained politically active, but his career and reputation were ruined.

Summary

Soviet society and culture saw significant changes during Gorbachev's tenure. The concept of *glasnost* (openness) was reflected in more candid comment in the Soviet press and public opinion. Film, drama, and art became more experimental and outspoken in subject matter and approach. *Glasnost* went far beyond previous decades of Soviet rule, but limits remained. The primary purpose was to admit old problems and work for solutions. Gorbachev encouraged this behavior, so long as it did not undermine national unity and security or his *perestroika* efforts. Soviet law and human rights issues also saw some improvement after late 1986. More citizens, especially Jews, were allowed to emigrate. Several punitive laws were not used as they had been in the past to punish those who criticized the lack of human rights in the Soviet Union. Andrei Sakharov, for example, banished to Gorky by Brezhnev in early 1980, was permitted by Gorbachev to return to Moscow in December, 1986.

Time, however, worked against his reform program. Gorbachev and his advisers admitted that the problems were greater than originally identified. Public inertia, the stifling ideological system, and the bureaucratic opposition to *perestroika* proved too difficult to overcome. In the meantime, the quality of life for many citizens became worse, and they increasingly blamed Gorbachev for their discomfort. The public admission of problems in the era of *glasnost* further heightened frustration and anti-Gorbachev feeling. The Soviet superpower was ultimately reduced to an assortment of struggling, underdeveloped nations, and Russia's devastation was laid largely at the feet of its reform-minded former leader.

Bibliography

Brown, Archie. *The Gorbachev Factor*. Oxford, England: Oxford University Press, 1997.

Butson, Thomas G. *Gorbachev: A Biography.* Briarcliff Manor, N.Y.: Stein & Day, 1985. A readable biography of the Soviet leader from early years to his selection as general secretary in 1985. Contains some information based on interviews not found in other sources. An adequate description and assessment.

Doder, Dusko, and Louise Branson. *Gorbachev: Heretic in the Kremlin*. New York: Penguin, 1991.

Gorbachev, Mikhail. *Perestroika: New Thinking for Our Country and the World.* New York: Harper & Row, 1987. A well-known account by the Soviet leader of the challenges his country faces. This candid assessment of strengths and weaknesses, with a minimum of rhetorical camouflage or self-serving defense, reveals the man and his outlook.

Medvedev, Zhores A. *Gorbachev.* New York: W. W. Norton, 1986. A careful biography by a noted Soviet intellectual and former dissident now living in Great Britain. Penetrating assessment of Gorbachev's values and priorities, with predictions of the success or failure of Gorbachev's reform efforts.

Morrison, Donald, ed. *Mikhail S. Gorbachev: An Intimate Biography.* New York: Time, 1988. Very readable and complete biography, taking the story to the Washington summit in December, 1987. Gorbachev's personality and leadership style are effectively presented. An important source for the general reader. Illustrated.

Murarka, Dev. *Gorbachev: The Limits of Power.* London: Hutchinson, 1988. An important and useful biography by an Indian journalist stationed in the Soviet Union for many years. Reveals independent judgment about Gorbachev and his nation. Includes his rise to power with emphasis on the first several years in office, attempted reforms, and results.

Schmidt-Haüer, Christian. *Gorbachev: The Path to Power.* Topsfield, Mass.: Salem House, 1986. A readable account of Gorbachev's life with the focus on the 1980's. Relates Gorbachev's reform efforts to Peter the Great and others. Very good coverage and assessment of his political leadership and policies as general secretary. Includes helpful appendices.

Wieczynski, Joseph L., ed. *The Gorbachev Encyclopedia*. Salt Lake City, Utah: Schlacks, 1993.

Zemstov, Ilya, and John Farrar. *Gorbachev: The Man and the System.* New Brunswick, N.J.: Transaction, 1989. The most current and thorough analysis of Gorbachev as general secretary, in a detailed presentation. A daunting source to read but illuminating. Excellent charts, chronologies, and appendices. Focus is on 1985 to 1987.

Taylor Stults

HAILE SELASSIE

Tafari Makonnen

Born: July 23, 1892; near Harar, Ethiopia
Died: August 27, 1975; Addis Ababa, Ethiopia

During his long rule as emperor (1930-1974), Haile Selassie instituted programs for unification and modernization at home, while striving to open up Ethiopia to the world outside its formidable borders.

Early Life

Haile Selassie was the last in a long line of emperors of Ethiopia which, according to the legendary history, originated with Menelik I, the son of Makeda, the queen of Sheba, and King Solomon. He was born Tafari Makonnen on July 23, 1892, near Harar, Ethiopia. His father, Ras (duke) Makonnen, was the governor of Harar and adviser to his cousin, Emperor Menelik II. Young Tafari, born as he was in one of the oldest Christian domains, was baptized while only a few days old and, according to custom, given a Christian name, Haile Selassie (power of the trinity)—a name he would use in church and later as ruler.

Tafari was reared in the Coptic Christian faith and educated by European tutors. His father, an important influence on Menelik II and, finally, on young Tafari, had traveled to Rome on state business, and this exposure helped convince him that Ethiopia could benefit from education, modernization, and development. He died in 1906 before he could complete Tafari's political education, which he had only recently begun. He had, however, made Tafari a district governor in Harar province in 1905, giving him the title *dejazmatch* (count). Passed over by Menelik to succeed his father as governor of Harar because of his youth and inexperience, Tafari stayed instead at the palace at the emperor's request. During this eight-month period, he observed much, learning the ways of rulers and much about palace intrigue. His political education advanced rapidly, even without his

Haile Selassie *(Library of Congress)*

powerful father. Tafari spent the next year continuing his education in Addis Ababa.

In 1908, Tafari was made governor of Darassa, a subprovince of Sidamo. He moved there with three thousand troops and several trusted officers. In April, 1909, he returned to Addis Ababa because Menelik, who had suffered a minor stroke in 1908, experienced a more crippling one in January, 1909. As his condition worsened, Empress Taitu's power increased, but so did the plotting by some powerful rases against her. Aware of intrigues by various factions against various members of the royal family, Tafari managed to remain on good terms with all. In 1910, Taitu, who had gained more power following Menelik's third and worst stroke in October, 1909, was overthrown, and Lij Iyasu, Menelik's grandson and Tafari's cousin, assumed power. Taitu had promoted Tafari to governor of Harar, and Iyasu confirmed the appointment. Tafari entered Harar on May 12, 1910, and began to restore the reforms begun by his father.

In 1911, Tafari married Waizero Menen, a wealthy, attractive woman of twenty-two who, as it happened, was the crown prince's niece. The crown prince, meanwhile, was creating problems for his rule even before the death of Menelik II in 1913, favoring Islam in this historically Christian country and not fully tending to the affairs of his office. Tafari, who had been undercut by some of Iyasu's policies, was at the center of a plot to overthrow the crown prince. The coup came in September, 1916. Iyasu was removed from power, Menelik's daughter, Zauditu, was named empress (October, 1916), and Tafari, at age twenty-four, was made ras, heir presumptive, and regent. He was also invested with the Grand Cordon of the Order of Solomon.

Life's Work

Tafari proved to be an able and progressive ruler. Even early in his regency he showed his interest in modernization and reform, despite the more conservative and religious preoccupations of the empress. These early efforts were capped by the seating of Ethiopia in 1923 in the League of Nations. Resistance to accepting Ethiopia was based on objections to its slavery and slave trade. Tafari promised to abolish the slave trade, which he did the next year and then began implementation of a program for the gradual emancipation of Ethiopia's slaves.

Tafari became the first Ethiopian ruler to go abroad when in 1924 he traveled to Rome, Paris, and London, among other European capitals. This trip only increased his determination to bring change and modernization, however gradual, to Ethiopia upon his return.

Ruling Ethiopia, once a group of separate kingdoms, was made difficult not only by the extremes of terrain, the ethnic diversity, and the primitive communication and transportation facilities, but also by the continuing independence of a number of its provinces. In the mid-1920's, Tafari began to move to exert more control over these provinces. In 1926, he took control of the army and by 1928 had increased his authority while the power of Empress Zauditu and of a number of the provincial governors had lessened. On October 7, 1928, amid much pomp and ceremony, Tafari was crowned negus (king).

In late March, 1930, Ras Gugsa Wolie, the estranged husband of Zauditu, led a coup attempt against Tafari. Wolie was killed in a battle at Ankim on March 31, 1930, and the coup died with him. Zauditu died suddenly the next day. Tafari, with an endorsement by the archbishop, declared himself negusa nagast (king of kings) and took his baptismal name, Haile Selassie. Then, in a grand ceremony on November 2, 1930, to which world leaders and monarchs specifically were invited, Haile Selassie was crowned His Imperial Majesty Haile Selassie, King of Kings of Ethiopia, Conquering Lion of Judah, and Elect of God. The event and the refurbishing of Abbis Ababa to host it were, among other things, calculated to symbolize Haile Selassie's determination to bring modernization and reform to Ethiopia and to open it up to the rest of the world.

In July, 1931, Haile Selassie proclaimed a new constitution. The "constitutional monarchy" that was established vested all final power and authority in the emperor. It also increased the power of the central government in an attempt to unify what had been little more than a collection of interacting provincial governments. Haile Selassie then began his efforts at modernization, introducing programs for road building, public works, education, and public health.

These long-overdue changes would be abruptly halted by actions taken against Ethiopia by Italy from bases it had established in Somalia and Eritrea. Benito Mussolini had designs on the horn of Africa, and the conquest of Ethiopia was crucial to the realization of those designs. Haile Selassie was not unaware of the threat that Italy represented but trusted in the League of Nations to protect Ethiopia against aggression. On October 3, 1935, Mussolini telegraphed instructions to open the attack against Ethiopia. The league did nothing. Haile Selassie led his warriors against the invading Italian army. They fought bravely but were gravely overmatched. The Italians, using planes, poison gas, and sophisticated weapons, crushed the Ethiopian resistance, capturing Addis Ababa on May 5, 1936. Haile Selassie fled his country, living in exile, ultimately, in England. This represented the first loss of national independence in recorded history.

On June 30, 1936, Haile Selassie addressed the League of Nations. A decade earlier, protests to that body opposing some 1926 Anglo-Italian accords which infringed on the sovereignty of Ethiopia had fallen on deaf ears. Now Haile Selassie's personal appeal for military sanctions to help stop Italy's aggression brought similar results. His warning that "God and history will remember your judgment" struck a chord but produced no immediate result. Only mild sanctions were voted and were never really enforced. By late 1938, the horn was being recognized as Italian East Africa.

When World War II broke out and Italy joined the Axis Powers, Great Britain recognized Haile Selassie as an ally, then, in January, 1941, joined with him and his army in exile in Sudan. They, with the assistance of freedom fighters still in the country, drove the Italian army out of Ethiopia. On May 4, 1941, Haile Selassie reentered Addis Ababa. By November, he once again ruled Ethiopia, now with a new set of circumstances and problems. His absence and the struggle against the Italians at the local level had revitalized some provincial power bases. At the same time, the Italians had constructed roads, bridges, and a bureaucracy that would facilitate unification.

Haile Selassie moved quickly to reassert his authority, extending his administrative and military control over the country by regulating the church, the government, and the finances of the nation. He also put down uprisings in Gojjam and Tigre provinces. Unification as he envisioned it would not be easy, nor would the establishment of proper relations with foreign nations. Haile Selassie wanted foreign assistance in the development of Ethiopia but not interference in its internal affairs. In fact, however, Great Britain, then other Western nations including the United States, especially while World War II raged, were deeply involved in Ethiopia's modernization and, almost necessarily, its internal affairs.

In 1947, Haile Selassie began to press for annexation of Eritrea. Arguing that it had been a part of Ethiopia before the 1890's, that Eritreans shared with Ethiopia a common language, dress, and set of social customs, and adding Ethiopia's need for a Red Sea port (Mesewa), Haile Selassie took his case to the United Nations. In December, 1950, the United Nations General Assembly voted to federate an "autonomous Eritrea" with Ethiopia "under the sovereignty of the Ethiopian crown." This arrangement would remain, Eritrea's objections notwithstanding, until Ethiopia absorbed Eritrea in 1962. Eritrea's struggle for independence would present problems for Haile Selassie for the rest of his rule.

In 1954, Haile Selassie, who would be among the most widely traveled of world leaders, visited the United States, Canada, and Mexico. He was an overnight guest of President Dwight D. Eisenhower at the White House, he addressed a joint session of Congress, and he received honorary degrees from Howard, Columbia, and Montreal universities. He was less fortunate during another series of state visits in December, 1960. While he was in Brazil, a number of important and highly placed individuals attempted to overthrow Haile Selassie's government. His supporters managed to defeat the conspirators, but the very challenge to his authority suggested the growing tensions in the changing if still delicately balanced society.

Haile Selassie would continue to keep a high profile in his country, on the continent, and in the world. In 1963, he helped found the Organization of African Unity, whose headquarters opened that year in Addis Ababa. He helped mediate disputes on the continent, such as the Algerian-Moroccan border war (1963), and continued his rounds of state visits.

By 1970, he seemed more involved in foreign affairs than in domestic concerns. In February, 1974, a military coup, this time successful, was mounted against Haile Selassie's government. On September 12, a provisional military government was established and Haile Selassie was deposed and made a prisoner in his own palace. Crown Prince Asfa Wossen was named king-designate, but then in March, 1975, the military rulers issued a proclamation abolishing the monarchy entirely. Haile Selassie died in Addis Ababa on August 27, 1975.

Summary

During his rule first as regent and then emperor, Haile Selassie sought to unify and modernize Ethiopia and involve it in the larger world. This meant moving, within the period of his rule, from an isolated, preindustrial, feudal society, still with the institution of slavery, to a unified nation-state growing in wealth and exercising influence throughout the continent and the world. His efforts at unification, based on control of a standing army, the institution of a centralized fiscal system, and the reorganization of provincial governments under a more powerful "constitutional monarchy," were successful, unleashing new forces less easily controlled. The same result was obtained through his efforts at modernization. Foreign aid was sought but not foreign intrusion. For a time the Italians provided the most and worst of both, but even friendly nations would leave their stamp.

For Haile Selassie modernization included three priorities, which he articulated in 1950: expansion of education, development of communications, and secure employment for all Ethiopians. Progress in these areas, which would involve restructuring Ethiopian society and the creation of an intelligentsia, would also give rise to groups less content to live under the limitations and restrictions of Haile Selassie's autocratic rule. It seemed inevitable that the forces of change unleashed in Ethiopia should one day challenge the ancient system of rule that had first set them in motion. It is a tribute to Haile Selassie that he was able to balance competing claims and remain in power for as long as he did.

Bibliography

Greenfield, Richard. *Ethiopia: A New Political History.* New York: Frederick A. Praeger, 1965. Another survey, and a good one, this study emphasizes the complexities of Ethiopian politics, especially in the twentieth century, all building toward the 1960 coup attempt. Greenfield devotes a quarter of the book to the failed coup and makes no effort to hide his sympathy for it.

Hess, Robert L. *Ethiopia: The Modernization of Autocracy.* Ithaca, N.Y.: Cornell University Press, 1970. This is a good introductory survey of prerevolutionary Ethiopia, including some two thousand years of history. The second two-thirds of this book, which includes a good bibliography, concentrates on the rule of Haile Selassie.

Lockot, Hans Wilhelm. *The Mission: The Life, Reign, and Character of Haile Selassie I.* New York: St. Martin's Press, 1989.

Marcus, Harold G. *Haile Selassie I: The Formative Years, 1892-1936.* Berkeley: University of California Press, 1987. The first of a three-volume biography, this is an excellent account of Haile Selassie's life up to the time of the Italian occupation. It is illustrated and includes an extensive bibliography.

Mosely, Leonard. *Haile Selassie: The Conquering Lion.* Englewood Cliffs, N.J.: Prentice-Hall, 1965. A generally sympathetic book by a British journalist who covered the liberation of Ethiopia and who knows his subject well. Illustrated.

Rasmussen, R. Kent. *Modern African Political Leaders.* New York: Facts on File, 1998. Biographies of eight twentieth century African leaders, including Haile Selassie, that emphasize the place of each man in his country's history.

Spencer, John H. *Ethiopia at Bay: A Personal Account of the Haile Selassie Years.* Algonac, Mich.: Reference Publications, 1984. A detailed study of Haile Selassie's Ethiopia written in the first person by an American who was an adviser to that country's government during the Italian invasion and who later served as principal adviser to the Ethiopian Ministry of Foreign Affairs for much of the period 1943-1974. Though its maps and illustrations are welcomed by the general reader, its prose and detail make it more appropriate to the specialist.

David W. Moore

DAG HAMMARSKJÖLD

Born: July 29, 1905; Jönköping, Sweden
Died: September 18, 1961; near Ndola, Northern Rhodesia (later Zambia)

As secretary-general of the United Nations (U.N.) from 1953 to 1961, Hammarskjöld vastly increased both the influence and the prestige of the United Nations. He oversaw the explosive growth of the organization among Third World nations, prevented the United Nations from becoming a pawn of the major Cold War rivals, and initiated the U.N. peacekeeping role.

Early Life

Dag Hjalmar Agne Carl Hammarskjöld grew up in a home dominated by the ideals of public service and faith in one's own convictions. The youngest of four sons, he watched his father, a former prime minister of Sweden, sacrifice his political career by defending Sweden's neutrality during World War I. Certainly his father's subsequent devotion to the principles of the League of Nations, the world's first genuine collective-security organization, influenced the young Hammarskjöld's later career. His mother's influence was less apparent, although her skepticism of rational thought can be discerned in his later poetry and religious writings.

Educated at the University in Uppsala, Hammarskjöld first studied social philosophy and French literature, later turning to the fields of economics and political economy, in which he did exceedingly well. In 1927, he studied at the University of Cambridge under the great English economist John Maynard Keynes, receiving his degree the following year and a doctorate in economics from the University of Stockholm in 1933. After teaching for a year, he went into government service. First employed on the staff of the National Bank of Sweden, he then became permanent undersecretary of Sweden's Ministry of Finance. During World War II, he combined this latter post with service as board chairman of the Swedish National Bank, retaining that position until 1948.

When the war ended in 1945, Hammarskjöld left the Ministry of

Finance for the cabinet, in which he served as an adviser on financial issues. This was an exciting period for a young economist, for the Swedish government was breaking new ground in shaping a socialist economy. Hammarskjöld thrived in an atmosphere in which he could emphasize practical measures rather than economic theory and soon achieved a genuinely national reputation.

It was shortly after the war that he entered the field of diplomacy. As a cabinet adviser, he helped to shape many of Sweden's trade and financial policies in negotiation with foreign governments. In 1949, he became the Swedish delegate to the Organization of European Economic Cooperation and served on its executive committee, a post that launched his work in the field of international organization.

Life's Work

Hammarskjöld's reputation would be forged in the world of diplomacy, not economics. Between 1947 and 1953, however, the future secretary-general of the United Nations straddled both the economic and the diplomatic worlds. Becoming undersecretary for economic affairs in the Foreign Ministry in 1947, Hammarskjöld supervised Sweden's role in discussions leading to the Marshall Plan for the economic reconstruction of Europe. Two years later, he became secretary-general of the Foreign Office, and, in 1951, he received a cabinet appointment as minister without portfolio in which he specialized in economic matters.

Characteristically, Hammarskjöld thought of himself as a civil servant and not as a politician. Even after he entered the cabinet, he refused to join a political party, believing that his only real loyalty other than to Sweden should be to the ideal of public service. In this he shared the attitude of many men in the professional foreign services. The principle of public service also proved to be central to the United Nations, chartered in June, 1945, to keep the world from again fighting a world war.

When Trygve Lie of Norway, the first secretary-general of the United Nations (U.N.), found himself crippled in office by Soviet opposition to his support for the U.N. role in the Korean War, and by anticommunist American supporters of Senator Joseph McCarthy, who denounced the United Nations as a hotbed of communist activity, he announced his retirement. The Security Council in a compromise vote then selected Hammarskjöld as Lie's successor.

The new secretary-general was still not well known outside economic circles, his U.N. experience limited to once having served

Dag Hammarskjöld *(Library of Congress)*

as head of Sweden's U.N. delegation. Nevertheless, neither his lack of reputation nor his inexperience interfered with his desire to reinvigorate the United Nations secretariat. Retaining the best of Lie's aides, he surrounded himself with an exceptionally able group of subordinates and quickly addressed issues that affected the morale of U.N. employees. He asserted successfully the independence of the United Nations as an international civil service when he protected American employees against efforts to subject them to political tests by the Dwight D. Eisenhower administration. In the process, Hammarskjöld would gain the respect of the previously demoralized secretariat, increasing both his prestige and his authority.

After addressing internal U.N. matters, Hammarskjöld turned to the more complex rivalries among the great powers. It was there that the relatively unknown Swede first displayed his extraordinary negotiating skills. After months of frustrating effort, he helped gain the release in August, 1955, of seventeen American flyers held prisoner by the new communist government in China. Having proved himself to skeptical officials in both power blocs, he thereafter became a major factor in international diplomacy.

In 1956, Hammarskjöld encountered two of his three most challenging crises as secretary-general. The emotional and historic rivalries in the Middle East pitting Israelis against their Arab neighbors erupted in full-scale war in November, a situation complicated when British and French paratroopers wrested control of the Suez Canal from Egypt's President Gamal Abdel Nasser, who had recently nationalized that international waterway. The crisis combined colonial politics with ethnic hatreds. Reestablishing peace between Israel and Egypt would have tested Hammarskjöld's talents in the best of times. With both Great Britain and France possessing a permanent veto on the Security Council, a peaceful settlement looked all the more remote. Taking advantage, however, of the opposition of both the United States and the Soviet Union to the Suez invasion and skillfully implementing the proposal of Canada's Lester Pearson for the creation of an international peacekeeping force (the U.N. Emergency Force), Hammarskjöld not only helped to resolve the crisis but placed the United Nations into a much more active and creative role than its founders had ever anticipated.

However, Hammarskjöld was much less successful when seeking to moderate the effects of a Soviet invasion of Hungary that occurred at the same time. A revolutionary anti-Soviet government in Budapest sought to withdraw from the Warsaw Pact, the Soviet security system in Eastern Europe, and the Russians responded by sending in their tanks. The Hungarian situation exposed the real limits of U.N. action, for there was no possibility of challenging a superpower squarely within its own geographical sphere of influence. Moreover, the General Assembly's action appeared to make Hammarskjöld personally responsible for the failure of the organization's efforts. As observers credited him with the Suez success, so he had to absorb criticism (most of it unjustified) for the Hungarian failure.

From 1957 to 1960, Hammarskjöld's tenure as secretary-general witnessed a number of lesser successes (as in Lebanon, where he succeeded in using the United Nations to minimize the intrusion of foreign powers) and failures (as in Laos where a civil war introduced great power rivalries). Yet his greatest challenge came after the Congo received its independence from Belgium in the summer of 1960. There he extended the authority of his office far beyond its original parameters, conveying to observers the creative possibilities as well as the dangers of U.N. initiative. His efforts helped to stabilize an exceptionally dangerous situation that threatened to convert central Africa into a Cold War minefield, but he paid a high price.

The Soviet leader Nikita Khrushchev called for Hammarskjöld's resignation and demanded a "troika" system to weaken the secretary-general (it would have effectively allowed an East-West veto of the secretary-general's action), while France's President Charles de Gaulle joined the Soviet Union in refusing to pay its U.N. assessment. More important, it was during the Congo Crisis that Hammarskjöld tragically died in a plane crash when seeking to end the secession of mineral-rich Katanga province in September, 1961. He was posthumously awarded the Nobel Peace Prize of 1961.

Summary

Although the U.N. Charter made the secretary-general's office nonpolitical, Dag Hammarskjöld after 1953 converted it into a dynamic and highly political instrument. In the process, he injected new life and controversy into a U.N. seriously weakened by the Cold War rivalry between the United States and the Soviet Union. The timing was right, for he took advantage of the diplomatic thaw that followed the death of Joseph Stalin and the end of the Korean War. By the same token, he made the most of his extraordinary intellect, his great confidence, and his phenomenal endurance. Hammarskjöld came to symbolize unusual integrity, singlemindedly devoting his energies to the United Nations. Even his harshest political critics, such as Khrushchev and Israel's David Ben-Gurion, personally held him in high esteem. Virtually all observers understood that his imaginative use of both his own office and the United Nations in general by creating U.N. peacekeeping forces and a U.N. "presence" in troublespots made the organization into a major factor in international political life.

Bibliography

Cordier, Andrew, and Wilder Foote, eds. *The Quest for Peace: The Dag Hammarskjöld Memorial Lectures.* New York: Columbia University Press, 1965. Essays by many of the leading personalities at the U.N. Contains much rhetoric but much useful information as well.

Cruise O'Brien, Conor. *The United Nations: Sacred Drama.* New York: Simon & Schuster, 1968. An insightful and somewhat controversial history of the United Nations by an Irish official deeply involved in the Congo operation. Highly critical of Hammarskjöld's political activity.

Fredriksson, Gunnar, et al. *Sweden at the UN: Eight Profiles.* Stockholm: Swedish Institute, 1996.

Hammarskjöld, Dag. *Markings.* New York: Alfred A. Knopf, 1964. A meditative, even religious, work that provides great insight into the author's mind, though offering no direct comment about his political activity.

Jordan, Robert S., ed. *Dag Hammarskjöld Revisited: The U.N. Secretary-General as a Force in World Politics.* Durham, N.C.: Carolina Academic Press, 1983. Recent scholarship on the secretary-general, including an excellent bibliographical article by B. L. S. Tractenberg.

Kelen, Emery. *Hammarskjöld.* New York: G. P. Putnam's Sons, 1966. Organized topically rather than chronologically, Kelen's book is lively though sometimes inaccurate. The author headed television services for the United Nations.

Lash, Joseph P. *Dag Hammarskjöld: Custodian of the Brushfire Peace.* Garden City, N.Y.: Doubleday, 1961. Based mainly on published sources, this is an admiring though superficial biography.

Urquhart, Brian. *Hammarskjöld.* New York: Alfred A. Knopf, 1972. The most important study of Hammarskjöld, written by his undersecretary-general for special political affairs. Sympathetic yet not uncritical.

Van Dusen, Henry P. *Dag Hammarskjöld: The Statesman and His Faith.* New York: Harper & Row, 1964. A somewhat superficial biography by a leading Protestant theologian.

Wallensteen, Peter. *Dag Hammarskjöld.* Stockholm: Swedish Institute, 1995.

Zacher, Mark W. *Dag Hammarskjöld's United Nations.* New York: Columbia University Press, 1970. A bit dull, but plenty of good analysis of Hammarskjöld's strategy and tactics for settling disputes.

Gary B. Ostrower

WARREN G. HARDING

Born: November 2, 1865; Caledonia, Ohio
Died: August 2, 1923; San Francisco, California

As president of the United States from 1921 to 1923, Harding adopted compromise politics in economics and foreign affairs in an attempt to guide the nation through readjustment to great social and economic changes.

Early Life

Warren Gamaliel Harding was born on November 2, 1865, in Caledonia (modern Blooming Grove), Ohio. His father, George Tryon Harding, was a homeopathic doctor who practiced for a few years in the town of Caledonia before moving the family to Marion when Warren was sixteen. His mother, Phoebe (Dickerson) Harding, after bearing eight children, attended the same Cleveland homeopathic institute as her husband and joined him in practice in Marion. Harding's youth was occupied with family chores and working for nearby farmers. After ascending the grades in the one-room schoolhouse in Caledonia, he attended Ohio Central College, an academy a few miles from Caledonia, graduating from the two-year institution in 1882. He was quick-witted and did well in school, although he was never studious. Following graduation, he taught school for a single term, a period long enough to convince him of an aversion to teaching, just as a few months of reading law were sufficient to dispel interest in the legal profession.

When Harding moved to Marion, it was a growing town with a booster mentality. Harding contributed to the city's reputation by playing in the local brass band at nearby towns and in Chicago, an excursion he arranged. With financial assistance from his father, he acquired the failing *Marion Daily Star* in 1884. Two young friends from Caledonia who had entered this venture with him left the enterprise within a few months. By hard work, attention to detail, modernization of the production facilities, and constantly supporting civic progress in Marion, Harding built the *Marion Daily Star* into a successful paper by 1890. In addition, he joined an array of civic and service organizations and was among the best-known citizens of the town by the time he married the widow Florence Kling DeWolfe in 1891.

As the town of Marion and the *Marion Daily Star* grew apace, Harding's political influence also increased. He was a leader in the Marion County Republican organization during the 1890's and entered politics as a candidate for the Ohio Senate in 1899. He won that election and subsequent reelection in 1901; in 1903, he was elected as lieutenant governor under Governor Myron T. Herrick. He was a popular figure in Ohio Republican circles from the outset, as his political style of conciliation and persuasion appealed to leaders of a party that was rancorous and bitterly divided for three decades prior to World War I.

From 1905 to 1910, Harding left the political arena to run the *Marion Daily Star*, which now assumed statewide importance because of the reputation of the owner. He lost as the Republican gubernatorial candidate in 1910, largely because of the emerging rift between Progressives and regular Republicans. He achieved national recognition two years later, when he nominated William Howard Taft at the Republican National Convention, although he alienated many of the Progressives forever by derisive references to Theodore Roosevelt. In 1914, he handily defeated both Democratic and Progressive candidates in the election for the U.S. Senate; off to Washington, he left behind a reputation for amiability and achievement.

Life's Work

Harding was not an outstanding senator. He did not make any memorable speeches during his term, he introduced no legislation of national importance, and he had one of the highest absentee rates on roll-call votes. He continued to make friends, however, including another freshman senator, Albert B. Fall of New Mexico, and the wealthy Ned and Evalyn McLean, owners of the *Washington Post*. His prestige within the party increased following his keynote address at the Republican convention in 1916. He generally supported Woodrow Wilson's wartime legislation but voted after the war with Senator Henry Cabot Lodge's strong reservationists against the League of Nations. His political strategy on Prohibition, a popular issue in Ohio, was to vote in favor of the amendment, while acknowledging that he was a "wet" who thought that the people in the states had the right to decide the issue.

Harding announced his presidential candidacy in 1919, at the urging of several of his friends, and, on the advice of political ally Harry M. Daugherty, he set forth with a cautious strategy to win support. When the Republican National Convention of 1920 became

Warren G. Harding *(Library of Congress)*

deadlocked between Governor Frank O. Lowden of Illinois, General Leonard Wood, and Senator Hiram Johnson of California, Harding received the nomination for several reasons—he was from the key state of Ohio, he was well known, if not distinguished, he was not associated with strong stands on controversial issues, and he was acceptable to most elements within the party; he was, in the political parlance, "available." Harding made an effective campaigner. Speaking mainly from his front porch in Marion, the handsome candidate with classic features and silver hair looked statesmanlike. He promised a return to "normalcy" and had little trouble defeating the Democrat, James M. Cox, as he received the greatest majority of popular votes of any preceding presidential election.

As president, Harding launched the era of normalcy by supporting financial initiatives which posed an alternative to the prewar Progressive policies of Woodrow Wilson. His appointment of Pittsburgh banker Andrew Mellon as secretary of the treasury presaged a conservative financial program, which included cuts in government spending, higher tariff rates (the 1922 Fordney-McCumber Tariff), and corporate tax reduction. Shortly after entering office, Harding signed the Budget and Accounting Act, which created a Bureau of the Budget accountable to the president; bureau director Charles Dawes immediately implemented a program to reduce government expenditures. As a fiscal conservative, Harding vetoed the 1922 soldier's bonus bill, a plan designed to pay a cash bonus to veterans of World War I. A compromise tax reduction plan emerged from Congress as the Revenue Act of 1921, which Harding signed. Secretary of Agriculture Henry C. Wallace successfully pressed for the passage of farm relief legislation in 1921 and 1922.

The implementation of much of Harding's program for normalcy was a result of strong cabinet members and Harding's tendency to allow much latitude to congressional leaders. His conciliatory approach to presidential-congressional relations, however, was unsuccessful in some areas. Midwestern senators and congressmen, who formed the so-called Farm Bloc, fought the administration's agricultural policies and urged stronger measures; Progressives in both parties opposed the Fordney-McCumber Tariff and repeal of the excess-profits tax. Harding's defense of Truman Newberry, accused of gross overspending in his Senate race in 1918, also stirred controversy. By early 1923, Harding was more often a congressional antagonist than mediator.

In foreign policy matters, Harding for the most part followed the lead of his legalistic-minded secretary of state, Charles Evans Hughes, and the Senate leadership. Following a general policy of nonintervention in matters under consideration by the League of Nations, the administration nevertheless assembled the Washington Disarmament Conference in 1921, which dealt boldly with problems of naval development in the Far East. In addition, the administration settled some remaining problems from World War I, such as peace treaties with Germany, Austria, and Hungary, and adopted a noninterventionist policy toward Latin America.

The Harding administration is, however, best remembered for its improprieties, notably the Teapot Dome Scandal, in which Secretary of the Interior Albert B. Fall improperly leased government oil reserves in Teapot Dome, Wyoming, and Elk Hills, California, to private interests. While Harding himself was not directly linked to the wrongdoing, he bears much of the blame, owing to his appointments of the men responsible for these affairs—Fall, a former Senate colleague and friend; Veterans' Bureau director Charles Forbes, who bilked his agency until discovery by a congressional investigating committee; and Harry M. Daugherty, Harding's attorney general, who was accused of selling government favors, along with his and Harding's "Ohio gang" friends, from the infamous "little green house on K Street." Harding had a penchant for appointing his cronies to these and other positions, which were well beyond their abilities.

Accusations about these scandalous affairs and a subsequent Senate inquiry drove a tired Harding from Washington in June of 1923. With other government officials and Mrs. Harding, he took a train across the country to look into developments in the Alaska territory. After a hectic trip to Alaska, the party came back via California; Harding suffered what was later diagnosed as a mild heart attack on the train but seemed much improved upon arrival the next day in San Francisco. He died a few days later, however, on August 2, while resting in his hotel. His body was taken to Washington for funeral services on August 8, and to Marion for burial on August 10.

Summary

Harding's career was a reflection of midwestern life in the nineteenth century. A product of a small town in Ohio, he adopted the virtues for success in that environment. He demonstrated his sense of civic responsibility by joining merchants and businessmen in local organizations, and he used the columns of the *Marion Daily Star* to boost Marion's economic growth. He was popular, both socially and as a speaker, although his forceful speeches were often ponderous. His success in this narrow arena, as well as his likable personality, helped lead to political success. As he ascended the ladder of Ohio politics, his availability for national office became apparent. Yet in the larger context of national politics, Harding lacked the intellect and training to understand and deal adequately with the forces for change, which propelled many of his contemporaries into the prewar reform movement.

In some ways, though, Harding's administration compared favorably to that of his predecessor, Woodrow Wilson. For example, aside from miscalculated choices of friends for some appointments, Harding did surround himself with men of high caliber in his Cabinet. Herbert Hoover, as secretary of commerce, was the liberal of the cabinet and was instrumental in organizing the Unemployment Conference of 1921; Henry C. Wallace, secretary of agriculture, was a friend of the farmers, who thoughtfully pursued progressive agricultural policies during the farm crisis of the early 1920's; Charles Evans Hughes, secretary of state, fashioned a better record in Latin American policy than did his predecessors; and Andrew Mellon, secretary of the treasury, John W. Weeks, secretary of war, and James J. Davis, secretary of labor, were all competent men.

The policies of normalcy represented a somewhat old-fashioned response to the upheavals of war and economic and social change; while Harding pursued his policies as an adjustment to these changes, his program was carried on by Calvin Coolidge and, to a lesser extent, Herbert Hoover. In pressing policies to allow for economic expansion and economy in government, Harding applied his political talents for compromise and melioration to assuage congressional opponents. While some historians have pointed to his growth in office and more effective leadership of the nation by early 1923, he did not live to develop any newfound talents. Had he lived, he undoubtedly would have been hamstrung by the scandals that broke shortly after he died. Hampered by his background and limitations, he did his best in a difficult time. However, this was an area where his availability could be of no use.

Bibliography

Adams, Samuel Hopkins. *Incredible Era: The Life and Times of Warren Gamaliel Harding*. Boston: Houghton Mifflin, 1939. An early biography of Harding, based on the author's interviews with Harding family members, associates of the president, and journalists of the Harding era. Mainly concentrates on the sensational aspects of the time, including scandals, amorous affairs, and the rumor of Harding's black ancestry.

Anthony, Carl S. *Florence Harding*. New York: William Morrow, 1998. Biography of Harding's wife.

Buckley, Thomas H. *The United States and the Washington Conference, 1921-1922*. Knoxville: University of Tennessee Press, 1970. Ably assesses the major foreign policy event of the Harding years. Describes the Four-, Five-, and Nine-Power Treaties as necessary first steps in achieving lasting peace, which later administrations failed to follow up.

Downes, Randolph C. *The Rise of Warren Gamaliel Harding, 1865-1920*. Columbus: Ohio State University Press, 1970. A detailed, lengthy (640-page) study of Harding's early career. Valuable for its coverage both of Harding's rise in Ohio politics and of the issues and strategies of the election of 1920.

Frederick, Richard G., comp. *Warren G. Harding: A Bibliography*. Westport, Conn.: Greenwood Press, 1992.

Grieb, Kenneth J. *The Latin American Policy of Warren G. Harding*. Fort Worth: Texas Christian University Press, 1977. Indicates that Harding was active in promoting goodwill in United States-Latin American relations through a commercial approach rather than the armed intervention of previous administrations.

Murray, Robert K. *The Harding Era: Warren G. Harding and His Administration*. Minneapolis: University of Minnesota Press, 1969. The major revisionist work on the Harding era: Attempts to evaluate the Harding presidency objectively by examining major policies and events apart from the scandals and Harding's sometimes indecorous personal life. The best-researched and most detailed of the works dealing with the Harding presidency.

__________. *The Politics of Normalcy: Governmental Theory and Practice in the Harding-Coolidge Era*. New York: W. W. Norton, 1973. Analyzes and interprets the approach of Warren G. Harding to the presidency and to national affairs. Murray stresses the positive aspects of the Harding administration and demonstrates Harding's growth in office, especially in congressional relations.

Potts, Louis W. "Who Was Warren G. Harding?" *Historian* 36 (August, 1974): 621-645. Examines the historical writing on Warren G. Harding from the time of his death until the early 1970's.

Shows that the textbook writers and other generalists have usually described Harding in the worst terms, while students of his life and administration have responded more favorably in analyzing his accomplishments.

Russell, Francis. *The Shadow of Blooming Grove: Warren G. Harding in His Times*. New York: McGraw-Hill, 1968. A lengthy biography which tends to be anecdotal rather than analytic, particularly in treating the presidential years. Well detailed in the sections on Harding's amorous affairs.

Sinclair, Andrew. *The Available Man: The Life Behind the Masks of Warren Gamaliel Harding*. New York: Macmillan, 1965. Sinclair was the first researcher to publish a book based on the Harding papers opened by the Ohio Historical Society in 1964. He questions many of the myths surrounding Harding's career and is particularly adept at explaining the times as well as the life of Warren G. Harding.

Trani, Eugene P., and David L. Wilson. *The Presidency of Warren G. Harding*. Lawrence: Regents Press of Kansas, 1977. A review of the Harding administration based almost entirely on published sources. The authors conclude that the achievements of the Harding administration were short-term, stopgap measures during a time made difficult by transitions in American life. Harding, they assert, had no real strength as president and failed to achieve any personal stature.

Richard G. Frederick

HATOYAMA ICHIRŌ

Born: January 1, 1883; Tokyo, Japan
Died: March 7, 1959; Tokyo, Japan

Hatoyama was the architect of the postwar conservative coalition which began an uninterrupted period of ruling Japan as the Liberal Democratic Party (Jiyu-Minshuto) in 1955.

Early Life

Hatoyama Ichirō was the son of Hatoyama Kazuo, who graduated from Kaisei Gakko (later Tokyo University), studied at Columbia and Yale universities, and returned to Japan to pursue a distinguished career in diplomacy and party politics, being elected to the Diet in 1892 and rising by 1896 to become Speaker of the House. Hatoyama's mother, Haruko, was a leading educator of women who founded Kyoritsu Joshi Shokugyo Gakko (later Kyoritsu Women's University) and served as the school's president from 1922 until her death. Hatoyama's younger brother, Hideo, represented Japan at the League of Nations, served in the Diet like his father and brother and was a respected legal scholar. The family was wealthy and well positioned to make significant contributions to the development of modern Japan.

Life's Work

Hatoyama graduated from Tokyo Imperial University in 1907 with a specialty in English Law. In 1915, he was first elected to the Diet as a member of the Seiyukai Party. As a protégé of Tanaka Giichi he served as chief cabinet secretary from 1927 to 1929, when Tanaka was prime minister. Hatoyama became embroiled in controversy when, as Tanaka's cabinet secretary, he helped draft legislation applying the death penalty to anyone proposing changes in the *kokutai*, or "national polity," the term used to denote Japan's prewar political system, thus foreshadowing the thought control characteristic of the 1930's. This early display of conservatism was followed in the 1930's by several additional incidents that came to haunt him for the rest of his life.

In 1930, after the government of Prime Minister Hamaguchi Yuko agreed to a new round of naval arms reductions at the London Naval Conference, Hatoyama emerged as a vocal member of the Seiyukai opposition by demanding an end to the government's bargaining with the West over the security of Japan. By arguing that the Hamaguchi cabinet had violated the principle of autonomous command for the navy—the principle that the navy itself should determine its requirements without being subject to cabinet control—Hatoyama took a position which was later used by other rightists throughout the 1930's to defeat civilian control of the military. Hamaguchi himself was wounded in an assassination attempt and had to resign in 1931.

From December, 1931, until March, 1934, as minister of education under Prime Ministers Inukai Tsuyoshi and Saitō Makoto, Hatoyama further established his reputation as an arch-conservative by instituting curbs on freedom of speech and ordering the revision of textbooks to reflect the prevailing nationalist ideology. In May, 1933, he ordered the dismissal of Takigawa Yukitoki, a professor of law at Kyōto Imperial University, for harboring "dangerous thoughts" which Hatoyama believed were detrimental to the *kokutai*. Takigawa had argued that society bore some responsibility for the acts of criminals and had criticized the relegation of women to inferior social and legal status. Takigawa's dismissal sent shock waves across Japan. The president and thirty-six members of the Kyōto University faculty resigned in protest. A subsequent search for more "dangerous thoughts" among state employees led to more dismissals and arrests of teachers at all levels. In 1934, Hatoyama himself was forced to resign after being charged with bribery and tax evasion.

Hatoyama's prewar public positions were not always antidemocratic. He is remembered for having opposed the military's removal of Saito Takeo from the Diet in 1940 for giving an antimilitary speech on the floor, his refusal to join the Imperial Rule Assistance Association, the combined party of wartime Japan, and his candidacy in the 1942 election as a supporter of constitutional government.

The more common view of Hatoyama, however, is that he remained committed to the policy first expressed by Tanaka in the late 1920's, to promote Japan's special destiny on the mainland of Asia—the so-called positive policy toward Manchuria and China. In 1937, he toured the United States and Europe as Prime Minister Konoe Fumimaro's personal representative to explain Japan's objectives in the war. In 1938, he wrote a book in which he commented favorably on Nazism and compared it with Japanese *bushido*. He also recommended Nazi-style labor controls for Japan. These activities associated him with Japanese militarism in the eyes of the occupation authorities after 1945, when they accused him of having "aided the forces of obscurantism, reaction and militarism" and of having paid only lip service to democracy.

With Japan's defeat in 1945, Hatoyama organized his followers into the Jiyuto, the "Liberal Party," and together they won a 140-seat plurality (out of 466 contested seats) in the Diet election of April, 1946. It was at that point, on the eve of his assuming the prime ministership, that the American occupation authorities stepped in and removed him from the political arena by labeling him a "militarist and ultranationalist." In his place, Yoshida Shigeru, a wartime peace advocate and foreign minister under the liberal leader Shidehara Kijuro, became prime minister. Hatoyama was allowed to resume public life in 1951, in the waning months of the occupation. His supporters, who had been temporarily in Yoshida's camp, now returned to him and became the nucleus of the Democratic Party. Their defection cost Yoshida his majority in the Diet, and he was forced to resign in December, 1954.

Hatoyama became the next prime minister, but his Democratic Party proved unable to win an absolute majority in the Diet. Consequently, he was forced to engineer a merger of his party, which won 185 seats in the election of February, 1955, with the Liberals, who had 112, forming the Liberal Democratic Party (LDP), the conservative coalition that has ruled Japan since November, 1955.

As prime minister, Hatoyama had two major objectives: the pursuit of an independent foreign policy and the revision of the constitution. The first involved a readjustment of Soviet-Japanese relations and the second entailed an effort to have Article IX, the famous "no more war, no more military forces" article, removed from the constitution. He started talks with the Soviet Union, and, though the talks nearly foundered over the issue of ownership of the Kuril Islands, Hatoyama was able to conclude a peace treaty with the Soviets during a trip to Moscow in October, 1956, thereby normalizing relations. Trade and fisheries agreements followed. Ironically, it was the right wing in postwar Japan that attacked Hatoyama at the end of his career for dealing with the Soviet Union, and there were vociferous patriotic demonstrations against the agreements.

There were three Hatoyama cabinets between 1954 and 1956. Being based on the Liberal Democratic coalition, his governments were perhaps more democratic than those of Yoshida, but they were also weaker. For example, he strongly opposed the diffusion of political authority that had taken place under the occupation and fought to reassert central government control over such functions as local administration, civil service appointments, police, and education. Powerful opposition from within the LDP and the bureaucracy forced him to accept many compromises in the area of administration. He was successful, however, in centralizing the police and broadening their powers to include internal security and in getting the Ministry of Education to appoint local school committees instead of having them elected. He also asserted government control over the content of school textbooks.

In December, 1956, Hatoyama resigned because of ill health and was succeeded by a journalist, Ishibashi Tanzan, who also fell ill, and then by Kishi Nobusuke, who served until 1960. Although Hatoyama and Kishi were arch-conservatives and sought to restore much power to the central government, what they accomplished was more on the order of adjustments to the massive reforms already effected by the occupation. Many of the reforms could not be undone. For example, despite Hatoyama's sentiments against universal suffrage, including voting rights for women, most Japanese supported it. The old-fashioned values reflected in the conservatism of Hatoyama and Kishi, together with their records of service to militarist governments before the war, made them ideal targets for charges by the socialists that they were trying to take Japan back to the repression of the 1930's. Prime ministers who followed Kishi's resignation in 1960 and who had not served in government before 1941 were much less vulnerable to that kind of criticism.

Summary

Hatoyama Ichirō was one of several Japanese political leaders whose careers survived World War II. His contributions were in the area of party politics, and the postwar history of Japan owes much to the way Hatoyama forged the conservative factions in postwar Japan into an effective political force. Yet his actions at key moments during the Japanese government's rightward drift in the 1930's associated him with the curse of militarism and handicapped his postwar governments by denying him the full measure of legitimacy necessary for strong leadership. Personal ties, therefore, were his stock-in-trade and have been the key to understanding Japanese politics ever since the end of the American occupation.

Bibliography

Baerwald, Hans. *The Purge of Japanese Leaders Under the Occupation*. Berkeley: University of California Press, 1959. The basic source on the purge that robbed Hatoyama of the prime ministership in 1946.

Dower, John W. *Empire and Aftermath: Yoshida Shigeru and the Japanese Experience, 1878-1954*. Cambridge, Mass.: Harvard University Press, 1979. A basic book on prime minister Yoshida, especially useful for comparisons of the way Yoshida and Hatoyama were seen by the American occupation authorities.

Fukui, Haruhiro. *Party in Power: The Japanese Liberal-Democrats and Policy-Making*. Berkeley: University of California Press, 1970. A detailed study of the inner working of the LDP factions, useful for understanding the political genealogies of modern Japanese leaders before and after the war.

Gayn, Mark. *Japan Diary*. Rutland, Vt.: Charles E. Tuttle, 1981. Events in occupied Japan from the point of view of an outstanding journalist. Especially useful for the election of 1946 and the events surrounding Hatoyama's purge.

Hellmann, Donald C. *Japanese Foreign Policy and Domestic Politics*. Berkeley: University of California Press, 1969. A basic study useful for Japan's alignment with the United States and Hatoyama's attempts to settle the peace treaty negotiations with the Soviet Union.

Masumi, Junnosuke. *Postwar Politics in Japan, 1945-1955*. Translated by Lonny E. Carlile. Berkeley: Center for Japanese Studies, University of California, 1985. Includes a detailed account of Hatoyama's political career after the war, from the purge through his election as prime minister.

Morris, Ivan I. *Nationalism and the Right Wing in Japan: A Study of Postwar Trends*. New York: Oxford University Press, 1960. A discussion of the continuities in Japanese politics between the pre- and postwar eras.

Thayer, Nathaniel. *How the Conservatives Rule Japan*. Princeton, N.J.: Princeton University Press, 1969. The classic work on the coalition of conservatives that formed the LDP in 1955.

Yoshida, Shigeru. *The Yoshida Memoirs*. Translated by Kenichi Yoshida. Boston: Houghton Mifflin, 1962. Prime Minister Yoshida's own version of political events before and after the war, with surprisingly gentle treatment of his rival Hatoyama.

Donald N. Clark

ÉDOUARD HERRIOT

Born: July 5, 1872; Troyes, France
Died: March 26, 1957; Lyons, France

One of the most important French statesmen of the first half of the twentieth century, Herriot served nearly four decades in the French parliament, headed three governments between 1924 and 1933, held posts in six other cabinets between 1916 and 1936, was mayor of Lyons (France's second-largest city) from 1905 to 1957, and was leader of the Radical-Socialist Party for much of his career.

Early Life

Édouard Herriot was born into a humble provincial family less than two years after republican rule returned to France. Education was the key to his personal success. While both of his parents came from military backgrounds, none of his relatives was prominently connected or wealthy; consequently, the young Herriot had to rely on native intellectual ability and scholarship grants to gain educational opportunities. Tutored at an early age by a village priest, Herriot at age fifteen received a scholarship to a prestigious Paris *lycée* from a local official whom he happened to impress. Four years later, he won admission to the École Normale Supérieure, where he received training as a teacher. In 1905, he completed his doctorate at the Sorbonne.

Herriot's rich educational experience instilled in him a deep commitment to rational investigation and inspired him to work throughout his political career to expand educational opportunity for all Frenchmen. It also cultivated a love of literary pursuits, which made him one of the most brilliant orators and prolific writers of his day. Before he died, Herriot published nearly fifty books and articles—historical and political tracts, literary essays, works based on his own travels abroad, and memoirs. He composed his first scholarly treatise, *Philon le Juif* (1898), a study of the important Hebrew philosopher who was a contemporary of Jesus Christ, in the barracks at Nancy while completing his mandatory military service in 1898. In 1947, his writings would win for him election to the Académie Française.

Herriot's early and enduring affiliation with the Radical-Socialist Party at the municipal and national levels followed naturally, in his view, from his concern for the defense of basic human rights and his faith in the power of rational thought. As he wrote in 1931: "Radicalism appears as the political application of rationalism." It was also, Herriot believed, the best embodiment of France's democratic tradition. Herriot's political philosophy solidified at the time of the Dreyfus affair and the vicious anticlerical campaign that followed it. A spirited Dreyfusard and anticlerical himself, Herriot claimed to have entered public life under the patronage of Émile Combes, the Radical prime minister from 1902 to 1905 who spearheaded the controversial separation of church and state. Herriot first gained public office by winning election to the Lyons city council in 1904. The following year, he was elected mayor of Lyons (at thirty-three, he was the youngest mayor in the country), and, as chief executive of France's second largest city, he gained a voice in Radical politics at the national level. In 1912, he began a seven-year term as France's youngest senator, and, in 1919, he won election to the Chamber of Deputies. In the latter year also, he was chosen president of the Radical-Socialist Party, and his career as a statesman was under way.

Life's Work

Herriot's life's work focused on city hall in Lyons and the cabinet rooms and legislative chambers of Paris. In the first setting, Herriot's disposition toward social activism may be most easily seen. As mayor, he improved hospitals and schools, expanded housing for working-class citizens, enhanced libraries and museums, constructed numerous public buildings, renovated and enlarged port facilities, and undertook municipal beautification programs. Despite the heavy responsibilities of national office for most of his career, Herriot emphasized that nothing was as important to him as Lyons and said once: "I loved Lyons as one adores a woman."

His service in Lyons and the publication of a collection of his lectures earned for Herriot recognition by the national leadership and resulted in his first appointment to ministerial office in December, 1916, in the cabinet of Aristide Briand. He held the post of minister of public works, transports, and supplies for barely four months, however, and his decision to ration bread and limit the number of courses allowed in restaurant meals was not popular despite its importance to the war effort. Herriot did not hold governmental office again until 1924, when he was named prime minister after the ruling center-right majority was overthrown in national elections by a coalition of left-wing parties (Cartel des Gauches), in which his own Radical-Socialist Party constituted the largest group.

It was as head of the government from June, 1924, to April, 1925, that Herriot established himself as an important national leader. During this brief term, Herriot directed the end of France's Ruhr Valley occupation, the implementation of the Dawes Plan, and the preliminary negotiations to the Locarno Pact. In all of this, he manifested a more conciliatory approach to Germany and a significant change in tone from earlier postwar French foreign policy. In 1924, he became the first head of a French government to address the League of Nations in Geneva, an occasion he later termed the "most solemn moment" of his life. He also established full diplomatic relations with the Soviet Union in 1924, a move paralleled by Great Britain's Labor government in the same year.

In 1925, Herriot became the first minister of any major European government to advocate publicly some form of European federation. His domestic agenda favored the standard left-wing (though non-Marxist) program of social insurance, educational reform, reorganization of the tax structure, and reduction of the length of military service. The conservative senate ended his premiership when he tried to enact a tax on capital. Herriot's colleagues in the Chamber of Deputies, however, rewarded him with the presidency of the lower house when his government was overthrown, and he held this post—generally viewed as the third-highest office under the French republics—on several occasions during the next quarter-century.

Herriot's appointment as minister of public instruction in July, 1926, led to his most enduring achievements in cabinet politics. As a trained teacher of humble origins, Herriot appreciated the importance of equal educational opportunity for all Frenchmen regardless of their wealth or social status. He also believed that the democratic state had an obligation to finance and universalize public education in the interest of creating an informed citizenry. Accordingly, among Herriot's accomplishments as minister in the 1920's were laws admitting students to primary and secondary schools without charge, equalizing instruction for girls and boys, and standardizing course content nationwide.

Perhaps Herriot's greatest triumph in educational reform may be seen in the preamble to the constitution of the Fourth Republic, which he helped to frame in 1946, which guaranteed "equal access of children and adults to education, professional training and culture" and affirmed as the "duty of the State to provide free, secular, public education at all levels."

In the 1930's, Herriot headed one more government and sat in four others. His major accomplishment as premier in 1932 was a nonaggression pact with the Soviet Union, which paved the way for a full-scale anti-Fascist alliance with Moscow four years later. During this troubled decade, Herriot held such influential positions as president of the Radical-Socialist Party, president of the Chamber of Deputies, and president of the Foreign Affairs Committee of the Chamber of Deputies. After 1936, however, he was excluded from cabinet posts and was opposed to the official policy of appeasement of the Fascist dictators.

The fateful year of 1940 found Herriot, as presiding officer of the chamber, in the midst of events surrounding national defeat and the dissolution of the Third Republic. Herriot became one of the most outspoken defenders of parliamentary rights during the authoritarian Vichy regime. He was arrested in 1942 and spent the remainder of the war in captivity, ultimately in Germany. After the defeat of Adolf Hitler and Herriot's own liberation by Russian troops, he returned to France, resumed his mayoral duties in Lyons, and restored himself and his Radical-Socialist Party to national prominence.

With so many French politicians discredited by collaboration with the Nazis, Herriot's example of passive resistance to the wartime tyranny won vast public admiration. He emerged during the postwar years as a primary shaper of France's new republican regime and served as president of the National Assembly from 1947 to 1953. These years also afforded Herriot the opportunity to champion another of his long-standing goals: European federation. In November, 1948, he became president of the international study commission for European unity, and, when the Council of Europe was founded as the first common political institution for Europe in 1949, Herriot delivered the inaugural address in Strasbourg.

Summary

Édouard Herriot's life coincided with one of the most tumultuous periods of French history. Born two years into the Third Republic, itself the offspring of catastrophic defeat in the Franco-Prussian War, Herriot became one of the most important leaders of the last three decades of that regime. His first ministerial post came in the midst of one world war; his tenure as president of the Chamber of Deputies ended with France's defeat at the beginning of the next. His death preceded by one year the end of the Fourth Republic, a regime he had helped to found. While his specific political and literary achievements speak for themselves, Herriot's ultimate contribution may lie in what he symbolized. His rise from ordinary beginnings to extraordinary prominence bore witness to republican France's emphasis on careers open to talents. As a statesman, he confronted the problems of war and recovery on two momentous occasions. Above all, Herriot stands out for his unyielding commitment to parliamentary government, the ideals of the French revolutionary heritage, and international harmony. For his defense of these principles, he fell momentary victim to the Nazi tyranny. Once vindicated, he regained the opportunity to move his nation toward the elusive vision of "liberty, equality, and fraternity." In the aftermath of World War II, Herriot became to many the "Patriarch of the Republic" and the symbol of what was best in France's entire political tradition.

Bibliography

De Tarr, Francis. *The French Radical Party: From Herriot to Mendès-France.* New York: Oxford University Press, 1961. Contains an entire chapter on Herriot as the "symbol of Radicalism" and is especially informative on Herriot's importance as party leader after World War II.

Herriot, Édouard. *In Those Days.* Translated by Adolphe de Milly. New York: Old and New World Publishing, 1952. An English translation of the first volume of Herriot's memoirs covering to the outbreak of World War I. Offers useful insights into Herriot's formative years as a writer and a politician.

Jessner, Sabine. *Édouard Herriot, Patriarch of the Republic.* New York: Haskell House, 1974. The only full-length Herriot biography in English. Based solidly on Herriot's own writings and the wealth of scholarly literature about him in the French language.

Larmour, Peter J. *The French Radical Party in the 1930's.* Stanford, Calif.: Stanford University Press, 1964. A scholarly treatment of radicalism that provides extensive material on Herriot's role in the Radical-Socialist Party during the turbulent decade before the outbreak of World War II.

Morgan, Ted. *An Uncertain Hour: The French, the Germans, the*

Jews, the Klaus Barbie Trial, and the City of Lyon, 1940-1945. New York: William Morrow, 1990.

Talbott, John E. *The Politics of Educational Reform in France, 1918-1940*. Princeton, N.J.: Princeton University Press, 1969. Contains a good summary of Herriot's achievements in the field of education.

Thomas H. Conner

HIROHITO

Born: April 29, 1901; Tokyo, Japan
Died: January 7, 1989; Tokyo, Japan

Hirohito, in an unprecedented action, made the decision that ended World War II in the Pacific. Thereafter, he provided the symbolic leadership that facilitated the recovery of Japan from the devastation of the war, while first renouncing a divine status for himself and then promulgating the new democratic constitution for his nation.

Early Life

Hirohito was born barely three decades after the fall of the Tokugawa system that had ruled Japan from 1603 to 1867. His grandfather, posthumously known as the Emperor Meiji, was the symbol of the new order that succeeded the feudal Tokugawa regime. As with emperors and heirs apparent of the time, the newborn was given the suffix "hito" (benevolence) and a name by which his reign would be known posthumously: Showa (Enlightened Peace). Again following custom, only a few months after birth, the infant was placed in the care of a trusted aristocratic family—and eventually, a second.

Showa, as he should now be called, had an elitist education. In 1906, a private school was organized for him, his younger brother, and selected classmates. In 1908, he was sent to the Gakushuin or Peers' School, an elementary school for aristocratic offspring, similar to Britain's Eton. There, he came under the influence of Count Marusuke Nogi, a naval hero and Hirohito's first role model. Yet the direct influence was short-lived: In 1912, on the eve of Emperor Meiji's funeral, Nogi and his wife committed ritual suicide to express their grief. This had a lasting impression on Hirohito and was said to be an important factor in leading him to question traditional military values.

After six years, Hirohito graduated from the Gakushuin and became the sole pupil at a special school created for him. Although efforts were made to imbue him with military values, he gradually spent more time on science, especially marine biology, and while a teenager he discovered a new species of marine life.

By this time, his father (then known as Yoshihito, but subsequently as Emperor Taisho) was demonstrating erratic behavior, a result of mental illness, that would lead to his retirement from public life and in 1921 to the appointment of Hirohito as prince regent, assuming the duties of his father. These new responsibilities came soon after he returned from his 1921 tour abroad—the first by a Japanese heir apparent. Years later, he would say his visit to Great Britain was the happiest time of his life.

In 1918, his engagement to Princess Nagako was announced. Despite her being the explicit choice of her fiancé, who customarily would not be consulted, and his mother, her selection was opposed by leaders of the Choshu clan, who expected to have one of their own be the empress-designate. The Choshu circulated information that Nagako had a genetic tendency for colorblindness, grounds for which the engagement could be terminated. Yet the prince regent and his supporters were insistent, and Nagako became his bride on January 26, 1924. Since the imperial line, in modern times, could only pass through the male side, disappointment was widespread when four daughters were born. Pressure grew that the emperor consider a concubine, but that issue was resolved when in 1933, a son, Akihito, was born. Later a second son and a fifth daughter joined the family, and Japan had its first deliberately monogamous emperor.

Life's Work

At Emperor Taisho's death, December 25, 1926, his eldest son immediately succeeded him, although the formal ceremony of enthronement did not occur for nearly two years. During Taisho's life, Japan had moved from a feudal society, similar to that of Europe centuries before, to a modern one, ranking just below the United States and Great Britain in many measures of industrial development. Major efforts were made to provide mass education, to generate capital for economic investment, and to organize a system whereby private and public management could be coordinated in pursuit of priorities established by the government. As would be the case throughout the twentieth century, the benefits of this modernization were dispersed unevenly among the population. Especially in rural areas, hardship continued to be common.

A principal motive for this drive to modernize was the desire not to be humiliated by the Western powers, as China and other Asian nations were. Japanese leaders were convinced that military prow-

Hirohito *(Library of Congress)*

ess was essential to dissuade the occidental nations from exploiting Japan. Japan had achieved remarkable success in creating a modern military apparatus. One indication of that was manifested in the naval conferences of the 1920's, wherein Japan's naval power was recognized as falling into a category just below that of the United States and the major European powers, excluding Germany, which was denied rearmament by the Treaty of Versailles. Yet Japanese military leaders were offended that their nation had not been placed in the highest category.

Unmistakably in the 1920's and continuing into the 1930's, advocates of militarism, glorifying Japanese successes in the Sino-Japanese War of 1894-1895 and the Russo-Japanese War of 1904-1905, promoted larger military expenditures and aggression on the Asian mainland. China was the main target of those ventures as Japanese militarists fabricated one "incident" after another with the intention of provoking the Japanese people to support a vengeful retaliation.

Thus, the new emperor Hirohito was confronted with a rising militarism that would eventually bring devastating destruction to his nation. His position was paradoxical: Symbolically, he had unlimited powers as a god-ruler, but, throughout most of recorded history, Japanese emperors had rarely exercised power. Instead, the power had been used in their name by various other officials, the Shogun of the Tokugawa being an excellent example. Until the Meiji Restoration, emperors had for centuries resided in Kyōto, while effective governmental authority was wielded at Edo (later Tokyo), hundreds of miles away.

It was customary before the Meiji Restoration for emperors to abdicate while relatively young men and bestow the office upon their, in many cases, minor sons. With Meiji, the emperor became more visible and increasingly informed about affairs of state. Whether the 1889 Meiji constitution made Japan a constitutional monarchy is debatable. The document gave the nation the appearance of a parliamentary system, but Taisho certainly did not decide governmental policy. No emperor has wielded the powers attributed to Hirohito by British and American propaganda during World War II.

Hirohito, while a retiring personality, was aware of major actions leading up to and during World War II. Prince Kimmochi Saionji, who was for years the chief imperial adviser, concurred with Hirohito's advice of moderation to the military. In several instances, Hirohito reportedly expressed reservations and even anger about actions taken or planned by the military. Given the imperial tradition, it is nearly inconceivable that the emperor would have directly countermanded decisions of duly authorized officials, although he did move swiftly to halt the attempted military coup of 1936. In August, 1945, after two atomic bombs had been dropped on Japan and faced with the inevitable invasion of the Japanese islands, the war cabinet deadlocked. Only then did the emperor decisively move to stop the war.

At the close of World War II, there was considerable sentiment in the victorious nations to try Hirohito for war crimes. Others contended that at least he should abdicate. These positions were founded on the view that even if he was not directly responsible for Japan's military aggression, he was morally responsible. In his famous visit of September, 1945, to General Douglas MacArthur, Hirohito voluntarily assumed responsibility for the war. The relative positions of the two men were dramatized in the photograph of the emperor in formal Western dress standing beside MacArthur in casual military attire with an open-shirt collar.

MacArthur chose not to bring Hirohito to trial or have him abdicate. It is unlikely that MacArthur did this because of a profound comprehension of the actually limited powers of Japanese emperors. Rather, MacArthur's decision was motivated by his desire to use the emperor to develop popular support for conversion of the Japanese governing system and for rebuilding the economy. To have punished the emperor might have fomented widespread opposition to occupation programs.

The end of the war did not complete Hirohito's remarkable efforts. In 1971 and 1975, he and the empress traveled abroad, to Europe and to the United States, respectively. These precedent-setting events, combined with his 1921 tour, secured his place as the first emperor to have direct knowledge of foreign nations. The wide television coverage of the later imperial tours abroad gave the Japanese far greater exposure to the royal family than was conceivable for any of his predecessors on the Chrysanthemum Throne. This was in line with a policy that Hirohito pursued with the end of World War II to make the imperial office more accessible to the Japanese populace. The reticent emperor was uncomfortable in his initial efforts to move among his subjects shortly after the war, but he persisted. The intention was not to make the imperial office as visible as the British monarch but to emphasize its human rather than divine status. Once that was established, imperial walkabouts were cut back. In later years, Hirohito's public appearances were largely restricted to formal occasions, such as opening the 1964 Olympic Games in Tokyo. Hirohito thus continued as the symbol of the Japanese nation but with a human face and with far less mystery and reverence than his office accrued before Japan's surrender.

Until near the end of his life, Hirohito pursued his youthful enthusiasm for marine biology, being recognized as an authority on the hydroza. Of the more than one dozen books that he published, some translated into English, four dealt with that topic.

Hirohito's final years were occupied with the heavy ceremonial functions of his office, many of which dated from his earliest ancestors; presiding at the renowned New Year's poetry reading, initiated by his grandfather; following sumo wrestling; and in general being a father figure for his people. He retained some distinctly non-Japanese habits for his generation, such as his love of golf and a daily breakfast of toast and eggs, two by-products of his 1921 visit to Great Britain. His funeral, however, was a reminder of the elaborate ritual associated over the centuries with the direct descendant of the Sun Goddess.

Summary

Hirohito lived longer and reigned longer than any of his 123 predecessors. Neither of these, however, was the major achievement of his reign—that was his transformation of the imperial office. In transforming that role, he continued to be not only a primary symbol of Japanese nationhood but also a manifestation of the democratic principles of the postwar regime imposed by the occupation under MacArthur. Ironically, rather than using the democratic mechanism of a referendum to enact the new constitution, MacArthur had the emperor announce it. Years before, Hirohito had quietly indicated his preference for a more liberal system, reservations about imperial divinity, and an envy of the less restrictive manner of royal rule that he had observed in Great Britain. Yet with the firm emphasis on duty and tradition in which he had been trained, he would never have initiated these changes. His duty was to serve.

Bibliography

Behr, Edward. *Hirohito: Behind the Myth*. New York: Vintage Books, 1990.

Bergamini, David. *Japan's Imperial Conspiracy*. New York: William Morrow, 1971. Bergamini, born in Japan and a prisoner of war in the Philippines, presents a massive (1,277-page) book that purports to demonstrate that Hirohito was the driving force behind

Japanese militarism in the 1930's and 1940's. Few Japanologists concur.

Hoyt, Edwin. *Hirohito: The Emperor and the Man.* New York: Praeger, 1992.

Irokawa, Kaikichi. *The Age of Hirohito.* New York: Free Press, 1995.

Kanroji, Osanaga. *Hirohito: An Intimate Portrait of the Japanese Emperor.* Los Angeles: Gateway, 1975. Kanroji was an imperial attendant for seventy years, retiring in 1959, and a classmate of Taisho at Peers' School.

Kawahara, Toshiaki. *Hirohito and His Times: A Japanese Perspective.* Tokyo: Kodansha International, 1990.

Large, Stephen. *Emperors of the Rising Sun: Three Biographies.* Tokyo: Kodansha International, 1997.

Manning, Paul. *Hirohito: The War Years.* New York: Dodd, Mead, 1986. Focuses on the planning, conduct, and immediate aftermath of World War II. Assumes that Hirohito had a commanding role in that event. Appendix has a list of key figures who advised him.

Mosley, Leonard. *Hirohito: Emperor of Japan.* Englewood Cliffs, N.J: Prentice-Hall, 1966. Perhaps the most readable and detailed biography in English, but misses the final quarter century of the subject's life.

Packard, Jerrold M. *Sons of Heaven: A Portrait of the Japanese Monarchy.* New York: Charles Scribner's Sons, 1987. The last 250 pages concern Hirohito. Contains a seven-page bibliography, a list of all Japanese rulers, various documents pertaining to the imperial office, and the preface to a 1977 scientific paper by Hirohito.

Severns, Karen. *Hirohito.* New York: Chelsea House, 1988. Part of the World Leaders: Past and Present series, this work was written for young adults but is useful for a broad audience. There are photographs or other graphic material on nearly every page. Names are given in Asian fashion: family name first. An excellent starting point to examine Hirohito's life.

Takeda, Kiyoko. *The Dual-Image of the Japanese Emperor.* New York: New York University Press, 1988. In less than two hundred pages, this book examines American, British, Canadian, Australian, and Chinese views of the Japanese emperor from 1942 to 1952. Also contains a chronology of this period.

Thomas P. Wolf

ADOLF HITLER

Born: April 20, 1889; Braunau am Inn, Austro-Hungarian Empire
Died: April 30, 1945; Berlin, Germany

As leader of the National Socialist German Workers' Party in Germany and as dictator of the Third Reich, Hitler was responsible for many of the events that led to World War II. His belief in Teutonic racial superiority and his anti-Semitism also resulted in the Holocaust.

Early Life

Adolf Hitler was born on April 20, 1889, at Braunau am Inn, which is near Linz, in the Austro-Hungarian Empire. His father, Alois, was a customs agent whose primary concerns were his work, his status, and himself. When he was forty-seven, Alois married Klara Pölzl, his third wife. Even though eight children were born of his marriages, he took little interest in his family, preferring to devote his time to his work. He was a rigid and taciturn man who was especially severe to his sons. Klara, on the other hand, was an indulgent and loving mother, whose children and stepchildren loved and respected her deeply. Alois's position in the petite bourgeoisie provided the family with a good income and a secure standard of living. Even after his retirement in 1895, the family was able to live comfortably on his pension and inheritances.

Young Adolf was a sickly child who was overprotected by his mother. His father became a direct influence in his son's life only after he retired, for he then determined to impose his ideals on his children. When Adolf finished the Volksschule in 1900, Alois decided that the boy should attend the Realschule and prepare for a career in the civil service. The son rebelled at this treatment, for he considered himself to be an artist, not a member of the bourgeoisie. His father forced him to attend the Realschule, and Adolf's grades, which had been excellent, became quite poor. The boy became sullen, resentful, uncooperative, and withdrawn, both at home and at school.

During this period, the boy became enamored of Germanic myths, especially those presented in Wagnerian opera and in historical romance. It was not an unusual interest for boys of that era, as Austria-Hungary was greatly divided over various issues of nationality. German nationalists believed fervently that all German people should be bonded together in a single German Reich. The schools of the time were a place where Teutonic national superiority and an emphasis on social Darwinist views of the "survival of the fittest" were constantly taught. By the age of sixteen, Hitler had become what he was to be until his death—a fanatical German nationalist.

Adolf Hitler (right) riding with Benito Mussolini in a Munich motorcade in 1940 *(National Archives)*

In 1903, Alois died, leaving an adequate income for his family. His son did complete the *Realschule* in 1905, although he did not receive a certificate of graduation. In 1906, he moved to Vienna but twice failed to gain entry into the Imperial Academy of Fine Arts. For several years he eked out a precarious, solitary existence in Vienna by painting postcards or advertisements, drifting from one men's home to another.

The Vienna in which he lived was a veritable hotbed of anti-Semitism. Hitler read widely, but shallowly, preferring to read that which buttressed his own opinions about life. During this time he manifested many of his later characteristics: a quick temper that erupted when he was contradicted, an inability to form ordinary relationships with others, a passionate hatred of non-Germans and Jews, the use of violent rhetoric to express himself, and a tendency to live in a world of fantasy in an effort to escape his own poverty and failure. In 1913, he left Vienna for Munich, hoping to gain admission to the art academy there. Again he met with failure. He was twenty-four, with no marketable skills and little prospect for the future.

Life's Work

With the outbreak of World War I in August, 1914, Hitler immediately volunteered for and was accepted into the Sixteenth Bavarian Reserve Infantry Regiment. He served on the Western Front as a dispatch runner in the frontline throughout the war. That he served courageously is evidenced by his decorations for bravery. He received the Iron Cross, Second Class, in December, 1914, and he was awarded the Iron Cross, First Class (a rare distinction for a mere corporal), in August, 1918. He was wounded in October, 1916, and was gassed in October, 1918. The war was critical for his development, for it gave to him a sense of purpose, of comradeship, and of discipline. It also confirmed in him his belief in the heroic nature and necessity of war as well as his belief in the need for an authoritarian form of government.

War's end found him convalescing from his gassing. As there were few jobs available in postwar Germany for a young man of thirty with few skills, Hitler remained in the army. Serving in the army's political department, his primary job was the political education of soldiers. Hitler quickly learned that he could control large audiences with his oratorical skills. His other job was that of spying on various Bavarian political groups that the army wanted controlled. In September, 1919, he visited one such group, the German Workers Party, a violently anti-Semitic group. Finding that his ideas closely matched those of the group, he resigned from the army and began working with the party. Within a year, he had become its chief propagandist and, soon thereafter, its leader. In 1920, the renamed National Socialist German Workers' (or Nazi, a shortened form of the German name) Party issued its program: the union of all Germans in a greater German state, the expulsion of Jews from Germany, the revocation of the Treaty of Versailles, and the "creation of a strong central power of the State." Hitler introduced the swastika as the symbol of the party and created a private army of brown-shirted storm troopers. Force and violence quickly became a trait of the new party.

The double shock of military defeat and economic humiliation had left many Germans prepared to listen to anyone who promised a better national future. To be sure, Hitler's earliest adherents were the poor and dispossessed, but his message was also appealing to many middle-class Germans. In 1923, during the French occupation of the Ruhr Valley, which had resulted in the collapse of the German economy, Hitler attempted to overthrow the Bavarian government. This Beer Hall Putsch was a fiasco, for the army remained loyal to the government. Hitler was sentenced to five years' imprisonment, of which he served nine months. While in prison, he dictated *Mein Kampf* (1925-1927; English translation, 1933), an autobiographical account of his life and his political philosophy.

Mein Kampf is a rambling, turgid statement of Hitler's biases, of which there were many. To Hitler, the goal of the National Socialist German Workers' Party was to create a highly centralized state of and for the master race, that is, the Germans. The reason for this state was the rectification of the injustices perpetrated upon the German people by the decadent Western powers at Versailles. Only through war, Hitler believed, could the illegalities of that imposed settlement be erased. In this state, his racial policies would result in the rooting out of those who were not of Aryan blood. His most venomous statements were reserved for the Jews. To them he ascribed the blame for all of Germany's misfortunes, especially the loss of World War I. Jews, and their underlings, the Bolsheviks, were internationalists bent on destroying the purity of the German race. These "malignant tumors" had to be eradicated.

By the time Hitler was released from prison, economic and political conditions in Germany had improved dramatically. Gustav Stresemann, the Weimar Republic's chancellor, made the government more respectable, both at home and internationally. The Dawes Plan and currency reform resulted in German economic stability. Moreover, without Hitler's leadership, the Nazi Party had virtually disintegrated. Hitler himself was forbidden to speak publicly in Bavaria until 1929. As a result, the Nazi Party played an insignificant role in German politics until the Depression caused German economic and political instability once again.

Between 1929 and 1933, the Nazi Party grew from one of the smallest to the largest single party in Germany. Hitler made alliances with the army, with the magnates of business and industry, and with other conservative elements in German society. Still, the Nazis would not have been victorious had not Hitler's speeches regarding the future of Germany struck a responsive chord in the German electorate. Hitler's demagogic tactics and the failure of the Weimar government to mount effective opposition resulted in his being named chancellor of Germany in January, 1933.

The Reichstag fire of February, 1933, led to the destruction of the German Communist Party and to decrees that limited personal freedom in Germany. Hitler was given virtually unlimited power. Hitler's rearmament program quickly stimulated the German economy and put Germans back to work. Hitler and his minions thus restored German confidence and power at the expense of the democratic liberalism of the Weimar Republic. Those who opposed him were ruthlessly eliminated. Concentration camps were established to incarcerate enemies of state, especially Bolsheviks and Jews.

Hitler himself was not as interested in creating a totalitarian state as he was in establishing German hegemony in Europe. In October, 1933, Germany walked out of the international disarmament conference in Geneva as well as left the League of Nations. Two years later, Hitler proclaimed Germany's repudiation of the disarmament clauses of the Treaty of Versailles and began rearming. In 1936, he further repudiated Versailles by remilitarizing the Rhineland. In 1938, after witnessing Italian successes in Ethiopia, Japanese successes in China, and Francisco Franco's success in Spain, Hitler ordered an Anschluss with Austria. This too was successful. In September, 1938, at Munich, further appeasement by the Western democracies left Czechoslovakia truncated, with the Sudetenland being given to Hitler.

Hitler had now achieved, through bluff and diplomacy, part of the program set forth in *Mein Kampf*. In March, 1939, Germany dismembered the rest of Czechoslovakia, thereby shattering the myth of appeasement. Hitler then shrewdly maneuvered a German-Soviet nonaggression pact, which neutralized the threat of a two-front war. On September 1, 1939, the war that Hitler had wanted and for which he had planned erupted. Success quickly followed success as Poland, Denmark, Norway, the Low Countries, and

France were defeated by the German juggernaut. The Blitzkrieg (lightning war) resulted in German domination of Central and Western Europe. When German forces were unsuccessful in swiftly conquering Great Britain, Hitler's attention quickly turned to the East. First Yugoslavia, then Greece were annexed. Finally, it was the turn of the Soviet Union. In June, 1941, in a massive surprise attack, Hitler launched his attack on Bolshevism. Despite enormous early victories, the size and weather of the Soviet Union prevented an outright German victory.

While the war was being waged, Hitler concerned himself primarily with military matters, leaving domestic policies to his subordinates. These henchmen continued implementing the Nazi totalitarian program as well as creating for themselves powerful bases. To many Nazis, the domestic issue that was of greatest concern was the so-called final solution of the Jewish question. Before the war, Jews had been allowed to emigrate or had been expelled; war ended this option. The next stage was concentration, and numerous concentration camps and ghettos were established to hold the Jews of occupied Europe. This, however, was viewed as only a temporary measure; extermination was to be the final solution. Some six million Jews were systematically eliminated during the Holocaust. In addition, millions of others perished in concentration camps or labor camps, or as the result of Nazi activities or atrocities.

Hitler himself became ever more preoccupied with the running of a war that was quickly becoming unwinnable. As the Allies could outproduce Germany six to one, Germany could make do only by relying upon slave labor and total mobilization of the German population for war. Hitler became increasingly irrational during 1943 and early 1944, as Allied armies in North Africa, Italy, and the Soviet Union pushed German armies backward. Hitler's vegetarian diet and his living conditions led to a precipitous decline in his health. His personal physician, Theo Morell, prescribed huge doses of medication that resulted in a marked deterioration of Hitler's nervous system. The assassination attempt of July 20, 1944, merely accelerated the physical decline of the Führer.

As the Allies closed in from Italy, France, and the East, Hitler completely lost touch with reality. He sincerely believed that secret weapons would save Germany and that a rupture of the Grand Alliance was merely a matter of time. Even the Battle of the Bulge, which was merely a recapitulation of the 1940 offensive against

France, resulted in the shattering of the German forces on the Western Front. Early 1945 found Hitler maneuvering nonexistent armies on maps in his bunker and issuing orders that could not be carried out. Finally, when the Russian guns were within firing distance of the Reichs-Chancellery in Berlin, Hitler realized the finality of the situation. On April 30, 1945, he and Eva Braun, his mistress whom he finally married, committed suicide. It was ten days after his fifty-sixth birthday. Hitler's Thousand Year Reich survived him by only eight days. It had lasted for only twelve years and four months.

Summary

The appalling statistics from the end of World War II can only begin to itemize the legacy of Adolf Hitler. To Germany he bequeathed more than 6.5 million dead and more than twice that number as refugees. Germany itself was in ruins, partitioned, and occupied. The European balance sheet was similar. The total number of civilian and military dead from World War II probably exceeded fifty million. Direct and indirect costs from the war are virtually impossible to calculate. Europe was prostrate, both economically and politically. War damage was in the trillions of dollars, and most governments were either unstable or nonexistent because of the dislocations of war. While Germany in particular and Europe in general rebuilt themselves with the aid of the Marshall Plan and through the European Community, the scars of war and fears of Nazism/Fascism remain. Despite denazification, fear of a strong Germany continues to temper the attitudes of European neighbors toward a revitalized Germany. Germans fear that they will never be forgiven for the nightmare that was Hitler.

The destruction of Germany and the impact of the war on other European powers left a weak Western and Central Europe overshadowed by the military power of the Soviet Union and the United States. The Cold War that emerged from the ashes of World War II stemmed from two sources. The memory of Munich in 1938 left a fear of appeasement of the Soviet dictator by the West and resulted in a hard-line policy of containment of communism. The Cold War was also a competition between the United States and the Soviet Union over control of the Europe that had been devastated by Hitler's war. The artificial barrier, the so-called Iron Curtain that separated Eastern and Western Europe resulted in dislocation and scarcity as well as political instability. Hostile alliances and competition between the superpowers along the line of 1945 continue to exist.

One final significance of Hitler would be an understanding of totalitarianism. The totality of defeat for the Third Reich in 1945 meant that the state documents of the Third Reich fell into the hands of the victors. This documentation was used initially to prosecute war criminals at Nuremberg and elsewhere. It has since been used to study the megalomania of the Nazi leaders. No other dictator has ever been so well documented or thoroughly studied. An understanding of the situation that brought Hitler to power as well as an understanding of the forces that drove the man could help in dealing with future threats of his type. Although Hitler was, perhaps, the greatest megalomaniac in history, it does not mean that he was or will be the only one.

Bibliography

Bracher, Karl Dietrich. *The German Dictatorship: The Origins, Structure, and Effects of National Socialism.* Translated by Jean Steinberg. New York: Praeger, 1970. This is the best introduction to the theory and practice of National Socialism.

Bullock, Alan. *Hitler: A Study in Tyranny.* Rev. ed. New York: Harper & Row, 1964. This biography is a solid account of the life of Hitler that combines excellent research with lucid writing. With an emphasis on political narrative, it remains one of the best single-volume accounts of Hitler's life.

Carr, William. *Hitler: A Study in Personality and Politics.* New York: St. Martin's Press, 1979. This study of Hitler focuses upon the interrelationship between Hitler and the social forces that existed in Germany between World War I and World War II.

Fest, Joachim C. *Hitler.* Translated by Richard Winston and Clara Winston. New York: Harcourt Brace Jovanovich, 1974. This German biography is considered by many to be the standard biography of Hitler from the German point of view.

Langer, Walter C. *The Mind of Adolf Hitler: The Secret Wartime Report.* New York: Basic Books, 1972. In 1943 psychoanalyst Langer wrote a psychological profile of Hitler for the Office of Strategic Services. This long-classified work was finally released in 1972 and is considered to be the best psychohistory of Hitler.

Lukacs, John. *The Hitler of History.* A. A. Knopf, 1997. Revisionist study of Hitler's life through a critical examination of his numerous biographers.

Marrus, Michael Robert. *The Holocaust in History.* Boston: University Press of New England, 1987. As literature pertaining to the Holocaust is considerable, this work provides a broad survey of the causes and events of the Holocaust as well as a bibliography of literature about the Holocaust.

Shirer, William L. *The Rise and Fall of the Third Reich: A History of Nazi Germany.* New York: Simon & Schuster, 1960. Written by a journalist who covered the Third Reich during the 1930's, this single-volume account of the period is one of the best and most readable introductions to the many issues and personalities of National Socialism.

Smith, Bradley F. *Adolf Hitler: His Family, Childhood, and Youth.* Stanford, Calif.: Hoover Institution on War, Revolution, and Peace, 1967. There is little primary material extant that pertains to Hitler's formative years, but Smith attempts to provide a background for Hitler's development prior to World War I. It is primarily a chronological narrative.

Steinert, Marlis. *Hitler: A Biography*. New York: W. W. Norton, 1997.

Toland, John. *Adolf Hitler.* Garden City, N.Y.: Doubleday, 1976. While there is little new in this biography of Hitler, Toland achieves an intensity lacking in other biographies, perhaps because of the 250 oral interviews with personalities closely associated with Hitler, which gives a new perspective to the personal nature of the dictator.

William S. Brockington, Jr.

HO CHI MINH

Nguyen That Thanh

Born: May 19, 1890; Kim Lien, Vietnam, French Indochina
Died: September 3, 1969; Hanoi, North Vietnam

Ho was the chief architect, founder, and leader of the Indochinese Communist Party (1930), an organizer of the Viet Minh (1941), and president of the Democratic Republic of Vietnam (North Vietnam) from 1945 until his death. An ardent proponent of his country's independence, Ho was recognized as one of the twentieth century's greatest anticolonial revolutionaries and most influential communist leaders.

Early Life

Ho Chi Minh was a native of the village of Kim Lien, in the province of Nghe An, in central Vietnam (then part of French Indochina), an area long noted for its poverty, rebellious spirit, antiforeign leaders, and anticolonial activity. He was originally named Nguyen Sinh Cung and called by several others, before adopting the name Ho Chi Minh in the early 1940's. Ho's father, Nguyen Sinh Sac (sometimes Nguyen Sinh Huy), was a Mandarin and man of letters like his father before him. Nguyen Sinh Sac was dismissed from his civil service post for anti-French activities and nationalist leanings. Ho's mother, Hoang Thi Loan, was the eldest daughter of a village scholar with whom Ho's father studied as a young man.

Ho was the youngest of three surviving children. Like both his brother, Khiem, and his sister, Thanh, Ho espoused anticolonial ideas in his youth. He was sent initially to a public school to study the Vietnamese and French languages in addition to Chinese ideograms. At the age of nine, Ho, his siblings, and his mother, who had been charged with stealing French weapons for rebels, fled to Hue, the imperial city. Ho's father had left for Saigon, where he earned a meager living by practicing Oriental medicine.

Ho's stay in Hue was short. His mother died suddenly, and the young boy (age ten) found himself back in Kim Lien. Also, at age ten, according to custom, Ho's birth name was changed to Nguyen That Thanh (Nguyen who is destined to succeed). At age fifteen, Ho started attending Quoc Hoc Secondary School studying *Quoc Ngu* (the romanized form of Vietnamese) and French. The school was then considered the best in the country. While there, he was involved in some insurrectional movements that swept across central Vietnam in 1908. After four troubled and disappointing years of study, Ho headed southward to the town of Phan Tiet, where he taught French and Vietnamese at an elementary school.

After several months Ho went to Saigon, was enrolled in a vocational school, and then decided to leave Vietnam after the first Chinese Revolution broke out in October of 1911. Under the name of Ba, he took work on a French steamer. He was a seaman for more than three years, visiting ports in France, Spain, North Africa, and the United States. At the outset of World War I, Ho gave up his seafaring career and took up residence in London. In 1917, he moved yet again. When he set foot on French soil toward the end of World War I, he saw his future mapped out before him.

Life's Work

Ho's life was dedicated to improving conditions in his own country, working to force colonial regimes to introduce reform, and promoting revolution (ultimately worldwide revolution) against imperialism. Adopting the new name of Nguyen Ai Quoc (Nguyen the patriot) in Paris, Ho immediately took up the struggle for the political rights of the Vietnamese people, a struggle which lasted five decades. During the six years Ho spent in France (1917-1923), he became an active socialist, and then a communist. In 1919, he organized a group of Vietnamese living in France and, with others, drafted an eight-point petition addressed to the Versailles Peace Conference that demanded that the Vietnamese people be given legal equality with the French colonials; freedom of assembly, press, speech, and emigration; better educational facilities; and permanent Indochinese representation in the French parliament. He also requested a general amnesty for political detainees. There was, in the modest document, no explicit mention of independence or of self-determination.

Because the petition brought no response, except to make Ho a hero among certain Vietnamese, he took more drastic measures. In 1920, he became a founding member of the French Communist Party. He then began to denounce the evils of British and French colonialism in his new French journal, *Le Paria* (the outcast). The journal was the voice of the Intercolonial Union founded in 1921 to acquaint the public with the problems of the colonial people. When Ho went to Moscow at the end of 1923, his friends considered him a

Ho Chi Minh *(National Archives)*

thoroughgoing revolutionary. He participated in revolutionary and anti-imperial organizations and took an active part in the Fifth World Congress of the Communist International. Under the name of Nguyen Ai Quoc, Ho was the first of a series of Vietnamese revolutionaries to attend Moscow University for Oriental Workers, studying political theory. Although throughout his life Ho considered theory less important than revolutionary practice, he felt at home at the university as his emotional ties with the Soviet communists grew stronger.

In December, 1924, Ho's first visit to Russia ended when he departed for the southern Chinese port of Canton. This area was a hotbed of agitation and a center of Vietnamese nationalist activities. There he organized the Vietnamese Revolutionary Youth Association known as the Thanh Nien. Almost all of its members had been exiled from Indochina because of anticolonial beliefs and actions against the French. Canton became the first real home of organized Indochinese nationalism.

After expulsion from China at the hands of Chiang Kai-shek, Ho sought refuge in the Soviet Union. In 1928, he was off again to Brussels, Paris, and finally Siam (Thailand), where he spent two years as the Southeast Asian representative of the Communist International Organization. In February of 1930, Ho was brought back from Siam to Hong Kong to preside over the founding of the Indochinese Communist Party. Ho's achievement was his unification of three separate communist groups into one organization. Ho, still using the name of Nguyen Ai Quoc, summarized and published the results of his and others' efforts by issuing a call for support of the new Communist Party among the workers, peasants, soldiers, youth, and students of Vietnam. This document also contained Ho's first demand for the complete political independence of Indochina.

In the summer of 1930 there occurred the first mass revolutionary uprising in Vietnam brought about by the peasants (something Ho had advocated earlier). It followed on the heels of a less successful rebellion in February of 1930 and originated in the provinces of Ha Tinh and Nghe An (where Ho was born). The French reacted brutally, executing without trial some seven hundred anticolonials and torturing others. Though Ho was outside the country during the summer rebellion and his role was probably nil, the French condemned him to death in absentia. In June, 1931, Ho was arrested in Hong Kong, where French officials arranged with the British to have him extradited. He was finally released, but not before he had spent one year in prison and had contracted tuberculosis.

In 1934, Ho returned to Moscow, and in 1935 he participated in the Seventh Congress of the Communist International as chief delegate for the Indochinese Communist Party. The congress sanctioned the idea of the popular front (an alliance of leftist organizations to combat fascism), which Ho had advocated for some time. Relations eased in 1936 between communists in Indochina and the French because of the formation of Premier Léon Blum's Popular

Front government in France. With the fall of the Blum government in 1937, however, French repression in Indochina returned, and Ho's era of relative quiet (1934-1938) came to an end.

In 1938, Ho returned to China, stayed with Mao Zedong for a time, and traveled throughout the land. With the German defeat of France in 1940, and Japan's attempt to occupy and rule Indochina, Ho returned to his homeland for the first time in thirty years in January, 1941. With the help of his lieutenants, Vo Nguyen Giap and Pham Vam Dong, Ho organized in May, 1941, the League for the Independence of Vietnam, better known as the Viet Minh.

This new organization promoted Vietnamese nationalism with renewed zeal. In June, 1941, Ho issued the clarion call for national insurrection and liberation. In an important letter published at that time to all Vietnamese, Ho pledged his modest abilities to follow them in their revolutionary efforts. Although the concrete results of the June appeal were not immediately apparent—the Viet Minh had few guns—the events of 1941 were the most important in Vietnamese revolutionary history. For Ho, who had celebrated his fifty-first birthday on the day of the founding of the Viet Minh, those events meant the end of thirty years of leadership of revolution from outside his own country, with the exception of some time he spent in a Chinese prison. Ho's new organization sought help from China in 1942. When Ho crossed the border in the summer of 1942, he had already taken the name of Ho Chi Minh (Ho who enlightens). Because Chiang Kai-shek distrusted Ho, the latter was imprisoned for eighteen months. During this time, he wrote his famous prison diary as friends were arranging his release.

In 1945, Ho established his first contacts with Americans and began to collaborate with them against the Japanese who had overrun Indochina and imprisoned or executed all French officials. At the same time, Giap and his commandos, under Ho's direction, moved against Hanoi, the Vietnamese capital. The moment Ho had been waiting for finally came following Japan's surrender to the United States after the atomic bombings in August. On September 2, before an enormous crowd gathered in Ba Dinh square, Hanoi, Ho declared Vietnam independent and proclaimed the inauguration of the Democratic Republic of Vietnam, which included the entire country. The declaration, drafted by Ho himself, opened with words intended to garner United States support. After September 2, 1945, Ho became more than merely a revolutionary, he became a statesman. Nationwide elections held on January 6, 1946, conferred the presidency on Ho. In July, 1946, a liberal constitution was adopted, modeled in part on the U.S. Constitution.

France, under the leadership of Charles de Gaulle, did not accept Vietnamese independence, nor did the Chinese. The Chinese were supposed to replace the Japanese and occupy Vietnam north of the sixteenth parallel. Ho persuaded the French, who were attempting to reassert their authority over Vietnam, to force the withdrawal of the Chinese; he then began negotiating with the French to secure Vietnam's autonomy and unification. After many months, negotiations broke down when a French cruiser opened fire (November 20, 1946) on the town of Haiphong after a clash between French and Vietnamese soldiers. Almost six thousand Vietnamese were killed.

On December 20, 1946, Ho declared a national war of resistance and called on his countrymen to drive out the French colonialists and save the fatherland. Ho sought refuge in northern Vietnam while the first Indochinese war was fought. Finally, in May of 1954, the French were thoroughly defeated at Dien Bien Phu and had no choice but to negotiate. The meeting between representatives of eight countries in May-July, 1954, yielded the Geneva Accords, in which it was finally concluded that Vietnam was to be divided at the seventeenth parallel into northern and southern sections. The north was to be led by Ho, the south by Bao Dai (later Ngo Dinh Diem), until elections could be held in 1956 and a unified government be established by the vote of the people.

In September, 1955, Ho, who had been both president and premier of North Vietnam, relinquished the premiership to Pham Van Dong. He continued to be recognized as the real leader of North Vietnam (still officially called the Democratic Republic of Vietnam). The 1956 elections that were to guarantee the country's reunification were postponed by the United States and by South Vietnam, which was created on a de facto basis at that time. In September, 1960, Ho was reelected president of his country, and a new constitution, adopted that year in the north, gave him unlimited power and placed greater emphasis on communist principles.

Ho never lived to see the fulfillment of his vision—a unified, autonomous, peaceful Vietnam. In 1959, there emerged in South Vietnam the communist-oriented Viet Cong guerrilla force supported by Ho and the North Vietnamese government. They began conducting an armed revolt against the American-sponsored regime of Ngo Dinh Diem. In response, the United States sent military aid to South Vietnam. The conflict escalated to full-fledged war which lasted until 1975, when the Vietnamese communists unified their country as a totalitarian state. Ho had died six years before, on September 3, 1969, at the age of seventy-nine.

Summary

Ho Chi Minh was a man of many facets: a shrewd calculator, a consummate actor, a patient revolutionary, and a relentless agitator. Above all, he was a successful leader. He did not hesitate to resort to any means to achieve his political objectives, but his popularity seems never to have waned. Throughout the villages of North and South Vietnam he was referred to as Uncle Ho, a name symbolic of the affection he engendered in the public mind. Behind the scenes, he ruled increasingly with an iron fist and, for reasons of state, ultimately silenced forever half a million adversaries during the infamous period of land reform in North Vietnam (1953-1956).

Ho was not the intellectual genius that some of his admirers claimed him to have been. Rather, he worked to improve his knowledge of men and things as part of the pursuit of his ideal. Being in the company of international revolutionary theorists (in France, Russia, and China) made him keenly aware of his shortcomings. While in France (1917-1923), he suffered from his relative lack of education (because of a wretched childhood) and sought to correct this by reading the works of William Shakespeare and Charles Dickens in English, Lu Hsün in Chinese, and Victor Hugo and Émile Zola in French. His favorite author became Leo Tolstoy. Ho's ability to create and motivate groups and organizations was surpassed only by his ability to continue to influence them, as was demonstrated in 1954 when he persuaded the Viet Minh radicals to accept, for a time, the Geneva Accords. His death in 1969 ruined chances for an earlier settlement of the Vietnam War.

Ho was one of the most important leaders of the twentieth century. His continual battle against foreign control of Vietnam caused grave crises in two of the West's most powerful countries, France and the United States. As one of the leading communists internationally, he emphasized the role of the peasantry in the success of revolutionary struggle.

Bibliography

Fenn, Charles. *Ho Chi Minh: A Biographical Introduction.* New York: Charles Scribner's Sons, 1973. As a correspondent and friend of Ho, the author brings an important perspective to his work. This book attempts synthesis rather than completeness by culling, from previous biographies, scholarly studies, and personal knowledge, essential information on the life of Ho. It presents to the reader extensive quotations from these other sources.

Halberstam, David. *Ho.* 2d ed. New York: McGraw Hill, 1986.

Ho Chi Minh. *On Revolution: Selected Writings*. New York: Praeger, 1967.

Huyen, N. Khac. *Vision Accomplished? The Enigma of Ho Chi Minh.* New York: Macmillan, 1971. A native of Indochina, Huyen lived under Ho's regime for seven years. The book represents a scholarly contribution to the literature on Ho. It is well documented and contains appendices, a bibliography, and an index which are helpful to the researcher or serious student. Written from the perspective of respect for Ho, it nevertheless attempts a balanced view.

Karnow, Stanley. *Vietnam: A History.* New York: Viking Press, 1983. Written by a distinguished journalist who reported on Southeast Asia during his career, this extensive volume covers the first (1946-1954) and second (1959-1975) anticolonial Indochinese wars. Three introductory chapters trace the history of Vietnamese nationalism and help the reader to understand the context of Ho's nationalistic ideas.

Lacouture, Jean. *Ho Chi Minh: A Political Biography.* Translated by Peter Wiles. New York: Random House, 1968. Originally published in French in 1967, this is one of the best-known biographies of Ho written by French journalist Lacouture two years before the leader's death. Its style is popular rather than scholarly and focuses on the political activities of Ho and how they had been viewed up to the time of the book's publication.

Neumann-Hoditz, Reinhold. *Portrait of Ho Chi Minh: An Illustrated Biography.* New York: Herder and Herder, 1972. This volume presents the essential events of Ho's life, with special attention given to his early political training in France and his visits to China and Russia. Written in an engaging style, the book contains many informative photographs as well as extensive quotations taken from the translated writings of Ho Chi Minh. It does not say much about Ho's activities from 1954 through 1969.

Sainteny, Jean. *Ho Chi Minh and His Vietnam.* Translated by Herma Briffault. Chicago: Cowles Book Company, 1972. This work tells of Ho's life from the standpoint of a noted French diplomat who engaged in negotiations with the Vietnamese leader and became his close personal friend. It is an easy-to-read translation of a succinctly written study.

Tin Bui. *Following Ho Chi Minh: The Memoirs of a North Vietnamese Colonel.* Honolulu: University of Hawaii Press, 1995.

Tonnesson, Stein. *The Vietnamese Revolution of 1945: Roosevelt, Ho Chi Minh and de Gaulle in a World at War.* Thousand Oaks, Calif.: Sage Publications, 1992.

Andrew C. Skinner

HERBERT HOOVER

Born: August 10, 1874; West Branch, Iowa
Died: October 20, 1964; New York, New York

As the president whose presidency ushered in the Great Depression, Hoover has long been castigated as a failure. Nevertheless, his career both before and after his presidency and the accomplishments of his administration give final judgment of Hoover as a great American.

Early Life

Herbert Clark Hoover, or "Bertie" as he was known to his family, was born in West Branch, Iowa, on August 10, 1874. He had an older brother, Tad (Theodore), and a younger sister, May (Mary). His father, Jesse Hoover, was a businessman who worked as a blacksmith and operated a farm implement store. He died in 1880, at the age of thirty-four. Herbert's mother, Hulda Minthorn Hoover, worked as a seamstress to pay the family's debts after the death of her husband and was vigorously active in the Quaker Church, speaking at meetings throughout the area. She died of pneumonia in 1884, at the age of thirty-five.

The three orphaned children were separated and parceled out to other family members. Herbert stayed briefly with his uncle Allan Hoover and his aunt Millie before moving to Oregon at the age of eleven to live with Laura and John Minthorn. John Minthorn was a medical doctor and a businessman, and the family provided a more cultured environment for young Hoover than he had found in Iowa. In 1891, Herbert became the youngest member of the first class to attend the newly established Stanford College in California. Nearly six feet tall, thin, and muscular, with thick, light hair, Hoover had the brusque, retiring manner which also characterized him as an adult. Even as a youth he had the plumb cheeks, which, as an adult, became the familiar jowls that dropped down to the stiff white collars he wore, long after they had gone out of style. He worked his way through the University, where he met his future wife, Lou Henry, who, like Hoover, was majoring in geology.

Hoover graduated in 1895 and the following year left for a mining job in Australia, where he began a highly successful career in mining. In 1899, he married Lou Henry, who accompanied him to China, where they were both actively involved in aid for those civilians caught in the Boxer Rebellion. Hoover moved up the ladder of success, returning to Australia and then to London, where his son Herbert, Jr., was born in 1903, followed by another son, Allan, in 1907.

By 1908, Hoover had built a home in Palo Alto, California, developed mines in Burma, and established a consulting business which allowed him to exercise his managerial and organizational talents as well as enlarge the fortune he had already earned. In 1909, Hoover published his *Principles of Mining*, which was the standard textbook in the field for many years. In 1912, he was named a trustee of Stanford University, an institution to which he was always loyal. He later established the Hoover Institute on their campus.

Hoover was in Europe at the outbreak of World War I and immediately plunged into the organization of Belgian relief. His committee was credited with saving several hundred thousand persons from death. After the United States entered the war, Hoover turned his organizational talents to directing the United States Food Administration with remarkably effective results. He next accompanied President Woodrow Wilson to Paris, where Hoover acted as head of the European Relief Program and as one of Wilson's economic advisers at the Paris Peace Conference.

Life's Work

At the end of World War I, Hoover had both a national and an international reputation. As the Great Humanitarian and as the Great Engineer, Hoover seemed to combine the best of both worlds, a practical idealist. In 1920, both the Democrats and the Republicans considered him to be a presidential possibility. When he declared himself to be a Republican, he allowed friends to pursue his possible candidacy, but the Republican leadership was cool, and he did not do well in early primaries. In 1921, he accepted the position of secretary of commerce in the cabinet of President Warren G. Harding, and he remained there under President Calvin Coolidge as well. He was an activist secretary, certainly one considered a Progressive in the context of the 1920's.

Under Hoover's direction the Commerce Department made major gains in gathering and distributing information on a wide variety of subjects of interest to the business community. Hoover was also reasonably sympathetic to labor unions. He effectively used two tactics which had served him well in his earlier activities—voluntary cooperation and widespread publicity for his goals. Once again responding to crisis, Hoover directed relief efforts for victims of the 1927 Mississippi River flood. In that program, and throughout the Commerce Department, Hoover began an effective program of racial desegregation.

When Calvin Coolidge chose not to run again in 1928, Hoover became a candidate for the Republican nomination—which he re-

Herbert Hoover *(Library of Congress)*

ceived and accepted on his fifty-fourth birthday. His campaign focused on progress through technology and, on major issues, differed little from that of his Democratic opponent Alfred E. Smith. Hoover, his reputation enhanced by his Cabinet years, and the country ready to continue the prosperity which seemed tied to Republican leadership, was a comfortable winner in 1928.

As president, Hoover was more progressive than most contemporaries recognized. He supported both civil liberties and civil rights. The Wickersham Commission on Crime and Prohibition gave a mixed report on the constitutionally mandated abstinence from alcohol. Hoover chose to enforce the law, though he was apparently not in full agreement with it. Although Lou Hoover would tolerate no alcohol nor, while in the White House, would the Hoovers attend functions where alcohol was served, after leaving the presidency, Hoover was partial to one martini after dinner. Hoover, as president, supported conservation of natural resources, aid to the economically distressed farmers, and, in 1930, supported the Hawley-Smoot Tariff. A high tariff had long been a Republican tradition, but the Hawley-Smoot Tariff became highly politicized as the Democrats charged that it had helped to spread the Depression.

Hoover had little opportunity to initiate a program before the stock market crash of 1929 launched the Great Depression. He had been concerned about the speculative fever of the stock market before he took office and, after the initial crash, worked closely with the nation's major banks to alleviate the crash. Hoover believed that the decline would, like the other panics in America's past, be relatively brief in duration. The idea that prosperity was "just around the corner" (actually said by Vice President Charles Curtis, though often attributed to Hoover) quickly proved false, and the nation rejected Hoover both for the crash itself and for what was perceived to be false optimism.

Hoover endeavored to follow the pattern of his earlier success—voluntary activity and publicity. Despite his holding biweekly press conferences and participating in ninety-five radio broadcasts during his four years in office, Hoover never was able to restore public confidence. His bland, unemotional voice conveyed neither his genuine concern for the suffering caused by the Depression nor his underlying confidence in America and its people. Voluntary action similarly proved to be inadequate in the face of the ever- worsening Depression.

In spite of a philosophy and a personal experience which emphasized individualism, Hoover did provide active leadership to meet the emergencies of the Depression. In 1932, he encouraged the establishment of the Reconstruction Finance Corporation (RFC) to provide economic aid for the banks, which Hoover believed would then "trickle down" to help provide funds for business and thus jobs for the unemployed. Hoover, throughout his administration, feared direct relief on the part of the federal government, believing that it would damage the concept of local self-government as well as deprive the recipients of the desire to work. The RFC was maintained and expanded by the New Deal; indeed, many of the concepts held by Hoover became part of the New Deal. Franklin D. Roosevelt, however, carried many ideas further and faster than Hoover could have tolerated.

In foreign policy, Hoover was something of a pacifist. He met face-to-face with British prime minister Ramsay MacDonald and French premier Pierre Laval. He supported the World Court and continued the pursuit of disarmament at the 1930 London Naval Conference and, in 1932, at the Geneva Peace Conference. He opposed the kind of "dollar diplomacy" which led to intervention in Latin America, anticipating here the Good Neighbor Policy of his successor, Franklin D. Roosevelt.

The Japanese invasion of Manchuria produced the Stimson Doctrine, which provided nonrecognition of such aggression. The Hoover Moratorium in 1931 suspended payment for one year of both the Allied war debts and the German reparations from World War I. The continuing downward spiral of the economy had the result of making the suspension of payments permanent.

In 1932, Hoover was renominated by the Republicans but without noticeable enthusiasm. The Democrats chose New York governor Franklin D. Roosevelt, who promised the nation a "new deal." The two men were of dramatically different personalities, which made them seem further apart in philosophy than they often were. Hoover appeared even more aloof from the problems of the common man as he failed to repudiate the excessive actions of General Douglas MacArthur in driving the Bonus Army (World War I veterans who marched to Washington to seek early payment of their promised bonus) out of the capital city. The outcome of the election was easily predicted—a Democratic victory.

Hoover and his wife briefly returned to their home in Palo Alto, California, but in 1934, moved permanently into a suite in the Waldorf-Astoria Hotel in New York City. Hoover wrote many books, traveled to Europe, and, over the years which made him the longest lived former president except John Adams, collected eighty-five honorary degrees and 468 awards. With the outbreak of World War II, he once again raised funds for relief. He opposed United States participation in the Korean War in spite of a growing and rigid anticommunist outlook. President Harry S Truman brought Hoover back into government to do what he had always done best—organize and manage. Hoover chaired the 1947 Committee on the Organization of the Executive Branch of Government and brought much needed reform and coherence to that branch of government. At the age of eighty, he chaired a second committee to which he was appointed by President Dwight D. Eisenhower. He died at his home in New York at the age of ninety.

Summary

Throughout his long life and varied career, Hoover's outlook was dominated by his Quaker heritage. He believed in an orderly universe and in the beneficial results of cooperation among men of goodwill. He also held strongly to the belief, grounded in experience, in individualism. It was a self-help philosophy tempered by his belief in cooperative action. His engineering background gave him a strong faith in technology and statistics. His many humanitarian activities reveal a deep and abiding concern for his fellow man—revealed also in his opposition to foreign intervention and his desire for peace.

In any other time, Hoover would have been a superior president. He had abundant leadership and managerial skills, but few political talents. His pompous physical appearance, his dry wit, and undynamic demeanor were suitable for the chairman of the board, not for an elected executive who on occasion needed to persuade both the Congress and his countrymen of the value of his policies. Generally nonpolitical (he had never voted for president before 1920, because he was so often out of the country), Hoover never acquired the skills which came so easily to Franklin D. Roosevelt (and which made the contrast between the two of them so painfully denigrating to Hoover).

Hoover's experience and philosophy limited the extent to which he could involve the government in the lives of citizens. Yet when it was clear that voluntary and local relief had failed, Hoover first set the federal government on the path of response to the public need—down which it traveled so much more rapidly under the New

Deal. In the context of the 1920's Hoover was a classic Progressive in the programs he supported; it was the Depression and the vigorous activism of Roosevelt which made him seem to be a conservative.

Hoover lived long enough to see himself rehabilitated in public esteem. He advised many presidents, and his enormous managerial skills were again used for the national good under Truman and Eisenhower. In spite of his stalwart anticommunist stance, he never supported the excesses of Senator Joe McCarthy during the Red Scare of the 1950's (nor had he tolerated the similar excesses of the 1920's). He was a good man, indeed a great man, who was overpowered by the awesome circumstances of the Great Depression. Unable to articulate and communicate his concern for the people and his optimism for the future, Hoover's reputation, like the stock market, plunged down—and, like the economy, eventually revived.

Bibliography

Best, Gary Dean. *The Politics of American Individualism: Herbert Hoover in Transition, 1918-21*. Westport, Conn.: Greenwood Press, 1975. An excellent work on Hoover's early public service. Best has also written on Hoover's postpresidential years, and his excellent research is useful in rounding out the story of this president.

Burner, David. *Herbert Hoover: A Public Life*. New York: Alfred A. Knopf, 1979. Probably the best single biography among the many available on Hoover. It covers his entire life and career admirably and strikes a balance between admiration and criticism.

Emerson, Edwin. *Hoover and His Times*. Garden City, N.Y.: Garden City Publishing, 1932. A useful book with a valuable immediacy of views concerning Hoover's presidency. Like several books published soon after Hoover left office, it suffers from a lack of perspective.

Fausold, Martin L. *The Presidency of Herbert Clark Hoover*. Lawrence: University Press of Kansas, 1985. One of the most valuable books on the presidency of Hoover. It does not do justice, nor does it attempt to do justice, to the other areas of Hoover's career.

Liebovich, Louis W. *Bylines in Despair: Herbert Hoover, the Great Depression, and the U.S. News Media*. Westport, Conn.: Praeger, 1994.

Lyons, Eugene. *The Herbert Hoover Story*. Garden City, N.Y.: Doubleday, 1948. Reprint. Washington, D.C.: Human Events, 1959. A favorable book in support of Herbert Hoover. Originally entitled *Our Unknown Ex-President*, its interest comes especially from the personal viewpoint of the author, who, in his youth, was sympathetic toward communism until a visit to Russia thoroughly disillusioned him. His philosophical travels from Left to Right provide an interesting perspective from which to view Hoover.

Nash, George H. *The Life of Herbert Hoover: Master of Emergencies, 1917-1918*. New York: W. W. Norton, 1996.

Smith, Richard N. *An Uncommon Man: The Triumph of Hoover*. New York: Simon and Schuster, 1984. Another excellent biography of Hoover, taking its title from one of Hoover's own inspirational articles on being uncommon. Smith picks up a theme many writers have used, that Hoover did triumph over the Depression, and that a dispassionate view of his administration will reveal this fact.

Warren, Harris Gaylord. *Herbert Hoover and the Great Depression*. New York: Oxford University Press, 1959. A relatively brief and easily read book covering the major facets of Hoover's life and concentrating on the Depression years.

Wilson, Jean H. *Herbert Hoover: Forgotten Progressive*. Boston: Little, Brown, 1975. Another relatively brief account of Hoover's entire career, focusing on the basically progressive character of Hoover and the many ways in which his ideas did, in fact, anticipate the New Deal. An interesting and provocative account.

Carlanna L. Hendrick

HUSSEIN I

Born: November 14, 1935; Amman, Transjordan
Died: February 7, 1999; Amman, Jordan

While holding power longer than any other contemporary world leader, Hussein, king of Jordan, maintained the autonomy of Jordan, contributed to Arab unity, and served as a stabilizing force in the Middle East.

Early Life

Hussein I (born Hussein ibn Talal) of Jordan is considered to have been a direct descendant of the Prophet Mohammed and the head of the "first family" of Islam, the Hashemites. The eldest of four children born to Crown Prince Talal and Princess Zein, he was born in Amman, the capital of Transjordan (later Jordan), on November 14, 1935. At that time, Jordan was a poor, feudal, Bedouin state, mostly desert, and even the royal family lived frugally. Hussein grew up in a five-room house in Amman, where, by his own account, he learned to mend his clothes and even sold his bicycle at one point to help with family finances.

Hussein's father suffered from mental illness, and his grandfather, King Abdullah, took a special interest in young Hussein's upbringing and exerted a significant influence on his character. Under his grandfather's supervision, Hussein was reared as an Arab prince and educated in both English and Arabic. At age five, he was enrolled in kindergarten in Amman, where he also attended the Islamic College. At age eight, he was sent to Victoria College in Alexandria, Egypt.

The Hashemites had played a key role in ending the Ottoman rule over the Arab states. As his reward, Abdullah was recognized by the British as emir of Transjordan, created as an adjunct of the British Mandate in Palestine in 1921, and received a British subsidy to maintain security and establish a central government over the Bedouin tribes. In 1946, Abdullah established the independent Hashemite Kingdom of Transjordan, with continued support and collaboration from the British. When the termination of the British

Mandate in Palestine on May 14, 1948, resulted in the creation of Israel and the Arab-Israeli War, King Abdullah took control of areas of eastern Palestine on the West Bank of the Jordan River and was proclaimed king of United Transjordan and Palestine (or the Hashemite Kingdom of Jordan) in December, 1948.

Hussein frequently accompanied his grandfather on his official duties. In July, 1951, on a trip to Jerusalem, King Abdullah was assassinated by a Palestinian extremist at El Aqsa Mosque (the Mosque of the Rock), and Hussein narrowly escaped death himself when he tried to capture the assassin and a medal on his uniform deflected a bullet. Witnessing his grandfather's murder and the panic that ensued among his loyal followers made a profound impression on the young prince. His firsthand experience with political assassination and the unreliability of the king's followers taught Hussein the risks of political life at an early age and instilled in him a determination to live purposefully and to be ready for death whenever it comes.

Crown Prince Talal, who had been receiving treatment in a mental hospital in Switzerland, was crowned king in September. Hussein, now crown prince, was sent to complete his studies at Harrow in England, where his cousin, Faisal II, heir to Iraq's throne, was also a student. When Talal suffered a relapse and was asked to step down from the throne in August, 1952, Hussein was declared king three months before his seventeenth birthday. He took a six-month accelerated course at the Royal Military Academy at Sandhurst, England, while the regency council exercised control of Jordan until his eighteenth birthday.

Life's Work

Hussein was crowned king of Jordan on May 2, 1953. His strong autocratic rule, strength of character, and personal charisma make it difficult to extricate his personal history from the history of the state of Jordan. Despite his youth and lack of political experience, he was able to survive multiple internal and international challenges during the economic and political instability of the early years of his reign. His commitment to Arab nationalism, his desire for peace in the Middle East, his search for a solution to the Palestinian problem, and his democratic ideals were not always compatible with consistent political decisions.

Jordan's incorporation of the West Bank under King Abdullah resulted in a sudden increase in population that strained the small

Hussein I *(Library of Congress)*

country's resources. Some 750,000 Palestinians, including an influx of more than 500,000 refugees from Israeli-occupied Palestine, outnumbered the Jordanians almost two to one. Although Jordan was the only Arab state to grant the Palestinians citizenship and participation in parliamentary and municipal elections, they were bitter and resentful. They resented Jordan's financial dependence on Great Britain, British influence on the Jordanian government and armed forces, and the parliament's token participation in government.

Jordan's desire for accommodation and peace with Israel, given its extended border with that country, contrasted dangerously with the demands for all-out war from the other Arab states. Left-wing Middle Eastern extremists, led by Egyptian president Gamal Abdel Nasser, fanned the fires of Palestinian resentment and labeled Hussein "a tool of the West." Confronting the first urban unrest and agitation in Jordan, Hussein yielded to demands for political liberalization and relaxed restrictions on the press, measures that temporarily enhanced his popularity but only served to increase the turmoil.

When the British insisted in 1955 that Jordan join the Baghdad Pact, part of a general Middle East defense system against the Soviet Union, riots followed. The king dissolved parliament, and the Arab Legion (the Jordanian armed forces), commanded by an Englishman, John Bagot Glubb, had to suppress the mobs. Hussein announced his unwillingness to join either the Baghdad Pact or the Egyptian-Syrian-Saudi Arabian bloc, but the demands for a scapegoat on whom to blame the disturbances resulted in his dismissal of Glubb in March, 1956; one of Glubb's replacements was Lieutenant Colonel Ali Abu Nuwar, the leader of the movement to eliminate foreign influence in Jordan. Relations between Great Britain and Jordan cooled.

In October, 1956, Hussein agreed to join the Unified Arab Command (UAC), a mutual defense pact, and in January, 1957, Egypt, Syria, and Saudi Arabia agreed to provide Jordan with financial support, replacing the British subsidy. The 1948 Anglo-Jordanian treaty was terminated in March, 1957; Great Britain's involvement in the Israeli attack of Egypt, October, 1956, made Hussein's break with Great Britain inevitable. By September, 1957, the last British troops had left Jordan.

Meanwhile, the Jordanian elections of October, 1956, led to a coalition government under Suleyman al-Nabulsi, the leader of the National Socialists. The king, aware of al-Nabulsi's Soviet leanings, demanded his resignation, suppressed all political parties, and imposed martial law. An attempted coup, allegedly instigated by Nuwar, head of the armed forces, followed; the king escaped being overthrown only through a courageous appeal to loyal Bedouin troops. Nuwar, together with leaders of the coalition, was exiled.

Egypt and Syria, now firmly aligned with the Communist bloc, had not fulfilled their financial commitments to Jordan, and their relations with Jordan worsened when Hussein accepted American aid. In February, 1958, they merged to form the United Arab Republic (UAR). In response, Hussein and his cousin, King Faisal II of Iraq, formed a federation between their two countries. That summer, Faisal and his family were massacred in a coup and Hussein narrowly escaped a military takeover by Nasser supporters. The armies of Iraq, Syria, and Israel threatened Jordan, and only the arrival of British troops, in response to Hussein's appeal, averted the collapse of his kingdom.

During the next two years, Hussein enjoyed relative peace and the financial support of the United States. He took a firm stand against communism but in August, 1959, renewed diplomatic relations with the UAR (broken off in July, 1958), in spite of frequent incidents on the Syrian border. In 1960, Prime Minister Hazza al-Majali, labeled "an imperialist agent" by Egyptian and Syrian sympathizers, was murdered. After his death, there were several attempts on the king's life, a succession of prime ministers, and cycles of repression, relaxation, and riots.

Relations with Israel were tense. Major issues included the future of the refugees, Israel's plan to divert the Jordan waters, and the future of Jerusalem. At the Second Arab Summit in August, 1964, Hussein mended relations with Nasser, recognized the Palestinian Liberation Organization (PLO), and agreed to the creation of a unified Arab military command. From the summer of 1965, however, border raids by the PLO increased, and in July, 1966, Hussein banned the organization in an attempt to stop Israeli counterattacks. A massive Israeli reprisal raid in November, 1966, led to violent demonstrations in Jordan. Worsening relations with Syria resulted in border clashes and calls by Syria and the PLO for Jordanians to revolt against Hussein.

Jordan boycotted the next meeting of the Arab Defense Council. Yet, concerned about an imminent war with Israel, Hussein signed a defense agreement with Egypt and joined forces in the June, 1967, Six-Day War. The war was disastrous for Jordan. It cost Hussein his entire air force, fifteen thousand troops, and all Jordanian territory on the West Bank, including the old city of Jerusalem. Refugees poured into the East Bank. Realizing that Jordan would bear the brunt of any war with Israel, Hussein helped to draft the United Nations resolution calling on Israel to give up occupied territory in exchange for Arab recognition (land for peace) following the war.

The PLO, supported by Syria, increased its presence within

Jordan (a "state within a state"), threatening Jordan's internal security. Bloody confrontations between guerrilla organizations and the official government increased between 1968 and 1970. Finally, in September, 1970 (Black September), after an assassination attempt on King Hussein and the hijacking of four Western airliners, Hussein drove the guerrillas from Amman. By August, 1971, the last of the PLO had been ousted from Jordan.

In 1972, again trying to resolve the Palestinian problem, Hussein proposed a United Arab Kingdom, a federation of autonomous Jordanian and Palestinian regions, united under the king and a federal council of ministers. Other Arab states criticized the plan and Hussein's handling of the PLO problem, and he was not apprised of Egypt and Syria's plans for the fourth Arab-Israeli War in October, 1973. Therefore, Jordan's involvement in the war was limited, although Hussein received credit from the other Arab states for going to Syria's assistance.

In another move to regain political standing in the Arab world, Hussein agreed to the 1974 Arab Summit resolution, which recognized the PLO as the only legitimate representative of the Palestinian people, thereby virtually abandoning his claim to the West Bank. In 1978, he denounced the Camp David accords that led to a peace treaty between Egypt (by then under Anwar Sadat) and Israel. Enjoying improved relations with the Arab states, in November, 1978, he received pledges of renewed support from oil-rich countries at the Baghdad Summit Conference.

By 1982, the United States was supporting the creation of a Palestinian state on the West Bank in confederation with Jordan, but Hussein met with repeated failures in his attempts to persuade the PLO to support a joint Jordanian-Palestinian negotiating team. Hussein maintained that he would not negotiate a separate peace. He called for an international conference to be attended by all concerned parties, including the PLO, requiring Israel to accept the principle of "land for peace" and giving the Palestinians the right to self-determination regarding the proposed confederation. His proposal was temporarily supported by Yasir Arafat, head of the PLO, but it did not gain the support of the Arab states or Israel.

Meanwhile, Hussein attempted to create a Palestinian constituency on the West Bank and introduced in 1986 a five-year development plan for the region. In December, 1987, following the Amman Summit, which agreed to support an international peace conference if the PLO was recognized as the "sole legitimate representative of the Palestinian people," there was a spontaneous uprising (*intifada*) on the West Bank, despite brutal security measures by Israel.

At the Extraordinary Arab Summit called in Algiers in June, 1988, in support of the uprising, Hussein denied any ambition to rule the West Bank, and, on July 28, 1988, he severed Jordan's legal and administrative ties with the West Bank, dissolving the Jordanian House of Representatives, where the West Bank occupied thirty of sixty seats; laying off about twenty thousand teachers and public servants; and terminating the West Bank Development Plan. This move placed the responsibility for peace negotiations and the administration of the West Bank squarely on the PLO and Israel. While persevering in his efforts to support any movement toward peace in the Middle East, Hussein devoted more time to internal affairs, responding to serious problems in the economy and a call for political reform. The first elections in Jordan in more than twenty years were held in November, 1989.

The 1990 Persian Gulf War forced Hussein to choose between allies. While his relationship with the United States cooled when he expressed support for Iraq's Saddam Hussein, relations with the Palestinians and with his own people were improved. By 1994 he had cultivated good diplomatic ties with both the West and the Arab nations, signing a formal peace treaty with Israel that awarded him custodianship of the Muslim holy sites in East Jerusalem. Frequently operating as a moderating influence in the Israeli-Palestinian peace process, his contribution to stability in the Middle East cannot be underestimated.

In 1998 Hussein went to the United States for cancer treatments. When he returned briefly to Jordan in early 1999, he altered Jordan's political future by announcing that his younger brother Hassan was no longer the heir to the throne. He returned to the United States for further treatment, leaving his eldest son and new heir, Prince Abdullah, in charge of the country. After he died in February, Abdullah became king of Jordan.

Summary

Hussein I was thrust onto the stage of world politics at the age of eighteen, when he came to the throne of Jordan, a country which occupies an important strategic position in the Middle East. His remarkable survival—he survived numerous assassination attempts, attempted coups, and four Arab-Israeli wars—was accredited to his undeniable courage and strength of character. He enjoyed an immense popularity within his own country and was respected throughout the world. Although he maintained the real authority in Jordan, he was committed to democratic ideals, and his anticommunist, moderate stance set him at odds with other Arab states during most of Jordan's turbulent political history.

Hussein was committed to preserving the state of Jordan and the Hashemite throne. His vision literally shaped the destiny of the nation. Although by the late 1980's the economy was burdened by foreign debt and a growing trade deficit (the result of the failure of some Arab states to give the financial assistance they pledged), Hussein brought about impressive economic progress in the country. Illiteracy had markedly declined, electrical power supplies were developed, irrigation projects multiplied, agricultural production increased, new roads were built, a national airline was created, and tourism increased during his reign. This progress is all the more remarkable considering that Jordan is a small state, poor in natural resources and dependent on foreign aid.

Hussein's policies were dictated by his commitment to Arab nationalism and, in part, by his desire not to alienate the Palestinians, who represent a considerable threat to political stability in Jordan. While attempting to integrate the Palestinians and to forge a national consciousness among the people of both the East and West Banks, he affirmed the Palestinians' rights to self-determination and to their own homeland. Many world leaders came and went during Hussein's reign. He was long one of the foremost spokesmen for peace in the Middle East, respected worldwide for his statesmanship and integrity.

Bibliography

Bailey, Clinton. *Jordan's Palestinian Challenge 1948-1983: A Political History.* Boulder, Colo.: Westview Press, 1984. Bailey focuses on the problems that the Palestinian nationalists have posed for the Hashemite monarchy since 1984 and concludes that Hussein's policies were dictated, for the most part, by his desire not to alienate the Palestinian majority in his country. Bailey sees Hussein's survival as a remarkable achievement in the light of PLO, Israeli, and Egyptian schemes to topple the king.

Hussein, King of Jordan. *Uneasy Lies the Head: The Autobiography of His Majesty King Hussein I of the Hashemite Kingdom of Jordan.* London: Heinemann, 1962. Hussein begins by recounting the details of his grandfather's assassination, then discusses his early life, including his school days of Harrow and Sandhurst, and devotes most of the volume to the turbulent years following his inauguration as king. His account of the many attempts on his life is presented against a political context in which communism and Zionism are regarded as the chief obstacles to peace and to Arab nationalism.

__________, with Vick Vance and Pierre Laver. *My "War" with Israel.* Translated by June P. Wilson and Walter B. Michaels. London: Peter Owen, 1969. The book consists, for the most part, of conversations with Hussein and the king's radio broadcasts and speeches. Hussein reveals his attitudes toward Israel and the Palestinians and provides his account of the events preceding, during, and following the June, 1967, war.

Lunt, James. *Hussein of Jordan: A Political Biography.* London: Macmillan, 1989. A comprehensive, well-documented biography of Hussein, Lunt's book reflects the author's long experience in Jordan and his personal knowledge of the king. Lunt provides a sympathetic, though not uncritical, view of the Arab character and Jordanian history. Lunt's scholarly biography is augmented by an extensive bibliography.

Moritz, Charles, ed. *Current Biography Yearbook.* New York: H. W. Wilson, 1986. The entry on Hussein is this rather general series is helpful in offering introductory biographical information and an assessment of Hussein's career to the date published.

Mutawi, Samir A. *Jordan in the 1967 War.* New York: Cambridge University Press, 1987. An account by an Arab journalist of the 1967 war with Israel, the "most shattering event in recent Arab history." The book discusses the causes of the war, exploring the motives behind King Hussein's decision to enter the war, inter-Arab rivalries, the events of the war itself, and Jordan's position in the postwar period. An extensive bibliography is included.

Satloff, Robert B. *From Abdullah to Hussein.* New York: Oxford University Press, 1994.

Seccombe, Ian J. *Jordan.* World Bibliographical Series 55. Santa Barbara, Calif.: Clio Press, 1984. More than eight hundred critical annotated entries on works from the nineteenth century to modern times, dealing with key aspects of Jordan's history, geography, economy, politics, culture, and social organization. Many entries provide invaluable background information for a study of Hussein's life. A comprehensive cross-referencing system and thorough author, subject, and title index are provided.

Snow, Peter John. *Hussein: A Biography.* Washington, D.C.: R. B. Luce, 1972. Though it is of the "popular" variety, Snow's biography, which is anecdotal rather than scholarly, is readable and persuasive about both Hussein and the Middle East situation. Snow is sympathetic toward Hussein, whom he presents in the complex political context that includes Zionism, the PLO, Arab nationalism, and Western ties.

Sparrow, Gerald. *Hussein of Jordan.* London: George Harrap, 1960. The first English-language biography of Hussein, Sparrow's relatively short book is highly anecdotal and exceptionally sympathetic toward the king. Though it has been superseded by Lunt's biography, Sparrow's book provides a valuable early assessment of the king's early life until 1959.

Edna Quinn

MOHAMMED ALI JINNAH

Born: December 25, 1876; Karachi, India
Died: September 11, 1948; Karachi, Pakistan

Jinnah led the movement that resulted in the establishment of Pakistan as a Muslim-majority state when the British granted the Indian subcontinent home rule in 1947. Jinnah served briefly as Pakistan's governor-general, and as Quaid-i-Azam (supreme leader) he represented the Muslim voice in British Indian affairs as Mohandas Gandhi had represented the Hindus.

Early Life

Mohammed Ali Jinnah was born into a wealthy Shi'ite Muslim family in Karachi, India. Although his first school record shows his birthdate as October 20, 1875, he later claimed to have been born on December 25, 1876, the official birthdate celebrated throughout Pakistan. The Arabic name Jinnah means "wing," as of a bird or army. He adopted this form of his family name Jinnahbhai while in London in 1893. Jinnah was the eldest of seven children, and his family belonged to a minor sect within Islam, the Khojas, representing a successful merchant community in South Asia. He early realized that he was part of the Muslim minority in India, which made up about 20 percent of that British colony's population.

As a young man, Jinnah was not a diligent student, and his tolerance for formal education was never high, but his natural intelligence caught the attention of one of his father's British business associates, Sir Frederick Leigh Croft. Croft recommended Jinnah for an apprenticeship at the Douglas Graham and Company home office in London. Barely sixteen, Jinnah left for Great Britain in January, 1893, after a hastily arranged marriage demanded by his mother. Both his bride and his mother died before his return from London.

The drudgery of his apprenticeship caused Jinnah to apply for admission to Lincoln's Inn during the spring of 1893. There he completed the process of legal certification and on May 11, 1896, at the age of twenty, was admitted to the bar as a barrister welcome to practice in any British court.

While in London, Jinnah had almost followed a theatrical career and also became fascinated by the glamorous world of politics. Because of this political exposure, he returned to India as a Liberal nationalist. He enrolled as a barrister in Bombay's high court on August 24, 1896, and joined advocate-general John M. MacPherson's firm in 1900 as the first native Indian lawyer. He sat on the municipal bench for a six-month interim term in 1901.

Life's Work

Involvement in India's congress politics was an integral by-product of his flourishing legal career. He favored Indian home rule through a gradual, constitutional process which would ensure unity of the various communities, especially Hindu and Muslim. Jinnah attended the twentieth Indian Congress in December, 1904. At this point, he opposed the formation of the Muslim League in 1906 and was a leading moderate voice during the nine years between 1907 and 1915 when congress divided into angrily conflicting parties, all claiming to be the heir to India's nationalist movement.

On January 25, 1910, Jinnah took his seat on the expanded sixty-member legislative council, which offered a voice to the Indian public regarding British colonial policy. Jinnah finally joined the Muslim League in 1913 but insisted that it did not overshadow his larger loyalty to an independent, unified India. He understood but did not share the Muslims' apprehension about their role in a Hindu majority population when self-government on Western parliamentary lines came to India. Jinnah was confident that he could safeguard the future of the Muslims by constitutional provisos.

It was during this period, at the beginning of World War I, that Jinnah met Mohandas Gandhi, who returned to India in 1915. From the beginning, their relationship was one of deep tensions and mistrust underlying superficially polite manners. Jinnah believed that Gandhi's Hindu ideology could never support a common Indian nationalism. In the push for Hindu-Muslim unity, Jinnah supported the general demands of congress for reforms from the British raj. These reforms focused on equal military treatment, extension of self-government, and development of local commerce and industry. It was during this period that Jinnah was able to negotiate with congress the 1916 Lucknow Pact, which guaranteed separate electorates and weighted representation for the Muslims in any future constitution. Hindu-Muslim unity declined when Gandhi supported British recruitment of Indian soldiers for World War I, and Jinnah opposed such a move without guarantees of equal citizenship in the empire. Nevertheless, there was a brief honeymoon between congress and the Muslim League after World War I.

During the World War I era, between 1916 and their marriage on April 19, 1918, Jinnah courted the young daughter of a wealthy Parsi merchant. Ratanbai Petit was eighteen and Jinnah more than forty when they wed. The marriage lasted until her death in February, 1929, but it caused her to be disowned by her family; during the last five years of Ratanbai's life, she was virtually estranged from Jinnah as well. A daughter, Dina, was born to the union, and she, like her mother, married outside her family's religious community. The marriage of Dina to a Parsi who had converted to Christianity led to an almost complete break between her and Jinnah. Fatima Jinnah, Jinnah's adoring spinster sister, served as housekeeper, hostess, and nurse to Jinnah until his death.

A period of discontent and withdrawal began for Jinnah in 1919 and lasted until 1934, when he undertook leadership of a reconstituted Muslim League and moved toward acceptance of the idea of Pakistan. During the 1920's, the Rowlatt Act, the Amritsar Massacre, the Khilafat Pan-Islamic movement, and Gandhi's growing following for nonresistance, *satyagraha*, caused division over methodology among advocates of home rule. Therefore, Jinnah's earlier successes at Lucknow and the desire for moderate nonconfrontational programs were rejected, and he withdrew from not only the Legislative Council but also the Muslim League and congressional leadership.

Jinnah's goal was to bring independence to India through a unified Hindu-Muslim state, so he led a Muslim League faction that opposed the radical Khilafat movement. He gradually regained positions of prominence in political circles and went to London in 1930 to participate in the Round Table conferences on India. These conferences ended without tangible results. Disillusioned over the failure to achieve communal unity in India or even unity among his Muslim colleagues, Jinnah moved to Great Britain in 1930 and transferred his law practice entirely to appeals before London's Privy Council, the highest court in the empire. Jinnah returned to Bombay in 1934 and began to help rebuild the Muslim League, planning appeals to congress to support Muslim demands and to present a common front against the British.

These unity efforts failed, and in October, 1937, Jinnah moved toward leadership of the All-India Muslim League and set off on a path that would lead to the formation of Pakistan. At this point, he became known as Quaid-i-Azam, changed to native dress, and soon adopted the black Persian lamb cap that would be known throughout the world as a "Jinnah cap." By the spring of 1940, in an address at Lahore, Jinnah lowered the final curtain on any prospect for a united India. This early advocate of unity had transformed himself into Pakistan's great advocate and became the father of that nation based on Muslim solidarity.

For the next seven years, until success came in August, 1947, Jinnah devoted himself to the establishment of Pakistan and the division of India. He resisted all compromise, whether offered by the British, the Hindus, or his fellow Muslims. He determined Pakistan a necessity, because he feared Muslims would be excluded from power or prospects of advancement in the close-knit structure of Hindu social organization and their majority state. Even during World War II, there was constant vying for position so that home rule for the Indian subcontinent would be quickly granted afterward. Jinnah upheld Muslim demands for Pakistan and bitter communal struggle characterized the whole process. With few options left, the British and Hindus acquiesced, and Pakistan was born, a divided state with the Bengali area in the east and the larger region on the western border.

With independence, Jinnah was the supreme authority and the symbol of the new state. He was governor-general of the dominion, while uniting in himself the ceremonial functions of a head-of-state and the effective power of a chief executive. He often presided over the deliberations of the cabinet or sent it directives and was president of the Constituent Assembly as well as its legal adviser. Provisions in the India Independence Act of 1947 and the Government of India Act of 1935 were adapted to give his office wide powers of discretion and special responsibility. Jinnah's leadership, however, lasted only thirteen months, and during that time he was seriously ill. He died September 11, 1948, in Karachi, the place of his birth, but now the city was a part of the state of Pakistan, carved from the India of the British raj for its Muslim citizens.

Summary

The founding of Pakistan as a Muslim majority state was the crowning glory of Mohammed Ali Jinnah's life. He first devoted himself to the goal of an independent, unified India with communal harmony achieved between Hindus and the various minorities by constitutional guarantees. Eventually he realized that his professional success as a leading barrister in colonial India and the high economic and social position he thus achieved would never allow him to participate fully in the Indian congress movement, because his status as a Muslim always provided an invisible barrier.

Jinnah's logical, precise, and self-controlled mind rejected communal violence and supported constitutional guarantees for all Indians. By 1940, however, Jinnah had determined that those guarantees would not protect Muslim interests in a Hindu-dominated state and that separate states must be formed when the British granted India home rule. Jinnah's position reflects the use of religious identification as a foundation of nationalism, a major force in the modern world. The rise of Islam as a nationalistic unifier was early evidenced in the Indian struggle. Although not particularly devout himself, Jinnah became the Quaid-i-Azam of Pakistan and headed a nationalistic movement that succeeded in dividing the Indian subcontinent based on religious identification. The bitter struggle and communal hatred engendered by that division has had long-lasting political and diplomatic repercussions.

Pakistan's founding in August, 1947, gave Jinnah the task of guiding the infant state through its earliest difficulties. He had devoted so much effort to the struggle for independence that a detailed plan of action for the new government had to be formulated after the fact. He survived only thirteen months, but he affixed his own indelible seal to the ideals of the new nation as he advocated law and order, elimination of bribery and corruption, and equal rights for all citizens regardless of religion. Achieving these goals presented problems for Pakistan, and the internal conflict that resulted in the eastern Bengali region, later Bangladesh, seceding from Pakistan have altered the dream he had for the future.

Jinnah spent his life as a freedom fighter: first, for freedom from British colonial rule; then, for civil freedom for the Muslim minority in India; and, finally, for guaranteed freedoms in the new state of Pakistan. He used his skills as a barrister to serve as the Muslim voice in India, to found the nation-state of Pakistan, and to build its early structure as the first governor-general. He was afterward revered as Pakistan's founding father, and he alone retains the title of supreme leader, Quaid-i-Azam.

Bibliography

Ahmad, Jamil-ud-Din, comp. *Historic Documents of the Muslim Freedom Movement.* Lahore, Pakistan: United Publishers, 1970.

The documents in this collection focus on the resolutions, speeches, and writings of the Islamic Indian community. They are organized in chronological order and provide an overview of the move toward home-rule and partition.

_________, comp. *Quaid-i-Azam, as Seen by His Contemporaries.* Lahore, Pakistan: United Publishers, 1966. Jinnah's work, personality, and influence are examined from several points of view by former associates. The recollections are generally positive but provide telling insights that reveal the man and his relationships.

Ahmed, Akbar S., and Ahmed Akbar. *Jinnah, Pakistan and Islamic Identity: The Search for Saladin.* New York: Routledge, 1997. Provocative study of the partition of India with a revisionist view of Jinnah's role in the creation of Pakistan.

Ali, Chaudhri Muhammad. *The Emergence of Pakistan.* New York: Columbia University Press, 1967. This historical study of the creation of Pakistan focuses on 1946-1948, but it also provides an examination of the social, economic, and political background. Jinnah is portrayed as a calm, logical, astute politician protecting Muslim rights, while the role of Hindus and Sikhs is criticized.

Collins, Larry, and Dominique La Pierre. *Freedom at Midnight.* New York: Simon & Schuster, 1975. A series of anecdotes and highly descriptive accounts depict the transition of power from British control to independence. The focus is on Gandhi and India with a negative presentation of Jinnah and the Pakistan movement as key hindrances to Indian unity.

Edwards, Michael. *The Last Years of British India.* New York: World Publishing, 1963. Beginning before the turn of the century, major forces that allied with the congress and the Muslim League are identified. The key factor in partition is depicted as Muslim determination for autonomy led by the dedicated guidance of Jinnah. Evidence of a less than positive opinion is evidenced when Jinnah is compared to Adolf Hitler.

Ispahani, M. A. H. *Quaid-i-Azam Jinnah as I Knew Him.* Karachi, Pakistan: Forward Publication Trust, 1966. The memoirs of one of Jinnah's closest personal friends represent the wealthy commercial and financial voice of Calcutta and the Bengali faction of the Muslim League. Jinnah's role in the East Pakistan region is particularly explored.

Jalal, Ayesha. *The Sole Spokesman: Jinnah, the Muslim League and the Demand for Pakistan.* Cambridge, England: Cambridge University Press, 1985.

Jinnah, the Founder of Pakistan: Through the Eyes of His Contemporaries and His Records at Lincoln's Inn. New York: Oxford University Press, 1998. Slim collection of speeches made at the inauguration of the Jinnah Society in London, with supplementary material on Jinnah's life.

Merriam, Allen Hayes. *Gandhi vs. Jinnah: The Debate Over the Partition of India.* Calcutta, India: Minerva, 1980. The leading figures in the Indian independence movement evidence the differing philosophies, conflicting methodology, and tense antagonism between the two who are heroic figures within their own communities.

Mujahid, Sharif al. *Quaid-i-Azam Jinnah: Studies in Interpretation.* Karachi, Pakistan: Quaid-i-Azam Academy, 1981.

Pandey, Bishwa Nath. *The Breakup of British India.* New York: St. Martin's Press, 1969. This study analyzes the origins of nationalism in the British raj and then examines the growing movement of Muslim separatism. There is a focus on religious and social issues while noting the strong influence of the leaders on each side.

Wolpert, Stanley A. *Jinnah of Pakistan.* New York: Oxford University Press, 1984. This objective, well-documented, comprehensive biography of the life of Jinnah portrays the complexity of his personality and his dedication to the Muslim voice in India. While always acknowledging his role as a major leader in twentieth century Indian affairs, his enigmatic character is evidenced.

Frances A. Coulter

JOHN PAUL II

Karol Jozef Wojtyła

Born: May 18, 1920; Wadowice, Poland

John Paul II is the 264th pope of the Roman Catholic Church and the first non-Italian pope since 1522. The first Slav to be named pope, the first pope from a communist country, and the youngest pope in modern times, John Paul II has a history of political involvement that predates even his religious vocation, having fought attempts first by Nazi Germany and later by the Soviet Union to weaken the power of the Church in Poland. During his reign as pope, he has sought to bring the Church back to some of the traditional values that he believed were lost after the Second Vatican Council.

Early Life

Karol Jozef Wojtyła, the future Pope John Paul II, was born on May 18, 1920, to Karol and Emilia (Kaczorowska) in Wadowice, a small town near Kraków, Poland. "Lolek," as he was affectionately known, was delivered by a midwife in the Wojtyła family apartment, a three-room residence on the second floor of a house across from the village church. The Wojtyła family originally came from Czaniec, a village near Andrychow. Wojtyła's paternal grandfather, Maciej, was a tailor who had settled in Biala Krakowska. Wojtyła's father, Karol, married in Wadowice and decided to settle there. The elder Karol Wojtyła had been a staff officer with the Twelfth Infantry Regiment of the Polish army. While Wojtyła was growing up in Wadowice, his father was retired, and the family subsisted on a meager army pension.

Wojtyła learned to speak German from his mother, Emilia, whose family had come from Silesia. Emilia died from a heart ailment when Wojtyła was nine years old. Four years later, Edmund, Wojtyła's only surviving sibling, a doctor, died after contracting scarlet fever from a patient. This left Wojtyła and his father, a stern but warmhearted man, alone. While Wojtyła went to high school, his father took care of the apartment. As time went on, Wojtyła's father became all but a recluse, with only his son to keep him company. As a result, the two became very close.

The younger Wojtyła was devout even as a boy, stopping each morning at the church to pray. His gifts for the humanities were evident early; he excelled in religion, Latin, Greek, German, and philosophy. Even in grammar school, he demonstrated a fierce enthusiasm for the theater and frequented the cinema. He also wrote poetry and took second prize reciting poems at a local speech festival. He loved the outdoors, especially enjoying skiing, hiking, and kayaking. Accounts of his youth reveal an irrepressible personality, a young man with a prankish disregard for authority, and a skilled raconteur. Naturally, he was likable, and he was popular even with the young girls. Like most of his teenage friends, he had a steady girlfriend. Wojtyła graduated from high school with distinction in 1938, and he and his father moved to Debniki Krakowskie, a district of Kraków. There they lived in a cramped, dark, cold, basement apartment, which was nicknamed the "catacombs."

Life's Work

Wojtyła was enrolled at Kraków's Jagellonian University to study for a degree in Polish literature. Always enthusiastic and energetic, the young student joined the Polish Language Society, a group of students who wrote poetry, held literary meetings, and went to the theater. He also joined the newly established Theatrical Fraternity. His first year of college completed, Wojtyła spent the summer of 1939 in military training, which was compulsory for all Polish young men. Before the fall term began, the Blitzkrieg offensive against Poland was launched. On September 1, 1939, Kraków, along with other Polish cities, was bombed by Adolf Hitler's army. While most of the citizens of Kraków sought cover from the bombing, Wojtyła spent that morning assisting the vicar in saying Mass. When the city fell to German forces a few days later, one of the first things that the occupying army did was to close the university and to make it illegal for Poles to seek a university education. The handful of teachers who had managed to avoid arrest were to establish an underground university by the end of the year. Wojtyła was immediately enrolled as a second-year literature student in one of the secret cells.

To support himself and his father, and to acquire the documents needed to avoid arrest by the Nazis, Wojtyła was able to secure a job at a quarry, breaking and hauling rocks. Later he worked at a water purification factory. During this time, he continued writing poetry, kept up his secret university studies, and even began studying French with a family friend. Because the Polish theater was outlawed, Wojtyła and his friends started an underground theater. Later, Wojtyła joined the clandestine Rhapsody Theater as an actor and coproducer. This small group was able during the war to give more than twenty performances of plays by Polish writers. Most of these plays were presented in the apartments of friends. One play was performed immediately after a Gestapo search. Wojtyła's daring extended beyond the theater, and he was eventually blacklisted by the Gestapo for providing many Jews with new identities and hiding places.

John Paul II *(AP/Wide World Photos)*

Wojtyła's father died of a stroke in the spring of 1941. Several months later, Wojtyła was enrolled at the clandestine theological seminary in Kraków. He distinguished himself academically at the seminary, where he finally moved in 1944, for safety, along with the other seminarians, under the orders of the archbishop. The end of World War II brought little in the way of political reprieve for the Poles, for Poland was immediately occupied by Joseph Stalin's Soviet army. The schools, however, were no longer outlawed, and Wojtyła was permitted to complete his education.

Karol Wojtyła was ordained on November 1, 1946, by the metropolitan archbishop of Kraków, Prince Adam Sapieha. Wojtyła was sent to Rome to study at the Pontifical University Angelicum under the Dominican Fathers. There he resided at the Belgian College, where he was able to further refine his knowledge of the French language. His studies first focused on the Spanish mystic Saint John of the Cross; later, he would concentrate on Saint Thomas Aquinas. He became a doctor of divinity, magna cum laude, on April 30, 1948.

Upon his return from Rome, Wojtyła was made pastor of a poverty stricken parish in the small country village of Niegowic. He soon became popular with the young people there. He organized a theater group and took many of the youth with him on hiking and kayaking trips. In less than a year, much to the disappointment of Niegowic's inhabitants, Wojtyła was transferred to the important parish of St. Florian, in Kraków. Again he gave much of his time to the youth of the parish, risking arrest by the Soviet-backed government, which had its own ideas about to which groups the Polish young people should belong. At this time, Wojtyła was also lecturing on Thomistic philosophy and Max Scheler at the Catholic University of Lublin.

In 1958, he was consecrated auxiliary bishop of Kraków. He officially became archbishop in 1964 and was elevated to the cardinalate by Pope Paul VI on May 29, 1967. Throughout his career, Wojtyła was a chief advocate of greater concessions by the communistic state toward the people. His main concerns have been human rights, better education, improved access to the mass media, the abolition of censorship and atheistic propaganda, and religious freedom, including freedom of religious instruction.

On October 16, 1978, Wojtyła was chosen pope by the Conclave of Cardinals. He chose the name John Paul after his immediate predecessor and began his reign by declining coronation, preferring to be installed simply during a pontifical Mass in St. Peter's Square on October 22, 1978.

In June, 1979, Pope John Paul II landed at Warsaw airport for a historic visit to his homeland of Poland. His trip stimulated processes of reform that almost certainly contributed to the fall of the communist regime in Poland ten years later. Relations with the communist leaders of Poland were quite tense during the visit. Two years later, in May of 1981, John Paul survived an assassination attempt by a Turkish terrorist in Vatican City's St. Peter's Square.

One of the many ways in which John Paul II has distinguished himself as pope is in his travels. He has been to Latin America, Ireland (becoming the first pope ever to go there), the United States, the Philippines, Brazil, and other countries, including his beloved homeland. During his first American tour, he addressed the United Nations on world problems, especially peace and disarmament. He confronted Church leaders and dissidents in the United States, listening patiently to their complaints. He admonished the Catholics in the United States to beware of excesses and wished for a more equitable share of wealth in the world.

Throughout his American tours, John Paul stressed the sanctity of unborn life, the Church's opposition to artificial means of birth control, and the sacredness of the marriage bond. His call for an end to the death penalty is credited with saving the life of a convicted murderer whose sentence was commuted following John Paul's visit to the United States in January, 1999. The pope has called for Christian unity but does not want to dilute the Church's essential doctrine or compromise essential practices. When Anglican leaders expressed an interest in intercommunion, John Paul refused, saying that fundamental differences needed to be resolved first.

With the fall of communism in the early 1990's, John Paul II focused on different threats to the dignity of humankind in the form of Western commercialism, liberalism, materialism, secularism, and hedonism. He increased his efforts to confront those who called for relaxation of Catholic norms regarding the use of birth control, the practices of abortion and euthanasia, priestly celibacy, and the ordination of women. To impose greater order in the Church, John Paul II issued a new *Catechism of the Catholic Church* in 1993. He also issued many encyclicals, including *Veritatis Splendor* (1993) and *Evangelium Vitae* (1995). *Evangelium Vitae* (gospel of life) seeks to clarify Catholic teachings concerning abortion, euthanasia, and the death penalty. In the encyclical John Paul stresses that respecting the dignity of the person calls for the respect of life as a gift of God.

Summary

John Paul II's enrollment at the secret university, his assistance to Kraków's Jewish population, and his affirmation of faith in the face of an atheistic government are the direct result of the environment in which he was reared, as are his traditionalist views concerning morality. As pope, John Paul has asked for less permissiveness in faith. His reign reflects a return to conservativism after the liberalism of Vatican Council II. In contrast to Paul VI, who laicized two thousand priests each year, John Paul II has reaffirmed the permanence of priestly vows and has refused to dispense a single priest. Despite the growing demand in the United States and elsewhere for the admittance of women into the episcopate, the pope stands firm on the side of an all-male priesthood.

John Paul II is, paradoxically, a sociopolitical liberal. He believes strongly in the inalienable rights of the individual and the peaceful coexistence of church and state. He is steadfastly opposed to communism. A savvy diplomat and sophisticated intellectual, he can hold his own in debate with Marxists. For these reasons, he is respected by friends and enemies alike. He is in constant contact, often physical, with his congregation and has traveled to more countries than any pope before him, thus expanding his visibility and modernizing his position. He has also canonized more saints than any other pope.

Bibliography

Bernstein, Carl, and Marco Politi. *His Holiness: John Paul II and the Hidden History of Our Time*. New York: Doubleday, 1996.

Blazynski, George. *Pope John Paul II*. New York: Dell, 1979. Although its prose suggests that the author's first language is not English, this biography is packed with accurate information on the pope's early life. Blazynski provides the reader with the social and political backdrop of John Paul's Poland. Suitable for a general audience.

Gronowicz, Antoni. *God's Broker: The Life of Pope John Paul II*. New York: Richardson and Snyder, 1984. Gronowicz skillfully weaves a portrait of John Paul from interviews with the pope himself and others who know him well. This book makes excellent reading, offering humorous and dramatic insight into the life and mind of the pope. Illustrated and indexed.

John Paul II. *Crossing the Threshold of Hope*. New York: Alfred A. Knopf, 1994.

Korn, Frank. *From Peter to John Paul II: An Informal Study of the Papacy*. Canfield, Ohio: Alba Books, 1980. Written by a Fulbright scholar, this volume, as its title suggests, covers more than two thousand years of papal history. It is illustrated and contains a useful chronological listing of all the popes.

Kwitny, Jonathan. *Man of the Century: The Life and Times of Pope John Paul II*. New York: Henry Holt, 1997.

Moritz, Charles, ed. *Current Biography Yearbook, 1979*. New York: H. W. Wilson, 1980. A comprehensive biographical reference, written in an easy-to-read style, this book provides information on people in the news. Published annually, it is illustrated and indexed.

National Catholic News Service, eds. *John Paul II: "Pilgrimage of Faith."* New York: Seabury Press, 1979. Pictorial account of the first year of John Paul's reign, with an emphasis on his October, 1979, visit to the United States. An appendix contains the texts of his major addresses and homilies.

Szulc, Tad. *Pope John Paul II: The Biography*. New York: Scribner, 1995.

Joyce M. Parks

LYNDON B. JOHNSON

Born: August 27, 1908; near Stonewall, Gillespie County, Texas
Died: January 22, 1973; en route to San Antonio, Texas

An astute, skilled, and compassionate professional politician, Johnson advanced the cause of civil rights and expanded the government's role in social welfare through his Great Society programs.

Early Life

Lyndon Baines Johnson, the thirty-sixth president of the United States, was born August 27, 1908, the first of five children of Rebekah Baines and Sam Ealy Johnson, Jr. His mother, a graduate of Baylor University, taught school briefly before her marriage to Sam Johnson, a Gillespie County tenant farmer, realtor, and politician. A frontier Populist, Sam Johnson demonstrated political courage as a member of the Texas legislature. During World War I, when anti-German sentiment ran to extremes, he rose to oppose a bill aimed at German-Americans. Later, he joined forces with Governor James Ferguson to oppose the Ku Klux Klan in Texas. A further claim to remembrance lies in the fact that he introduced in the legislature the bill that saved the Alamo from demolition. Johnson's gregarious and extroverted father represented a contrast to his sensitive and introspective mother.

Johnson began his education at age four in a country school near his home along the Pedernales River in the Texas hill country. Later, he attended a school in the small community of Albert and then transferred to high school in nearby Johnson City, where his parents had moved. He served as president of his six-member graduating class of 1924. After high school, Johnson, then fifteen years old, had not decided on a career for himself. He left with a group of friends to travel to California, where for two years he worked at odd jobs. Returning home, he worked as a laborer before deciding to enroll in college, as his mother had desired. She selected Southwest Texas State Teachers College in San Marcos, about sixty miles from his home. Johnson worked throughout his entire college career, for a time as the college president's assistant.

Lyndon B. Johnson *(Library of Congress)*

He left college for one year to teach school at Cotulla in the South Texas brush country, where he encountered for the first time the struggles and deprivations of the Hispanic Texans whom he taught. Despite his year of teaching, he completed his B.S. in history (1930) in three and a half years. The following year, he taught secondary public speaking and debate at Sam Houston High School in Houston, where his first-year debate team went to the state finals. His career as a teacher ended abruptly when Richard M. Kleberg of the

King Ranch family won an off-year congressional election in 1931 and selected Johnson as his secretary.

In Kleberg's Washington office, Johnson became, in effect, the manager. He mastered the operations of federal institutions and bureaucracies, took care of Kleberg's constituents, made as many influential contacts as he could, and found federal jobs for Texas friends and associates. A workaholic for whom the sixteen- or eighteen-hour day was normal, he set the pattern of diligence, commitment, and loyalty that he would later expect from his own staff. After the 1932 presidential election brought in the New Deal of Franklin D. Roosevelt, Johnson worked on behalf of the new programs and often influenced a reluctant Kleberg to support them. While a member of Kleberg's staff, he established several important working relationships with experienced political leaders who served him well later, the most significant being a fellow Texan, Sam T. Rayburn, later to become a powerful Speaker of the House of Representatives.

More important, following a whirlwind courtship, he married Claudia Alta (Lady Bird) Taylor on November 17, 1934. The daughter of a businessman and landowner from Karnack, Texas, she became a valued adviser, supporter, and counselor, as well as a gracious hostess and often his most effective personal representative.

After leaving Kleberg's staff in 1935, Johnson was selected by Roosevelt to head the Texas branch of the National Youth Administration, a New Deal organization designed to help young people remain in school during the Depression, largely through providing public works jobs in summers. In this office, Johnson came to understand the power of government programs to help needy people, including minorities. Continuing his torrid pace of work, he gained national recognition as an effective leader.

Life's Work

By the time Johnson enrolled in college, he was reasonably sure that his life's work lay in politics, though he was unsure as to how it would develop. His career in political office lasted thirty-two years and included every elective office within the federal government. It began with a congressional election in 1937, to fill an unexpired term in the Tenth District of Texas, which included the state capital of Austin and Johnson's home region. He ran on a platform of all-out support for Roosevelt. A tireless campaigner but not always an inspiring speaker, Johnson often included in his campaign catchy or novel elements that his opponents found corny. In 1937, his slogan, "Franklin D. and Lyndon B.," succeeded in identifying him with the popular president.

As a congressman, Johnson formed a close working relationship with Roosevelt, supporting the president's programs while looking out for his own district and the economic interests of Texas. More quickly than many others in Congress, he realized that the nation was on a course toward war and strongly supported the president's rearmament efforts. He took time out in 1941 to run for the Senate against Texas governor W. Lee O'Daniel, losing the race by a narrow margin. During World War II, he served briefly in the navy before Roosevelt summoned all congressmen in military service back to Washington.

Following the death of Roosevelt in 1945, Johnson realized that world conditions had changed considerably since the early days of the New Deal. Employment levels were high, and a victorious nation was prosperous once again. Perceiving the major challenge confronting the United States to be communist expansionism, he supported President Harry S Truman's efforts to rebuild the armed forces. Formerly a strong supporter of labor, Johnson cast his vote in favor of the restrictive Taft-Hartley Act.

When the opportunity came for another Senate race in 1948, Johnson ran against Governor Coke Stevenson, campaigning throughout the state in a helicopter, then a novel mode of transportation. With the support of the National Democratic Party, he won the primary by a narrow margin, and in the one-party state that Texas then was, this was tantamount to victory.

He selected as his Senate mentor Richard Russell, the Democrat from Georgia, whose guidance helped Johnson to advance quickly to positions of power and prominence. Senate Democrats chose him as party Whip in 1951, minority leader in 1953, and majority leader in 1955. Through his total commitment to success, his boundless energy, his own abilities as an organizer and leader, and his grasp of Senate operations and traditions, he became perhaps the strongest senatorial leader in American history. As a leader, his primary watchwords were: pragmatism, compromise, reason, bargaining, and consensus. During deliberations, he preferred face-to-face discussion and debate, including bargaining, for in this mode he usually held the advantage. Almost six and a half feet tall, long limbed with a broad forehead, large nose and ears, and prominent cheekbones, Johnson commanded a formidable presence. A complex man of many moods, known for homely language and abundant anecdotes, he was highly persuasive.

As Senate leader, Johnson forged the consensus that enabled passage of the Civil Rights Act of 1957, the first legislation of its kind in eighty-seven years. In foreign policy, he persuaded Democrats in the Senate to adopt a bipartisan approach in support of President Dwight D. Eisenhower. He believed that the opposition party should operate in a constructive manner, especially in foreign affairs.

In 1960, he sought his party's nomination for the presidency but lost in the primaries and at the convention to Senator John F. Kennedy. Kennedy chose the powerful Johnson as his running mate, hoping to carry the South, which had defected almost wholesale to Eisenhower in the two previous presidential elections. Despite his record on civil rights, Johnson had respect and strong support in the South and succeeded in swinging enough votes to win.

As vice president, Johnson undertook important missions and responsibilities. He represented the president in travels abroad, oversaw the high priority national space program, and pressed hard, with reasonable success, for equal opportunity employment. He gave speeches on foreign policy, indicating that he understood that many conflicts are regional or local, not the result of the East-West confrontation. Yet where Southeast Asia was concerned, he clearly perceived the conflict in the context of the larger ideological struggle. He accepted the view, a legacy of the Eisenhower years when John Foster Dulles as secretary of state shaped American policy, that the fall of one Southeast Asian nation would precipitate the fall of all the others—the so-called "domino theory."

Following the assassination of President John F. Kennedy in Dallas on November 22, 1963, Johnson became the thirty-sixth president and led the shocked nation along the course charted by his predecessor. Perhaps no other vice president was better prepared to assume the powers of the presidency. With a long career of public service behind him and with his energy undiminished, he undertook enormous efforts on both domestic and foreign fronts. The overwhelming support he received in the 1964 national election against the conservative Senator Barry Goldwater gave him a mandate to proceed with his own programs. He declared war on poverty and vowed to end it. He brought forward important legislation in almost every area on the domestic front, a cluster of programs together known as the Great Society. In health care, the environment, housing, inner cities, education at all levels, and, above all, civil rights, he proposed new and important legislation. The nation had not experienced anything like the amount of new domestic legislation since Roosevelt's first term.

In foreign policy, he continued to regard the East-West conflict as paramount. He met with Soviet premier Aleksei Kosygin to explore avenues of agreement. Yet the main foreign policy preoccupation remained the war in Vietnam. In an effort to secure a noncommunist South Vietnam, Johnson increased the level of American commitment to half a million men. Casualties mounted, little progress was discernible, the war became increasingly unpopular at home, and the president felt obliged to seek a negotiated peace that did not come until long after his term had ended.

Having decided not to seek a second full term, Johnson left the White House in January, 1969, to return to his Texas ranch in retirement. He died near there, within a mile of his birthplace, on January 22, 1973.

Summary

In the assessment of historians, Lyndon B. Johnson's legacy will be limited primarily to his presidency. Early responses suggest that he will be included among the strongest of American presidents. Placed in the larger context of American post-World War II foreign policy, his failure in Vietnam will become more understandable. In domestic affairs, it will be apparent that his influence has endured. His Great Society was in essence a continuation of Roosevelt's New Deal. It sprang from Johnson's deepest sympathies and concerns for the underprivileged, a reflection of his Populist roots.

The Civil Rights Act of 1964 and the Voting Rights Act of 1965 assured fundamental rights to millions previously denied them. Johnson championed federal support for education, from the preschool Head Start program, to job training programs and federal programs for higher education. Medicare and increased Social Security benefits brought greater financial security to older Americans; Medicaid and increased welfare appropriations improved the lot of those in need. Although some Great Society programs had limited or mixed results—housing and urban projects among them—the Great Society effectively extended the benefits of an affluent society to a larger number of people.

The tribute by Ralph Ellison at the time of Johnson's death

appears valid: "When all of the returns are in, perhaps President Johnson will have to settle for being recognized as the greatest American president for the poor and for the Negroes, but that, as I see it, is a very great honor indeed."

Bibliography

Barrett, David M. *Uncertain Warriors: Lyndon Johnson and His Vietnam Advisers*. Lawrence: University Press of Kansas, 1993.

Bornet, Vaughan Davis. *The Presidency of Lyndon B. Johnson*. Lawrence: University Press of Kansas, 1983. Bornet attempts a balanced assessment of Johnson's programs and his overall impact on the nation, including the economic cost of the Great Society and the Vietnam War. He includes a useful annotated bibliography.

Caro, Robert A. *The Years of Lyndon Johnson: The Path to Power*. New York: Alfred A. Knopf, 1982. A lengthy assessment of Johnson's early career down to 1948. Develops the thesis that Johnson's actions and decisions were calculated to increase and enhance his power.

Dallek, Robert. *Lone Star Rising: Lyndon Johnson and His Times, 1908-1960*. New York: Oxford University Press, 1991.

__________. *Flawed Giant: Lyndon Johnson and His Times, 1961-1973*. New York: Oxford University Press, 1998.

Dugger, Ronnie. *The Politician: The Life and Times of Lyndon Johnson, the Drive for Power from the Frontier to Master of the Senate*. New York: W. W. Norton, 1982. Traces Johnson's views on government to his family background and myths of the frontier. Emphasis upon Vietnam in Johnson's experience and political life.

Johnson, Lyndon. *The Vantage Point: Perspectives on the Presidency*. New York: Holt, Rinehart and Winston, 1971.

Kearns, Doris. *Lyndon Johnson and the American Dream*. New York: Harper and Row, 1976. The book contains a poignant account of Johnson's early family life. The author provides an account of his career and an assessment of his strengths and weaknesses as a leader.

Miller, Merle. *Lyndon: An Oral Biography*. New York: G. P. Putnam's Sons, 1980. Miller presents a chronological biography through the words of those who knew Johnson, recorded in interviews and arranged in sequence with little additional comment and explanation. The author interviews those who knew him best, from secretaries to cabinet members. A lively, multifaceted portrait of a complex subject.

Valenti, Jack. *A Very Human President*. New York: W. W. Norton, 1975. A sympathetic view of the Johnson presidency by a prominent member of the White House staff. It includes a perspective on the decision-making process, discussion of important issues, and an insider's account of the president's interaction with the staff.

White, William S. *The Professional: Lyndon B. Johnson*. Boston: Houghton Mifflin, 1964. A favorable retrospective of Johnson's career, beginning with his accession to the presidency. White attempts to shed light on Johnson's personality, political views, goals, and methods.

Stanley Archer

JOHN F. KENNEDY

Born: May 29, 1917; Brookline, Massachusetts
Died: November 22, 1963; Dallas, Texas

Combining intelligence with personal charm, Kennedy became a model to millions around the globe, inspiring them to seek new goals and to work toward those goals with self-confidence.

Early Life

John Fitzgerald Kennedy was born May 29, 1917, in Brookline, Massachusetts, an inner suburb of Boston. He was the second son of Joseph P. Kennedy, a businessman rapidly growing wealthy, and Rose Fitzgerald Kennedy, daughter of former Boston mayor John F. "Honey Fitz" Fitzgerald. He was educated at Choate School in Connecticut and graduated from Harvard in 1940. While his earlier years were plagued by illness, and his grades were often mediocre, he revealed himself to be an original thinker. His senior thesis was published as *Why England Slept* (1940), largely by the efforts of Joseph Kennedy's friends. John Kennedy was able to travel widely in Europe in 1937 and 1938 and to spend the spring of 1939 in Britain, where his father was United States ambassador. Still there when World War II began in September, he assisted in caring for American survivors of the first torpedoed passenger ship, gaining a sense of realism about war.

As United States entrance into the war became likely, he entered the U.S. Navy as an ensign, September, 1941, six feet tall but exceptionally thin and looking younger than his years. A thatch of often rumpled, sandy hair added to his boyish appearance. He was sent to the South Pacific where he commanded PT 109, a patrol torpedo boat. The boat was sunk in action on August 2, 1943, and Kennedy not only rescued survivors but also swam for help though badly injured. Awarded the Navy and U.S. Marine Corps medal, he briefly commanded another boat but soon went on sick leave and was discharged for disability as a full lieutenant in December, 1944. Because of his injury, coming in the wake of earlier illnesses, he was often a sick man.

Life's Work

Kennedy had thought of writing as a career and covered the United Nations Conference at San Francisco, April-July, 1945, and the 1945 British elections for the New York *Journal-American*. His older brother, Joseph, Jr., slated to be the family's political success, had been killed in the war in Europe, and John took up that task. In 1946, he ran for the House of Representatives from the Eleventh District of Massachusetts, narrowly gaining the Democratic nomination but winning the November election with 72.6 percent of the vote. The district sent him to Washington for three terms, during which time his record was mixed.

In favor of public housing and an opponent of the then reactionary leadership of the American Legion, Kennedy was friendly with Senator Joseph McCarthy of Wisconsin, whose "red-baiting" began in 1950. Plagued by a painful back, Kennedy was diagnosed in 1947 as having Addison's disease also, then usually fatal, and was often absent from the House. He showed more interest in national issues than local ones and became deeply interested in foreign policy. He rejected his father's isolationism, supported the Truman Doctrine and the Marshall Plan, but joined right-wing critics of the so-called loss of China to Mao Zedong. In 1951, he toured Europe and Asia for several weeks and returned better balanced regarding a Russian threat to Western Europe and the significance of Asian anticolonialism.

Unwilling to spend many years gaining seniority in the House, in 1952, Kennedy ran against Henry Cabot Lodge for the U.S. Senate. Despite illness, explained to the public as wartime injuries or malaria, he campaigned effectively, helped by family money and friends, building his own political organization. He won 51.5 percent of the vote and would be easily reelected in 1958.

He married Jacqueline Lee Bouvier on September 12, 1953, and they had two children, Caroline, born November 27, 1957, and John, Jr., born November 26, 1960. A third child, Patrick Bouvier Kennedy, born in August, 1963, lived only a few hours. Jacqueline Kennedy's beauty, charm, and linguistic skills helped the future president on countless occasions.

As a senator, Kennedy gained national publicity by working to cure the economic ills of all of New England. He continued to speak out on foreign policy, often against French colonialism in Indochina or Algeria. He finally turned away from McCarthy as the Senate censured the latter. During one long illness, he put together another

John F. Kennedy *(Library of Congress)*

book, *Profiles in Courage* (1956), based heavily on others' research, winning a Pulitzer Prize and good publicity. One result of Kennedy's growing national reputation was his almost becoming Adlai Stevenson's running mate in the 1956 presidential election. While older politicians often regarded him as a rich young man with no serious intentions, his popularity was growing among voters.

Kennedy began, in 1956, to work for the 1960 Democratic presidential nomination. His brother Robert observed the Stevenson campaign, and afterward, the brothers began building a national organization. Finding his health improving, thanks to the use of cortisone, Kennedy made speeches throughout the country and created a "brain trust" of academic and other specialists who could advise him on policy. To win the nomination and then the 1960 election, Kennedy had to overcome anti-Catholicism and his own image as too young and inexperienced. Campaigning hard both times, he convinced millions of voters that he was intelligent and prepared for the office as well as a believer in the separation of church and state. He named as his running mate Lyndon B. Johnson of Texas, Democratic majority leader in the Senate, who was strong where Kennedy was weak, especially in the South.

In televised debates with his opponent, Vice President Richard M. Nixon, Kennedy appeared competent and vigorous; Nixon, exhausted from campaigning, did poorly. Kennedy won the election by 303 electoral votes to 219, with a popular vote margin of only 119,450 out of 68,836,385, so narrow a victory that it limited his political strength. He named a cabinet representing all factions of the Democratic Party and including two Republicans. Despite the administration's "New Frontier" label, it was balanced between liberals and conservatives.

As president, Kennedy sought a constant flow of ideas of all shades of opinion. He held few Cabinet meetings, preferring the informality of task forces on various problems. To reach the public, he used "live" televised press conferences. A handsome face, no longer gaunt and pained, the thatch of hair, plus Kennedy's spontaneity and wit, captivated millions. His inaugural address had promised boldness, especially in the Cold War, and he acted on that in agreeing to a Central Intelligence Agency plan for an invasion of Cuba to overthrow Fidel Castro. When the CIA fumbled and the Cuban exile invaders were killed or captured at the Bay of Pigs, Kennedy publicly took the blame and found his popularity rising. He went to Europe to meet French president Charles de Gaulle, who warned against American involvement in Vietnam, and also Nikita Khrushchev of the Soviet Union, finding the communist leader tough, belligerent, and unwilling to help solve any problems.

In domestic matters, Kennedy accomplished little during his thousand days in office. He sought and obtained minor increases in the minimum wage and Social Security coverage, plus money for public housing, and forced a temporary rollback in steel prices. Jacqueline Kennedy supervised a notable redecoration of the White House in Early American style. Only late in his brief term did Kennedy take up the issue of civil rights, because of increasing violence in some Southern states. He took executive action where he could and proposed an anti-poll tax amendment to the Constitution, which passed the Congress while he was still president. He also called for increased federal power to enforce voting rights and a major civil rights act to include the opening of public accommodations and an end to job discrimination.

Kennedy was more active in foreign affairs. Concerned about Soviet moves in the Third World, he founded the Peace Corps and the Alliance for Progress. After the Bay of Pigs and his encounter with Khrushchev, he became "hard line," appointing such militant anticommunists as John McCone as CIA director and General Curtis LeMay as commander of the Air Force. He also vowed that the Western powers would remain in West Berlin.

The major event of Kennedy's foreign policy was the crisis that arose when Khrushchev tried to establish nuclear missiles in Cuba in 1962. Using all of the information and ideas he could get from another task force and forcing his advisers to debate their ideas in his presence, he chose to blockade Cuba and threaten Khrushchev, keeping in reserve an air attack on the missile sites. Khrushchev withdrew the missiles and countless millions around the world were relieved that no nuclear war took place.

Kennedy learned from the missile crisis. Afterward he was interested in "peace as a process," as he put it in the spring of 1963; the United States and the Soviet Union had to find ways to end the nuclear threat. Kennedy established a "hot line" for communication between the White House and the Kremlin and negotiated a treaty which stopped American and Russian outdoor nuclear tests, reducing radioactivity in the atmosphere. It is this, Kennedy's admirers say, that indicates how he would have acted in a second term. Yet Kennedy also listened to advisers who insisted that the United States send troops to Vietnam to go into combat and show the South Vietnamese army how to fight. Skeptical, Kennedy agreed, saying that if this did not work he could change his mind and withdraw the American forces.

Tragically, he did not live to follow that plan. In Dallas on a trip to heal a split in the Texas Democrats, he was assassinated on November 22, 1963.

Summary

Kennedy represented a new generation in American politics, for whom World War II and the Cold War were the major events, rather than the 1920's and the Depression of the 1930's. He brought with him a style different from that of Presidents Harry S Truman and Dwight D. Eisenhower, a contemporary style without formality and with wry, self-deprecatory humor. While his actual accomplishments were limited largely to proposing domestic legislation and to steps toward detente in foreign policy, he inspired millions in the United States and abroad to reach toward new goals in a spirit of confidence that they could make a difference. As did another assassinated president, Abraham Lincoln, he left a legacy of legend, in this case of Camelot or a new King Arthur's court of brave men and beautiful ladies engaged in serving good ends.

Bibliography

Beschloss, Michael R. *The Crisis Years: Kennedy and Khrushchev, 1960-1963*. New York: Edward Burlingame Books, 1991.

Fairlie, Henry. *The Kennedy Promise: The Politics of Expectation*. Garden City, N.Y.: Doubleday, 1973. The expectations created and left unfulfilled by John and Robert Kennedy.

Hamilton, Nigel. *JFK, Reckless Youth*. New York: Random House, 1992.

Manchester, William. *One Brief Shining Moment*. Boston: Little, Brown, 1983. The best of the memorials, with superb pictures and a moving text.

Matthews, Christopher. *Kennedy and Nixon: The Rivalry That Shaped Postwar America*. New York: Simon & Schuster, 1996.

Miroff, Bruce. *Pragmatic Illusions: The Presidential Politics of John F. Kennedy*. New York: David McKay, 1976. An incisive reassessment, showing the reality of Kennedy's presidency rather than the myth.

Parmet, Herbert S. *Jack: The Struggles of John F. Kennedy*. New York: Dial Press, 1980. The closest there is to a definitive biography, well balanced and based on exhaustive research; the story to 1960.

__________. *JFK: The Presidency of John F. Kennedy*. New York: Dial Press, 1983. The second volume of the best biography is also the best balanced view of Kennedy as president.

Reeves, Richard. *President Kennedy: A Profile in Power*. New York: Simon and Schuster, 1993.

Schlesinger, Arthur M., Jr. *A Thousand Days: John F. Kennedy in the White House*. Boston: Houghton Mifflin, 1965. Admiring tale of Kennedy's presidency by a friend and aide.

Sorensen, Theodore C. *Kennedy*. New York: Harper and Row, 1965. Even more admiring memoirs by Kennedy's closest aide.

_________. *The Kennedy Legacy*. New York: Macmillan, 1969. An early and favorable attempt to assess Kennedy's presidency.

Walton, Richard J. *Cold War and Counterrevolution*. New York: Viking Press, 1972. Harshly critical of Kennedy as a "cold warrior."

Robert W. Sellen

ALEKSANDR FYODOROVICH KERENSKY

Born: May 2, 1881; Simbirsk (later Ulyanovsk), Russia
Died: June 11, 1970; New York, New York

Kerensky was the leading figure in the short-lived Provisional Government that replaced the deposed Czar Nicholas II and was in turn displaced by the Bolshevik (Communist) Party of Vladimir Ilich Lenin during the Russian Revolution of 1917. He attempted unsuccessfully to establish a liberal democratic government in Russia.

Early Life

Born in Simbirsk (later Ulyanovsk), Russia, on May 2, 1881, Aleksandr Fyodorovich Kerensky was the eldest son of Fyodor Mikhailovich Kerensky, a schoolteacher and administrator, and his wife, Nadezhda Aleksandrovna (née Adler), the daughter of a prominent military officer and topographer. During their son's earliest years in Simbirsk, the Kerenskys' social and professional circle undoubtedly included Ilya Nikolaevich Ulyanov, another local school official, and his son Vladimir Ilich, who, under the pseudonym Lenin, was later to become Aleksandr's chief antagonist during the stormy days of the Revolution of 1917. Since, however, the future Lenin was more than ten years older than young Aleksandr, there is no evidence that the two were at all acquainted as children.

In 1889, Fyodor Kerensky moved his family from Simbirsk to the frontier city of Tashkent in distant Central Asia, where he had been appointed head of the Turkestan educational administration. Eleven years later, having completed his basic education in Tashkent, Aleksandr traveled to the then capital of Russia and enrolled in the faculty of history and law at St. Petersburg (later Leningrad State) University. As a student, young Kerensky came under the influence of the famous philosopher N. O. Losskii and the liberal jurist L. I. Petrazhitskii and became affiliated with the liberal constitutionalist movement, although his sympathies were more truly drawn to the radical populist party of Socialist-Revolutionaries (PSR).

Upon graduation from the university in 1904, Kerensky married Olga Lvovna Baranovskii, the offspring of a distinguished military family and cousin of several active Socialist-Revolutionaries. Thereupon, swept up in the turbulent events of the abortive Revolution of 1905, Kerensky soon joined the PSR, became editor of its newspaper, and even attempted, though unsuccessfully, to join the so-called Fighting Organization, the terrorist wing of the PSR. As a result of these activities, the young revolutionary was arrested and exiled from St. Petersburg for a period of some six months.

Returned to the capital in late 1906, Kerensky began a brief but sensational career as a defense lawyer in a series of highly publicized political trials. Beginning in 1906, Kerensky's legal activities attracted widespread attention throughout Russia and finally culminated in two celebrated cases in 1912: the first, involving the largely successful defense of the Armenian Dashnak Party, held before a special tribunal of the Imperial Russian Senate (supreme court), and the other, even more famous, embracing the official investigation and condemnation of the czarist government's mishandling of the tragic Lena Goldfields massacre. The notoriety gained by Kerensky in these two episodes set the stage for his brief but spectacular career in Russian politics.

Life's Work

In late 1912, taking advantage of the favorable publicity surrounding his legal exploits, Kerensky was elected to the Fourth State Duma (parliament), representing the Volsk district of Saratov Province. Elected as a member of the Trudoviki (Laborite) Party, an amalgam of moderate socialists loosely associated with the PSR, the young legislator at once became the leading spokesman for the Duma's radical opposition. Meanwhile, behind the scenes, Kerensky also joined the ranks of Russian Freemasonry, a secret but highly influential political movement dedicated to the creation in Russia of a republican government under liberal direction.

In 1914, Kerensky received an eight-month prison sentence for sponsoring a protest against the czarist government's support for the disgraceful trial of Mendel Beilis, a Ukrainian Jew who had been unjustly accused of ritual murder. Saved from incarceration by his parliamentary immunity, Kerensky continued his radical activities in 1914 by leading the Trudoviki refusal to support unconditionally Russia's entry into World War I. By 1915, Kerensky's deepening disgust with czarism drove him to the advocacy of a political revolution in Russia though, as yet, without success. Untracked by serious illness in early 1916, Kerensky returned to the Duma later in that year and began at once to agitate for the overthrow of the monarchy, including, if necessary, the assassination of Czar Nicholas II.

In March, 1917, the unexpected coming of the revolution thrust the youthful Kerensky into a position of political leadership during

Aleksandr Fyodorovich Kerensky *(Library of Congress)*

an eight-month period of more or less continual revolutionary chaos. For its part, to fill the vacuum created by the removal of the czar, the Duma promptly established a so-called provisional government headed by a cabinet made up entirely of middle-class liberals with the exception of Kerensky, who, as minister of justice, became the new government's sole representative of political radicalism. At the same time, the popular Kerensky was also elected vice chairman of the powerful Petrograd (formerly St. Petersburg) Soviet of Worker's and Soldiers' Deputies, an unofficial body representing the interests of political radicals and the poor. In these circumstances, the young revolutionary became the only common member of the two bodies, which had effectively replaced the fallen monarchy.

As minister of justice in the original provisional government, Kerensky introduced a broad program of civil rights in Russia, including the ending of ethnic and religious discrimination as well as the abolition of capital punishment and the long-established exile system. On the other hand, in late April and in May, Kerensky also became embroiled in a fierce debate with Foreign Minister P. N. Miliukov regarding Russian war aims, in particular the latter's alleged insistence upon Russian acquisition of Constantinople and the Straits of the Dardanelles. In the end, confronted by hostile street demonstrations, Miliukov was forced to resign from the cabinet, in which action he was soon joined by the minister of war, Aleksandr Guchkov.

As a result of the resignations of Miliukov and Guchkov, the provisional government was reorganized on May 18. Arranged by Kerensky and his Masonic "brother" Nikolai Nekrasov, the new cabinet included a combination of liberals and socialists and was thus called the Coalition, the first of three such reorganizations that were destined to occur over the next several months. As minister of war in this new cabinet, Kerensky became convinced that the government's declared goal of a "general democratic peace" could be achieved only by the undertaking of one last great Russian military offensive that would demonstrate the nation's continued military strength and thereby pave the way for successful peace talks. With this in mind, the war minister at once departed for the front, where he soon earned the title "Supreme Persuader-in-Chief" in token of his fiery speeches seeking to convince the Russian soldiery to support his planned offensive. Finally launched in early July, the so-called Kerensky Offensive, after some initial success, quickly turned into a disastrous rout, following which the Russian Army began rapidly to disintegrate.

On July 16, prompted by the failure of the Kerensky Offensive, popular demonstrations, led first by disaffected workers, soldiers, and sailors and later by the Bolsheviks, erupted in the capital city of Petrograd. In response to this "July Days" crisis, Kerensky assumed the prime ministership of Russia on July 20. Having defused the Petrograd uprising by releasing documents purporting to show that Lenin and the Bolsheviks were really German agents, Kerensky at length organized a new, second Coalition, which again consisted of a shaky combination of liberals and socialists. Thereupon, in late August, in an effort to reconcile all the contending factions in Russia, the new prime minister summoned the Moscow State Conference, which instead of arresting the country's deteriorating political situation merely emphasized its hopelessness.

Finally, in early September, the climax of the Kerensky era was reached in the form of the famous Kornilov Revolt. In this confusing episode, the prime minister became convinced that General Lavr Kornilov, the commander in chief of the army, had concocted a plot to overthrow the provisional government and establish a military dictatorship in Russia. Whatever the truth of this charge, which was never substantiated, Kerensky responded by ordering the commander in chief's dismissal and arrest. More important, to defend the government from the alleged danger posed by Kornilov's troops (who, in fact, were easily disarmed), Kerensky also ordered the relegalization and arming of the Bolsheviks, who had been proscribed and in hiding since the July Days.

In the wake of these developments, no expedient, including the organization in mid-September of still another, third Coalition in which Kerensky served as both prime minister and commander in chief, or the convocation in October of a so-called Council of the Republic (or Pre-Parliament) was sufficient to save the situation. Instead, on November 7, 1917, the Kerensky regime was overthrown in an easy, almost bloodless, revolution engineered in Petrograd by Lenin and his Bolshevik (later Communist) Party.

For his part, having escaped the capital on the eve of the revolution and led a brief, futile effort by a small band of Cossack troops to dislodge the new rulers, Kerensky was forced to flee Russia in May, 1918, never to return. Arriving in Paris, the former prime minister tried to convince the Western allies to support his return to power in Russia by military action. Having failed in this effort, Kerensky began more than fifty years of political exile, living first in Western Europe and later in the United States. During this long period, the former Russian leader engaged in a variety of anticommunist (and antifascist) activities and supported himself by writing and lecturing, much of the subject matter of which was devoted to the justification of his behavior in 1917.

In 1927, Kerensky visited the United States and published the first version of his memoirs, entitled *The Catastrophe* (1927). From 1928 to 1933, he worked in Paris and Berlin, where he edited the émigré journal *Dni* (days). In 1939, he divorced his first wife and married Lydia Ellen Tritton, the daughter of a prominent Australian industrialist. Having narrowly escaped the Nazi occupation of Paris in 1940, Kerensky moved to the United States, where he lived for the rest of his life, though not without frequent, often lengthy, visits to Western Europe. From 1956 to 1961, together with the American historian Robert P. Browder, Kerensky worked in the Hoover Institution at Stanford University, where he prepared for publication a large collection of documents on the provisional government that finally appeared in three volumes in 1961. In 1965, he published a second version of his memoirs, grandiloquently entitled *Russia and History's Turning Point* (1965). He died of cancer in New York City on June 11, 1970.

Summary

In addition to its enormous historical significance, the Bolshevik Revolution of 1917 was a great watershed in the life of Aleksandr Fyodorovich Kerensky. Thus, before the revolution, Kerensky's career represents an all but unbroken tale of personal and public accomplishment. Based on a philosophical commitment to liberal democracy combined with a kind of populist dedication to improving the welfare of the Russian people, Kerensky's early legal career, as well as his service in the State Duma, was devoted to the defense of individual rights and the struggle for a better society in the face of a corrupt and tyrannical state.

In 1917, however, primarily because of his great reputation as an implacable foe of czarism, Kerensky was abruptly thrust into a position of political leadership in conditions of revolutionary chaos. In these circumstances, although his personal magnetism and great oratorical skills enabled him for a time to hold his own, his essential political moderation was soon outstripped by the deepening radicalism of the revolution. In the end, therefore, insufficient ruthlessness and a stubborn refusal to sacrifice democratic principles to radical expedience spelled Kerensky's political doom.

Following the revolution, although he retained his faith in democracy and fought adamantly against both Soviet and, later, Fascist authoritarianism, Kerensky's always considerable ego caused him to spend much of his long time in exile defending his conduct in 1917 and developing various conspiratorial, almost paranoid, explanations for his failure. As a result of this inability to perceive that his fate was really the consequence of powerful social and economic forces largely beyond his capacity to control, the former prime minister alienated his friends, aggravated his enemies, and died in a state of splendid political isolation.

Bibliography

Abraham, Richard. *Alexander Kerensky: The First Love of the Revolution.* New York: Columbia University Press, 1987. This is the only full-length biography in English. Based on Kerensky's official papers as well as materials supplied by his family, the treatment is sympathetic but not uncritical.

Browder, Robert P. "Kerensky Revisited." In *Russian Thought and Politics*, edited by Hugh McLean et al. The Hague: Mouton, 1957. A positive reevaluation of Kerensky, particularly his role in the early period of the Revolution.

Elkin, Boris. "The Kerensky Government and Its Fate." *Slavic Review* 23 (1964): 717-736.

_________. "Further Notes on the Policies of the Kerensky Government." *Slavic Review* 25 (1966): 323-332. Articles hostile to Kerensky and the provisional government in practically every area of their endeavor. Written by a close associate of Miliukov, the treatment is especially critical of Kerensky's alleged submission to the radical leaders of the Petrograd Soviet.

Katkov, George. *The Kornilov Affair: Kerensky and the Break-up of the Russian Army.* London: Longman's, 1980. This slender volume constitutes an exhaustive analysis of perhaps the pivotal episode in Kerensky's political career. Based in part on interviews with Kerensky in 1963; the author places most of the blame for the Kornilov disaster on Kerensky.

Kerensky, Alexander F. *Russia and History's Turning Point.* New York: Duell, Sloan and Pearce, 1965. These are Kerensky's memoirs. In addition to his interpretation of events, Kerensky contends that he and Russian democracy were betrayed by virtually everyone, including the parties of the Left, Right, and center as well as the Germans and the Allies.

Vishniak, Mark. "A Pamphlet in the Guise of a Review." *Slavic Review* 25 (1966): 143-149. This article is a rejoinder to the above criticisms of Elkin. The author's support of the provisional government is more an attack on Miliukov than a defense of Kerensky.

John W. Long

RUHOLLAH KHOMEINI

Born: November 9, 1902; Khomein, Iran
Died: June 3, 1989; Tehran, Iran

Arguably the most famous postmedieval Muslim religious leader anywhere, Khomeini directed the Iranian Revolution of 1978 and 1979, established the Islamic Republic of Iran in April, 1979, and ruled the country thereafter for ten years. His legacy also includes inspiring fundamentalist Muslim activism throughout the world.

Early Life

Ruhollah Khomeini was born in the small town of Khomein to a local Shi'i cleric who was killed a year later in a quarrel with employees of an absentee landlord. Ruhollah was reared at an aunt's house, there apparently being insufficient money or room at home for him. At an early age, he began traditional religious education, partly under the tutelage of an elder brother. In 1919, shortly after the deaths of his aunt and his mother, Ruhollah went to the city of Arak to continue his theological studies. There Ruhollah joined the group around Shaykh 'Abdolkarim Ha'eri Yazdi and in 1920 followed Ha'eri to Qom, where he completed his basic theological education in 1926.

Meanwhile, in Tehran a military officer called Reza Khan participated in a 1921 *coup d'état* against the central government and later emerged as the strongest political actor on the national scene. In 1924, Reza Khan visited Ha'eri in Qom, which the latter was molding into a leading Shi'i theological center. Shi'i clerics, wary of Reza Khan's Persian nationalism, blocked a plan to replace the Qajar monarchy with a republic. In 1925, Reza Pahlavi deposed Ahmad Shah and brought the Qajar Dynasty to an end. A year later, he crowned himself *shahanshah* (emperor) and embarked on ambitious programs of Westernization and secularization, which made the Pahlavi monarchy Khomeini's lifelong arch enemy.

In 1930, returning from a pilgrimage to the Shi'i shrine at Mashhad, Khomeini visited Tehran and married a prominent cleric's daughter called Batul, who was ten years old at the time. In

1932, Khomeini's first son, called Mostafa, was born. Khomeini's second son, Ahmad, was born in 1936. By this time, Khomeini was an established instructor of Islamic jurisprudence in Qom and had even conducted some of the recently deceased Ha'eri's advanced theology classes. In 1937, Khomeini made the hajj, or pilgrimage to Mecca.

In the fall of 1941, upon the arrival of British and Russian occupation forces, Reza Shah Pahlavi was forced to abdicate the Iranian throne. The Allies allowed his son, Mohammad Reza Shah Pahlavi, to succeed him, despite efforts by Shi'i clerics to persuade the British to put an end to the monarchy.

By 1946, Ayatollah Mohammad-Hussein Borujerdi emerged as the leading Shi'i cleric and proceeded to advocate an apolitical course. Khomeini became a Borujerdi aide and taught in the Qom theological school system. At a 1949 meeting of leading clerics, while Borujerdi advocated withdrawal by leading clerics from active participation in politics, Khomeini sided with clerics advocating political activism. Later, these activists played a role in events that led in August, 1953, to an American-orchestrated *coup d'état* that toppled the nationalist prime minister Mohammad Mosaddeq and reestablished Mohammad Reza Shah Pahlavi on the throne. In 1955, now a prominent instructor of Islamic sciences, Khomeini supported, and Mohammad Reza Pahlavi allowed, the persecution of the Baha'is.

In 1960, Borujerdi and other clerics opposed a land reform law, which Mohammad Reza Shah Pahlavi was consequently obliged to have annulled. In 1961, Khomeini, now an ayatollah, published *Tawzīh al-masāʿil* (*A Clarification of Questions*, 1984). When Borujerdi died in the same year, no single ayatollah was recognized as his successor as the chief Shi'i leader, although Khomeini received support from clerics advocating, as he did, political activism on their part.

Life's Work

By 1962, Khomeini was being referred to by the title "grand ayatollah." In January, 1963, he published an attack on a government land redistribution proposal. In March, he was arrested after speeches in which he ordered the Shi'i faithful not to celebrate *Nowruz* (Iranian New Year). In April, Mohammad Reza Shah Pahlavi went regally to Qom and castigated the clergy. Then on June 3, which coincided with the anniversary of Shi'i Imam Husayn ibn ʿAlī's death at Karbala in 680, Khomeini again preached against the government, calling the shah an agent of Israel. After his arrest two days later, riots ensued.

Ruhollah Khomeini *(AP/Wide World Photos)*

Khomeini remained in jail in Tehran for three months and was thereafter kept under house arrest.

In October, Khomeini he was again arrested, this time for advocating a boycott of elections. In April, 1964, by now the leading opposition figure, Khomeini was allowed to return to Qom. In November, Khomeini gave a speech protesting an Iranian/American bill that would extend diplomatic immunity to American military personnel in Iran and asserting the shah's subservience to the American government. Again arrested, Khomeini was this time exiled to Turkey. In January, 1965, Khomeini settled in Najaf, Iraq, where he was allowed to go after protesting Western dress codes in Turkey. On January 20, Prime Minister Hasan 'Alī Mansur was assassinated at the behest of Khomeini aides, after a secret Islamic court condemned him to death. The social reformer Kasravi had been similarly assassinated by Shi'i activists in 1946, as had Prime Minister Haj Ali Razmara in 1951.

In June, 1967, after Israel defeated the Arabs in the Six-Day War, Khomeini discussed clerical political rule for Iran and an Islamic holy war against Israel. In 1968, Khomeini resumed his teaching of theology and thereafter implored Iranians to overthrow the Pahlavi monarchy. Based on that teaching, Khomeini's *Hokumat-e-Eslami* (*Islamic Government*, 1979) was published in 1971. In it, while arguing that Muslim jurisprudents were uniquely qualified to govern societies, he predicted the overthrow of the Pahlavi monarchy and the establishment of an Islamic state. About this time, Khomeini met the prominent Arab religious leader Musa Sadr, whose niece had become Ahmad Khomeini's wife. In 1975, Khomeini called for a boycott of the newly formed Rastakhiz Party, the basis for the shah's new, one-party state.

In October, 1977, Khomeini's son Mostafa died in suspicious circumstances in Iraq. In December, students in Tehran demanded that Khomeini be allowed to return to Iran. In January, 1978, an article planted by the government in a national daily newspaper slandered Khomeini. A series of protests, clashes with the government, and memorial services ensued throughout that spring. In July, the Rex Cinema in Abadan burned down, with hundreds of people locked inside. Clerical involvement in the tragedy was assumed, but Khomeini blamed the shah's security forces. In October, expelled from Iraq and denied entry to Kuwait, Khomeini traveled to Paris, from which, via television, he became a household name throughout the world. Demonstrations in Tehran in December, coinciding with the anniversary of Husayn ibn 'Alī's death, called for Khomeini to return to lead Iran. The magnitude of the demonstrations made it likely that the shah would not survive politically.

On February 1, 1979, Khomeini returned triumphantly to Tehran, two weeks after the abject departure of the shah. In March, the

Islamic Republic of Iran was established, with Khomeini as its leader. The execution of hundreds of Pahlavi government officials followed. Sensing the strict theocratic basis of the new social order, tens of thousands of educated, secular-minded Iranians began leaving the country. In November, 1979, a group of Iranians identifying themselves as followers of the "Imam's line" seized the American Embassy in Tehran and held some fifty hostages until January, 1981. Khomeini orchestrated the release of the hostages to take place the moment that Ronald Reagan was sworn in to succeed Jimmy Carter as president of the United States.

In September, 1980, Iraq invaded Iran, and a war commenced that served to unite some elements of the Iranian population behind Khomeini. By the time hostilities had ended inconclusively in mid-1989, it had cost hundreds of thousands of Iranian lives and devastated the economy.

In 1981, a longtime supporter of Khomeini called Sheik Mohammad Saduqi declared that Baha'i blood might be legally spilled. In June of that year, Islamic Republic's president, Abolhassan Bani-Sadr, was deposed as mullahs grew more powerful. A hundred or more clerical leaders and officials died in a bombing at a party headquarters in June, for which the subsequently outlawed Mujahedeen-e-Khalq-e-Iran (People's Combatants of Iran) claimed responsibility. In 1982, former Khomeini supporter and foreign minister Sadeq Ghotbzadeh was executed for plotting Khomeini's overthrow. In 1983, leaders and thousands of members of the Tudeh Party of Iran were arrested. An assembly of experts was charged in 1984 with planning for Khomeini's successor. His will and testament were deposited in a safe at the Parliament Building for publication the moment he died. In 1988, Khomeini declared edicts on governmental prerogatives which are binding for Shi'is. Early in 1989, Khomeini called for the death of India-born British author Salman Rushdie because of the latter's alleged insults to Islam in a novel called *The Satanic Verses* (1988).

Khomeini died on June 3, 1989. Millions of Iranians mourned his death and attended his funeral, one of the largest in history. The chant "Death to America" was an integral part of the proceedings. In late July, former Parliament speaker Hashemi Rafsanjani was elected president of the Islamic Republic of Iran, thereafter consolidating his position as Iran's most powerful political figure and sending signals that he might harmonize Islamic teachings with modern realities.

Summary

From his early adult years until 1979, Ruhollah Khomeini labored to achieve two ends, the collapse of the Pahlavi monarchy and the installation of an Islamic government. Incorruptible, ascetic, religious, single-minded, and self-confident in pursuing these goals, Khomeini proceeded in 1979 to show the world an authoritarian, autocratic leadership style (as an arguably traditional Iranian patriarch), intense xenophobia against the West and Israel, and ignorance of things beyond the pale of Islam. In asserting that U.S. president Jimmy Carter was a manifestation of Satan and consequently deserved assassination, and that women should be in their husbands' homes by the time they menstruate for the first time, among other things, Khomeini presented a challenge to the nonfundamentalist Muslim world and to the non-Muslim world: how to deal with a leader whose perspectives and thought processes are very different and who does not believe in compromise.

As the leader of a major revolution, as the architect of a fusion of theology and politics in the establishment of perhaps the first "fundamentalist" Islamic republic in the history of Islam, as the implementor of a historical alternative to secular rule, and as a thwarter of Western values, Khomeini stood as a successful political leader in the short term. As a pan-Islamic activist who argued for the substitution of the notion of the Islamic community for the Iranian nation or Iranian nationalism, Khomeini offered a political vision with serious consequences in the long term for nation-states with significant Muslim populations.

Bibliography

Arjomand, Said Amir. *The Turban for the Crown: The Islamic Revolution in Iran.* New York: Oxford University Press, 1988. A sociologist's explanation of the Islamic revolution of 1979 in Iran and "assessment of its significance in world history," this study details Khomeini's role as a chief actor in the Iranian political arena, compares him with other famous revolutionary leaders, and demonstrates the success of his Islamic revolutionary ideology.

Dorraj, Manochehr. *From Zarathustra to Khomeini: Populism and Dissent in Iran*. Boulder, Colo.: Lynne Rienner, 1990.

Ferdows, Adele. "Shariati and Khomayni on Women." In *The Iranian Revolution and the Islamic Republic of Iran*, edited by Nikki R. Keddie and Eric Hooglund. Syracuse, N.Y.: Syracuse University Press, 1986. A discussion of a most sensitive issue in modernizing

Muslim societies today, that of the continuing relegation of women in Islam, according to feminist observers, to inferior social status. Khomeini's conservative views receive treatment along with those of the Western-educated and anti-Pahlavi social reformer Ali Shariati.

Fischer, Michael M. J. "Imam Khomeini: Four Levels of Understanding." In *Voices of Resurgent Islam*, edited by John L. Esposito. New York: Oxford University Press, 1983. A biographical sketch and an analysis of Khomeini's public persona in an attempt to account for his success as a charismatic religious and political leader.

Mackey, Sandra. *The Iranians: Persia, Islam, and the Soul of a Nation*. New York: Penguin Books, 1998.

Mottahedeh, Roy. *The Mantle of the Prophet: Religion and Politics in Iran*. New York: Simon & Schuster, 1985. Intended for the "intelligent general reader of Middle Eastern history" and in the context of "an extended reading of Iranian culture," including historical interchapters, this study traces the life of a prominent contemporary Iranian Shi'a Muslim cleric given the pseudonym Ali Hashemi. Although not the explicit focus of the presentation, Khomeini figures prominently in it because Hashemi's life revolves around Khomeini's political activism and role in Iranian affairs as of the late 1970's.

Rose, Gregory. "*Velayat-e Faqih* and the Recovery of Identity in the Thought of Ayatullah Khomeini." In *Religion and Politics in Iran: Shi'ism from Quietism to Revolution*, edited by Nikki Keddie. New Haven, Conn.: Yale University Press, 1983. A sympathetic treatment of Khomeini's response to what he perceived as the Muslim world's identity crisis and pervasive alienation. With a review of the history of the concept of authority or governance of the Muslim jurisprudent over the affairs of the Muslim community, the essay describes Khomeini's view that Shi'ite Islam needs to be a revolutionary ideology.

Taheri, Amir. *The Spirit of Allah: Khomeini and the Islamic Revolution*. Bethesda, Md.: Adler & Adler, 1986. Although not a sympathetic portrait and not inclusive of Khomeini's last three years, this is the fullest and most informative treatment to appear.

Michael Craig Hillman

NIKITA KHRUSHCHEV

Born: April 17, 1894; Kalinovka, Russia
Died: September 11, 1971; Moscow, Soviet Union

Khrushchev ruled the Soviet Union for a tumultuous decade, during which he began de-Stalinization and released millions of his countrymen from the Siberian Gulag. In foreign affairs, the Sino-Soviet split, the suppression of the Hungarian Revolution of 1956, and the Cuban Missile Crisis characterized his time in power.

Early Life

Nikita Sergeyevich Khrushchev was born in Kalinovka, Kursk Region, Russia, on April 17, 1894. He started working in factories and mines of the Ukrainian Donets Basin when he was fourteen years old. In 1918, he joined the Communist Party and fought in the Russian civil war. By the mid-1920's, he had become a local party secretary, and he held various party jobs in the Ukraine over the next decade. In 1935, he became first secretary of the Moscow Communist Party. In 1938, he returned to the Ukraine as first secretary in that republic. In 1939, he became a full member of the Politburo. During World War II, Khrushchev was a member of the Military Council on the Southern Front.

When Stalin died on March 5, 1953, Georgi Malenkov became the senior Communist Party secretary and head of the Soviet government. Khrushchev, while one of the party secretaries, was still a secondary figure. Eight days after Stalin's death, Malenkov miscalculated. He had a picture of the signing of the 1950 Sino-Soviet Treaty cropped to show only Joseph Stalin, Mao Zedong, and himself, and published the picture. Malenkov's colleagues interpreted this maneuver as a bid for sole power. They forced him to relinquish his position as head of the party, although he remained the dominant governmental figure. The party leaders subsequently made Khrushchev the senior party secretary, apparently assuming that Khrushchev would pose no serious threat to their own power positions.

Life's Work

In March of 1953, Lavrenty Beria, the head of the secret police, was generally regarded as the second most powerful man in the Soviet Union, after Malenkov. Beria inspired both loathing and fear. In an action of notable courage, Khrushchev went secretly to his colleagues and convinced them that Beria was plotting a supreme power-grab that might bring a terror worse than that of Stalin. Beria was arrested in July of 1953 and executed in December. When Khrushchev was asked after his fall what his greatest achievement had been, he answered that it was the saving of his country from Beria.

The balance of power between Khrushchev and Malenkov shifted gradually in Khrushchev's favor. In the autumn of 1954, an open policy dispute erupted between them, with Malenkov advocating consumer goods and Khrushchev favoring heavy industry and military strength. Khrushchev won, and Malenkov was forced from his position as head of government on February 8, 1955.

It was not long before Khrushchev began to cut a wide swath in foreign affairs. In late 1954, Khrushchev visited Mao in Beijing, and the Chinese pressed unsuccessfully for the return to China of Mongolia, then a Soviet puppet state, and for other concessions. When Khrushchev returned to Moscow, as he reports in his memoirs, he told his colleagues that "conflict with China is inevitable." In Europe, Khrushchev visited Yugoslavia and tried unsuccessfully to undo the 1948 Stalin-Tito break.

West Germany was moving toward participation in the North Atlantic Treaty Organization (NATO) in 1954, and Khrushchev tried to convince the Germans that neutrality might open the door to German reunification. Perhaps as an example, he agreed to a neutral, unified Austria, and the withdrawal of Soviet forces.

Khrushchev also gave up the Porkkala Peninsula naval base in Finland. Vyacheslav Molotov opposed these concessions and was later forced out as foreign minister. West Germany did enter NATO, however, and the Warsaw Pact was the Soviet bloc's response. In 1956, twin crises erupted in Poland and Hungary. The Poles, led by Władysław Gomułka, faced down Khrushchev in a tense Warsaw confrontation and achieved half the loaf of their national autonomy. In Hungary, the crisis resulted in the crushing of the Hungarian Revolution by Soviet tanks and troops. In the Suez crisis, which broke out at the same time, Khrushchev waited until the worst was over before he threatened to support Egypt's Gamal Abdel Nasser with rockets.

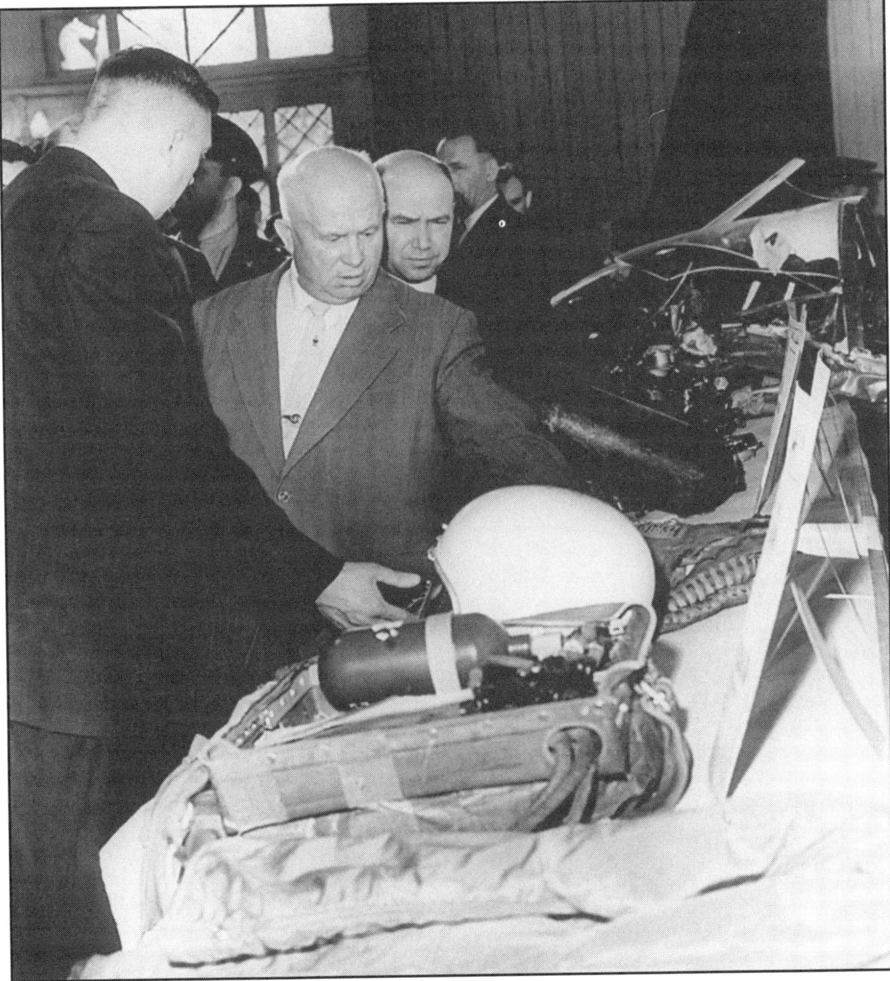

Nikita Khrushchev *(Library of Congress)*

In domestic affairs, Khrushchev encouraged a "thaw" and permitted greater literary freedom. Works by nonconformist writers, such as Aleksandr Solzhenitsyn, were published. Khrushchev was also notably, if not always consistently, liberal with cultural figures and scientists. In February of 1956, at a closed session of the Twentieth Congress of the Soviet Communist Party, Khrushchev delivered his "Secret Speech" denouncing Stalin's crimes. De-Stalinization swept the land, and statues and portraits of Stalin disappeared. Khrushchev followed up with an amnesty, which led to the release of millions of Soviets from the Siberian Gulag. In addition, Khrushchev restored national autonomy to Caucasian and other peoples whom Stalin had deported, and allowed most survivors to return to their homes. He launched a program to build apartments everywhere and more than doubled annual housing construction during his time in office.

In agricultural policy, Khrushchev abolished the machine and tractor stations that had served both as mechanized service units and centers of political control in the countryside. He transformed many collective farms into state farms (state-run factories in the countryside). He pushed a drive to plant corn for fodder with such vigor that underlings forced plantings where the corn would not grow. He also launched the Virgin Lands Program in Kazakhstan and Central Asia, forcing the planting of vast stretches of prairie in wheat. By 1956, Soviet wheat production had risen by 50 percent, but bad years, such as 1958 and 1963, reflected emerging dust bowl conditions. Khrushchev promised that the Soviet Union would soon overtake the United States in the production of milk, meat, and butter, but that program faltered.

In 1957, Khrushchev's opponents in the Communist Party Presidium (Politburo) combined against him. His opponents included Malenkov and Molotov (for reasons already indicated), Old Stalinists, and ambitious careerists. Khrushchev's adversaries formed a majority to oust him. Khrushchev appealed the decision to the party central committee.

Marshal Georgi Zhukov, the minister of defense and a World War II hero, helped Khrushchev fly in central committee supporters from distant places, and the Presidium vote was overturned. Key members of the Presidium majority were then publicly branded as an "anti-Party Group." Molotov was sent off as ambassador to Mongolia, and Malenkov became manager of an electric power station in Semipalatinsk. Khrushchev removed his erstwhile ally Zhukov in October.

Khrushchev decreed a system of rotation in party jobs and limits to incumbency. Later he split the Communist Party leadership in each region, constituting a separate agricultural and industrial party organization, to the deep resentment of many local party chiefs. Khrushchev reformed education, forcing adolescents to interrupt their academic studies to work in factories and farms. He launched an antireligious drive that resulted in the closing of more than 40 percent of the Russian Orthodox churches in the country. He turned from support of heavy industry to consumer goods, scrapped Navy cruisers and destroyers, reduced the Red Army by more than a million men, and cut the perquisites of military and police officers. Many of these initiatives made for Khrushchev new enemies in the establishment.

Relations with China worsened as the Great Leap Forward of 1957-1958 produced turmoil and failure. In 1959, Khrushchev scrapped the Sino-Soviet arms aid agreement and supported India during Chinese-Indian border hostilities. In 1960, the Soviet Union withdrew its technicians from China and sent Chinese students home. In Moscow in October of 1961, the Sino-Soviet split became public. Chou En-lai laid a wreath at Stalin's bier in the Red Square mausoleum and went home. Eight days later, Khrushchev had Stalin's body removed, cremated, and reburied by the Kremlin wall.

With respect to the West, Khrushchev issued a six-month ultimatum on Thanksgiving Day of 1958 to get out of Berlin. He let the ultimatum slide, however, as preparations went forward for a two-week visit to the United States in September, 1959. The visit proved a success, and President Dwight D. Eisenhower hoped that a planned return visit and the Paris Summit of May, 1960, would bring important new arms control agreements. The shooting down of Francis Gary Powers and his U-2 "spy plane" dashed these hopes. When Eisenhower refused to apologize, Khrushchev broke up the Paris summit. In the autumn of 1960, Khrushchev returned to New York for the United Nations General Assembly, banging a shoe on his desk in protest during a debate about the suppression of the Hungarian Revolution.

John F. Kennedy was inaugurated in January of 1961, and a series of incidents convinced Khrushchev that Kennedy was weak. First, there was an American humiliation in Laos. In April, there was the Bay of Pigs. In June, there was the Khrushchev-Kennedy summit in Vienna, where Khrushchev was able to browbeat Kennedy. In August, there was the erection of the Berlin Wall. All this no doubt influenced Khrushchev in his decision to place intermediate-range nuclear missiles in Cuba. The Cuban Missile Crisis ensued and, in Dean Rusk's words, Khrushchev blinked first. While the settlement guaranteed that the United States would not invade Cuba, the identity of the loser was clear. Nevertheless, Khrushchev did not withdraw into sullen isolationism but responded to Kennedy's initiative the next year and negotiated the Atmospheric Nuclear Test Ban Treaty—a blessing to the health of the world.

The seeds of discontent had produced dense thickets of opposition in the Soviet Union by the summer of 1964. Aleksandr

Shelepin, Chief of the Party-State Control Commission, reportedly argued with other Presidium members that Khrushchev would soon purge them. The head of the secret police Komitet Gosudarstvennoi Bezopasnosti (KGB), Vladimir Semichastny, joined the plotters. There was discontent among army and navy officers. The bad harvest of 1963 had produced bread rationing, and the Cuban Missile Crisis had been a humiliation. The shoe-banging had not helped. Old Stalinists smoldered, party bureaucrats grumbled, and defense-minded advocates of heavy industry fumed. Many blamed Khrushchev for the break with China. Perhaps the last straw was the knowledge in Communist Party circles that Khrushchev intended a new shake-up when he returned from his 1964 Black Sea vacation.

Leonid Ilich Brezhnev telephoned Khrushchev on October 13, 1964, and convinced him to cut short his vacation for an important meeting in Moscow. When Khrushchev drove to the nearby airport, he found an unfamiliar plane. In Moscow he found a different car, driver, and bodyguards, and he was met by KGB Chief Semichastny. When Khrushchev arrived at the Kremlin, he found the nine other members of the Presidium waiting. Mikhail Suslov, from a current copy of *Pravda* and one from Stalin's day, showed Khrushchev that he had promoted his own "personality cult," as Stalin had. As in 1957, Khrushchev demanded a central committee meeting. His colleagues, anticipating this, had already assembled a hand-picked quorum, the members of which had already waited for days in the Kremlin incommunicado, watching films to while away the time. Khrushchev was led to the meeting and obliged to resign.

Khrushchev retired to his country house in Petrovo-Dalnee, near Moscow. He planted a vegetable garden and began to dictate his memoirs into a tape recorder. The tapes were smuggled to the West and published. It is said that the ensuing pressure on Khrushchev to repudiate the memoirs hastened the two heart attacks that resulted in his death on September 11, 1971.

Summary

Nikita Khrushchev's flamboyant style left a residue of amusement, admiration, outrage, and fear. In some ways, Khrushchev did better by his country then either his countrymen or the world appreciated. The monument over his tomb displays a dramatic juxtaposition of black-and-white marble, as the sculptor correctly proclaims that Khrushchev's life was a contrasting mixture of darker deeds and gleaming white ones. He was a forerunner of Mikhail Gorbachev and his policies, including *perestroika* (economic restructuring) and *glasnost* (openness).

Bibliography

Crankshaw, Edward. *Khrushchev: A Career.* New York: Viking Press, 1966. This work by one of the foremost experts of the Soviet Union covers Khrushchev's career in its entirety. Includes a chronology, notes, and an index.

Fursenko, Aleksandr, and Timothy Naftali. *One Hell of a Gamble: Khrushchev, Castro, and Kennedy, 1958-1964.* New York: Norton, 1997.

Heller, Mikhail, and Aleksandr Nekrich. *Utopia in Power.* New York: Summit Books, 1986. Two prominent dissident émigrés have written a critical history of Soviet rule. They include about a hundred pages of description and commentary on the Khrushchev period, when they were intellectual leaders in the Soviet Union.

Khrushchev, Nikita *Khrushchev Remembers.* Edited and translated by Strobe Talbot. Boston: Little, Brown, 1970.

__________. *Khrushchev Remembers: The Last Testament.* Edited and translated by Strobe Talbot. Boston: Little, Brown, 1974. These are Khrushchev's own memoirs, spoken into a tape recorder after his fall from power. They represent more than eleven hundred pages of fascinating and indispensable commentary on Khrushchev's time in power.

Khrushchev, Sergei. *Khrushchev on Khrushchev: An Inside Account of the Man and His Era.* Boston: Little, Brown, 1990.

McCauley, Martin. *The Khrushchev Era: 1953-1964.* New York: Longman, 1995.

Medvedev, Roy A. *Khrushchev.* Garden City, N.Y.: Anchor Press/Doubleday, 1983. Medvedev has long been recognized as the leading dissident communist historian working in Moscow. His book has discerning judgments and much information about Khrushchev's period of rule.

Serov, Alexei, ed. *Nikita Khrushchev: Life and Destiny.* Moscow: Novosti Press Agency, 1989. This small volume brings together reminiscences by members of Khrushchev's family, a colleague on the Politburo in Khrushchev's time, and other prominent Soviet writers and political figures.

Shevchenko, Arkady N. *Breaking with Moscow.* New York: Alfred A. Knopf, 1985. Shevchenko became the senior Soviet diplomat at the United Nations Secretariat before he defected. Much of his diplomatic career was spent under Khrushchev, and his unvarnished account is rich in anecdotes and insights.

Tompson, William J. *Khrushchev: A Political Life*. Oxford, England: Macmillan, 1995.

Zubok, V. M. *Inside the Kremlin's Cold War: From Stalin to Khrushchev*. Cambridge, Mass.: Harvard University Press, 1996.

Nathaniel Davis